CAPITALISM IN CHAOS

CAPITALISM IN CHAOS

HOW THE BUSINESS ELITES OF EUROPE PROSPERED IN THE ERA OF THE GREAT WAR

MÁTÉ RIGÓ

CORNELL UNIVERSITY PRESS
Ithaca and London

First published 2022 by Cornell University Press

Library of Congress Cataloging-in-Publication Data
Names: Rigó, Máté, 1985 - author.
Title: Capitalism in chaos : how the business elites of Europe prospered in the era of the Great War / Máté Rigó.
Description: Ithaca [New York]: Cornell University Press, 2022. | Includes bibliographical references and index.
Identifiers: LCCN 2021048209 (print) | LCCN 2021048210 (ebook) | ISBN 9781501764653 (hardcover) | ISBN 9781501764677 (pdf) | ISBN 9781501764660 (epub)
Subjects: LCSH: Industrialists—Europe—History—19th century. | Industrialists—Europe—History—20th century. | World War, 1914–1918—Europe—Influence.
Classification: LCC HC53.R54 2022 (print) | LCC HC53 (ebook) | DDC 330.94—dc23/eng/20220304
LC record available at https://lccn.loc.gov/2021048209
LC ebook record available at https://lccn.loc.gov/2021048210

Contents

Acknowledgments

I started working on this book a decade ago and have amassed a huge intellectual debt to many colleagues and friends since then. Curiously, there is still moderate appreciation of collaborative scholarly work in the humanities, so I will try (and likely fail) to do justice to my intellectual interlocutors, friends, and mentors below. First and foremost, without the relentless encouragement, generous intellectual support, and selfless mentoring of Holly Case, the research on which this book is based would have been inconceivable. If you find this book readable and analytically sound at the same time, you can thank Holly, who was also the first one to prompt me to venture beyond the comfort of area studies, or my native Hungary's history. Vicki Caron and Isabel Hull showed me how to make a large, comparative endeavor feasible as a research project and went way beyond the call of duty to exchange ideas with a junior researcher. István Deák took time out to go on long walks through the meandering trails of Riverside Park and listen to my writing and offer advice and further readings, and continued to do so beyond age ninety-five as I prepared the book. Working with Pieter Judson and discussing the book on Piazza Santo Spirito and elsewhere in pre-pandemic Florence has profoundly shaped my thinking on nationalism, the First World War, and empires more generally. I am grateful for Tara Zahra for an invitation to a research group on the histories of deglobalization and for opening the field of East-Central European history to comparisons with France in general and Alsace-Lorraine in particular.[1]

I am grateful to Alison Frank Johnson, Laird Boswell, and Stephen Gross for reading an earlier version of this book and discussing it for a whole day (in person!) at Yale just a few months before a global crisis prevented such discussions. I received similarly generous comments from participants of the book workshop at the Institute of Political History in Budapest: Balázs Ablonczy, Anna Adorjáni, Ágoston Berecz, Zsombor Bódy, Péter Csunderlik, Gábor Egry, Mária Hidvégi, Attila Hunyadi, and György Kövér. Colleagues at Yale-NUS College offered advice in support of this book, and I am especially grateful to Naoko Shimazu, Wannes Dupont, Andrew Hui, Taran Kang, Emanuel Mayer and Tan Tai Yong.

Emily Andrew, my editor at Cornell University Press, has fully supported this book from the initial stages. I am grateful for her trust and the risk she took with a book of this sort; I also appreciate the work of Bethany Wasik, who managed the publication of this book till the final stages. Lianna Sanford Kazarian has proved essential in editing the manuscript at all stages, and the final text bears the imprint of her superb skills. I am grateful to Judit Bakonyi and Mike Bechthold for the maps, and to Ashley Chan, Anna Csicsics, Damien Kee Wei Hao, Grace Ow, and others for assisting with this book's publication. The anonymous reviewers, one of whom turned out to be the excellent historian Roland Clark, helped improve the manuscript toward its final form. I am grateful to the editors of *Central European History* and *European Review of History* for allowing me to republish newer versions of my articles that appeared as "Imperial Currencies after the Fall of Empires: The Conversion of the German Paper Mark and the Austro-Hungarian Crown at the End of the First World War," *Central European History* 53, no. 3 (September 2020): 533–563; and "The Long First World War and the Survival of Business Elites in East-Central Europe: Transylvania's Industrial Boom and the Enrichment of Economic Elites," *European Review of History* 24, no. 2 (March 4, 2017): 250–272. I am grateful to Henri Mellon, who granted me access to the de Dietrich family's archives and allowed me to reproduce family photos.

Writing the histories of businesses often requires more funding than actually operating some of these businesses. Despite two global crises, this endeavor persisted thanks to relentless support by public and private institutions dedicated to the survival of research in the humanities and social sciences. I am especially grateful for the fellowships and grants I received from Central European University's History Department, the Mario Einaudi Center for International Studies, the Judith Reppy Institute for Peace and Conflict Studies, and the Walter LaFeber Research Fund at Cornell, along with support from the Cornell Institute for European Studies, the Central European History Society, the Romanian Cultural Institute, and Cornell's Graduate School. The support of president László Sólyom's research grant proved crucial while drafting this book. While at the European University Institute in Florence, I benefited from the support of the Max Weber fellowship, as well as the support of the Department of History and Civilization. Yale-NUS College has supported this book with numerous subventions for research, workshops, and research leaves, and it has proved to be an excellent place to undertake a book. I am especially grateful for advice and support from Jeannette Ickovics. Finally, the manuscript may not have been completed in time were it not for a fellowship at the Imre Kertész Kolleg in Jena and its vibrant community of scholars, including Joachim von Puttkamer and Jochen Böhler.

Archivists and librarians in Arad, Budapest, Bucharest, Cluj-Napoca, Genova, Ithaca, Strasbourg, Timișoara, Vienna, London, Singapore and elsewhere were essential in allowing me to bring this project to fruition. The manuscript was greatly improved by conversations with Cornel Ban, Nándor Bárdi, Ludovic Báthory, Gergely Baics, Peter Becker, Antal Berkes, Dan Cirjan, Victor Demiaux, Cristina Florea, Regina Grafe, Jessica Hanser, Károly Halmos, Aaron Law, Sándor Horváth, Paul Hanebrink, Steve Keast, Tamás Kende, Zsombor Méder, Michael Laurence Miller, Shannon Monaghan, Bogdan Murgescu, Marta Musso, Robert Nemes, Zoltán Rostás, Chris Szabla, István M. Szijártó, Ksenia Tatarchenko, Balázs Trencsényi, Gábor Gyáni, Tamara Scheer, Tamás Vonyó, Ondřej Vojtěchovský, Nancy Wingfield, and other colleagues.

I am also grateful to my teachers and mentors in the *Pannonhalma Bencés Gimnázium* for nurturing my interest in history. I especially want to thank Fidél Nádai and Mátyás Varga, who shared their passion of intellectual pursuits with me. Partners along with friends and family in Budapest, Bucharest, Cluj-Napoca, Strasbourg, Paris, New York, and Ithaca were instrumental in striking a good balance between research and daily life. I am indebted to Rebecca Ahdoot, Shalini de Almeida, Shreya Atrey, Felix Binder, Péter Brezina, Kálmán Czeibert, Péter Cziráki, Mark Deets, Gergely Máté Éliás, Tayler Eaton, Sean Fear, Gábor Förköli, Imre Gérecz, Anikó Gregor, Máté Halmos, Cecília Hauer, Chris Hesselbein, András Hüttl, Ádam Ignácz, Márton Jankovics, Andor Kelenhegyi, Carmen V. Krol, Panni Kiss, András Lugosi, Viktor Marsai, Bálint Menyhért, Zsuzsi Molnár, Gergő Pulay, Tamás Réti, Irina Savinetskaya, Madhur Shrivastava, István Sinkó, Tamás Makány, Joseph Murray, Attila Mráz, Radu Pârvulescu, Marcell Szabó, Kata Tamási, Maria Taroutina, Balázs Varga, Benedek Varga, Kata Varsányi, Máté Veres, David Vichnar, Bart von Wassenhove, and János Zsiros. The home of Agnes and Ivan Sanders in New York has always provided a welcoming refuge from writing and research, as did the homes of my grandmothers Irén and Hajnalka in Hungary.

Even though I was very young when my mother, Andrea Máthé, completed her PhD, I am forever inspired by her dedication to scholarly work, along with my father István Rigó's work as a sculptor and my brother Bálint's work as an architect. This book is dedicated to them.

Abbreviations

AEB	Allgemeine Elsässische Bankgesellschaft (Alastian General Bank)
BMMB	Banca Marmorosch and Blank (Marmorosch and Blank Bank)
ElMaG	Elsässische Maschinenbau Gesellschaft (Alastian Mechanical Construction Company)
GCB	Magyar Általános Hitelbank (Hungarian General Credit Bank)
KLAG	Kriegsleder-Aktiengesellschaft (German War Leather Corporation)
KST	Kali Sainte Thérése Potash Mines
PHCB	Pesti Magyar Kereskedelmi Bank (Pest Hungarian Commercial Bank)
SCMC	Salgótarjáni Kőszénbánya R.t. (Salgótarjan Coal Mining Corporation)
UZMC	Urikány-Zsilvölgyi Kőszénbánya R.t. (Urikány and Jiu Valley Hungarian Coal Mining Corporation)
WNJ	Wolf, Netter, Jacobi Engineering Company

Note on Place-Names

The regions and towns of Central Europe were called a variety of names by states and inhabitants during the nineteenth and twentieth centuries. In order to honor this diversity, table 0.1 lists the most common designations of places mentioned in the book. For the sake of concision and clarity, in the main text I use the current French and English names of Alsace-Lorraine's towns, which were in official use before 1870 and between 1918 and 1940. For cities in Transylvania, I use the Hungarian names for the period before 1918, while in chapters pertaining to the period after the First World War, I switch to the official Romanian place-names, to reflect the official designations in each period. For instance, the Transylvanian city that is now called Cluj-Napoca is referred to as Kolozsvár in chapters 1–5, and in the following chapters, it is referred to as Cluj, the official Romanian designation in the interwar period.

Transylvania was a historical region within the Hungarian kingdom (map 1). Historical Transylvania was considerably smaller than the territories annexed by Romania from Hungary after 1918. While the Banat, Crișana, and Maramureș were not part of Transylvania before 1918, after Romania annexed parts of these territories, contemporaries started to refer to them as constitutive parts of this "greater" Transylvania. For simplicity's sake, this book refers to Transylvania as the ensemble of territories that Greater Romania annexed from Hungary after 1918, while highlighting the distinct trajectories of its various subregions whenever possible. Much like Transylvania after 1918, Alsace-Lorraine emerged as a distinct region as a result of annexation and encompassed different territories with autonomous histories of their own. Alsace-Lorraine (map 2) first appeared on the map of Europe after the Treaty of Frankfurt between France and Germany in 1871. It encompassed the vast majority of the historical region of Alsace, except for the city of Belfort, a few strategically important French villages in the Vosges department, and the eastern half of Lorraine.

Table 0.1 Place-names

ENGLISH	FRENCH	GERMAN	HUNGARIAN	ROMANIAN
Alba Iulia		*Karlsburg*	*Gyulafehérvár*	*Alba Iulia*
Alsace		Elsass / Elsaß		
Alsace-Lorraine		*Reichsland Elsaß-Lothringen*		
Arad			Arad	Arad
Austrian Littoral		*Österreichisches Küstenland*		
Baden	Pays de Bade	Baden		
Brașov		*Kronstadt*	*Brassó*	*Brașov*
Bucharest				București
Budapest			*Budapest*	
Bukovina		Bukowina	Bukovina	Bucovina
Chernivtsi		*Czernowitz*		*Cernăuți*
Cluj-Napoca		Klausenburg	Kolozsvár	Cluj[1]
Colmar	*Colmar*	*Kolmar*		
Geneva	Genève	Genf		
Jiu Valley		*Zsilthal*	*Zsil-völgy*	*Valea Jiului*
Karlovy Vary		Karlsbad		
Lingolsheim	*Lingolsheim*			
Lorraine		Lothringen		
Lower Alsace	*Bas-Rhin*	*Unter-Elsass*		
Maramureș			Máramaros	Maramureș
Mediaș		*Mediasch*	*Medgyes*	
Mulhouse	Mulhouse	Mülhausen		
Oradea		*Großwardein*	*Nagyvárad*	*Oradea Mare*
Periam			Perjámos	Periam
Reghin		*Regen*	*Szászrégen Regén*	
Rhineland	Rhénanie	Rheinland		
The Saar	Sarre	Saarland		
Satu Mare		Sathmar	Szatmárnémeti	Satu Mare
Sibiu		*Hermannstadt*	*Nagyszeben*	*Sibiu*
Strasbourg	Strasbourg	Straßburg		
Székely Land / Szeklerland		*Szeklerland*		*Ținutul Secuiesc Secuimea*
Timișoara		Temeswar Temeschwar	Temesvár	Timișoara
Upper Alsace	Haut-Rhin	*Ober-Elsass*		

[1]The Romanian name of Cluj-Napoca in the interwar period.

Map 1. Transylvania in 1918. Source: Judit Bakonyi.

MAP 2. Alsace-Lorraine after 1918. Source: Judit Bakonyi.

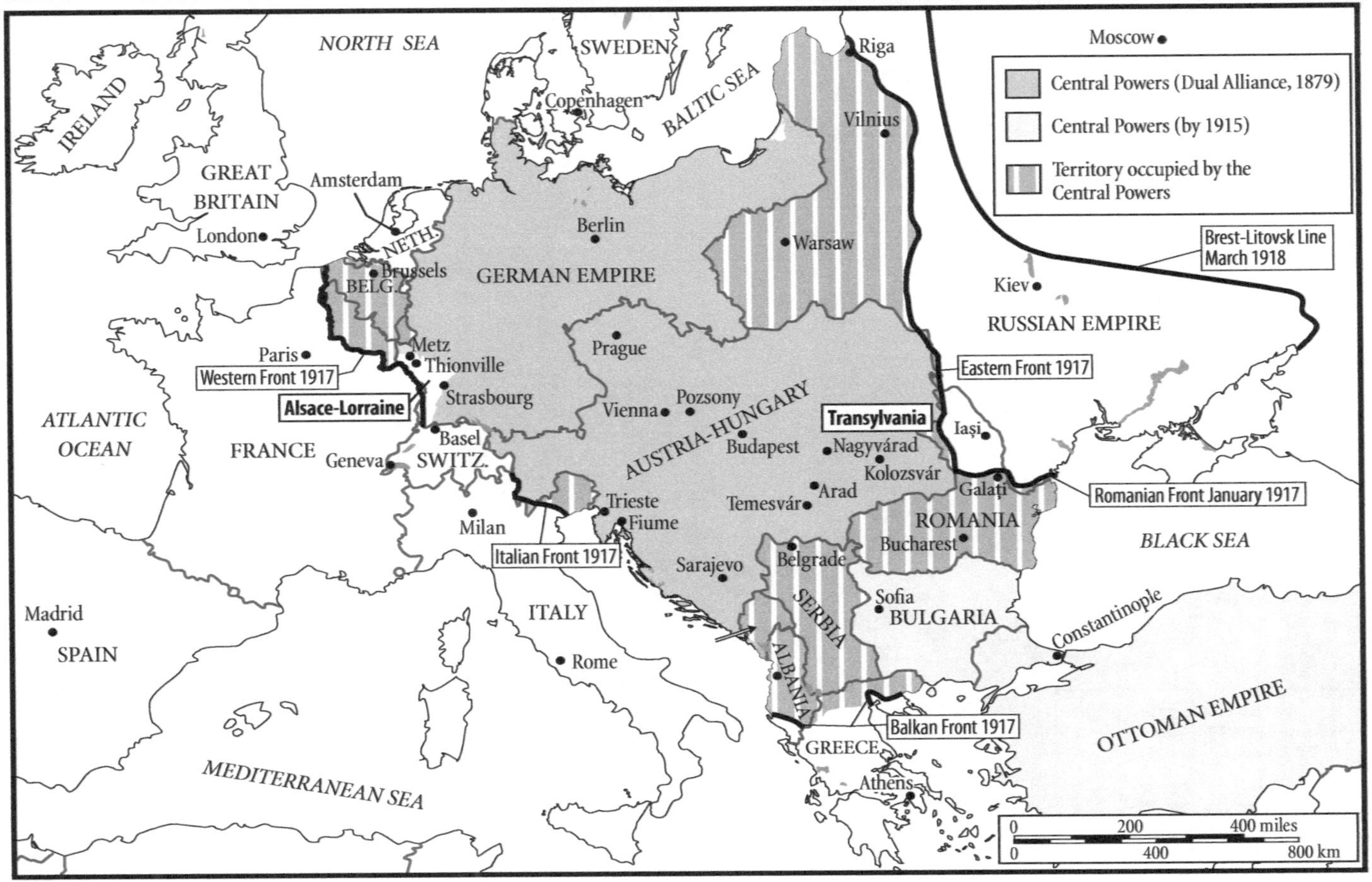

Map 3. The territorial gains of the Central Powers in Europe during the First World War, 1914. Source: Mike Bechthold.

Map 4. Europe's borders after the peace treaties that ended the First World War, 1918. Source: Mike Bechthold.

CAPITALISM IN CHAOS

Introduction

The First World War witnessed the mobilization of sixty-five million people, leaving nine million dead and twenty-one million wounded. By 1918, much of Europe lay in ruins or disarray, while the rest of the continent sank into poverty. Both the victorious Allied coalition and the defeated Central Powers emerged impoverished, as their gold reserves were shipped to the United States and neutral states in exchange for food and ammunition. In a matter of months, Germany and Austria-Hungary, the two empires that spanned much of Central and East-Central Europe, collapsed, replaced by ten smaller states and even more "wannabe" states and over ten thousand kilometers of new borders. Socialist revolutions erupted in most major cities from Strasbourg to Budapest in 1918–1919, while war continued between Poland and Soviet Russia and between Hungary and Romania, paramilitary groups terrorized Jews and borderland populations for years, and the Spanish flu decimated rich and poor alike.[1] The wave of revolutions and border changes that swept through the former Austria-Hungary and Germany after 1918, it seemed, would eclipse the influence of the two empires' bourgeoisie. The expectation of social change and a better life for peasants and workers after years of suffering for war aims that made little sense by 1918 threatened the basis of capitalism. Calls for revolutionary social change echoed the radicalism of Karl Marx and Friedrich Engels's 1848 *Communist Manifesto* and foreshadowed the fate of the bourgeoisie in Eastern Europe after 1948.

Even one of the wealthiest families in Europe, the multinational German-Hungarian steel tycoons the Thyssen-Bornemiszas, felt the impact of short-lived regime changes. Heinrich Thyssen-Bornemisza, the son of steel magnate August Thyssen, had to flee his Hungarian estate after the communist Béla Kun seized power.[2] Back at the family's headquarters in Germany, workers' councils had already subjected Heinrich's father and brother to a series of humiliating interrogations starting in November 1918.[3] The British expert at the Paris peace conference, John Maynard Keynes, who overtly empathized not just with defeated Germany but with the European bourgeoisie, noted that "we are thus faced in [continental] Europe with the spectacle of an extraordinary weakness on the part of the great capitalist class. . . . The terror and personal timidity of the individuals of this class is now so great, their confidence in their place in society and in their necessity to the social organism so diminished, that they are the easy victims of intimidation."[4]

Yet the First World War and its turbulent aftermath did not manage to destroy Central Europe's "capitalist class" as Keynes and others had predicted. Surprisingly, most tycoons returned to their villas or moved to new ones within months after sovereignty changes and revolutions. Tracing the fate of European business dynasties through French, Swiss, German, Austrian, Hungarian, and Romanian archives reveals glaring continuities across the dividing line of 1918, not just among the top "one percent" of local societies but also among middle classes, professionals, and workers. These continuities contradict still-dominant historical narratives that emphasize the victimhood of ethnic minorities, the "trauma" of vanquished states, and the ecstasy of "new beginnings" in victorious countries.[5] How did these families in Alsace-Lorraine—such as the de Dietrichs, who furnished trench equipment to the German army—become the darlings of the French regime after 1918? How did a Hungarian Jewish industrialist, Mózes Farkas, become one of the most influential businessmen in the openly antisemitic and anti-Hungarian Greater Romania? In short, how did so many industrialists and ethnic minorities thrive in countries where minorities were officially unwanted and even targeted for persecution or discrimination, and do so despite the havoc of total war, imperial collapse, and changes of sovereignty?

Our laser-like focus on the "episodic history" of events that fix our attention on ruptures such as the disintegration of empires and competing nationalisms has led us to overlook the slow-moving structures of social and economic life that belied the nationalist rhetoric of ethnically homogenous societies preached by governments after 1918.[6] From waning empires and nascent states as units of analysis, the present study directs our attention instead to industrialists whose fate cannot be understood within the familiar story of imperial decline, ethnic violence, and antisemitism alone. Relevant and prevalent as these processes were, they obscure the agency that ethnic minorities, especially powerful industrialists, possessed to delay, divert, or sabotage their effects, or even to re-create their fortunes. Understanding why some of these actors were especially apt at doing so does not mean downplaying ethnic violence or the corrupting effect of antisemitism on the social fabric of Central and East-Central Europe, nor does it imply nostalgia or praise for powerful business elites. Rather, analyzing these remarkable continuities in social hierarchies brings us closer to understanding the mechanisms of social change, or the lack thereof, during times of unprecedented crises and chaos, how war rendered states fragile and beholden to the bourgeoisie, and why it is difficult—or impossible—for new regimes to "dissolve the people and elect another," as Bertolt Brecht famously quipped.[7] Local resilience had its limits, and many businesses would not survive the disruptions and destruction of the late 1930s and 1940s. Yet it would be misleading to read history backward, from the perspective of the Holocaust or nationalizations in the Soviet bloc, because to do so is to overlook the remarkable resilience of European societies, even in hotly contested border regions.

Continuities in social hierarchies despite political ruptures and the weakness of ethnic nationalism are best studied in regions well known for their turbulent politics and violent nationalist clashes. Perhaps no two regions demonstrate the division of European societies along ethnic lines as vividly as Alsace-Lorraine and Transylvania. Even so, they are rarely compared, owing to their geographical distance and ingrained taboos against comparing the histories of "developed" Western Europe with those of "backward" East-Central Europe.[8] Yet case studies drawn from the two regions show how similar processes of total war, imperial collapse, and nationalist mobilization worked out in different parts of the continent.[9] Despite belonging to different states, Alsace-Lorraine and Transylvania shared many similarities beyond their strategic importance for multiple empires and nation-building projects and the outcome, if not the origins, of the First World War. Both were multiethnic, with Germans and Jews constituting a large proportion of industrialists, and both were integrated within the same alliance systems, initially the Central Powers spearheaded by Germany between 1914 and 1918, then France's nascent European alliance in the 1920s. The trajectory of industrialists in the two regions also speaks to multiple national and imperial histories, including those of France, Germany, Austria-Hungary, and Romania, and the history of modern Europe more generally.

While case studies come with inherent limitations, they add depth to statistical comparisons, especially in an era when statistics were scarce and organized along national rather than regional boundaries. Germany and Austria-Hungary and the era of the Great War are especially well suited for comparative and transnational investigation because, in part due to the military alliance of the two Central European empires or the blockade, many of the processes that affected the fate of industrialists, such as shortages, the centralization of production, and enormous demand for finished products, were not specific to a given national context but affected both empires, cut off as they were from global markets. The study of convergences and divergences in the era of the first total war can also help us avoid "methodological nationalism" and misleading "locally specific explanations"[10] of global processes such as the First World War or the transition from empires to successor states.

The businessmen studied in this book probably never met in real life, although they were swept up in similar processes of war, economic nationalism, border changes, and political integration under the hegemony of Germany, and after 1918, of France. Paris attempted to use its unchallenged military presence in Eastern Europe to supplant German hegemony in the region after the Allies defeated the Central Powers, becoming the new, albeit economically depleted, "poor imperialist" of the region, a move made possible by the temporary withdrawal of Russia and the United States from European politics.[11] French troops were present in both Alsace-Lorraine and Transylvania, while the commander of the French army in the Balkans, Henri Mathias Berthelot, noted in private correspondence before being transferred from Transylvania to Lorraine that "in Greater Romania we could have the nicest French colony in the world."[12] The stories of businessmen and commercial transactions in *Capitalism in Chaos* thus stretch from Paris to Strasbourg, Budapest, Cluj, and farther east to Bucharest, as well as to several smaller localities from the steel town of Hagondange in Lorraine to the mining town of Petroșani in Transylvania.

As the histories of Europe's distinct regions have been forced into the Procrustean bed of national histories, or into stovepiped histories of Eastern and Western Europe in the modern period, alternative units of territorial integration have been forgotten. Yet self-proclaimed nation-states only started to dominate the map of Central and Eastern Europe after the First World War, while German and French attempts to forge these regions into an alliance exercised a far-reaching influence on the economic life of these territories.[13] It may thus be time to recover connections between Eastern and Western Europe from under the rubble of the Cold War, which reinforced a sharp East-West split on the continent.[14] At a time when lifestyles and economies are slowly converging between the former Eastern Bloc and the founding states of the European Union in Western Europe, this history, which showcases an antecedent to this convergence, is timelier than ever.

The nine chapters of this book develop five main themes and arguments. First, they explore why business elites survived and occasionally thrived amid chaos and uncertainty, and second, why the economic ties that came into being under the German and Austro-Hungarian empires endured despite defeat in the First World War and the disintegration of the two empires. Third, the book reveals many similarities between two regions that are rarely thought to have much in common: Alsace-Lorraine and Transylvania, and throws light on the importance of Mitteleuropa or Central Europe as unit of analysis that preceded the more familiar Cold War division of the continent. Fourth, while I expected to find more upheaval in social hierarchies in Transylvania and Europe's East than in Alsace-Lorraine and the West, given the massive territorial reshuffling in the regions of the former during and after the First World War, I actually found more profound changes unfolding in the latter.[15] In this Franco-German borderland, the property of German industrialists like the Adlers and Oppenheimers was expropriated by the French state between 1918 and 1920, following similar anti-French attempts by the German imperial administration between 1914 and 1918.[16] At the same time, in "Eastern European" Transylvania, both the Hungarian and Romanian administrations adopted a less dogmatic approach to nationalism than in "Western" Alsace-Lorraine and were more receptive to business interests while following this pragmatic line. Finally, the chapters that follow explore why even powerful states like France and Germany could not push through their agendas on the local level. The impact of the First World War and its aftermath instead emerged from negotiations among business leaders, city officials, regional politicians, governments, and military officers as they wielded different levels of agency amid the chaos of war and accelerated political changes. As a result, the economic nationalism of Germany, France, Romania, and Hungary was often frustrated.

Given that statistical data on regional and local economies and even on industrial production and consumption are scarce and unreliable, especially for the period of the First World War, surviving company archives that house personal and business correspondence and corporate annual reports offer more clues for understanding how European family businesses fared amid political changes. By focusing on midsize family firms in the same branch of industry (tanning) on the eastern and western peripheries of Germany's Central European alliance, it is possible to contrast how comparable businesses fared during similar political processes in different parts of Europe. Perspectives from smaller, provincial family firms are coupled with analysis of the negotiations that took place in the smoke-filled rooms of government ministers and corporate headquarters of mines and steel plants. The divergence between the successful maneuvering of East-Central European businesses and the expropriation of Western European German firms is further confirmed by the fate of Lorraine's and Transylvania's steel plants and coal mines, the other major industry branches under scrutiny.

Over the past decade, my research on the history of European industrialists has taken me from the de Dietrichs' castle in Reichshoffen in Alsace to a cramped socialist-era flat in Cluj-Napoca in search of surviving photographs and company correspondence buried, often literally, under the rubble of the Second World War. Businesses never operated in isolation from the state and politics, and they were also embedded in society through laws that bound them. Therefore, political, social, and economic histories are blended with a cultural history of businesses and their contexts that draws not only on regional, national, foreign ministry, and international organization archives but also on press clippings and fiction in French, Romanian, German, Hungarian, and English.

The over one hundred boxes of letters, memoranda, receipts, production reports, and statistics of the Renner tannery housed in the Cluj county chapter of the Romanian National Archives were an especially comprehensive source, spanning as they do regime and sovereignty changes as Cluj shifted back and forth between Hungarian and Romanian sovereignty. While the socialist regimes of Eastern Europe preserved the business correspondence of companies like the Renners', the memorabilia of bourgeois families did not make it into public collections and much of it was destroyed or remained scattered even three decades after 1989. One consequence of expulsions and Nazi genocide is that the history of bourgeois family life and the stories of businessmen's wives and daughters who were not directly involved in business operations has to be pieced together from a scanty source base, including the less reliable tabloid press of the time. The Adler-Oppenheimer papers were scattered after the family's emigration from Nazi Germany, much like the family archive of the Chorins, who owned and managed Transylvania's coal mines; the de Dietrich firm is the only one that has remained, at least in part, in the hands of the same family.

Overview of the Book

During the First World War, the fate of industrial companies depended heavily on laws, institutions, and political practices rooted in the European order that came into being by 1871 with the creation of unified Germany, Italy, Austria-

Hungary, the French Third Republic, and independent Romania. The first and second chapters thus address the prewar origins of industrial companies' very different fortunes in Alsace-Lorraine and Transylvania, and Germany and Austria-Hungary more generally during the First World War; they explore why Hungarian businesses surprisingly had more backing from the state than did those on the western peripheries of the German empire when the First World War broke out, even as the latter surpassed them in industrial capacity and wealth. The German administration hindered the development of Alsace-Lorraine's industries by embracing German economic nationalism directed at "unfaithful" Alsatian companies. Economic nationalism escalated especially on the eve of the Great War, a trend illustrated by the incident at the Grafenstaden machine-building factory, which led to the withdrawal of state commissions from one of the largest Alsatian plants. Economic nationalism also rendered relationships between Alsatian firms and imperial authorities tenuous at a time when corporations' success depended heavily on state support. By contrast, the Hungarian state supported industrialists with protectionist economic measures and lavish industrialization subsidies before these became widespread all over Europe during the postwar period. Even as many of these initiatives failed to establish a modern industrial sector, they strengthened an industrial bourgeoisie loyal to the state that was eventually able to economically survive the collapse of Austria-Hungary. Furthermore, in contrast to the German government, the Budapest administration suppressed calls for economic discrimination against ethnic minorities, in part because minorities owned only a fraction of the wealth in contested multiethnic territories of Hungary such as Transylvania.

Chapters 3 and 4 address the economic winners and losers of the First World War, respectively; they trace why some industrial companies were enriched even as imperial treasuries were drained, and how the radicalization of the First World War made the Central Powers turn against the wealth of their "domestic enemies," including Alsatians, Lorrainers, and Transylvania's Romanians. As chapter 3, "Millionaires of Mitteleuropa," shows, the blockade of the Central Powers by the Allies led to an industrialization drive in East-Central Europe that bred its own class of the ultrarich that profited from low taxes and lax state supervision of businesses. German banks and industrial companies "discovered" Transylvania and Southeastern Europe after the Allied blockade barred them from colonial markets in 1914. The Renners' skyrocketing prosperity showcased the economic ascent of businessmen in a new, German-dominated Europe that decisively faced east as it thrived on the economic exploitation of the occupied Balkans and Ukraine. In the meantime, the economic downturn of Alsace and Lorraine stemmed from the self-destructive pursuit of "enemy" industrialists that hindered the German economy at a time when it needed all available resources to fight the war.

Chapter 4, "The Enemy's Money," explores why the vexation, expropriation, and internment of domestic and foreign industrialists in the German empire in general, and in Alsace in particular, hindered the German war effort and created an insecure business environment even for otherwise prosperous companies. Transylvania's ethnic minority elites such as Romanian bankers and landowners were in a significantly better position than were their Alsatian counterparts, as the Austrian and Hungarian governments postponed the implementation of economic discrimination against domestic and foreign enemies until late into the war. In-depth case studies direct our attention to the wasteful aspects of the war economy even as the Great War is often touted as the heyday of economic planning.

The third part of the book addresses the "economic consequences of the peace" as experienced by industrialists. Chapter 5, on "secret deals," showcases how the power vacuum that characterized Central Europe after the armistices was more a time of maneuvering industrialists than of ambitious economic planners. Entrepreneurs, speculators, and politicians scrambled to exploit sovereignty changes to seize enemy property or cement their positions among the "top 1 percent" by other means. Yet such dubious practices of wealth accumulation were more widespread in Alsace and Lorraine than in Transylvania, where no massive expropriations of industrialists took place after 1918. Instead, the incoming Romanian administration and the notables of Transylvanian society made a series of deals that often remained hidden from the Bucharest government, mitigating the impact of sovereignty change for ethnic minorities. As chapter 9 explores in further detail, despite the fierce antiminority stance of the Romanian administration, it tacitly relied on ethnic minorities—primarily Hungarians, including many Jews—to run the economy as it struggled to establish its rule over the newly conquered territories. These deals ensured the functioning of the Romanian state and cemented the positions of prewar elites even as the Germans of Alsace and Lorraine were expropriated and expelled by the French government.

Chapter 6 explores the disparate impact of French hegemony in Central Europe on industrialists in the former German and Austro-Hungarian empires. While in Alsace and Lorraine it led to total expropriation and expulsion of former enemies, in East-Central Europe the French government and corporations acted as mediators between the pre-1918 business elite and new sovereigns, which contributed to the continued influence of most Austro-Hungarian banks and industrial companies. Surprisingly, the industrialists of Austria-Hungary often became better allies of French expansion than did the protectionist states that France helped create.

Chapter 7 explores why forging new national communities by spreading national currencies on formerly Austro-Hungarian and German territories proved particularly challenging for successor states, and sheds light on how costly it was to annex and integrate territories. While the French government attempted to win over some Alsatian and Lorrainer industrialists with a favorable conversion rate on German currency, doing so nearly bankrupted its treasury and precipitated financial chaos in the banking sector. At the same time, the belated conversion of the Austro-Hungary currency by the Romanian administration ended up unintentionally benefiting the country's ethnic minorities.

Finally, the last two chapters, on the 1920s, document how those businessmen who were supposed to sustain losses from the postimperial transition emerged prosperous in the early 1920s, while those who were expected to benefit stagnated. In East-Central Europe, even those industrialists who became ethnic minorities benefited from economic protectionism despite the hardships brought on by the need to re-create states' markets and establish novel political alliances with the hostile political elites of successor states. The mining and steel magnates—the de Dietrichs and other Alsatian industrialists—initially profited from their "return" to France even as they subsequently struggled to find their place in France's European and colonial markets, while industrialists like Farkas did comparably well in an agrarian Greater Romania badly in need of industrial goods. Meanwhile, the expropriation of German industrialists in Alsace and Lorraine did not eliminate those business families as many of them managed to re-create their industrial empires in Weimar Germany by borrowing from private banks and tapping state support, in addition to relying on their domestic assets. The Great Depression and the rise of Nazism did not immediately upend the trajectories of the companies studied here, especially as industrialists often applied the strategies of maneuvering they had learned in the 1910s, as the epilogue to this book briefly describes.

Chapter 1

Industrialists and Consolidation in Central Europe (1867–1914)

While the history of late nineteenth-century Central and Eastern Europe often conjures up the image of crowded passenger ships leaving the busy ports of Trieste or Hamburg for the United States, migrants often remained on the continent and moved from smaller to larger towns, nearby regions, or other states on the continent. Isaac Adler (b. 1837) and Johann Renner (b. 1856) left their hometowns in Baden and Württemberg and settled in Alsace-Lorraine and Transylvania, respectively—regions that were integrated into Germany and Hungary in the 1870s.[1] Both were in the leather business: Adler was a merchant, and Renner had learned the trade of tanning. While Adler and his brother-in-law and business partner Ferdinand Oppenheimer headed west to Alsace, Renner moved east on his own and settled in Transylvania in the early 1880s.[2] At the time, German states were overpopulated, and "free towns" and urban commerce and industry remained the dominion of guilds and patricians, leaving few opportunities for newcomers.[3]

The lands of the Austro-Hungarian and German empires were far from homogenous at the end of the nineteenth century, yet the prevalence of the German language in cities, the temperate climate, the diplomatic alliance of Germany and Austria-Hungary, and commercial connections forged ties across the region from Strasbourg in Alsace to Kronstadt in Transylvania.[4] Germans who decided to immigrate to Alsace-Lorraine and East-Central European regions like Transylvania could join communities of fellow German-speaking

Lutherans and Catholics. Both Alsace and East-Central Europe were also traditional areas of settlement for Jewish immigrants from the German lands and Russian Poland.[5] As Tara Zahra has emphasized, the "great departure" to the United States was a risky and costly move that often ended in impoverishment and therefore tended to attract those who had few other options and lived on the margins of their societies: the millions of landless peasants, ethnic minorities, and especially the persecuted Jews of the Russian empire.[6] 'Small departures' within Central and Eastern Europe were safer alternatives that did not require giving up native tongues and ties to religious communities in the way that immigrating to the United States did. Thus, moving within Central and Eastern Europe was especially attractive for businessmen and craftsmen who had a vested interest in retaining and cultivating their family ties and commercial networks back home.

The general contours of Europe's borders on the eve of the First World War, with the exception of the Balkans, emerged between 1867 and 1871. The impact and geographical scope of the events of the late 1860s and 1870s are comparable to those of other momentous turning points in the history of these regions, such as the Napoleonic Wars, the 1848 revolutions, or 1914. The 1860s and 1870s saw the end of an era of substantial political transformations in Central Europe that had started with the 1848 revolutions and resulted in the creation of a unified Italy, imperial Germany, and the Austro-Hungarian empire. The German and Austro-Hungarian empires were also linked by a military alliance from 1879 onward, which would eventually serve as the basis of the Central Powers in 1914.

As measured by its long-standing stability, which went hand in hand with unparalleled economic development and industrialization, the Central European order between the 1870s and 1914 was a success, yet the suppression of regional autonomies, nationalist aspirations, workers' movements, and calls for land reform, along with a host of other interests in the two empires, left many workers, women, landless peasants, and nationalist activists dissatisfied.[7] This Central European order was a German order from the outset, conjured up in the study of the Prussian chancellor Otto von Bismarck. Accordingly, the fates of Alsace-Lorraine and Transylvania, as well as those of Hungary and other territories, were subordinated to German strategic interests. Bismarck's aim in the 1860s and 1870s was to unify German lands and to secure this empire from both the west and the east. Alsace-Lorraine's appearance on the map of Europe as a distinct region coincided with Transylvania's disappearance in the early 1870s, and both were related to Bismarck's goal of securing the German empire. The annexation of Alsace-Lorraine weakened France and also provided a protective buffer zone around Germany's western borders. Prussia defeated Austria in

1866, thus effectively barring the Habsburgs from influencing Prussia's unification of Germany. In part because of pressure from Bismarck after Austria's military defeats, the Austrian emperor Francis Joseph accorded full internal autonomy to his Hungarian crownlands, which kept Austria in check from the east and further limited Francis Joseph's German aspirations. The Austro-Hungarian Compromise of 1867 allowed Hungarian elites to reunite Transylvania with the rest of the Hungarian crownlands and embark on turning these disparate regions into a Hungarian nation-state within the Dual Monarchy.[8] A large and semi-autonomous Hungary strengthened by Transylvania also allowed Hungarian elites to systematically modernize the country's economy, including transportation, and develop its industries.[9] Despite the bloody civil war between pro-independence Hungarians and pro-Habsburg Romanians in Transylvania in 1848–1849, the integration of Transylvania and its majority Romanian population into Hungary was smoother than that of Alsace-Lorraine into the German empire—the latter the result of a brutal war that included the shelling of Strasbourg and generated four decades of diplomatic tensions between France and Germany along with long-term discontent in Alsace-Lorraine.[10]

Alsace-Lorraine was one of the most industrialized regions in Central Europe, but in the 1870s its industrialists were hard-hit by the tariff walls that cut them off from French markets shortly after the Franco-Prussian War. The region's limited autonomy, and its subordinate position within the "polycratic" German empire made up of federal states, all of which enjoyed more rights than Alsace-Lorraine, was a further disadvantage.[11] Despite considerable accommodation to German rule, mistrust between the region's industrialists and the German military still lingered in the early twentieth century. Franco-German tensions over Alsace-Lorraine, the unfulfilled political aspirations of Transylvania's Romanians in Hungary, the militaristic culture of imperial Germany, and other long-standing problems of the late nineteenth century influenced how industrialists fared during the First World War.[12] The business elites and industrial companies of Central Europe who were to shape economic life for decades to come and even up to the present day emerged in the late nineteenth and early twentieth centuries. Revisiting the political constraints and institutions that had come into being by the 1870s also sheds light on the political and economic environment in Central Europe that influenced the fate and prosperity of industrialists during the First World War.

The reason Transylvania emerged as a region with more prospects for industrialists than Alsace-Lorraine by 1914 despite its lower level of industrialization lies in the differences between the two regions' integrations into their respective empires. In 1878, even the liberal nationalist former mayor of Pest, Móric Szentkirályi, who regarded Hungary and Alsace-Lorraine as comparable victims of imperial expansion, noted the relative economic plight of the region after German annexation as compared with Hungary's position within the Dual Monarchy.[13] "The only pride of Alsace-Lorraine's industrialists is to be able to pay the bread of their workers and their production costs, but even this does not work out all the time. Several factories that had flourished [before 1871] had gone bankrupt or their owners had emigrated. . . . All these factors explain why the Alsatians are dissatisfied with the present situation."[14] Szentkirályi's views on Alsace were inspired by the writings of the Alsatian Francophile Reichstag deputy Charles Grad, who stressed the plight of the Alsatian economy after German annexation.[15] Yet Alsace-Lorraine's economy also remained a model to emulate for Hungarian observers even as they noted the region's political troubles: "Why aren't there at least twenty industry towns [like the Alsatian Colmar] in Hungary? How different the situation of our domestic industries would be then," lamented a Hungarian journalist in 1876.[16]

Szentkirályi contrasted the nationalist sentiments and economic interests of subdued populations and concluded that people cared more about their wallets than their politics. He argued that the Alsatian situation remained unstable because the German empire was undercutting the prosperity of Alsace-Lorraine, not because it annexed it from France: "If the reason for the alienation of Alsatians and Lorrainers from Germany were their love of the homeland [France] alone, they would have already surrendered their resistance, as people are more likely to accept grievances that affect their rights than those that harm their [economic] interests."[17] Szentkirályi's evaluation of the Alsatian situation echoed his views of Hungary's status within the Dual Monarchy. Although Hungarians had to renounce independence, the country prospered economically within the Dual Monarchy. Eventually, accommodation to the new political environment became a reality in both Alsace-Lorraine and Transylvania by the 1900s, pushing the dilemmas of imperial integration that Grad and Szentkirályi had articulated into the background.

Transylvania's Industrialists in the Dual Monarchy

Johann Renner was a Bavarian craftsman who immigrated to Transylvania in his early twenties with no capital. He had only his superior tanning skills, which during his first decade in Transylvania earned him a living as the assistant and then partner of a Saxon craftsman in Szászrégen, or Regen in German, a small town where he had lived for years before moving to Kolozsvár, Transylvania's central city, around 1900. Szászrégen was an ideal destination in terms of

Renner's future assimilation into the Hungarian business community of Transylvania: craftsmen in this town were bilingual, which enabled him to learn Hungarian while relying on his German.[18] His arrival also coincided with the top-down dismantlement of traditional society by the Budapest government, which curtailed the autonomy of craftsmen's guilds and opened up opportunities for newcomers. In addition, Renner's marriage to the daughter of a wealthy local butcher helped him start his own business.

The Dual Monarchy's tariff policy incentivized trade within Austria-Hungary, and as a result, Austria remained Hungary's main trading partner. By the turn of the century, trade outside the Dual Monarchy represented just one-eighth of Hungary's national product.[19] This meant low exposure to foreign markets and firms, which proved to be an asset during the First World War, when the Allied blockade and isolationism cut Central Europe off from global trade routes. Despite the diplomatic alliance that had linked Germany and Austria-Hungary, economic relations between the two empires were far from cordial in the late nineteenth century. Trade between Germany and Austria-Hungary reached a low after Germany implemented protectionist economic measures in the aftermath of the 1873 Vienna stock market crash, which was partly fueled by speculation with the 5 billion franc indemnity France was forced to pay Germany after the Franco-Prussian War.[20] The recycling of French reparations by German and Austro-Hungarian banks at first precipitated a boom that gave way to economic decline from Alsace-Lorraine to Transylvania.[21] In 1877, Germany introduced higher tariffs for Austro-Hungarian agricultural products, which prompted Hungarian landowners to lobby for comparable protection against Romanian, Bulgarian, Turkish, and Russian imports to the Dual Monarchy.[22]

Transylvania's increasing integration with the rest of Austria-Hungary thus went hand in hand with the Dual Monarchy's loosening economic ties with Southeastern Europe, which negatively affected the economic life of Transylvania's border regions.[23] Repeated tariff wars with Romania and Serbia between the 1880s and 1910 and the Balkan Wars of 1912 and 1913 hampered commercial relations and devastated southern Transylvania's industries that had exported to Romania. They also contributed to the minimization of economic ties between Transylvania and neighboring Romania and Serbia by 1914, which left Hungarian industrialists and craftsmen unprepared to conquer the markets of Southeastern Europe during the First World War, even as some Transylvanian firms relocated branches to Romania to fight restrictive tariffs.[24]

Despite the substantial Romanian and Serbian populations in Hungary near the Romanian and Serbian borders and intensive cross-border trade in prior decades, only 2 percent of Hungary's imports came from Romania, while combined Serbian and Bulgarian imports to Hungary failed to reach 1 percent in 1913.[25] In 1913, only 3 percent of Hungarian exports went to Bulgaria, Romania, and Serbia combined.[26] Still, commercial exchanges continued to sustain the prosperous Saxon border town of Brassó, at least as regards the textile and tanning industries, while small-scale transactions across the border remained relevant for the livelihood of border zones despite their overall insignificance for the respective national economies.[27] Much like the Alsatian firms that had relocated to France to avoid punitive tariffs, southern Transylvania's craftsmen and small manufacturers moved to Romania to retain their markets while a host of Hungarian male workers and peasant women working as maids followed them to escape the Szekler Land's economic crisis.[28] Ironically, the negative effects of Hungary's "tariff war" with Romania were felt mostly in the Hungarian-populated area of southeastern Transylvania, the Szekler Land, where the government had to invest in creating factory jobs for the unemployed, including single women whose emigration to Romania created a moral panic among Hungarian nationalist policymakers.[29]

Industrialization in Transylvania was modest until the 1890s, fueled mostly by railway construction, tax breaks, agricultural demands, and urbanization, which led to a construction boom of historicist tenement buildings in the region's major cities.[30] Relocating to Kolozsvár proved to be a prescient move on the part of the Renners, since the region had become the railway hub and administrative center of Transylvania by 1900. Government-subsidized railroads greatly contributed to connecting Transylvania's economy to that of the Hungarian interior and boosted economic development and commerce.[31] A trip on the Budapest–Kolozsvár line, which was completed in 1870, took eight hours;[32] thanks to the centralized tariff regime adopted in 1889, a train ticket from Budapest to Nagyvárad (190 miles) cost the same as a ticket from Budapest to the most remote city in Transylvania, Brassó (451 miles), which encouraged the orientation of Transylvania's commerce to the interior of Hungary.[33] In 1883, the Budapest government took railway lines into state ownership, which enabled it to extend advantageous freight rates to firms registered in Hungary, despite criticism from Austria.[34]

The outskirts of late nineteenth-century Central European cities, including Kolozsvár and Strasbourg, looked remarkably rural with their vegetable gardens, small houses, and dirt roads. The Renners rented a house with a long plot of land suitable for their manufacture, which became one of these rural peripheries of Transylvania's "capital." The community of farmers in the neighborhood of Hóstát did not accept the Renners (likely because they resented the foul smell of tanning), and their landlord was forced to auction the house they had rented in order to pressure them to leave.[35] Johann Renner could not afford to lose the plot as it was less than a mile from the new railway line and the Kis-Szamos River, both of which were essential for reasons of transport and the tanning process, respectively. Renner thus sold all his leather stocks and was able to place the highest bid at the auction, which enabled the family to remain in the house.

By the 1910s, the move to Kolozsvár also brought Johann Renner into contact with social milieus and business networks that were unavailable in Szászrégen, including regional bankers, leather merchants, and shop owners. Kolozsvár was the seat of Transylvania's landowning aristocracy and was the country's second university town after Budapest.[36] The city was an administrative center and a hub of the justice system, which drew well-paid civil servants, while Kolozsvár's Hungarian Jewish bourgeoisie was open to investing in industrial enterprises. Most importantly, Kolozsvár was home to over twenty bank offices, including those of the monarchy's largest credit institutions as well as the Civic Savings Bank, a smaller regional bank that eventually partnered with the Renners in the 1910s. The city's population doubled between 1880 and 1910 to around sixty-one thousand, giving industrialists like the Renners access to the labor of Kolozsvár's roughly seven thousand workers, who had been organized into trade unions since the 1890s.[37] There were over eighty industrial establishments in the city, including smaller tanneries, but just nine larger factories competed for most of the workers. These factories made matches, brick, and soap. While four-fifths of the city's population was Hungarian, Romanians and Germans made up 12 percent and 3 percent, respectively, of the population; the small Romanian middle class included lawyers, judges, and even some civil servants.[38] The Albina Bank of the Transylvanian Romanian bourgeoisie was headquartered in Nagyszeben in southern Transylvania, where the majority of the Romanian population was concentrated. This bank had been thoroughly integrated into the Austro-Hungarian banking system by 1914 and had no ties to Romania.[39] All over Transylvania, Romanian banks like the Albina sustained around five hundred bourgeois families, including clerks, accountants, and bankers; only one-fourth of the educated Romanian middle class, around a thousand men, managed to enter the municipal and state service, which constituted highly coveted, secure positions informally reserved for the sons of Hungarian Christian middle-class families. Thus, around seven thousand families of priests and teachers and a few hundred wealthier landowners and peasants constituted the backbone of the Transylvanian Romanian middle class and national movement, concentrated mostly in the smaller towns of southern Transylvania.[40] The Renners likely employed several Romanian workers and a few Romanian clerks, but most of their business contacts were restricted to the Hungarian, German, and Jewish bourgeoisie before 1918.[41]

The German and Austro-Hungarian empires did not favor the protection of regional economic interests, and separate customs lines were equally unavailable to Alsace-Lorraine, Transylvania, and Hungary before 1918. The Dual Monarchy's customs union between Austria and Hungary was advantageous to Austrian and Bohemian industries, which could export duty free to less industrialized Hungary, as well as owners of large agricultural estates in Hungary, who profited from selling grain and flour on the Austrian market at prices surpassing those of European grain markets glutted by North American imports.[42] The Hungarian state embraced policies of economic nationalism and state-led industrialization before these became widespread in the successor states of Austria-Hungary after 1918. In order to favor Hungarian industries over their Austrian counterparts, Budapest passed four Industry Acts between 1881 and 1907 that offered tax breaks, favorable freight rates, and even direct cash subsidies to Hungarian industries or companies willing to relocate a branch to Hungary.[43] The last industry promotion act even favored light industry "start-ups" and proved to be crucial to Johann Renner's transformation from craftsman to industrialist after 1910, when the family decided to establish a factory.

Furthermore, although Transylvania's regional administration was permanently discontinued after 1867, this did not entail the end of regionalist politics altogether. By the 1910s, Transylvanian politicians had established a powerful lobby group within the house of representatives, the Parliament, to promote both Hungarian national supremacy and the region's economic modernization.[44] This contrasted with the case of Upper Hungary, Vojvodina, the Banat, or the Transdanubian regions, which showed no comparable signs of regional political mobilization within Hungary, a centralized state modeled after France.[45] In comparison to Alsace-Lorraine, Transylvania enjoyed the privileges that came from being incorporated into a much smaller state than the German empire, one in which the more than five million inhabitants of the Banat, eastern Hungary, Máramaros, and historical Transylvanian made up more than one-fourth of the total population while these regions also constituted more than one-third of Hungary's territory.[46] Starting in the 1880s, Transylvania's coal, natural gas, and other natural resources attracted the interest of Budapest politicians and bankers who were crucial in promoting railway connections between Transylvania's industrial areas and the rest of Hungary. It was Budapest's powerful politicians, bankers, and businessmen who created Transylvania's modern mining and heavy industries, profiting neatly from the process. They also managed to act as mediators for French,

German, and Belgian bankers and industrialists who appeared with sizable capital from the 1880s on.[47]

French and German Investors, State Subsidies, and the Making of Transylvania's Business Elite

Where business elites did not exist, they had to be created by state subsidies from the ranks of loyal politicians and businessmen whose companies grew enormously thanks to government subsidies and commissions during the dualist period. Heavy industries, mining, and railways were especially dependent on state support, which explains why governments were able to promote politicians as managers or board members of those companies. The massive expansion of heavy industries led to the prevalence of stock-exchange companies over family businesses because the former were able to attract new capital more easily. This process was more apparent in Transylvania, which was in the process of developing its modern heavy industries than in Alsace-Lorraine, where the long-standing industrialist families, such as the de Wendels and de Dietrichs, retained their prominent positions even as the Thyssen and other German corporations also expanded.[48] In Transylvania, coal mining and ironworks were overwhelmingly in the hands of publicly traded Budapest or Vienna-based companies by 1900 that took over state concessions and the few smaller manufactures. In Lorraine, Belgian and Luxembourg capitalists made forays into the steel industry as French investors avoided Germany and looked farther east. Notably, by 1900 Transylvania outstripped Alsace-Lorraine as a destination for French foreign investments in mining and steel plants as part of a broader flow of French capital to Russia and East-Central Europe.[49]

German investments were concentrated in gold mining, the sugar industry, timber extraction, and, on the eve of the First World War, natural gas.[50] German banks and corporations either took over smaller manufacturers or established brand-new ones with sizable investments in equipment and buildings and often partnered with Austrian and Hungarian business elites who had existing investments and knew where capital might provide the best returns. Saxon industrialists such as the Czell family also served as a link between German and Hungarian investors in Transylvania.[51] The Harkort'sche Mining Company bought up gold mines between 1884 and 1889 and accounted for one-third of Hungary's gold extraction by the end of the century, while the Bleichröder Bank, Disconto-Gesellschaft, and the Hungarian General Credit Bank jointly established a large sugar factory near Brassó.[52]

The first investors in southern Transylvania's iron ore and coal mines and steel plants in the mid-nineteenth century were Viennese firms and the Austrian treasury, which owned them before the 1867 Compromise. French investors developed an interest in Transylvania owing to the extraordinary importance of coal for nineteenth-century industrialization and their avoidance of Lorraine's iron ore and the Ruhrland's coal mines after the Franco-Prussian War. The Hungarian Pallas Encyclopedia, a fixture in bourgeois salons and gentlemen's offices, stated with confidence in 1895 that "there is no other mineral, apart from iron, that plays such an important role in the life of the civilized man (*kulturember*) as coal. Almost every branch of industry can thank it for its rise; hardly is it possible to conceive humanity's rise to such high level of civilization (*művelődés*) without coal."[53] The use of coal as a major energy source in industries and households spread rapidly beginning in the early nineteenth century, and by 1900 it met between 80 and 90 percent of Europe's energy needs.[54] Owning coal deposits was a guaranteed path to prosperity as demand for coal grew faster than its output. France had to import one-fourth of its coal in 1900, which prompted French companies to invest in coal mines abroad, including in the Jiu valley or farther afield in the Donbass region in Russian Ukraine, where even the future Soviet first secretary Nikita Khrushchev worked for a French-owned mine as a mechanic in his youth.[55] In continental Europe, Germany and Austria-Hungary were the largest coal producers with output of 173 and 42 million tons, respectively, in 1905.[56] Hungary's coal mines accounted for only 18 percent of Austro-Hungarian production, but the country opened up new mines for exploitation and increased production of existing mine fields throughout the 1880s and 1890s, which put it on the map for European investors.[57]

Despite the Pallas Encyclopedia's optimism about the importance of coal, the exploitation of this natural resource encountered numerous difficulties in both Transylvania and the rest of Hungary until the fin de siècle.[58] Just as in Lorraine, political instability dissuaded both foreign and domestic investors until 1867, while the lack of railway routes and state subsidies contributed to the demise of traditional forge masters and family businesses by the 1860s. The Viennese and Bohemian investors behind the Kronstadt Mining Company, which had bought coal fields in the valley, tried to curry favor with the new Budapest administration in the 1870s to obtain subsidies for railway construction.[59] Unfortunately for the company, its Austrian managers were unfamiliar with the camarilla politics of the governing National Liberal Party and recruited a powerless deputy, Ágost Pulszky, to its governing board, who failed to achieve concessions.[60] The rise of coal mining in the Jiu valley only took off when powerful industrial companies with government connections took over production in the region. The incident also shed light on a broader phenomenon: railway construction with massive guarantees and investments by the state preceded most mining and heavy industrial investments by private companies.

After years of recession resulting from the 1873 Viennese stock market crash, Hungarian agriculture and light industries were booming in the 1880s and 1890s, and as in Lorraine, the major expansion of heavy industries and mining characterized the last decade of the nineteenth century. The two major Budapest banks—the General Credit Bank (GCB), with its ties to the Rothschild's Creditanstalt, and the Pest Hungarian Commercial Bank—had amassed enough capital to surpass their Austrian and French counterparts as the country's primary investment banks.[61] These two banks backed the mining corporations that scrambled to seize the concessions of the Kronstadt Mining Company and other firms to exploit the Jiu valley's coal deposits. The Urikány-Zsilvölgyi Hungarian Coal Mining Corporation (UZMC), which produced around 30 percent of the valley's coal, was backed by the GCB as well as French investors from Lyon, while the Salgótarján Coal Mining Corporation (SCMC) produced 60 percent of the valley's mining output.[62]

French investors had been present in the Transylvanian iron ore mining and steel industries since 1855, when the Parisian Crédit Mobilier bank of Émile and Isaac Pereire successfully "privatized" the Austrian State Railway Company and acquired vast industrial territories in the Banat.[63] The French group behind the UZMC had less clout than the Pereires; it was made up of a motley group of notables in and around Lyon connected to the Crédit Lyonnais. Some, like the UZMC's director viscount Fernand Bellescize, had minimal experience in business and mining. Bellescize was a member of Lyon's high society and acted as a guarantor of the trustworthiness of this remote Transylvanian company.[64] Léon Boussand was a speculator and banker who had gone bankrupt in the 1880s; he had also lost 5 million francs on Caucasian oil and Russian timber investments.[65] The Lyon investment banker Paul Morin Pons, a relative of the Alsatian Koechlins, and mine and railway company manager Jean Neyret, on the other hand, had a history of successful investments in the Loire valley's coal mines and forges.[66]

The Hungarian partners in the Charbonnage d'Urikany had considerably more political connections and business experience than the French group. The corporation's vice president was none other than Adolf Ullmann, the managing director of the GCB. Ullmann was ennobled by Francis Joseph in 1889, just two years before the founding of the UZMC. *In labore virtus*, "virtue lies in work," was the inscription on the Ullmann family's coat of arms.[67] Following the government's line was an equally important "virtue" of Adolf Ullmann, who became a member of the Budapest Upper House in 1908 and was made a baron ten years later. In sum, the French group also gained a guarantor of its investments from the highest circles of Hungarian finance and politics. Comparably high levels of government guarantee for the security of investments were unavailable in Madagascar, Tunis, and other colonial destinations where some of this group of Lyon businessmen had invested in the past, highlighting the advantages of East-Central European investments over colonial ventures.[68] As a result, French investments in Central and East-Central Europe were already four times the amount of French colonial investments by the 1880s.[69] The UZMC also had no trouble collaborating with the German-owned Oberschlesische Kokswerke to cofound a coke factory in 1899 in the Jiu valley.[70] The Franco-German economic cooperation documented by Raymond Poidevin and Volker Berghahn also went more smoothly in East-Central Europe than in Alsace-Lorraine and the rest of the Wilhelmine empire, especially as diplomatic tensions escalated in the 1910s.[71]

The French investors brought capital and an international reputation to the Jiu valley that would later provide crucial "brand recognition" in the chaotic era after the 1918 armistices when French investors resurfaced in Transylvania. The stock exchanges in Paris, Geneva, and Lyon regularly quoted both the UZMC's and the SCMC's prices, which speaks to Europe-wide economic integration in the late nineteenth century, although it remained limited to a few industries.[72] Both specialized papers targeted toward the savvy bourgeois investor and broadly circulated tabloids such as the *Voleur Illustré*, *La Caricature*, and the *Journal du Dimanche* reported on the Jiu valley's mines, which suggests that a broad section of the French provincial bourgeoisie invested in the UZMC and other lucrative East-Central European companies.[73] Thus, by 1914, a dense web of economic investments connected broad swathes of French society, and not only its elites, to booming Central and Eastern European companies that offered on average 5–12 percent returns on invested capital, an attractive premium at the height of the gold standard.[74]

Investing in Hungary was attractive for several reasons. One French journalist explained the results of late nineteenth-century economic development in what may have been a paid article given its jubilant tone: "Industry in every state intensifies its upward movement; but in no country does it manifest itself with such force as in Hungary."[75] Rather than a unique phenomenon, Hungary's growth rate was characteristic of the rest of East-Central Europe and the industrialized areas of European Russia. The country's coal production tripled and the length of its railway lines doubled, while the growth of the Hungarian domestic product was on par with or even surpassed Germany's.[76] Despite the gradual convergence of welfare benefits in Austria and Germany, the suppression of trade unions and the Social Democratic Party formed the background of Hungary's economic growth. In addition, what made the UZMC especially attractive to French investors, as compared with British and French firms, was cheap labor, which gave East-Central and Eastern European businesses their competitive edge at a time when even Western European miners faced unenviable conditions, as portrayed in Émile Zola's *Germinal*; the miners in *Germinal*, however, were able to resort to strikes to better their condition. Further east, "in Urikány, extraction of coal costs almost nothing, . . . and one does not have to fear crises caused by strikes," argued a journalist in the Parisian magazine *Voleur Illustré*.[77] But he was mistaken, as southern Transylvania's mining districts were rattled by strikes in 1897, 1901, and 1903. The 1897 Jiu valley strikes left eleven miners dead after clashes with the gendarmes, while the 1901 strikes on the Pereires' estates in Resica involved four thousand workers.[78] Nonetheless, given that the government banned national unionization by miners, labor unrest remained geographically fragmented and achieved only modest results as compared to the achievements of French strikes.[79] As the rise of the Jiu valley's major industrialist family the Chorins showed, the liberal nationalist governments of Budapest actively intervened in the "free market" to create a group of domestic industrialists by handing over the exploitation of state property to them, suppressing the workers' movement, and passing a series of legislation on taxes, tariffs, and freight rates that favored domestic industrialists and their French, German, Belgian, and Austrian partners.[80]

From Rabbis to Politicians and Industrialists: Social Mobility in Fin de Siècle Hungary

In Hungary, domestic capital gained prominence over foreign, mostly Austrian, French, and German investors by 1914, and no other family better embodied the state-sponsored rise of the Hungarian bourgeoisie than the Chorins, whose investments stretched from the Jiu valley in Transylvania to Budapest, Upper Hungary, and most industrial regions of the country.

The Chorins perfectly embodied the rising Budapest business elite that acquired key positions in the Transylvanian economy through close ties to the government, despite having no personal connection to the region. Their relationship to Transylvania is analogous to that of the Thyssens and Krupps, who emerged as major investors in Lorraine and yet never became part of the Lorraine business elite. Transylvania's first "coal baron" was Ferenc Chorin Sr. (1842–1925) who, like Johann Renner, became a wealthy man and industrialist only later in life. Chorin, the grandson of reform rabbi Áron Chorin and the son of a physician from Arad, a prosperous commercial center in the borderland between Transylvania and the interior of Hungary, started his career as a provincial lawyer.[81] Like most educated Jews who came of age during and after the failed revolution and anti-Habsburg war of independence in 1848 and 1849, Chorin was a liberal Hungarian nationalist.[82] The 1867 compromise catapulted this onetime provincial lawyer into a career in national politics.[83] In 1871, Chorin became one of the first Jewish deputies to be elected to the Budapest Parliament. He continued to serve as a deputy until 1901 with only a few years of absence, and in 1903 he became a lifelong member of the Upper House as well. He was an ascetic and strong-willed man whose career as an industrialist started at the age of thirty-nine, when the SCMC invited him to serve on its board. Chorin took over management of the company in 1890, and within a few years it was controlling 40 percent of the country's coal output.[84] After a state bailout in 1868 and years of troubles, the SCMC finally enjoyed steady development that stemmed in part from the generous state subsidies secured by Chorin.[85] Chorin's son, also named Ferenc, emerged as the second most powerful manager of the SCMC by 1914. Father and son were equally active in the National Association of Industrialists, which Chorin Sr. had founded in 1902 to press for the interests of heavy industrialists.[86]

The SCMC's takeover of the Jiu valley mines in 1894 was a safe investment, as the Hungarian state had already built the railway lines to the mines at the treasury's expense. The nationalized railway company, in the meantime, pledged to purchase the output of the SCMC's coal mines in the Jiu valley. The Hungarian state also leased out its own Jiu valley coal mines to the SCMC for the minimal annual fee of 250,000 crowns (or US$50,000 at the time).[87] When the lease was contracted, it was an open secret that the SCMC was not going to exploit the newly acquired fields of the treasury in order to keep coal supplies low and its coal prices high.[88]

The SCMC increased its profits from 2.5 to 3.2 million crowns ($500,000–$637,000) at the time and its turnover from 21 to 46 million crowns ($4.2 million–$9.1 million) between 1899 and 1907; around one-fourth of this nationwide corporation's revenue came from its Transylvanian mines.[89] The SCMC became one of the top nine industrial corporations in Hungary, three of which were in the coal business and two in the iron industry, with beer, sugar, textile, and electric companies making up the rest of the list.[90] The reduction of the SCMC's bank debts, a widespread phenomenon among large corporations, also shows that Transylvanian heavy industrialists had gained enough momentum by the fin de siècle to operate independently from the government, the labor movement, and investment banks, much like Thyssen, Krupp, and other large firms in Central Europe.[91]

Chorin Jr. already belonged to a new class of business managers that started to dominate the landscape of European heavy industries in the 1890s.[92] Although these managers did not own the companies they ran, they wielded considerable power. The tax authorities assessed the Chorin family's net worth at 1.7 million crowns, or around a quarter of a million dollars, a sizable fortune in the 1910s.[93] This sum was significantly smaller than the fortunes of the de Wendels, Thyssens, and Schlumbergers, and even family dynasties that ran midsize companies such as the de Dietrichs, who lived in an eighteenth-century chateau in Alsace. Yet thanks to the particularly close relationship between the Hungarian governments and heavy industrialists like the Chorins, the family's power surpassed that of many Austrian, German, and French industrialists. Father and son lived in a four-story home in the heart of Budapest's financial district, overlooking the domes of the St. Stephen Basilica and the Parliament, icons of the power of the Catholic Church and the government in Hungary (figure 1.1).

Although heavy industries failed to produce a class of industrialists based in Transylvania, they contributed to the creation of the region's working class, whose multiethnic makeup was similar to that of Lorraine's steel and mining towns. By the end of the nineteenth century, the Jiu valley had become one of Austria-Hungary's boomtowns, much like the Galician oil town of Drohobycz.[94] The population of the valley's coal district increased from sixteen thousand to fifty thousand;[95] the largest expansion took place between 1900 and 1910, when the valley's population nearly doubled, in line with the rapid expansion of German and Austro-Hungarian heavy industries in the two decades preceding the First World War.[96]

The valley's mines acted as magnets that drew the monarchy's population, even from distant areas like Austria, Bohemia, Silesia, Galicia, and other parts of Transylvania. There was a small foreign, mostly Italian, mining population as well, although it was not as significant as in Lorraine.[97] The built environment of industry towns, their relative proximity to rural areas, their diverse, mostly immigrant workforce, and the workers' quality of life were similar across the industrial hubs of Transylvania, Galicia, and Lorraine. Like the de Dietrichs' factories in the Alsatian Niederbronn or the Thyssen steel plants in Hagendingen, Lorraine, the coal towns of the Jiu valley were surrounded by forests and sparsely inhabited mountains that attested to the rapidity of industrialization on both the western and eastern peripheries of Central Europe (figure 1.2). Around one-fourth of the Jiu valley's population made a living from agriculture, while employees of the de Dietrich factories were explicitly encouraged to cultivate vegetable gardens.[98]

The technologies, financing, number of workers, and output of heavy industrial companies in the two regions were remarkably similar, although

FIGURE 1.1. Ferenc Chorin Sr. and his son Ferenc Chorin Jr. around 1900. Source: *Az Andrássy úttól a Park Avenue-ig*, 24; Daisy Chorin Strasser's personal collection.

Alsace-Lorraine had a considerably larger share of urban working-class inhabitants (32 percent) than did Transylvania (6 percent).[99] While workers' salaries in Alsace-Lorraine were higher than in Transylvania, the lifestyles of the proletariat were converging across Central Europe as ownership of heavy industries and mines became concentrated in the hands of a few large corporations and banks. Despite these similarities, the underlying political context of industrialization differed between the two regions and in many respects was less favorable for industrialists in Alsace-Lorraine than in Transylvania.

FIGURE 1.2. The cable system that transported the Jiu valley's coal; note the pastoral landscape and farmers working in the background. Source: Photograph by Mór Erdély Co., in 1904; Magyar Földrajzi Múzeum, Budapest and Fortepan database, image no. 96261.

Longing for France, Profiting from Germany

Given the lack of an Alsace-Lorraine identity at the time of the German annexation of these disparate French territories, it was the condemnation of "German aggression" that forged a common political platform among the populations and political elites of this newly formed Reichsland or imperial territory, the official German name of Alsace-Lorraine. The local elites of the Reichsland were the wealthy class of industrialists or *notables* whose sway over municipalities, chambers of commerce, and local politics dated back to the early modern period.[100] The Franco-Prussian War united industrialists and their workers behind the French flag, forging ties that relegated the "social question" and the labor movement to the background until the 1890s.[101] The Treaty of Frankfurt enabled Alsatians and Lorrainers to opt for French nationality, and many of the region's industrialists gradually left, usually by sending the younger generation to study and live in France as the first step. Capital flight from the city of Strasbourg alone amounted to around 100 million francs.[102] In total, fifty thousand to sixty thousand people, or 4 percent of the two regions' population, immigrated to France.[103] Three-fourths of the optants who emigrated to France lived in larger towns, and industrialists, civil servants,

Catholics, Jews, and the francophone middle class were more likely to leave than other sections of society, including German-dialect speakers, Protestants, peasants, and workers.[104] This showed that the decision to leave was equally driven by Francophile sentiments, religion, and class status. As Christopher Fischer noted, "For the vast majority of Alsatians . . . the question of national belonging was less pressing as a major political theme. They conditioned their support for the cause of Alsace based upon other important issues, notably religion, language, and the economy."[105] Even among industrialists, religion played a part in their attitude toward the new ruler. As Vicki Caron emphasized, many Jews feared losing the rights they had gained in France in Germany, while Catholics resented the budding Kulturkampf of the new empire.[106]

After 1871, many of the region's industrial companies faced economic problems that stemmed from the subordination of Alsace-Lorraine to the interests of German federal states and to a lesser extent from French economic protectionism. French governments did not need Alsace-Lorrainers without Alsace-Lorraine. Even as the return of Alsace-Lorraine became the focal point of French nationalist mobilization, France applied the same trade restrictions on Alsatian and Lorrainer products as on imports from the rest of Germany as soon as the grace period in the peace treaty expired.[107] Spinners and weavers in the French northeast looked at Alsatian textile industries with envy, while heavy industrialists in Central France such as the Schneiders feared Lorraine's competition.[108] In 1892, Paris introduced high tariffs on products imported from Germany. As Dan Silverman noted, these tariffs "may have been as much of a shock to the economy of Alsace-Lorraine as the annexation itself in 1871."[109] This French policy, ironically, proved crucial in the reorientation of most Alsace-Lorraine businesses toward Germany. Only the wealthiest notables could afford to relocate part of their production to France and avoid tariffs. These included the de Wendels, the de Dietrichs (who built a plant in Lunéville in French Lorraine), and the Alsatian Mechanical Construction Company (Elsässische Maschinenbau Gesellschaft), which built a factory in Belfort, French Alsace. By 1914, however, both companies decided to legally separate from their French branch and concentrate on German markets.[110]

Germany was unwilling to adjust its commercial and industry laws to Alsace-Lorraine's interests as it had to balance them with those of politically more powerful federal states. The Reichsland's ambiguous legal status within the Reich gradually became the main problem of Alsace-Lorraine industrialists by the 1910s as federal states, the military, and the empire infringed on their economic interests. As one German legal scholar put it at the time, the Reichsland was an "anomaly" and a legal exception within the German empire.[111] The most important political rights within the empire were reserved for federal states, a status Alsace-Lorraine did not achieve until October 1918, a sign of a last-ditch attempt to save the region for Germany in the final days of the First World War.[112] Unlike federal German states, the territory had no autonomous internal administration, and the Kaiser and his appointees had the right to nominate both top-ranking and lower-level "imperial civil servants" for the region.[113] The Reichsland thus had considerably fewer political rights than other German states. It could not send representatives to the powerful federal council, or Bundesrat, the "formal executive authority" of the Reich, which was controlled by Prussian delegates.[114] It was represented by fifteen elected deputies to the Reichstag, corresponding to its share of the population within Germany (4 percent), but this did not translate into actual political power.[115]

The chief administrators of the region, the Statthaltern, functioned as lieutenants of the Kaiser.[116] The Reichsland enjoyed even fewer privileges within Germany than most of the comparable multiethnic border regions in East-Central Europe within Austria-Hungary by 1914. Galicia, Bukovina, and Croatia had territorial autonomy, while Hungary was a quasi-independent state within the Dual Monarchy that shared only its foreign affairs and defense with Austria.[117] Alsace Lorraine was a *corpus separatum* that had a different legal status and administration than the rest of Germany and an unenviable position when compared with federal states.[118] Even so, Alsace-Lorraine's industrialists had a more enviable position within Germany than that of the Danish and Polish notables of Schleswig-Holstein and Posen, who faced the consequences of the two regions' incorporation into Prussia.[119] Both regions became mere provinces within a federal state, a move that entailed their complete subordination to the Prussian government.[120] The forced Germanization policies of the Prussian administration, culminating in the deportation of Danish elites in 1900 and the expulsion of forty-eight thousand Poles and the forced sale of Polish estates in Posen in the 1880s, were unimaginable in Alsace-Lorraine until the First World War, thanks in part to the region's limited autonomy.[121]

The 1871 Treaty of Versailles, which ended the Franco-Prussian War, had left the private property of French citizens in unified Germany intact, unlike the treaty that the Allies concluded in the same palace with the German empire in 1919.[122] The German administration never carried out mass expulsions or expropriations, a fact that was significant for Alsatian and Lorrainer industrialists who opted for French citizenship since they were able to retain their sizable property. The partly France-based de Wendel family, for instance, retained its steel plants in Lorraine despite their strategic location on the Franco-German border.[123] Alsatian notables such as Eugene de Dietrich, who had fought on the French side in 1870–1871 but decided to return to German-ruled Alsace, also faced no retaliation. The protection of Alsatian property reflected prevalent liberal ideas in nineteenth-century international law on the sanctity of private property, and also attested to Bismarck's intent not to further alienate France from Germany after 1871.[124] Given the German administration's disinterest in remaking the region's social hierarchies and breaking the backs of Francophile notables, the first two decades of German rule left the political and economic power of Alsatian industrialists unchanged.

Alsatian and Lorrainer industrialists had shifted from the politics of protest that characterized the 1870s and 1880s to accommodation to the German political system by 1900. Eugene de Dietrich was elected to the Reichstag in 1881 on a protest ticket and remained a Francophile regionalist until his death in 1917 (figure 1.3). Most industrialists, however, did not follow his example. Textile industrialist Jean Schlumberger was ennobled by Wilhelm II for his services as head of the regional consultative assembly, while in 1900 his relative Théodore Schlumberger became a deputy of the federalist National Liberal Party, which was especially popular among German industrialists in Alsace-Lorraine and the rest of the Reich.[125] German industrialists like Eugen Jacobi of the Wolf, Netter, Jacobi (WNJ) engineering company and foundry advocated

FIGURE 1.3. Paternalism of the notables: Eugene de Dietrich with workers from his factory. Source: De Dietrich Company Archives (DCA), Reichshoffen, France, Box 43, Photo 1.76.

German imperialism, *Weltpolitik*, and economic expansion in the colonial world; his views matched those of nationalist liberals in other parts of the German empire.[126]

The lives of Alsace-Lorraine's native bourgeoisie changed surprisingly little after the region's annexation by Germany, even as they lost their influence over the regional administration.[127] As they did before 1871, they tended to marry within their own circles and their peers of the same religion in France. Unlike among liberal professionals and the middle bourgeoisie, intermarriages with immigrant Germans were unheard of, although Protestants were more likely to socialize with the top administrators of the Reichsland; these relationships were often mediated by their wives and the church. For instance, the Swedish wife of Statthalter Karl von Wedel (1907–1914), Stephanie, served as a link with the industrialist Herrenschmidt family.[128] At the same time, even Francophile notables like the de Dietrichs and de Wendels managed to establish extensive ties to German firms and reoriented their products toward German markets. The trajectory of the de Dietrich family offers a clear illustration of the discrepancies between pro-French politics and economic prosperity in the German empire. Originally named Didiers, this patrician Huguenot family had emigrated from Lorraine to Strasbourg in the sixteenth century to escape religious persecution in France.[129] Soon thereafter, the family changed its name to the German-sounding Dietrich, and its members emerged as wealthy burghers and owners of a foundry. While the family was ennobled by Louis XVI, it was the Holy Roman emperor Francis I, Duke of Lorraine and husband of Hungarian queen Maria Theresa, who bestowed a baronial title on the family in the 1760s.[130] The making of the de Dietrichs into one of the primary pillars of Francophile nationalism and regionalism in Alsace by 1870 was thus not a straightforward process.

The baron Frédéric de Dietrich served as mayor of Strasbourg during the French Revolution and was one of the people who commissioned Rouget de Lisle to write a song for the Rhine army after declarations of war on the "King of Hungary and Bohemia," the Austrian emperor, in 1792. This song eventually became the "Marseillaise," which has represented both Alsatian and French loyalties in Strasbourg ever since.[131] Despite Frédéric de Dietrich's support for the revolution, the Jacobins sent him to the guillotine in 1793 and expropriated the family's assets.[132] The de Dietrichs later regained full possession of the company and remained active in regional and French political and economic life. By midcentury, the company's railway carts, steel tires, steam engines, and rolling mills became sought-after products all over France. Despite the family's former Orléanist politics, the firm continued its rapid expansion during the reign of Napoleon III (1852–1870), tripling its workforce between 1852 and 1866 to two

FIGURE 1.4. The monument of the French army (1875) in German Alsace. Source: Strasbourg National Archives.

thousand.[133] Eugene de Dietrich, the third son of the company's chief manager, Albert, was a prisoner of war during the Franco-Prussian War and was finally released in 1871. He was elected to the Reichstag soon after.[134] This deputy of the German Reich kept a French flag in his office and was also the first to commission a hexagon-shaped monument to the French army in the Alsatian Woerth in 1875 (figure 1.4). In a further display of allegiance, he changed the spelling of the family's name to the Gallicized version Diétrich, although most of the family continued to use the old version of the name.[135]

Despite their pro-French politics, the de Dietrichs developed extensive ties with companies headquartered in Germany and drew most of their profits from selling to German states and corporations. By 1914 the firm's major business partners were located on the other side of the Rhine and included not only the imperial railways, but also German chemical giants Agfa, Bayer, and BASF.[136] Most Alsatian industrialists thrived in the rapidly booming economy of the late Wilhelmine empire and profited from Chancellor Leo von Caprivi's bilateral trade agreements, which opened up Russian and Austro-Hungarian markets for the region's industrial companies.[137] These examples demonstrate why political convictions and nationalism are misleading indicators for understanding economic activity in the region, even in the case of German industrialists. Industrialists like the Adlers and Oppenheimers invested in France as well as in Germany and entered business deals with their Alsatian colleagues, such as the Herrenschmidts, despite their divergent political views.

Business Ties and Social Separation: German Industrialists in Alsace

The Adlers and Oppenheimers and other German industrialists who immigrated to Alsace after 1871 joined a long line of immigrant entrepreneurs from nearby Germany who settled in Alsace. The textile industrialist Schlumbergers were originally from Swabia, while the Adt family, which ran a bank and a paper factory in Lorraine, had emigrated from the Sarre in the mid-nineteenth century.[138] Strasbourg, with its port on the Rhine, was an integral part of the Rhineland's economy; it is no surprise, therefore, that its industrial companies had hosted apprentices and recruited partners and spouses from Baden, Württemberg, and Hessen before 1871.[139]

German annexation boosted prevailing trends of immigration to Alsace and Lorraine from German states. Immigrants from neighboring German states made up most of the German population that settled in Alsace-Lorraine. Religious, regional, and social differences among immigrant Germans were so great as to defy simple generalizations of Alsace-Lorraine's Germans, even though for many contemporary Alsatians they appeared as a uniform group of intruders. In fact, German identity emerged gradually in the Reichsland, in part as a reaction to interactions with local society. Many Alsatians cast German immigration as "colonization," which was an exaggeration, yet it reflected the rapid rise of German populations in Alsace-Lorraine after 1871, which substantially transformed the demography of larger Alsatian towns in less than a decade. By 1914, 220,000 German immigrants had settled in Alsace-Lorraine, making up 11 percent of the region's population.[140] In Strasbourg, immigrant families like the Adlers and Oppenheimers made up almost one-third of the population from the 1880s; their numbers increased to 46,000, or 35 percent of the population, by 1905.[141] Germans lived in newly built, elegant neighborhoods outside the city center. German urban planners had redesigned Strasbourg so that its railways station, public buildings, and newly built avenues resembled other cities of the German empire by 1900.

The Adlers and Oppenheimers were part of this first large wave of German immigration to Alsace. They set up a leather business as early as 1871 in cooperation with the Alsatian business dynasty of the Herrenschmidts. Like other German businessmen in the Reichsland, they filled economic niches left by optants or companies that closed down during the economic downturn that followed the Franco-Prussian War. In 1889, they purchased an abandoned starch and sugar factory that had belonged to a native Alsatian businessman who had gone bankrupt seven years earlier. In sharp contrast to this small firm's 25 workers, they established a modern tannery that soon employed 350 people, with numbers increasing by leaps and bounds to 500 in 1900 and over 1,100 by 1908.[142] Alsatian tanners profited from the presence of large German garrisons in Alsace regardless of their political convictions. The Adlers and Oppenheimers furnished leather to the military—by 1905 there were thirteen thousand soldiers stationed in the city who needed boots, straps, and other leather products—while the WNJ engineering company profited from selling materials for the reconstruction of Strasbourg after shelling by the German army.[143] German companies were not alone in turning a profit from reconstruction, however, and most Alsatian firms also entered into business partnerships with the German army, railways, and other companies.

Despite the surge of German "colonists" in Alsace-Lorraine, German big business was slow to benefit from the annexation of Alsace-Lorraine, which defied contemporary expectations. The historian of unified Germany Heinrich von Treitschke lamented that "nature has dealt with our country much more like a step-mother than a mother"; as a result, "we are by no means rich enough to be able to renounce so precious a possession" as Alsace-Lorraine.[144] Similarly, looking back to the recent past from the perspective of French victory in 1918, polemicist Georges Delahache conflated the goals of the Franco-Prussian War and the First World War and maintained that Germany "was determined to carry out an economic conquest, as brutal as the other conquests, involving an entire plan of expropriation of the defeated by the victor, a return to the barbarity of ancient times, signaling fanatic material ambitions" after 1871.[145]

Yet Alsace-Lorraine sparked little interest among German investors for many decades after its annexation. German investments not only failed to increase but actually declined precipitously in the 1880s and 1890s, especially in Lorraine's heavy industries and mines, which showed that German annexation of the region served primarily military objectives while the war set back economic ties.[146] Before 1871, several German industrialists, including the iron master Roechlings, had invested in Lorraine and the rest of France, while Lorrainers established factories in the Sarre because borders were not a barrier to foreign investments.[147] Political and economic instability after the Franco-Prussian War, however, cooled interest in such investments.

The reappearance of German capital in heavy industries and mining was a gradual process and at first centered on light industries and small family businesses abandoned by French emigrants.[148] It was as late as the 1890s, in line with the region's political accommodation to German rule and the rapid industrialization of the Reich, that tycoons from the Ruhrland, Rhineland-Westphalia, and Belgium started to rediscover Lorraine's iron ore mining and steel production. The French businessmen behind the Dreyfus Dupont Company, for instance, sold their property to the Viennese Creditanstalt, which became the sole representative of Austro-Hungarian capital in the region.[149] Between 1890 and 1911, German investments even extended beyond the Franco-German border into the French steel town of Briey, despite diplomatic tensions between the former victor and the vanquished.[150]

Technological innovation also helped the rise of Lorraine's steel mills. The Thomas-Gilchrist process enabled the production of steel from Lorraine's lower-quality, phosphorous cast iron; on the eve of the First World War, Lorraine corporations produced one-fifth of the Reich's iron ore and 12 percent of its steel.[151] Yet the steel plants of the Francophile Lorrainer de Wendel family "dynasty" remained the most prominent in the region, rivaled only by the most modern plant that the Thyssen corporation had built in Hagondange in 1911.[152] Like the Thyssens, other German corporations had built plants in areas that had previously been sparsely populated and left unexploited by Lorrainer and French capital. By 1914, formerly Catholic and French villages had been transformed into bustling mining and steel towns, home to twenty-six thousand mostly unskilled Italian workers, and even more who had come from the federal states of Germany and constituted a majority of skilled workers.[153] The majority of the twenty-three hundred company clerks, managers, and engineers at the steel plants were from German federal states; only one-third were from Lorraine.[154] The demographic transformations precipitated by German corporations were felt mostly in these isolated communities and larger towns, while rural Alsace-Lorraine remained comparatively untouched by German immigration. Natives of Alsace-Lorraine remained prominent in most of the region and most professions. Even according to the exaggerated estimates of contemporary German economist Werner Wittich, German industrialists constituted a minority in Alsace; Wittich claimed they owned 1,500 of Strasbourg's 4,500 industrial companies, and 1,150 out of 3,300 corporations active in commerce and transport in 1895.[155]

Unlike German industrialist Eugen Jacobi, who became a public intellectual on economic matters, the Adlers and Oppenheimers limited their public engagement to charity and the Jewish community. Even so, their political views were likely similar to Jacobi's liberal nationalism; books in their tannery's library praised German colonial expansion and dissuaded workers from the Left. For instance, workers and white-collar employees could borrow the *Guide for the Non-Social Democratic Voter* and the *Campaign against the Hereros* by Paul

Rohrbach if they were looking for books on political life. Jingoist works on the German campaign against France in 1870 and 1871 stood side by side with volumes by Honoré de Balzac and other French classics, which the firm's librarian did not pull from the shelves, even during the First World War.[156]

After the relative political stabilization of the 1890s, large factories like the Adler and Oppenheimer tannery served as the main fora for social interaction between Germans and Alsatians, in part because workers and low-ranking clerks were less prone to observe the social separation practiced by the bourgeoisie and the majority of the Alsatian business elite.[157] Most mixed marriages between the two groups occurred among workers as well; altogether, at the peak of intermarriages between 1890 and 1905, one in five Germans married an Alsatian, which explained the difficulties that the French and German armies would face when trying to separate German and Alsatian populations during the First World War era.[158] Furthermore, Alsace-Lorrainers were five times more likely to marry a German than to marry a French citizen, attesting to the region's integration with Germany and its loosening ties to France by 1914.[159] Rapprochement between Germans and Alsace-Lorrainers was an urban phenomenon made possible by the similar social composition of the two societies. Industrial occupations characterized both populations: 41 percent of Germans and 34 percent of Alsatians and Lorrainers worked in industry jobs, and the ratio of workers to white-collar employees was also similar, at 35 percent and 28 percent, respectively. Independent businessmen were more prominent within immigrant German society (12 percent) than among native Alsatians and Lorrainers (8 percent), yet Germans clustered far less into specific middle- and upper-middle-class professions than Alsatian or East-Central European Jews.

German business families remained a more closed social group that tended to marry among their own ranks, but this was hardly an Alsatian or German specialty.[160] Prominent notables and industrialists in Alsace such as the de Dietrichs or Schlumbergers married members of the French or Alsatian bourgeoisie.[161] The two wives of Ferdinand Oppenheimer's son Julius were Jews from Germany whose families were active in the leather trade.[162] Karl Adler married Rosa Jacobi, whose family owned the WNJ engineering company.[163] While the Francophile orientation of Strasbourg Jews decreased after the Dreyfus affair, political and religious differences persisted between Alsatian and German Jewry and likely motivated the Adlers' and Oppenheimers' spousal choices, apart from business interests.[164] On the eve of the First World War, the first generation of German businessmen born in the Reichsland, such as the metal industrialist Eugen Jacobi, Karl Adler, and Julius Oppenheimer, assumed leadership roles in their companies, which further blurred differences between native and immigrant business elites. The younger generation became vocal advocates of Alsatian economic interests within the German empire in part because they gradually realized that the region's ambiguous legal status within the German Reich undercut its economic interests.[165]

Despite the families' recent history in Alsace and intermarriages with other German Jewish business dynasties, the Adlers and Oppenheimers became just as important in the economic and social life of Strasbourg as some of the native Alsatian industrialists. Strasbourg's working-class suburb Lingolsheim was largely built up by the Adler and Oppenheimer tannery, which commissioned a new office building, workers' housing, and industrial buildings that formed a city within the city by 1914 (figures 1.5 and 1.6). The continuous expansion of the tannery provided revenue for the municipality to modernize its infrastructure.[166] The Alsatian mayor of the township cooperated with the firm, and tax revenue and the sale of land to the tannery allowed for the introduction of tram service, electric lighting, gas, and a new water pipe system in Lingolsheim. The family founded a Jewish vocational school in association with the Alsatian Jew Georges Schmoll, the head of the Lower Alsace Jewish con-

FIGURE 1.5. The Adler and Oppenheimer tannery's new building complex.
Source: *Adler&Oppenheimer Lederfabrik A.G., aus Anlass der Fertigstellung ihres Neuen Verwaltungsgebäudes: Ende März 1914* (Strasbourg: A.O., 1914).

FIGURE 1.6. The Adler and Oppenheimer tannery's new dining hall, completed in 1914. Source: *Adler&Oppenheimer Lederfabrik A.G., aus Anlass der Fertigstellung ihres Neuen Verwaltungsgebäudes: Ende März 1914* (Strasbourg: A.O., 1914).

sistory, who was to play a key role in the company's history throughout the First World War.[167] The Adlers and Oppenheimers, who were prominent members of the Kléber Street synagogue in Strasbourg, also financed the clockwork of the Catholic church in Lingolsheim, as a gesture to the municipality and to their workers, most of whom were Catholic.[168]

As the German empire increased its welfare benefits for workers, paternalist industrialists had to provide more and more services to dissuade workers from striking. Tanners at the firm received subsidized company housing and benefited from the library, theater hall, discounted grocery store, and several charity funds set up by the Adlers and Oppenheimers.[169] Yet the Reichsland's German and Alsatian industrialists shared a fierce opposition to the labor movement. In promotion of traditional ideas on gender and family life, the de Dietrichs built small family homes for their workers that were suitable for raising multiple children and laid off female workers as soon as they got married.[170] The firm banned trade unions from its factory floors, yet every metal worker received a copy of the Bible personally from Eugene de Dietrich (figure 1.3).[171] In the same spirit, the Adler and Oppenheimer tannery's workers had to lead morally impeccable lives and refrain from drinking in excess in order to receive health care benefits.

On the eve of the Great War, the Adlers and Oppenheimers completed a new office building that also provided numerous services for workers (figures 1.5 and 1.6). Managers and visitors entered a spacious foyer furnished with bulky club chairs made of fine polished leather, an Adler and Oppenheimer product.[172] The slightly oversized hall and its monumental interior, broken up by thick columns, offered respite for employees and signaled the corporation's stability to traveling agents and business partners.[173] The new building's four floors housed the management's offices, a large dining hall for workers, and a "casino" for employees.[174] This social club prided itself on a library and a bathhouse where workers and their relatives could bathe after the work day. The bathhouse was an important benefit because when most workers' apartments lacked bathrooms.[175] The casino also housed a company store where employees could purchase canned food and basic necessities.[176] In February 1914, workers and employees at the Adler and Oppenheimer tannery had every reason to believe that, for them, the most life-changing event of the year would be the availability of services that were considered a rare luxury in prior decades.

Whereas in the 1870s many observers were skeptical whether the empires that came into being would be able to bring prosperity to the variety of territories they integrated, the four decades of political stability that ensued brought about remarkable economic prosperity for industrialists throughout Central Europe, not unlike in the rest of Europe and North America. This development defied some of the skeptical predictions of the 1870s that had pointed to the suppression of democratic politics and the rigidity of the administrative and political institutions of Germany and Austria-Hungary as potential sources of future economic problems. In the 1870s, Hungarian liberal Móric Szentkirályi noted that "when one compares our [Hungary's] situation to the Alsatian one, . . . we encounter the same apathy toward political life in Alsace as in our country."[177] Reflecting on the integration of Hungary into the Dual Monarchy and Alsace-Lorraine into Germany, Szentkirályi warned that "if institutions do not adapt to social relations, society will have to take up the mold of institutions, and in this case, the balancing of differences will take quite a long time."[178] Ironically, Szentkirályi proved to be a better predictor of Alsace-Lorraine's future than of that of his native Hungary, which adapted to the Dual Monarchy remarkably fast despite the memory of the 1848–1849 anti-Habsburg revolution and war of independence. Accommodation to German rule took at least two decades in the Reichsland, while the traditional, caste-like separation of business elites from the rest of society and from German rulers and businessmen changed slowly. Alsatian family firms proved to be resilient in times of political turmoil and sovereignty change, and they were also remarkably adaptable to rapid modernization in the late nineteenth century, yet they provided few opportunities for outsiders and newcomers to join them as partners.[179] By contrast, in post-1867 Hungary, the centralizing state destroyed the traditional frameworks of economic life, including guilds, the autonomy of Transylvania's Saxons, and other commercial barriers within the new state. Top-down nation building and modernization hurt numerous local interests but enabled immigrants like Johann Renner to integrate not only into Transylvania's German society but also into Hungarian economic life more generally; this was also true for Jewish families like the Chorins, who became the de facto business elite of the new state and enjoyed close relations with government politicians. The German government neither supported nor explicitly hindered Alsace-Lorraine's economic development, and the region's economy did expand after the 1880s in the climate of relative political stability and accommodation to German rule, even as Alsatian business elites lost their political influence to fight for regional economic interests.

Hungarian sociologist Karl Polányi (b. 1886) and Ferenc Chorin (b. 1879) were part of the same prewar generation of Budapest's Hungarian Jewish bourgeoisie. From the vantage point of the Second World War and implicitly, that of British history, Polányi labeled the pre-1914 period as the "liberal age" that culminated in the "self-regulating market system";[180] his assessment matched Stefan Zweig's, Hannah Arendt's, or John Maynard Keynes's take on the prewar period, which Zweig and Arendt labeled as the "golden age of security."[181] In Central Europe, however, as Polányi very well knew, markets were far from self-regulating, and states wielded considerable influence over markets. Alison Frank noted, for instance, that "Even powerful multinational corporations with global pretensions were associated with—and in some instances beholden to—national governments. . . . International capitalism did not diminish the significance of states."[182] Companies' domestic economic activity offers a particularly clear illustration of why states emerged as key actors even for such multi-million-dollar enterprises as Lorraine's steel plants or the SCMC mines. Through the tariffs, railway line construction, and freight rate manipulation practiced by France, Germany, and Austria-Hungary, states were able to favor loyal and domestic companies over foreign corporations and considerably hinder or support entire industry branches, putting the importance of government ties for business elites into stark relief in both the German and Austro-Hungarian empires.

CHAPTER 2

Costly Nationalism

Industrialists on the Eve of 1914

The decade before the outbreak of the First World War was an economically prosperous era for Central European industrialists despite periodic crises of capitalism. Yet the rise of economic nationalism, including political mobilization against industrialists, foreshadowed the breakdown of the liberal regime of property rights between 1914 and 1918 in Central Europe and worldwide. The prewar years provided belligerents with a blueprint for their treatment of domestic and enemy businesses after 1914 as courts, municipal and national administrations, and nationalist activists articulated plans that promoted economic discrimination even as these plans cost national economies dearly at the least in the short run. A closer look at the 1910s offers valuable insight as to why the seemingly solid system of private property rights broke down in a matter of weeks in August 1914. The study of contested border regions where calls for economic discrimination were especially salient puts policies of economic discrimination that became widespread in most of Europe between 1914 and the early 1920s into relief.

In the early twentieth century, economic discrimination centered on contested territories like Alsace-Lorraine and Transylvania, as was the case during the First World War. While both regions were thoroughly integrated into their respective imperial economies, nationalists cast them as "borderlands" where the futures of Germandom and the Hungarian nation were at stake.[1]

In addition to cultural and educational discrimination, nationalists demanded the reorganization of economic hierarchies based on perceived national interest. In many respects, these demands were not new and in fact dated back to the making of the Austro-Hungarian and German empires in the late 1860s and early 1870s.[2] By the early 1910s, however, France had reemerged as a great power intent on regaining Alsace-Lorraine, while Romania had become independent from Ottoman tutelage in 1878 and emerged more powerful than before from both the First and Second Balkan Wars of 1912 and 1913. Much like Serbian elites after 1903, the Romanian national liberals around Prime Minister Ion I. C. Brătianu, who were in power between 1909 and 1910 and from January 1914 until 1918, preferred the Entente to Germany and Austria-Hungary. The Franco-Russian alliance simply had more to offer Romania than the Central Powers at a time when the annexation of Transylvania with its Romanian population of three million emerged as one of Bucharest's war aims. Faced with these developments, German and Hungarian nationalists thus made purging "foreign" economic interests from territories like Alsace-Lorraine and Transylvania a priority.

While historians have recognized that the First World War failed to end in 1918, mobilization against domestic enemies and their private property in the years preceding 1914 points to the relevance of the "long First World War" concept even as regards the early 1910s.[3] In Central Europe, the rapid and seemingly unprecedented actions against enemy aliens, domestic enemies, and their property between 1914 and 1918 would have been unimaginable without the rise of political mobilization against domestic enemies in the early 1910s. "Laws of exception for times of war" were already in place in Hungary by 1912 in reaction to the First Balkan War, while in Alsace the boundaries between "enemy" industrialists and the Reich solidified during the same period.[4]

Given the similar domestic and international pressures on Germany and Austria-Hungary, which undermined the prevailing status quo on the sacrosanct nature of private property rights, a comparison of the situations in Alsace-Lorraine and Transylvania reveals how the German and Hungarian administrations responded differently to pressures to introduce economic discrimination against "domestic enemies." It also shows that economic nationalism centered on industrial property ownership both before and during the First World War in Western and Central Europe, including Great Britain, France, and Alsace-Lorraine. In East-Central Europe, on the other hand, it was landownership that captured the imagination of peasants and middle-class nationalists, and concentration of industrial wealth in the hands of a few key families remained unchallenged.[5] While German authorities in Alsace-Lorraine exaggerated a mundane nationalist conflict at the Grafenstaden machine building factory and turned it into a political crisis, Budapest tried to marginalize political efforts to Hungarianize Transylvania's economy to the detriment of Romanian landowners, instead rallying the public against Austrian industries and channeling sizable funds to Hungarian industrial companies. This support eventually contributed to the Hungarian economy's ability to sustain the war effort between 1914 and 1918.

Ironically, while Germany escalated tensions with France via economic discrimination against partially French-owned industrial companies in Alsace-Lorraine, it also urged moderation when it came to nationalist mobilization in East-Central Europe. For instance, it pressured the Hungarian government to make concessions to Transylvanian Romanians in order to win Romania over to the Central Powers, which also contributed to maintaining the status quo and relative political stability in the region until 1916.[6] This led to the growing divergence between Alsace-Lorrainer and Transylvanian firms and industrialists; while the former operated under increasingly dire circumstances, Transylvania's emerging businessmen and landowners enjoyed the backing of the government even amid the radicalization of domestic politics and diplomatic tensions. A short-lived attempt to limit the economic and political power of large industrial companies and banks between 1906 and 1909 also failed, further strengthening Transylvania's industrialists.

Failures and Successes of Economic Nationalism in Hungary before the Great War

After 1867, Hungary was ruled by the Liberal Party of Hungarian nationalist modernizers, which promoted the interests of domestic industrialists, banks, and landowners while suppressing ethnic minority political parties and the many Hungarian voters who preferred "independentist" candidates who followed in the footsteps of revolutionary Louis (Lajos) Kossuth, rejecting the Austro-Hungarian Compromise and favoring an independent Hungary. The government was only able to remain in power through systemic manipulation of elections and the limitation of suffrage. Open suffrage in the countryside readily lent itself to coercion of the electorate, and the voting census meant that only around 12 percent of the adult male population was able to vote, a lower proportion than in Germany and Austria.[7] Yet by the 1880s, the dualist regime enjoyed the support of a substantial portion of the population.[8]

When the governing party eventually lost the elections in 1905 and the Hungarian "independentist" opposition gained power in a coalition government with the liberals, the renegotiation of the 1867 Compromise in order to favor

Hungarian interests, including Hungary's economic interests, took center stage in national politics.[9] The new government faced an uphill battle as it tried to promote the interests of ethnic Hungarian landowners and small to midsize industrial companies, to the detriment of Hungary's partner state, Austria, all while attempting to curb the power of domestic big business. The government also attempted to introduce a uniform public education system that made the teaching of the Hungarian language mandatory, including in Romanian and German towns in Transylvania, which generated a backlash.[10]

The call for a separate customs zone around Hungary to protect domestic industries from Austrian competition was a long-standing demand of Hungarian nationalists dating back to the 1820s and 1830s, but little progress was achieved before 1918. Although a law introducing customs duties between Austria and Hungary was eventually passed, its implementation was postponed until 1917 and it was never actually applied.[11] In the meantime, a customs treaty concluded with Germany allowed German industrial products easier access to Hungary, simultaneously undercutting protectionist measures and Austro-Bohemian interests.[12] While economic ties within Central Europe intensified, the monarchy was moving toward economic fragmentation by 1914 that foreshadowed wartime debates on the distribution of food and raw materials within the Dual Monarchy and the Central Powers more generally.[13]

The Budapest coalition government, at least in its rhetoric, sided with the downwardly mobile landowning gentry and small and midsize entrepreneurs in their battle against the corporations that had been the darlings of liberal governments. A clampdown on a coal mining corporation like the Salgótarján Coal Mining Corporation (SCMC), which was tied to the ousted liberals through its director, Ferenc Chorin Sr., could show the electorate that the government was taking back control from large corporations. Prime Minister Sándor Wekerle and commerce minister Ferenc Kossuth were also invested in taking back the management of state-owned mines from the SCMC as part of their push for national energy independence. Loyal Hungarian commentators at the time compared the Budapest government's agenda with Germany's protracted attempts to transfer its coal mines to state ownership. In their view, German federalism, bureaucratism, and weak governments compared unfavorably with Budapest's efficiency and authority. Whereas in Germany, state ownership "may only be accomplished through lengthy negotiations and large state loans confirmed by legislation, by us [in Hungary], the self-conscious and firm actions of the government . . . led to [its] complete realization within a few months," noted a mining expert at the time.[14] In fact, Budapest took back the management of only three coal mines with moderate production capacities in 1907.[15]

Among the mines that Wekerle wanted to take back under state administration were fields that the treasury had leased to the SCMC in the 1890s. The pro-government press announced in early 1908 that the liberal administration had signed a disadvantageous deal when it leased the Jiu valley mines to the SCMC in 1895.[16] This was true, although the papers were slower to acknowledge that the new government was replacing one bad deal with another. During negotiations in 1907, Wekerle and Chorin agreed that the SCMC would surrender the mines before the lease expired in 1916. In exchange, however, the government pledged to purchase three-fourths of the SCMC's entire coal production at a rate favorable to the company. This deal showed that by 1907 the government was unable to challenge large corporations like the SCMC, which had grown into financially independent behemoths. Industry acts in previous decades had quadrupled funding for heavy industries.[17] The formation of the government's Council of Industry in 1907 also reflected business elites' continued influence on the government; this consultative organ led by Kossuth, son of the 1848–1849 anti-Habsburg revolutionary, counted Ferenc Chorin Sr. and several other industrialists and bankers among its members.[18] The new government's agenda to reclaim the management of natural resources like coal had failed in less than a year.

What proved to be a more successful initiative, in part because it did not hurt the interests of big business, was the government program that provided subsidies to help craftsmen expand their manufactures. After its failure to protect Hungarian industries from Austrian competition with a customs union, Budapest decided to channel funds toward support of domestic light industries.[19] In line with the government's nationalist rhetoric, the 1907 Industry Act strongly favored smaller and midsize companies over mines, steel plants, engineering firms, and foreign corporations. It also made the expropriation of land for industrial use easier and provided additional tax breaks and transportation subsidies for new companies.[20] In the spirit of economic protectionism, three-quarters of the managers and workers in these new companies had to be Hungarian.[21] The law did not, however, exclude Austrian and Bohemian companies from the Hungarian market. Instead, it prompted them to relocate a branch to Hungary in order to enjoy the benefits of the Industry Act.[22] New firms also had to acquire their machines domestically; this requirement was both impossible and unenforced since companies imported a large portion of their industrial machinery from Germany, Switzerland, France, and Austria.

For the Renner firm, the key aspect of the Industry Act was that it enabled the Commerce Ministry to give out "state subventions" of up to 50,000 crowns ($10,000) for the establishment of new factories with relative ease. These benefits were reserved for businessmen who refrained from "anti-state behavior" and "propaganda against the constitution."[23] These and similar charges had served as an excuse to clamp down on Romanian nationalists in Transylvania in the mid-1890s, and the provision may therefore have discouraged some Romanian-owned firms from applying.[24] However, the proportion of Romanians among Transylvanian craftsmen and industrialists was low, which also contributed to their relative underrepresentation among grantees.

On the whole, the 1907 law channeled state support worth 7 percent of all private capital invested in industries by 1912.[25] While between 1867 and 1907 a total of 14.5 million crowns ($2.9 million) in subsidies went to industrialization, subsidies in the eight years before the First World War alone amounted to 54 million crowns or $11 million.[26] The Industry Act went hand in hand with initiatives to encourage consumers to prefer Hungarian products over Austrian and Bohemian ones. Charismatic Catholic bishop Ottokár Prohászka encouraged small businesses and craftsmen to use the tulip logo to signal the Hungarian origins of their products. The "tulip movement" produced an impressive array of paraphernalia including postcards and home décor and also gave rise to a series of domestic industry fairs, while the tulip became associated with the coalition government.[27]

The tulip movement made little overall difference economically, however, and the tulip logo was soon adopted by Austrian firms that then generated stellar sales in Hungary. The Vienna branch of the German William Prym company, for instance, started to mass-produce pens decorated with the tulip logo and saturated the Hungarian market.[28] While the coalition government pushed to have Hungarian firms commissioned as suppliers of the Austro-Hungarian military, few companies were actually able to fulfill the army's requirements. So when some Hungarian firms won contracts to furnish horseshoe nails for the army, the nationalist press was jubilant.[29]

Support for craftsmen to expand their businesses was a more successful endeavor. By promoting light industries in previously less industrialized regions of Hungary such as Transylvania, the Industry Act boosted small and midsize businesses as well as the development of the provincial business elites who were to become the backbone of the local economy for decades to come. Partially as a result of the prewar industrialization drive, Hungary's industrial production reached almost one-third of Austria's by 1913.[30] In 1910, the city of Kolozsvár was home to more than seventy tanners, many of them with multigenerational ties to the city.[31] Yet it was the sons of a German immigrant to Hungary who established the city's first modern leather factory under the most nationalist Hungarian governments of the pre-1914 era.

The Renner tannery's rise to prominence shows how the benefits of the 1907 Industry Act had to be paired with political connections to municipalities and chambers of commerce, assertive management, a centrally located factory in a major urban center and railway hub, and finally, continuous commissions by the state and the army. Powerful managers and local politicians who acted as mediators between the Budapest government, the municipality, and industrialists were key to gaining state subventions. These managers, mediators, and politicians came from the ranks of the Hungarian and Hungarian Jewish urban bourgeoisie or lower-middle class and had often studied law but had family ties or other connections to the world of business. The politicians Ferenc Chorin Jr. and Sr., the businessman Zsigmond Szana, the modernizing mayor of Marosvásárhely György Bernády, the lawyer Elemér Gyárfás, and the Renners' partner Mózes Farkas all emerged as key mediators of Transylvanian local interests and Hungarian national lobby groups, banks, and industrial companies.[32] Their careers illustrate how dualist Hungary's society was "stratified but dynamic, in which generational differences and family strategies require as much attention as modes of production and property relations," as Robert Nemes has noted.[33] Given Hungary's rapid economic development after the 1880s, the lifestyles, wealth, and social circles of fathers and sons in Hungarian economic life differed radically, considerably more than in Alsace-Lorraine, where long-standing business dynasties held fast to their companies and status even as Bonaparte rule gave way to Wilhelm II's empire.

Mózes Farkas's career illustrates the opportunities available for agile newcomers to early twentieth-century Hungary's business elite. Farkas was born in 1881, the son of an upwardly mobile Jewish cobbler in the town of Huszt in northeastern Hungary, a region that Nemes characterized as being on "the linguistic and religious fault lines of Central Europe: . . . where eastern and western Christianity met, and where Hasidism bumped into other Jewish traditions."[34] In Huszt, a town of seven thousand, Ruthenians constituted the majority, while German and Hungarian speakers, including Jews, each made up around one-fourth of the population. Opportunities for craftsmen and businessmen were limited in this larger village, although Huszt became a stop on a secondary railway line shortly before Mózes was born. While Mózes was still a student, the family moved to Kolozsvár, where his father opened a shoe and leather business. While the family did not convert to Christianity, Mózes was enrolled in the competitive *gimnázium* of the Unitarian Church, which showed the family's loosening ties to Judaism and its concern for social advancement.[35]

Mózes Farkas completed his apprenticeship as a cobbler, but his family, like so many other Hungarian Jewish families, groomed him for a professional career that would allow him entry into the city's social elite. He enrolled at the law faculty of the University of Kolozsvár, which attracted young Jews and Christians alike who wanted to enter civil service or start a law firm. His studies also allowed him to socialize with the sons of German and Hungarian state and municipal officials and impoverished landowning gentry as well as those of the Romanian intelligentsia.[36] In other words, law school was an ideal place to acquire connections to the men who would be the movers and shakers of local society for decades to come. For a young man intent on going into finance and business, connections were important because they could be converted into financial capital at a time when Hungary was run by an old boys' network of state, bank, and private company clerks.[37]

Farkas's university years coincided with Hungary's first major political crisis after the 1867 compromise, which ended the era of political apathy and galvanized university students around anti-Austrian nationalism. The pillars of the Compromise, including the commercial and tariff treaty with Austria and the articles pertaining to the joint army, were due to be renegotiated in the early 1900s. Industrialists including Ferenc Chorin Sr. formed a lobby to protect the interests of domestic big business from Austrian competition, while a large swathe of the opposition wanted protective tariffs to shield Hungarian industries. Austrian-Hungarian negotiations on the expansion and modernization of the joint army prompted Hungarian nationalists to reignite demands to introduce Hungarian in addition to German as a language of command for recruits from Hungary in exchange for more soldiers and an expanded military budget.[38]

During his Kolozsvár years in the early 1900s, Farkas made his first forays into politics at the age of twenty-two on the side of the Hungarian nationalist opposition.[39] The opposition that would soon come into power constituted the most appealing choice on the limited political spectrum available to young middle-class Transylvanians like Farkas at a time when the liberals were increasingly identified with the cynicism of the István Tisza government. Many upwardly mobile Jews also embraced Hungarian nationalism because the country offered emancipation and social mobility to Jews who were willing to learn Hungarian, change their German last names, and shed the traditional elements of their religion.[40] The contemporary census recorded mother tongue rather than ethnicity, and since by 1910 most Jews, who made up 5 percent of the total population, spoke Hungarian, they were recorded as Hungarians. Hungarians constituted 54 percent of the total population of Hungary by 1910; thus, the promotion of Jewish assimilation also served to maintain the Hungarian statistical majority.

In 1903, along with twenty-one other recent law graduates, including members of illustrious Transylvanian noble families, Farkas signed a declaration titled "Greetings to the warriors" in support of the nationalist opposition's efforts, including its goal of introducing Hungarian as a language of command in the Austro-Hungarian army. Signatories invoked the "god of Hungarians" and offered their services, even as they acknowledged that "our word is insignificant, our power is weak."[41] The declaration was at best naive and offered no concrete suggestions, but the fact that Farkas signed it showcased his ambition, attested to his acceptance in the circles of up-and-coming liberal professionals, and also garnered him some attention in regional politics, since the declaration was printed in the national opposition daily.

Hungary descended into a political crisis in the following two years as the governing liberals around Prime Minister István Tisza lost the election in 1905. Despite the election results, Francis Joseph refused to tolerate a government that promised to continue the agenda of the 1848–1849 revolutionary Louis Kossuth, whom the emperor himself had defeated half a century earlier. The impasse of the country's political life and Farkas's limited prospects in national politics prompted him to concentrate on establishing himself as a lawyer specializing in finance and business. He counseled the Civic Savings Bank after he passed his bar exam in 1907, got married to his first wife Ilona Rózsa, and in 1909, the couple's first daughter, Gabriella, was born. Farkas thus lived the comfortable family life of the urban upper middle class of Austria-Hungary, yet there was nothing out of the ordinary in his trajectory and no indication of his future success.[42] His name cropped up again in the Kolozsvár press in the early 1910s when he cofounded a factory with the Renners, which would turn out to be the major business venture of his life and would sustain him and his family for decades.

After a difficult start on the outskirts of Kolozsvár, Johann Renner established a modest tanning business and even won a prize at an industry fair promoting Hungarian craftsmen that was organized by the tulip association in the mid-1900s.[43] Yet his small tannery was far from adequate to ensure the futures of his six adult sons, and Johann Renner was looking into expanding his business. He and his wife sent two of their sons, Emil and Friedrich, back to his native Bavaria to serve as apprentices at large tanneries. According to an interview recorded by Johann's grandson Ervin Renner after 1945, their mission also included industrial espionage in Germany and France; yet there is no indication of this in the company's papers.[44] In 1911, members of the Farkas and Renner families and the Hechts, a local Hungarian Jewish bourgeois family, formed a listed company to build, equip, and run a modern tannery on the outskirts of Kolozsvár. Farkas was aware of the Budapest government's grant calls for the establishment of new factories, and he also knew that the Kolozsvár Chamber of Commerce and municipal government were eager to attract industries to the city to boost tax revenue.[45] Farkas applied for and received a cash grant of 30,000 crowns, or $6,060, to purchase factory equipment, and he also successfully lobbied the municipality for a free plot of land.

The 1907 Industry Act was really an industrialist act since it channeled public funds to the private accounts of grantees without requiring them to repay the funds if their businesses went bankrupt. An intricate mechanism enabled by the act turned the commons of Kolozsvár and Hungarian taxpayers' money into private capital. When Farkas and the Renners formed the company, they had no capital of their own to invest in the venture. However, they issued 30 percent of shares in the new company to themselves, representing the value of the plot they had obtained from the municipality and the state's cash grant, for a total of 60,000 crowns ($12,000).[46] State subsidies thus became private capital. Friedrich and Emil Renner, however, received fewer shares than Mózes Farkas and his father, which showed from the outset that the real manager of the company was to be the young lawyer and not the craftsmen who gave the company its name.

Figure 2.1 is a photograph of the company founders taken in a downtown studio in Kolozsvár. Johann Renner is seated in the center, and Mózes Farkas, with his white attire and piercing gaze, stands apart from the rest of the founders. The bourgeois elegance of the men's three-piece suits and silk ties contrasts

FIGURE 2.1. The founders of the Renner company around 1911. Back row (*left to right*): Emil Renner, Frigyes Renner, József Farkas, Dezső Hecht, and an unidentified man; front row (*left to right*): Richard Hecht, Johann Renner, Mózes Farkas. Source: Iván Rohonyi's personal collection.

starkly with the modest financial prowess of their company, which at that point was entirely dependent on Hungarian state subsidies and bank credit.

Despite generous state support, the start-up founded by the Renners and Farkas almost went bankrupt by 1913 because consumers in Kolozsvár showed no interest in fine leather in a time of crises.[47] The factory was initially built to produce refined box and chevreux leather, the main materials used in the shiny footwear worn by middle-class men. The Renners and Farkas also aimed to build a separate shoe factory while Farkas Sr.'s downtown store handled distribution. This business model, aimed at Transylvania's still-thin layer of clerks and urban middle-class consumers, proved to be a failure. Furthermore, the Hungarian and Transylvanian economies entered a recession after the Balkan Wars of 1912 and 1913 when foreign investors withdrew their capital from the country. While the Renners sought ways to export to Southeastern Europe, the war closed down their trade routes. Worse yet, the shortage of capital propelled an increase in the cost of borrowing while bad harvests threw the economy further into recession.[48]

After the company registered a 264,000 crown profit in 1912, profits dropped to 27,000 crowns the following year and the company was unable to attract shareholders to increase its capital to 500,000 crowns.[49] The 1914 annual report asserted, "We worked with strong faith and will, and we believed in the value of conscientious careful work. Instead of pursuing instantaneous profit, we made our business more economical and our products more refined."[50] The audience of the annual report, however, was the firm's distressed shareholders, which explains why management used optimistic language to cover up a sharp decrease in profits. Farkas and the Renners found themselves facing the prospect of years of stagnation, aggravated by the news from Berlin, Vienna, and Budapest in July 1914.

Land and Nationalism in Transylvania

The rise of the Renner tannery as a result of state subventions did not spark animosity in Transylvanian politics or among Hungarian industrialists, in part because it fit neatly into the agenda of Hungarian economic nationalism. While Kolozsvár's social-democratic press and trade unions criticized child labor and twelve- to fourteen-hour workdays in the city's factories, the lack of a universal, secret ballot provided few opportunities for workers to bring these issues into mainstream national politics.[51] The "social question" centered on land ownership in the region, as it did in most of East-Central Europe. The fact that public debates were focused on the plight of the landless peasantry and land purchases by Romanian banks in Transylvania indirectly benefited industrialists and craftsmen because their enrichment failed to elicit political mobilization.[52] Their situation in Austria-Hungary contrasted sharply with that of Jewish industrialists in the Kingdom of Romania, who were denied citizenship until 1919, while Jewish tenants of agricultural estates were subjected to persecution in the 1907 peasant uprising that was "the most violent and destructive episode in Romanian history ever to occur in peacetime."[53]

Rather, what emerged as a contentious issue was landownership in Transylvania, overshadowing questionable enrichment by a few, well-connected industrialists. There was pressure in and outside of the house of representatives to limit land purchases by Romanians in Transylvania and to salvage the economically unviable estates of the region's Hungarian gentry. László Bizony, a self-proclaimed Transylvania expert, compiled a volume that featured contributions by leading Hungarian politicians, bankers, and businessmen calling for joint action to "defend" the "eastern frontier." As Bizony argued, "On the peripheries, the minority [Romanian] capitalists chain the Hungarian land to themselves, refashioning what villages look like, and their latest goal is to conquer industry and commerce and to chain the cities to themselves, as well."[54] Romanians made up around half of Transylvania's population but owned less than one-third of midsize estates and one-fifth of large estates, which undermined Bizony's thesis of large-scale economic expansion by Romanians.[55] The author included interviews with Transylvanian bank directors as well as advertisements of the same banks at the end of the pamphlet, which suggests that the volume was sponsored by the regional rivals of Romanian banks.

Hungarian nationalists had paid particular attention to purchases of land by Transylvania's Romanian banks since the 1890s, becoming a central rallying point in the years leading up to the First World War. Gusztáv Beksics, who represented the nationalist, Hungarianizing wing of the governing Liberal Party, raised a false alarm as early as 1895 that "the silent workers of the Romanian national cause now want to replace . . . the Hungarian gentry with the Romanian gentry,"[56] using rhetoric not unlike that of Bizony's pamphlet on the eve of the First World War.[57] In Miklós Bánffy's interwar *Transylvanian Trilogy*, set in the pre-1914 era, the Romanian lawyer Timisan reveals the hidden key to Romanian economic expansion in Transylvania to the novel's protagonist, Count Abády. As Timisan explains to Abády, "We need a wealthy middle class and up until now this class has not existed. . . . Our bank furnishes the original funds and, apart from other businesses, it lends money to certain people we believe can be trusted firstly to build up their own fortunes and then to use those fortunes for political purposes."[58] Statistics failed to back up Bánffy's tale of the economic expansion of the Romanian peasantry, but this did not detract from the salience of these arguments among radical nationalists in both the government and its opposition.

Despite political mobilization, Beksics' endeavors to impose economic restrictions on Romanians in Transylvania received no support from Budapest. What these plans did achieve was the establishment of the Altruista Bank in 1911, inspired by German practices against Poles in Posen.[59] The bank, however, was unable to achieve its mission of promoting Hungarian landownership in ethnic "borderlands" such as Transylvania; it primarily served as a tool to bail out loyal landowners under the guise of promoting the interest of the Hungarian nation.[60] The agenda of economic discrimination against the Romanian bourgeoisie lived on within the Transylvanian Alliance, a political pressure group that united government and opposition politicians and regional notables; its members opposed Tisza's reconciliatory line with Romanians and proposed additional subsidies for the region's economic modernization. The alliance's anti-Romanian agenda was significant as it would become government policy by 1917, following the political radicalization brought about by Romania's attack on Hungary in 1916.[61]

After 1910, the previous liberal political establishment returned to power and showed no interest in economic policies that discriminated against Romanian banks and landowners. Moreover, István Tisza, who served as prime minister after 1913, actively sought to cooperate with Transylvanian Romanians. In part as a result of German pressure on the Dual Monarchy at a time of escalating tensions between the Entente and the Triple Alliance of Italy and the two Central European empires, Tisza attempted to cement the Kingdom of Romania's alliance with the Central Powers by making concessions to the Romanian National Party of Transylvania, the political organization of the region's Romanians represented in the Budapest parliament. Unsurprisingly, Elemér Hantos (1880–1942), a leading banker, governing Party of National Labor deputy and director of the National Association of Credit Institutes, openly contested allegations of nationalist business practices of Romanian banks. He framed the problem of land as centered exclusively on profit and rational investment.[62] "I believe that the competition between the Transylvanian Hungarian and Romanian banks is just like the competition among any other banks. I have never encountered aggressive behavior by a Hungarian bank simply for national goals, and business comes first for the directors of Romanian banks, too. I know of actual deals in which Romanian banks offered the land they own to the state or to the *Altruista Bank* [Altruistic Bank]. In sum, economic motivations characterize the land policy of Romanian banks, not the achievement of national goals."[63]

Some doubt may be cast on the good faith of Hantos's strict separation between the market and politics in light of Budapest's massive economic interventions in the form of subsidies, concessions, and other measures. Yet research has confirmed that Romanian banks were more concerned with maximizing profits for their shareholders than with pooling resources to achieve national goals, unlike the Saxon banks in the region.[64] Ironically, as Germany pressed the Hungarian government to pursue reconciliation with Romanian elites in Transylvania, it further exacerbated relations with France by its persecution of Alsatians and Lorrainers. By the time the First World War broke out, there was relative domestic peace in Transylvania but considerable turbulence in Alsace-Lorraine.

The Economic Consequences of Singing the Marseillaise

The years preceding the Great War in Alsace-Lorraine showed how the regional and federal administrations precipitated political turmoil in one of Germany's most prosperous regions. Even before the onset of the First World War, the administration started to treat many Alsace-Lorraine businesses as enemy companies, and the German army and administration created conflicts that had no inherent connection to the Reichsland's economy. The "Grafenstaden affair" in 1912 showed Alsace-Lorrainers that the military and civilian authorities were willing to sacrifice their interests for the economic benefit of other regions of the German Reich. The events undergirding the affair started on a spring night in 1912, when the workmen's theater group of the Alsatian Mechanical Construction Company (ElMaG), a train-building factory in Grafenstaden near Strasbourg, performed a comedy about the recent adventures of the French army in Morocco.[65] After the performance, the actors and audience, mostly men, started to drink on the premises and the crowd spontaneously burst out singing the "Marseillaise."[66] Instead of going unnoticed, as had several previous performances and singings of the "Marseillaise," this event led to a political crisis and economic difficulties for the firm. Subsequently, the federal and Prussian governments retaliated against the ElMaG, which had served as the venue for the incident, and withdrew state commissions from this prosperous firm, sending shockwaves through the regional economy.[67] During these events, the Reichsland's weak authorities, which were in a position to defend the interests of firms like the ElMaG, capitulated to the army and sacrificed the interests of a major regional company to curry favor with Prussian interests.

Grafenstaden was a working-class suburb of Strasbourg and the location of the ElMaG's largest factory in Alsace, which mostly produced train carriages for the Prussian and federal railways. The singing of the "Marseillaise" was an ordinary and regular occurrence in prewar Alsace. Workers in the Grafenstaden plant had actively participated in cultural associations that included the St. Cecile choir, gymnastic associations, and theater groups with decades of tradition behind them.[68] As was the case with previous performances, the audience had peacefully left the factory for their neighboring quarters after the festive evening and resumed work the following day.

The actual "Grafenstaden affair" started weeks after the performance, when the German press and politicians retroactively turned the event into a major political crisis. In April 1912, the *Rheinisch Westphälische Zeitung*, a radical nationalist weekly based over 250 miles north of Grafenstaden in the steel town of Essen, published an article that attacked the Francophile attitude of the company's managers.[69] In a spirit of industrial paternalism, the paper accused one of the technical directors of the firm, Frédéric Théophile Heyler, of misleading the workers and encouraging Francophile sentiments. Essen was the seat of the Krupp steel company, which was in fact one of the sponsors of the paper.[70] The article demanded to know why the Prussian state railways acquired its locomotives and railway carts from such an anti-German corporation as the ElMaG. On the basis of this denunciation, the Prussian Landtag requested retaliation.[71]

The Grafenstaden affair showed how an Alsatian heavy industrial company could find itself at the center of the Franco-German tussle due to a mundane incident that involved drinking and the singing of a contentious song, both key components of nationalist incidents in late nineteenth- and early twentieth-century Central and East-Central Europe. The "Marseillaise" had been the national anthem of France since the French Revolution, and as such it evoked French sympathies, the Franco-Prussian War, and resistance to German rule in the Reichsland. In this regard, German authorities and the press were right to treat the incident as anti-German, even as regional actors at times less convincingly tried to play down its nationalist significance. Yet in many respects, they had a reason to do so. In Alsace, the "Marseillaise" also evoked regional and urban patriotism, which points beyond the interpretation of the incident as simply the expression of pro-French and anti-German sentiments, a clear yet not exhaustive meaning of what transpired. Eugene de Dietrich served on the board of the ElMaG; it was his paternal ancestor, the baron Frédéric de Dietrich, who had encouraged army engineer Rouget de Lisle to come up with an anthem for the impending battle with the Austrian emperor.[72] Aided by Mayor de Dietrich's generous provisioning of champagne, de Lisle composed a song overnight for the Rhine army, and de Dietrich and his fellow Strasbourg citizens were the first to hear it performed.[73] The song was thus the pride of both Strasbourg's Alsatian bourgeoisie and the region's *notables*, even though the French administration was later to exploit the Alsatian origins of the "Marseillaise" after 1918 to underpin its claims on this largely germanophone region (figures 2.2 and 2.3).

In 1911, the German emperor granted a limited constitution and a legislative assembly to Alsace-Lorraine, bringing about the rise of regionalist political mobilization accompanied by frequent singings of the "Marseillaise" in Grafenstaden and elsewhere. In the cold of a February night in 1912, for instance, just a few weeks before the performance at the ElMaG factory, a crowd of 150–200 men took to the heart of Strasbourg around midnight, whistling the "Marseillaise" until they reached the statue of Jean-Baptiste Kléber, the Alsatian general of the French revolutionary wars.[74] Even though a journalist from the *Illkirch-Grafenstadener Anzeiger*, a German nationalist newspaper, spotted Hugo Haug, secretary of the Strasbourg Chamber of Commerce, in the crowd, his angry article prompted no retaliation.[75] The workers who participated in the singing of the "Marseillaise" thus had good reason to believe that their spontaneous performance behind closed doors would incur no punishment, especially since the ElMaG was deeply embedded in the German economy.

FIGURE 2.2. The inauguration of the "Monument of the Marseillaise" in 1922 by Strasbourg's mayor Jacques Peirotes. Source: Agence Meurisse and Rol, c. BNF.

FIGURE 2.3. The inauguration of the "Monument of the Marseillaise" in 1922 with Baron de Dietrich. Source: Agence Meurisse and Rol, c. BNF.

The ElMaG appeared to be an unlikely target for a German nationalist campaign. The corporation had factories in Grafenstaden and Mulhouse as well as a smaller factory in Belfort in French Alsace.[76] It employed around two thousand German and Alsatian workers and two hundred white-collar employees. The ElMaG's employment of workers born in Germany set it apart from the de Dietrich firm, tucked away in the Alsatian countryside, which employed only a few German managers, clerks, and workers because immigrant Germans concentrated in cities. If anything, the ElMaG was the poster child for Alsace's integration into the German economy. It was a midsized company at the time of Alsace-Lorraine's annexation by Germany. The rapid industrialization of the Reich, however, turned it into one of the most important machine-building companies in southern Germany as its turnover increased 400 percent by 1910.[77] By then, the company's Reichsland branch had become more relevant than its factory in Belfort, French Alsace. In the early 1890s, 73 percent of the company's output still went to the French market, but after the 1892 implementation of protective tariffs by the Paris government it switched to German consumers. In 1912, two-thirds of the ElMaG's production was absorbed by the Prussian and imperial railways.[78]

The ElMaG's production and distribution networks reached France, Switzerland, and Germany on the eve of the First World War. This lucrative business's turnover increased from 46 to 67 million marks, or $11 to $16 million, between 1901 and 1911. Given that this increase in revenue stemmed from commissions by the Prussian and imperial railways, the company was exposed to state and imperial governments on the other side of the Rhine.[79] The ElMaG also specialized in the production of custom-made blowing engines, blast furnaces with gas motors, and steam turbines for the Rhineland's steel plants and factories, such as Krupp, Stinnes, and the Augsburg-based MAN mechanical engineering company.[80] In 1903, specifically at the request of the Krupp firm, the company designed and produced a powerful rolling mill engine for the Essen-based industrial giant.[81] It is thus doubtful that the Krupps were behind the denunciation of the *Rheinisch Westphälische Zeitung*, although large commissions by the Prussian and state railways to the ElMaG did irk many companies outside of Alsace.

The company's managers included prominent Alsatian notables who had cooperated with German authorities for decades and were also respected among German businessmen. Its director, Rudolf Albert Koechlin, was born to a distinguished Alsatian-Swiss family in Baden, Germany, in 1859 and grew up in Basel, Switzerland.[82] Like Walther Rathenau, Eugen Jacobi, Ferenc Chorin Jr., and most of continental Europe's business elites, Koechlin was well traveled, had received his training in Europe's major metropoles (including Berlin, Vienna, Paris, and London), and specialized in the finance and management of the cutting-edge industries of his day: electricity and railways. Thanks to his family connections, agility, and marriage to a member of the La Roche family (owners of the Basel chemical giant of the same name), Koechlin became a key figure in electrical development projects and banking from Paris to Vienna by the turn of the century. He served as the director of the Basler Handelsbank and sat on the boards of numerous Swiss-German industrial companies, as well as the Franco-Swiss, Credito Italiano, and Wiener Bankverein banks.[83]

The company's previous director, Théodore Schlumberger, came from a family of established Mulhouse textile industrialists.[84] As the city's wealthiest notable and president of the Alsace-Lorraine industrialists' syndicate, Schlumberger had worked with the Statthalter Prince Chlodwig von Hohenlohe-Schillingsfürst (1885–1894), who had subsequently become German chancellor (1894–1900). As Statthalter, Hohenlohe-Schillingsfürst attempted to bring Alsace-Lorraine and Germany closer to each other through commerce and viewed the region's business elites as natural allies.[85] Schlumberger also had extensive ties to other German politicians.[86] Schlumberger's networks among Germany's political elites expanded further in the 1900s when he moved to Berlin to attend the sessions of the Reichstag as a member of the National Liberal Party.[87] Notably, Schlumberger joined a mainstream German party that had no ties to Alsatian regionalism. National liberals received their support from the Reich's wealthy industrialists and the liberal professions and pushed for a more prominent place for Germany in world trade.[88] They enjoyed the support of the Pan-German League, a radical nationalist organization whose ideas were often voiced in the *Rheinisch Westphälische Zeitung*.[89] Given Schlumberger's role as president of the Alsatian Industrialist association and a founding member of the Franco-German Chamber of Commerce, he had excellent connections among German businessmen and had worked with Emil Guggenheimer, director of the MAN engineering company, and Konrad Borsig, owner of a locomotive production factory, among others.[90] By the time the *Rheinisch Westphälische Zeitung* started its campaign against the ElMaG, the septuagenarian Schlumberger had received the title of commercial adviser and emerged as a link among Alsatian business dynasties, the regional administration, and the Reich's government. The attack on the ElMaG was thus also a politically unproductive attack on the few Germanophile industrialists in Alsace, like Schlumberger.

It is likely that employees of the ElMaG passed information about the singing of the "Marseillaise" to the Essen newspaper, given that the performance had taken place on the factory's premises behind closed doors.[91] On April 20, 1912, citing the newspaper's article criticizing the disloyalty of the Grafenstaden factory's management, members of the Prussian Landtag demanded the cancellation of contracts and technical director Heyler's firing.[92]

The general secretary of the Prussian conservatives, August Strosser (1848–1915), who advocated for Heyler's removal, was himself from the industrial region and echoed the *Rheinisch Westphälische Zeitung*'s article when he stated that "Germans are neither employed as workers nor as officials" at Grafenstaden, which was far from the truth.[93] Furthermore, Strosser claimed that the company had adopted French as the language of business and that "Germanness and German culture are not cultivated" in the factory; as a consequence, "Germandom has lost many young men recently."[94] "It is hardly believable," continued Strosser, "that this is not known to our government, which extends contracts worth millions through the Prussian and imperial railways."[95] In fact, Alsatian companies like the ElMaG and the de Dietrich firm had already switched to the German language in the 1890s.[96] Strosser, who acknowledged that he had brought up the issue "in the interests of our German (*altdeutsche*) industrialists," warned Alsatian businessmen "that if factory directors are openly anti-German and Francophile, then it will be very difficult for these companies to compete on German markets."[97] While Strosser was right to note the Francophile culture of Alsatian industrialists, his comments attested to his ignorance of the region's society and economy, as he failed to notice that French sympathies went well together with economic orientation toward Germany. German observers also missed the differences between Frenchness as imagined in Alsace-Lorraine and the foreign policies of France, and mistakenly conflated the views Francophile Alsatians with those of the French government.

The Prussian administration adopted a hostile attitude toward the ElMaG even before the investigation began, which put pressure on the Alsace-Lorraine administration to produce the expected results. In response to Strosser's challenge, Edouard Stieger, who served as undersecretary at the Ministry of Public Works and had been employed as a top railway official, confirmed that his minister had read the *Rheinisch Westphälische Zeitung*'s article and promised that adequate retaliatory measures would follow.[98] This put the regional administration in a bind as it harbored close and good relations with the ElMaG and had to choose between protecting regional interests and yielding to political pressure from its superiors.

This affair erupted at the worst possible time for the regional administration. Discontent with the 1911 constitution among Alsace-Lorrainers prompted the mercurial Wilhelm II to threaten "ungrateful" Alsace-Lorrainers with the incorporation of the region into Prussia. Such an act would have undercut the interests of the Reichsland's German businessmen, who were locked in competition with Prussian companies over state commissions and markets.[99] Furthermore, heightened diplomatic tensions between France and Germany prompted the administration to take as few risks as possible. The result of the investigation showed that even loyal industrialists and politicians like Koechlin and Schlumberger were unable to sway an inflexible and authoritarian administration. The new constitution granted the Reichsland its own regional legislative assembly, the Landtag, but this affair painfully highlighted its limited power. As it turned out, the Landtag's protest could easily be marginalized by the imperial government. The elected Landtag's authority was dwarfed by the power of the government-appointed regional administration, which called the relevance of the new constitution into question.[100]

There were two investigations, an official one and an unofficial one, that ran parallel to each other. First, following the bureaucratic chain of command of imperial Germany, the Berlin government charged its representative in Alsace-Lorraine, Undersecretary of State for the Interior Karl Wilhelm Mandel, with carrying out a formal inquiry. Mandel's office operated as part of the government's Alsace-Lorraine Ministry, and Mandel was a loyal bureaucrat of the federal government. This pro forma investigation was hasty and superficial. It seemed to Alsatian observers that Heyler's condemnation was in accordance with the wishes of the Rhineland-Westphalia newspaper's article and the Prussian Landtag. Notably, the regional administration did not even summon Heyler himself although he was one of the witnesses of, and probably participated in, the Marseillaise incident. Instead, the administration gathered evidence from Heyler's enemies.[101]

The investigation thus discovered that, as a fourteen-year-old at the time of passive resistance to German rule in Alsace, the technical director had been sentenced for lèse-majesté. Even decades later, this charge was used to prove his anti-German attitudes as an adult. The second, unofficial investigation attempted to pressure Alsatian industrialists to resolve the issue on their own by firing Heyler; in exchange, the administration promised to clandestinely restore commissions to the firm.[102] The endeavor attested to the informal political power of the region's native industrialists, yet it also called into question the promise of democratization of Alsatian politics through the new constitution.[103] Alsace, as one historian put it, remained the "Alsace of the notables."[104]

Eugene de Dietrich, who sat on the supervisory board of the ElMaG, was at the center of Mandel's efforts to strike an informal deal. The old baron, however, refused to enter into negotiations with the weak regional administration as he probably realized that Mandel had no power over the Prussian government, let alone the federal administration.[105] Mandel's clumsy handling of the affair resulted in a perfect storm for the regional administration at the newly elected Landtag. Center-party, liberal, regionalist, and social-democratic candidates united to criticize the government's "dictatorial" measures and the inadequacy of the recently granted constitution.[106] The German social-democratic representative Bernhard Böhle castigated the administration for serving the interests of top German industrialists. The Francophile regionalist Abbé Émile Wetterlé asked, "Did you notice that in Pan-Germanist papers, it is always the Alsace-Lorraine *notables* that are attacked? They criticize [the *notables'*] harmful influence on the crowds. It is their domination that [the Germans] want to break."[107] While Wetterlé was far from an unbiased observer, he correctly pointed to the central role of industrialists in Alsatian nationalist polemics.

Wetterlé's allies, the Francophile regionalists, insisted that practical rather than political considerations drove business practices in Alsace.[108] Even the openly Francophile Daniel Blumethal maintained that the ElMaG had "scrupulously avoided adopting a political stance since 1870; [the company] knew all too well that it is no use parading around ideas that collide with the interests of its [German] customers."[109] Schlumberger gave his "word of honor" that he "never witnessed any anti-German manipulation or anything that came close to that. . . . To the contrary there is a Germanophile attitude among workers in Grafenstaden."[110]

In his response, Mandel poured oil on the fire when he indicated that unless the ElMaG fired Heyler, it would be impossible to persuade the Prussian Ministry to renew its contracts. The undersecretary also called for a "thorough cleaning" of the company, which implied the requirement to vet its workers and managers on the basis of loyalty to the Reich. Eugene de Dietrich, the doyen of Alsatian notables, personally intervened with the German administration in favor of Heyler; de Dietrich went so far as to admit that Heyler had made a mistake, but rejected the charges that the management ran the company in a manner hostile to Germany.[111] In the end, Mandel's office concluded that the ElMaG's management was responsible for inciting anti-German sentiment. The ElMaG fired Heyler; in response, Eugene de Dietrich resigned from the company's board of directors.[112] The following year, the ElMaG's top management decided to separate the company's branches in France and Germany. This separation was intended to reassure the Prussian and federal governments of the firm's loyalty. However, only the imperial railways renewed its contracts with ElMaG; the Prussian railways broke off business relations.[113]

The ElMaG's decision to try to please the administration by formally cutting ties to France was part of a broader trend among Alsatian firms. The escalation of diplomatic tensions between France and Germany negatively affected the businesses of Alsace-Lorraine's Germans as well—even the Adler and Oppenheimer tannery followed suit and shed its French branch; this was an indication of the escalation of economic nationalism before 1914.[114] The German administration's persecution of the firm cost the Reich's economy dearly, however, since the ElMaG's management transferred the majority of the firm's capital to France. While the German branch's capital was reduced from 18 to 13.5 million marks, the new French company in Belfort was founded with a capital of 20 million marks drawn from reserves accumulated mostly by the German branch.[115]

The investigation also showed that two years before the outbreak of the First World War, both the regional and imperial administrations were ready to sacrifice the interests of even loyal Alsace-Lorrainer industrialists without gaining any practical economic or political benefits. The tribulations of the ElMaG prefigured the waste of precious resources in the Reichsland and the rest of Germany during the First World War, when the administration and the army created thousands of "Grafenstaden affairs" as they pursued enemy property and liquidated companies that came under suspicion of having Allied interests. Lack of backing by the government became especially crucial during the First World War when the state wielded increased power to allocate raw materials, set prices, and extend commissions to firms.

If the Grafenstaden affair was a minor tragedy for Alsatian industrial companies, the Zabern affair that followed also excelled in farcical details that had grim consequences for Alsace-Lorraine's industrialists. The Zabern incident of 1913 attested once more to the subordination of the region's interests to the all-powerful military and the federal government. It involved a nineteen-year-old Prussian officer, Freiherr Günter von Förstner, who had insulted Alsace-Lorrainer recruits. After the regionalist newspaper *Der Elsässer* reported the incident, protests followed in front of the barracks, which the military mishandled by arresting numerous civilians, including a prosecutor and judges who were simply leaving their offices when the protests erupted.[116] Pressure from the Statthalter—General von Wedel—was unsuccessful in securing the transfer and punishment of the increasingly aggressive Förstner, who emerged unscathed. Even loyal politicians and industrialists had no power to influence the authoritarian and chauvinistic military leadership. Furthermore, just as it had during the Grafenstaden affair, the regional administration proved to be a puppet of the federal government. The Zabern incident thus showed that the military formed a state within a state in Germany.[117]

The incident not only alienated many locals from the German army and administration in the critical months preceding the war but also raised international consciousness of the issue of Alsace-Lorraine.[118] Even Vladimir Lenin pondered in a Russian newspaper whether the Zabern affair was an event that revealed the deep-seated "order of things" in German society.[119] The historian Hans Ulrich Wehler claimed that the affair was like a "flashlight" that revealed "for a moment, the fundamental conflicts inside [the Reich] that contributed to its collapse."[120] To some extent, the Zabern affair was the inverse, German version of the Dreyfus affair: while the Dreyfus affair led to the affirmation of civilian leadership over the military in France, the Zabern affair confirmed the privileges of the army over private corporations, elected representatives, and the civilian administration in Germany.

Convergences between Germany's and Hungary's industrial regions and companies were noticeable, even as the former continued to concentrate more workers and capital. Despite these remarkable economic advantages over other regions of the German and Austro-Hungarian empires, the industrialists of Alsace-Lorraine lost the backing of both the French and the German governments at a time when state commissions, favorable tariff laws, and protection from politicized attacks became crucial for the success of industrialists all over Europe. The early 1910s showed that industrialists in one of the most economically developed regions of the continent, Alsace and Lorraine, had considerably more difficulties with the rise of economic nationalism than did their competitors in East-Central Europe, even though they were sheltered from the economic consequences of the Balkan Wars, which precipitated a recession in Hungary and Southeastern Europe. As the Grafenstaden affair and the generous subsidies to the Transylvanian Renner tannery highlighted, economic nationalism could be both detrimental and advantageous to industrialists. While the German government and army exploited nationalist incidents to settle old scores with Francophile regionalist elites in Alsace, Budapest shielded business elites from fierce critics of ethnic minorities and social inequality; the price to pay included voter suppression and harsher conditions for workers, grievances that came to the fore during the revolutions in the aftermath of the First World War.[121] Furthermore, Budapest also handed out sizable subsidies to craftsmen and industrialists, which it justified by appeals to the "national interest" of enhancing Hungarian industrial production. As the near bankruptcy of the Renner tannery showed, government subsidies alone were inadequate for the industrialization of an overwhelmingly agrarian region: it was easier to create industrialists than to create viable industries, and Transylvania's new class of entrepreneurs would have to wait until the First World War.

Chapter 3

Millionaires of Mitteleuropa

The First World War ushered in a period of shortages and suffering for the populations of Austria-Hungary and Germany: it left more than four million soldiers and civilians dead and almost eight million ex-servicemen of the two empires wounded.[1] Yet the Great War was also the era of German-Austro-Hungarian empire building with the goal of long-term domination of Central and Eastern Europe.[2] Industrialists and businessmen scrambled to profit from this imperial expansion and amassed fortunes that contributed to their continued influence after 1918. The impressive gains of military suppliers were not unusual—past wars had contributed to the enrichment of the Fuggers, Rothschilds, and other financiers.[3] However, the First World War required the mobilization of considerably more resources than previous conflicts, broadening the circle of suppliers and those who were able to turn a profit. While governments wielded the language of collective sacrifice in their discourse toward ordinary women, men, and soldiers on the front, they condoned the privatization of wartime profits by businessmen and industrialists, a trend that successor states of both empires would continue after 1918 as they passed on the fruits of victory to loyal economic elites.[4] The question of how to finance a war was marginal during the July Crisis of 1914, which led to the First World War, and neither Austria-Hungary nor the German empire moved to tax excessive corporate profits.[5] Instead, they condoned populist anti-semitism that deflected responsibility for rising social inequality from governments by pinning it on enriched Jewish army suppliers or Jews more generally; they did this even as most of the Jewish populations of the two empires suffered from the same shortages as everyone else on the home front, Jewish soldiers fought on the war front, and tens of thousands of Galician and Polish Jews became homeless refugees and fled toward Vienna, Budapest, and Berlin, putting them among the most helpless of the two empires' populations.[6]

The enrichment of industrialists was systemic, the result of low corporate taxes and the lack of adequate supervision of industrial companies in both Austria-Hungary and Germany that benefited industrialists and businessmen, Jews and non-Jews alike.[7] Both the members of the Entente and the Central Powers remained "liberal political economies" that refused to nationalize even industries that were vital for the war effort and regarded the state's wartime influence over private enterprise as an exception rather than a model for postwar reconstruction.[8] Historians such as Niall Ferguson and Gerald Feldman have also highlighted the overtly bureaucratic and inefficient economic administrations of the Central Powers.[9] During the war, not only did the exploitation of lower-paid women and forced labor by POWs become widespread, but states were also unable to prosecute questionable accounting practices and product falsification.

Large industrial companies emerged as the primary beneficiaries of the war economy as the Great War accelerated the trends of vertical integration and capital concentration that were already apparent before 1914.[10] Similar to how the Central Powers conquered territories between 1914 and 1918 that they were unable to "digest," so did large corporations acquire majority shares in smaller firms on the home fronts of Germany and Austria-Hungary without having the capacity to control the management of these firms. The expansion of state intervention into private enterprise masked the control that large companies exercised over war corporations that the German, Austrian, and Hungarian governments established to centralize production and distribution of goods for their armies and civilians.[11]

The years between 1914 and 1918 proved to be a learning opportunity that industrialists would leverage during the post-armistice period, since it taught them how to react to rapidly changing political and military situations and profit from economic and political crises. Modern crises, according to Reinhart Koselleck, imply "a new sense of time" and denote either "perceptions . . . of epochal change" (that is, rupture) or a "state of greater or lesser permanence, as in a longer or shorter transition towards something better or worse or towards something altogether different."[12] From this perspective, the experience of the Great War was a prolonged yet accelerated period of transformation that nonetheless hewed close to the pre-1914 geopolitical and economic order.[13] The building blocks of capitalist economies remained in place after 1914, but the substitution of global supply chains for continental economic integration ratcheted up the value of readily available domestic resources while governments intervened massively in the production and distribution of a variety of assets.[14]

Business elites were fast learners at a time when state apparatuses were comparatively slow to adapt and pursued reactive rather than proactive economic policies, especially in the first months of the war.[15] The ascent of Transylvanian lawyer Mózes Farkas is emblematic of the opportunities that the Great War opened up for agile, well-placed business leaders. In the summer of 1914, the thirty-three-year-old Farkas was the director of a small Transylvanian tannery on the brink of bankruptcy. Three years later, the tannery was one of the largest in Hungary and Farkas was the head of the national leather industry syndicate.[16] Farkas took advantage of German and Austro-Hungarian economic expansion in Southeastern Europe to attract Viennese and Budapest capital to his firm and replaced Asian and Latin American suppliers with suppliers from neutral Switzerland and Norway.[17] The rise to prominence of industrialists like Farkas would have been unimaginable without the Central Powers' military victories in Eastern and Southeastern Europe, which made Hungary in general and Transylvania in particular springboards for postwar economic expansion while traditional centers of European industrialization on the western edges of Mitteleuropa, such as Alsace-Lorraine, declined. His meteoric rise highlights the fact that there were several corporations beyond the familiar circle of large industrialists like the German steel magnate Krupps that managed to profit from total war, especially in Hungary where the industry sector was smaller than in Germany and Austria and more independent from the interference of the army.[18]

The prosperity of German and Austro-Hungarian businessmen may seem surprising, since accounts of the two empires' war economies usually adopt the perspective of state treasuries, focusing on statistics that even renowned economic historians label as "incomplete," and stressing the increasing hardships and impoverishment of the Central Powers.[19] Unsurprisingly, the economic history of Germany's war effort is summarized as "the chronicle of disappointed expectations, painful adjustment, and . . . [of] insufficient resource base, and probably of misallocation and disingenuous economic planning."[20] These studies have greatly expanded our knowledge of the war finance and economic organization crisis faced by German, Austrian, and Hungarian leaders as their resource pool shrank during the war. It is clear that the governments of the Central Powers experienced increasing economic difficulties that surpassed those faced by the Entente that was able to rely on North American and colonial resources. A statistical view of the war economy, nonetheless, may reinforce the tendency to read history backward, from the perspective of the collapse of the two empires in 1918, a reading that was already popular among Central Europeans in the aftermath of the Great War, in part because the majority of society was indeed doing worse than before the war. Yet this evaluation did not pertain to industrial companies and the industrial capacity of the Dual Monarchy more generally. As economic historian Max Schulze has noted, Oszkár Jászi's interwar assessment, according to which the monarchy "was already a defeated Empire from the economic point of view" as early as 1913, was false since Austria-Hungary in fact "proved broadly capable of sustaining the war effort until 1917."[21] A shift from national to regional perspectives, and from politicians to industrialists integrated into local societies, nuances this picture by revealing regional and sector-specific variations in the war's economic impact. Turning our attention to the business elites who prospered shows a different side of the home front, one that experienced enrichment as a result of low taxes and lenient bureaucracies and territorial conquests in Southeastern Europe and the Russian empire that also fueled expectations of a favorable conclusion of the Great War.

The Rise of Mitteleuropa

The war did not start well for the Central Powers in 1914, as they failed to make a breakthrough on any of the front lines. Italy joined the Allies in 1915, while in August 1916 Romanian troops burst into southern Transylvania. Yet by Christmas of 1916, the German army occupied Romania's capital, Bucharest, and had seized the country's vast oil reserves, which enabled the Central Powers to continue fighting the war despite the blockade until 1918.[22] Russia collapsed under pressure from the Central Powers and revolution in 1917, leading to the unquestioned hegemony of Germany and its allies over Eastern and Southeastern Europe. The enrichment of German and Austro-Hungarian military suppliers resulted from the increased demand for their products created by the exit of much of Central Europe from the global economy, and the economic exploitation of over one million square kilometers of occupied territories stretching from northeastern France to Romania, Serbia, and Ukraine.[23]

The First World War intensified economic integration and industrialization among both the Allies and the Central Powers. In 1914, Great Britain initiated a comprehensive economic blockade of the Central Powers in retaliation for German war measures and blocked the shipment of a variety of raw materials and food to Central Europe.[24] This blockade, along with the stalemate on the western front, turned even advocates of German global domination or *Weltpolitik* toward Eastern and Southeastern Europe. In 1915 and 1916, a series of conventions were held in Dresden, Vienna, and Berlin that were attended by the leading German and Austro-Hungarian industrialists and trade organizations. This included the German-Austro-Hungarian Trade Association; the industry organizer Gustav Stresemann, who was an advocate of annexations; Kurt Sorge, who was the general director of Krupp; and Ferenc Chorin and Gusztáv Gratz as representatives of the Hungarian Alliance of Industrialists.[25] These economic conventions were based on the need for increased cooperation between the two empires during the war as regards the procurement of raw materials and the organization of production. German liberal imperialist Friedrich Naumann's 1915 book *Mitteleuropa* (*Central Europe*) went further to advocate the necessity of both economic cooperation and political integration, a considerably more contentious issue. Naumann believed that the war revealed the deep-seated economic dependence of conquered Eastern Europe on the Central Powers and made a customs union between Germany and Austria-Hungary an inevitable necessity. "You must think of these stretches of country as unity, as a brotherhood of many members, as a defensive alliance, as a single economic district! All the traditional separatism of these lands must be so effaced in the stress of the Great War as to make the idea of union tolerable. . . . History speaks to us of it [Mitteleuropa] in the thunder of the guns, but it rests with us whether or no[t] we listen."[26] Naumann's work was an instant best seller and was immediately translated not only into Hungarian but also into English. The book's broad readership, however, was mainly due to the controversial reception of such ambitions for German hegemony over Austria and Hungary, let alone in conquered territories or among ethnic minorities like Transylvania's Romanians.[27]

The question of Mitteleuropa's wartime integration deeply divided socialists, progressives, the nationalist Right, and industrialists more generally in both Austria and Hungary. Leaders of industries with sizable German capital welcomed the idea, while industrialists and bankers with ties to British and French capital remained skeptical, as did those who feared German competition. Hungarian coal magnate Ferenc Chorin Sr. supported economic integration with Germany but warned that a tariff union with the German empire would lead to "great disappointments,"[28] which showed that even Hungarian advocates of Mitteleuropa defined the alliance differently than their German counterparts, and somewhat wishfully interpreted it as the alliance of sovereign nations rather than German expansion. The "westernizer" intellectual and politician Oszkár Jászi devoted a special issue of his journal *Huszadik Század* (Twentieth Century) to the discussion of plans for Mitteleuropa, in which he interpreted

Austria-Hungary's integration with Germany as a harbinger of modernization that "accelerates the rhythm of intellectual and political contacts" with an economically and politically more developed state, Germany.[29] As regards economic life, Jászi idealistically expected that German capital would flow to support Hungary's industries, competition within the customs union would boost productivity, and German welfare policies would spread throughout Mitteleuropa. This positive vision of the future Mitteleuropa stemmed from Jászi's unfamiliarity with German practices of occupation and exploitation and his hostility toward tariff walls and *Kleinstaaterei*, the particularism of small nation-states that he associated with monopolistic and uncompetitive industries in Hungary.[30]

The main shortcoming of Naumann's plan for Mitteleuropa was characteristic of advocates of both formal and informal German imperialism. Namely, Naumann had nothing to offer non-Germans in Eastern and Southeastern Europe, who were expected to accept Germany's hegemony as a historical necessity rooted in the Wilhelmine empire's economic and civilizational superiority. Both the lofty ideas of Naumann's Mitteleuropa and actual German occupation practices offered few incentives even to Austrian and Hungarian industrialists.[31] While the integration of the two empires' economies progressed rapidly, the First World War also gave rise to Austrian and Hungarian plans to shore up their economic independence, autonomy, and interstate competition for resources, as part of trends of "re-territorialization" or "deglobalization" during the First World War; this entailed the increased importance of national borders, customs lines, and a heightened awareness of national "resources, livelihood, output and energy"[32] even as economic integration increased at the same time. Hungarian attempts to shield the interests of domestic industrialists played a part in German chancellor Theobald von Bethmann-Hollweg and foreign minister Gottlieb von Jagow's inability to convince the monarchy's foreign minister István Burián and its prime ministers of the need to increase and formalize economic integration in November 1915.[33] While expert committees continued to formulate proposals for economic integration of the two empires, it was never to materialize.[34]

The Allied response to plans for Mitteleuropa, developed at the Paris Economic Conferences of March and June 1916, was harsh and showed that the Allies took the plans more seriously than many politicians and industrialists in Austria-Hungary and Germany.[35] The conference also highlighted the Entente's superiority in economic warfare as it fostered closer economic cooperation among the Allies and the long-term exclusion of the Central Powers, especially Germany, from the global economy. The conferences led to the escalation of measures against the private property of enemy subjects and prompted the liquidation of German and Austro-Hungarian assets on Allied territory.[36] The Paris Economic Conferences rejected the prewar practice of free trade, with plans to maintain tariff walls around the two camps even after the war had ended, thus preserving the economic benefits of globalization and integration to the Allies while drawing rigid borders around the Central Powers. Accordingly, the Entente was to secure "raw materials and manufactured articles essential to the normal development of their economic activities" in order to "render themselves independent of enemy countries."[37] They also pledged "to adopt measures facilitating mutual trade relations, both by the establishment of direct and rapid land and sea transport service at low rates and by the extension and improvement of postal, telegraphic, and other communications."[38] The Allies' resolutions at the conferences were particularly beneficial to French interests, since the pact promised the long-term commercial isolation of Germany. In the meantime, economic cooperation and financial support from Great Britain promised to make up for France's loss of foreign income from its Austro-Hungarian, Russian, and Balkan investments.[39]

German propaganda touted the convention as proof of "England's" greed and envy targeting industrialized Germany; in this view, the pact revealed the true aim of the Entente war effort, the economic "annihilation" of the Kaiserreich.[40] This official German viewpoint was also a widespread interpretation of the Great War among Alsatian and Hungarian industrialists at the time, who failed to notice the relationship between excessive Allied economic measures and excessive German military strategy. English observers at the time regarded economic retaliation via the blockade as the only means in the hands of the Entente to curb Germany's disregard of international law and unconventional warfare, including the violation of Belgian sovereignty, the use of civilians on occupied territories in German munitions factories, and the use of poison gas.[41]

While the business elites of Germany and Austria-Hungary had no say in the outbreak of the First World War in 1914, and most of them lost out during the months of mobilization and the transition to the war economy, they publicly endorsed the war agenda early on, even though they had the opportunity to express divergent views, especially in Hungary. German propaganda on the causes of the Great War was remarkably effective among both Alsatian German and Hungarian business elites. Like their governments, they maintained that the conflict was inevitable because it was caused by inherent geopolitical and economic tensions between the two camps. For instance, the director of the Salgótarján Coal Mining Corporation (SCMC), Ferenc Chorin Jr., wrote in December 1914 that the real war had been started in the early 1910s by the Allies, which had forced a financial "crisis" on Germany and

Austria-Hungary.[42] According to Chorin, even if the Central Powers had been able to avoid open conflict during the July Crisis that followed the assassination of Franz Ferdinand, this paralyzing economic war "would have diminished our resources."[43] In his view, the war was thus precipitated not by diplomats and politicians but by British materialism, which set in motion a gargantuan struggle for Central Europe's economic resources. The Alsatian heavy industrialist Eugen Jacobi maintained that "England without doubt pursues her war effort not because she is convinced of her ability to conquer us, but in order to achieve her plan to destroy our global economic positions."[44] While Jacobi and Chorin rightly identified economic warfare as a crucial aspect of the British war effort, they failed to see how Germany and Austria-Hungary exacerbated and in many respects triggered these British policies.

Chorin's and Jacobi's acceptance of the official line of the German and Austro-Hungarian governments, which reduced the war to a simple conflict over economic resources, however, was really an attempt to find meaning in a war that had found both men unprepared. Industrialists' lofty statements in the press on the inevitability of the war contrasted with the apologetic tone of annual reports issued to worried shareholders. The brief report of Chorin's SCMC explained away difficulties in production by pointing out that "Hungary's industry and commerce remained uninformed as events were unfolding" in the summer of 1914.[45] Despite their initial difficulties, Hungarian industrialists emerged as major beneficiaries of the war effort, since the country's location adjacent to occupied Romania, Serbia, and Ukraine made it an attractive springboard for postwar reconstruction by 1917. At the same time, Allied military and economic pressures were felt less acutely in Transylvania and the rest of Hungary than in Alsace-Lorraine and Germany or in war-torn regions like Galicia or the Adriatic Littoral, indicating significant regional differences in the experience of the Great War within the German-Austro-Hungarian alliance.

Hungary's Empire in Southeastern Europe

The Central Powers' military conquests gave rise to an often-overlooked Austro-Hungarian, and even a specifically Hungarian, imperialism that defined their aims in remarkable separation from German ambitions for Mitteleuropa, even though Hungarian and Austrian imperialist agendas resulted from victories that were largely owed to the German army.[46] Hungarian bankers and industrialists posited themselves as equals to their German counterparts and believed that German and Hungarian plans to build an informal empire were compatible and based on economic and civilizational superiority over Southeastern Europe. At a time when Hungary had unique leverage over Austria because of its strategic food reserves, successive Hungarian governments also attempted to shore up the country's economic and political independence from Austria, although they achieved only modest results during the renegotiation of the 1867 compromise in 1917.[47]

According to the contemporary public intellectual Vilmos Laurentzi, Hungary was to emerge as the focal point of Eurasian commercial flows in the new global order after the war. He wrote that "the deep-seated [economic] integration of the West and the East" was only possible through Hungary, which was to be the central node in the "trans-Eurasian" railway network, the headquarters of a new stock exchange for Eurasian trade, and a new logistics and transshipment hub.[48] Laurentzi suggested in 1915 that the "world historical mission of Hungary," the proliferation of "culture" in Eastern Europe, found new meaning "on a grander scale through a monumental economic expansion" in Southeastern Europe, the Middle East, and Asia.[49] Eastern expansion turned into an Orientalist "civilizing mission" led by Hungarian entrepreneurs and politicians who were ready to replace expropriated French capital and culture in Southeastern Europe: "We [Hungarians] go to Germany to study. In the Balkans, however, we must become teachers ourselves," as the official journal of legal scholars put it in 1916.[50]

The Turanian Society, the Oriental Commercial Academy, Masonic lodges in Transylvania, and Kálmán Balkányi's Hungarian-Bosnian Center were the most vocal advocates of eastern economic expansion.[51] The Hungarian administration wanted to cement its alliance with Bulgaria and Turkey by expanding cultural and economic ties. The exhibition of Austrian and Hungarian industrial art opened in Sofia in 1917 by Ambassador Ottokar Czernin in the presence of the Bulgarian king and prime minister, and it was the most prominent cultural manifestation of economic expansion plans targeting Southeastern Europe and Turkey.[52]

While the war meant that few of these plans for economic expansion came to fruition, Transylvanian industrialists and businessmen prepared detailed plans for postwar reconstruction; chambers of commerce, for instance, petitioned for railway links that would connect Arad and Temesvár to "Balkan" markets.[53] The leather industry association noted that "the eastern markets that had so far been under the domination of French and English competitors will open up. English and French hegemony will cease and we [Hungarian industrialists] will be able to appear with our products in eastern markets without having to face French and English competitors."[54] At the same time, the Budapest-based Oriental Academy that was established in 1891 launched three-month courses on the culture, economy, and customs of Southeastern

Europe for Hungarian artisans and businessmen, while a separate program offered language courses not only in Serbian, Bulgarian, and Turkish but also in the true lingua franca of Balkan trade, French.[55] The courses used the latest results-oriented educational techniques, *en plein air* as one newspaper noted.[56]

The Hungarian government also sponsored the educations of Turkish and Bulgarian students, along with students from occupied Balkan territories, in Hungarian elementary and high schools. Temesvár, the largest city in the Bánát, and its vocational school became the second most popular destination for foreign students. While Turkish and Bulgarian students enjoyed a Hungarian government scholarship, it was the military administration of occupied Montenegro that sponsored the study of students from Cetinje in order to boost morale and its own popularity among occupied populations; these young "enemy students" studied alongside the more than two hundred Turkish and Bulgarian scholarship holders.[57] This "civilizing mission" extended beyond purely educational opportunities for students from the Balkans. It also aimed at the eventual emancipation of the "captive women of Stambul" in Hungarian schools for young women, much like the emancipation of Romanian Jews by the German occupiers under the Treaty of Bucharest, which ended the war between the Central Powers and Romania in May 1918.[58]

Ultimately, this eastern economic and cultural expansion remained a collection of ambitious plans that were out of touch with wartime shortages and the actual capacity of Hungarian industries. István Bárczy, the mayor of Budapest, harshly criticized the applied arts exhibition in Sofia as a manifestation of an "impatient [attitude] that would first like to conquer Sofia for our furniture, textiles, jewelry and chandeliers" before these products had conquered Hungarian provincial towns that still relied on Austrian and German imports, painfully pointing out how Hungarian plans to conquer Balkan markets were undermined by a lack of competitive production capacities and Austro-German economic expansion in Hungary.[59] While Hungarian companies were unable to gain a permanent foothold in Bulgaria, Romania, and Turkey, Transylvanian companies did benefit from this cultural and commercial shift from imperial capitals and Western Europe toward the Balkans because it attracted investments to the region, leading to a boom in industrialization.

Wartime Industrialization in Transylvania

The Renner tannery in Kolozsvár, Transylvania, was one of the companies that profited from the Allied blockade of the Central Powers, as well as Hungary's plans for an informal empire in Southeastern Europe after the war. The blockade forced both Germany and the Dual Monarchy to embark on import substitution industrialization. According to political economist Stephan Haggard, import substitution is "the economic process through which local production displaces, or substitutes for, previously imported goods"[60]—in this case, from Allied powers and their colonies. The practical result of this process was Hungary's increased economic independence from the industrialized core of the Dual Monarchy, Austria and Bohemia. Hungarian governments and politicians had been taking measures to support domestic industries against Austrian competition since the 1880s, and taking indirect measures since the 1820s, yet it was not until the Great War that they gained an opportunity to expand these protectionist measures into full-blown programs to explicitly favor Hungarian companies over their Austrian competitors.[61] This was paradoxical, since the Dual Monarchy constituted a single state that until 1916 was ruled by Emperor Franz Joseph, who in 1849 defeated Hungarian revolutionaries who had articulated similar, if politically more radical, demands for economic independence. All in all, the economic competition between Austria and Hungary resembled the rivalry among the German federal states over the allocation of raw materials and the planned partition of Alsace-Lorraine's natural resources during the Great War, even as the relationship between Austria and Hungary was more equal than that of Prussia and other federal states in Germany.[62] In some cases, Hungarian industrialists and even the government bypassed Austria and exported grain, cattle, minerals such as aluminum, and other goods directly to the war corporations of the German Reich, which paid higher prices than Austrian firms.[63] Austria, for its part, banned the export of certain industrial products to Hungary, including finished leather, and introduced a tax on a variety of Hungarian export items.[64]

Aside from the internal economic competition within Austria-Hungary, the enormous needs of the joint army also required the intensification of Hungarian industrial production. Even the least efficient factories and the smallest scraps of leather, metal, and timber became essential amid enormous shortages of finished products.[65] In response, the Budapest War Ministry attempted to maximize production and channeled commissions to regions like Transylvania, which had historically received less state support than the central regions of Hungary or Austria.

The outbreak of the war immediately put the Renner factory on an upward trajectory, despite its small size and recent founding. It is no surprise that a 1917 memo from its director Mózes Farkas on the future of European reconstruction was optimistic in every respect. Farkas noted that the war had depleted the resources of both the Central Powers and their enemies and that "in the foreseeable future . . . the sale of finished products is guaranteed" owing to high postwar civilian demand. The memo also noted that "it seems advisable for industrial companies to start to prepare now to meet global demand." The end of the war was expected to bring about a "peace boom" that the Renner factory was ready to exploit by rapidly expanding its production facilities.[66] As early as the fall of 1914, the company had switched to catering exclusively to the demands of the Austro-Hungarian military, attracted large pools of capital from Budapest banks, and received support from the municipality while paying minimal taxes.[67]

Between 1914 and 1915, the company's yearly profits increased from 27,000 crowns to 189,000 crowns, reaching 1 million crowns in 1918.[68] Inflation and the rising cost of raw materials undercut profits, even though inflation was slower in Hungary than in Austria.[69] Wartime gains enabled the construction of new factory units and worker housing on a twelve-acre plot that the firm purchased at a bargain price from the city of Kolozsvár in 1917.[70] Mózes Farkas used the more than 4.5 million crowns (equivalent to a half million dollars at the time) in capital from Budapest investors to build a three-level factory complex.[71] In the same year, the tannery increased its capital to 2 million crowns, and in the most economically difficult year of the war, 1918, it managed to raise an additional 3 million crowns, ratcheting up its paid-up capital to 5 million crowns, which represented around $500,000 or 120,000 Swiss francs at the time.[72] A contemporary journalist based in Kolozsvár noted that "capital has become an enormous lord. Wartime prosperity has placed it on a pedestal. It grew up and developed huge muscles. Capital lives in a shining palace, sits on a purple throne, claims royal prerogatives, rules, and commands."[73] The journalist likely knew about the enrichment of the Renners and the Farkases, who had become two of Kolozsvár's wealthiest and most powerful families thanks to their connections to the government, the municipality, and Budapest banks.

During peacetime, profit figures showcased companies' prosperity, enabling them to attract and retain investors and lenders; however, after 1914, corporations successfully hid their prosperity in order to avoid the attention of the authorities and the increasingly antisemitic popular press, which castigated "speculators," "war profiteers," and "war millionaires" in Germany, Austria, and Hungary.[74] Corporate profit accounting was also the subject of heated debates among politicians and industrialists.[75] As historian Jonathan Levy has pointed out, "Since accounting always involves accountability, it is also social. . . . Profit is no obvious, neutral, or timeless economic benchmark. Rather, it is a calculative practice open to interpretation. Corporations decide what profit is."[76] During the First World War, however, corporations had even more leeway in calculating their profits than they had before 1914 because the courts and tax authorities were forced to audit companies even as most of their personnel were fighting on the front lines.

For instance, corporations avoided reporting gains from the employment of POWs, unskilled laborers, and overpriced military contracts while the majority of society experienced various forms of destitution. Instead, profit reports and shareholder dividends were tailored to keep up appearances and stick to the templates and neutral narratives of the prewar period to suggest that nothing substantial had changed. The enormous and immediate demand for industrial products gave industrialists tremendous leverage in their negotiations with wartime governments.[77] One example of their influence on economic legislation is particularly revealing: in 1916, the Hungarian finance minister János Teleszky sent the outline of the war profits tax bill to the National Association of Industrialists for comments before the bill was sent to the house of representatives.[78]

The Central Powers had decided early in the war that rather than relying on taxes on individuals and corporations, they would finance the war economy by issuing war bonds that constituted long-term loans by populations to governments that were payable by the two empires after the conflict had ended. Thus, both Germany and Austria-Hungary discounted the taxation of corporate profits as a significant contribution to their war efforts, which also explains their lenient attitude toward questionable accounting practices by military suppliers. In Germany, the conservative-dominated Bundesrat prevented state secretary of the treasury Karl Helfferich from introducing any corporate taxes until the budget of March 1916.[79] Siegfried von Roedern, who succeeded Helfferich at the Finance Ministry, favored war bonds and indirect taxes over direct taxes as a means of financing the war and did not renegotiate the continuation of the strict terms of the 1916 tax law; as a result, Reich revenues from war-profit taxes fell from 4.8 to 2.5 billion marks in 1918.[80] The 1916 tax law required firms to deposit half of their war profits from 1914 in a special reserve account from which state authorities were to deduct taxes once the wartime tax code was complete. Companies, however, had plenty of time to hide profits and decrease their book value through dubious accounting practices before this legislation went into effect.[81] In Alsace, the Adlers and Oppenheimers paid out just 16 percent of their total net profits for the 1915–1916 business year in taxes, while the company's books show no signs of taxes paid in the other war years. It was the Reichsbank and public companies that were the most affected by the tax law, not private corporations.[82] In the meantime, France began taxing companies heavily in 1917, when the Paris government started confiscating half of war profits over half a million francs.[83]

The Hungarian government followed the example of Germany and Austria, passing its first war profits tax law in 1916, which provided several loopholes for companies while easing some of the pressure on the government to curb war profiteering.[84] While the law levied a tax of up to 35 percent on corporate profits, it also condoned the widespread practice of hiding gains in so-called secret reserve funds that enabled companies to substantially decrease their tax obligations.[85] In the parliamentary debate, Teleszky admitted that taxes on industrial companies were low, but he appealed to national interests and anti-Austrian sentiments to defend the government's fiscal policy that favored the small group of Hungarian industrialists. According to Teleszky, Hungarian industries deserved the same state support that Austrian companies enjoyed from their government in order to remain competitive.[86]

With industrial companies attempting to hide their operations rather than reporting on them to outsiders during the First World War, the corporate profit figures reported in specialized journals were utterly confusing even for contemporary accounting specialists and can hardly be considered accurate indicators of companies' actual gains.[87] The Renner factory's new accountant, for instance, begged the company in August 1918 to "simplify" its profit and loss statement to provide "a more realistic picture" of the company's operations, which seemed to bear no resemblance to the firm's performance on paper.[88] The desperate accountant warned that if the company did not follow his advice, it would face fines from the Ministry of Finance. Ironically, while the collapse of Austria-Hungary was a shock to most industrial companies, it was imperial collapse that saved many corporations from the consequences of a serious audit after the war had ended.

The accounting clerk of the Albina Bank in Transylvania, whom prosecutors tasked with making sense of a regional investment bank's accounts during litigation in July 1916, complained that "the handling of affairs was below all expectations, there was no controlling of accounts, and the company's bookkeeping was so convoluted that even after a meticulous investigation it was simply impossible to find out the real state of affairs."[89] The outcome of this investigation and that of the Renner factory's profit and loss statement are unclear. Despite these irregularities, Transylvanian companies continued to attract investments because the region was widely regarded as the springboard for German and Austro-Hungarian economic expansion in Southeastern Europe.

By 1917, Budapest banks constituted the majority of the Renner tannery's shareholders but did not take over corporate leadership positions. Thus, they did not economically "colonize" companies in the countryside as post-1918

Transylvanian regionalists would argue. As was the case before the war, banks' ownership of stakes in industrial companies did not entail the takeover of family businesses or large companies by a small group of bankers; large Budapest banks had neither the personnel nor the desire to micromanage their new possessions.[90] Banks even allowed the original founders—the Renners, Hechts, and Farkases—to retain the directorship of the company, and Mózes Farkas continued to make all major decisions even as he managed a company in which Budapest-based banks and companies acquired the majority of shares by 1917.[91]

Banks invested in industrial companies during the First World War because their other options were limited. Trading in gold was no longer an option as states monopolized precious metals, while housing construction had ground to a virtual halt and war bonds offered low returns and carried considerable risk in case of military defeat; wartime legislation also limited the ratio of dividends paid out to shareholders, forcing businessmen and bankers to reinvest their profits.[92] As a result, reinvesting profits in industrial companies was the best option available, especially as constant demand from war corporations guaranteed a fast return on investments in industrial companies.[93] With the help of capital from Budapest, Farkas transformed the Renner factory from a provincial enterprise into one of Hungary's largest tanneries, one that vigorously asserted its interests in both Budapest and Vienna. The Renner tannery's rise to prosperity was partially linked to the decline of its regional rivals, such as the S. Karres and Sons tannery of Medgyes and the Brassó-based Scherg brothers' firm following the Romanian army's attack on southern Transylvania between August and October 1916, during which Kolozsvár remained out of the reach of Romanian troops.

Simon Krausz's Hungarian Bank and the Anglo-Austrian Bank of Budapest financed two-thirds of the new capital that flowed to the Renner factory during the First World War. The rest came from József Löbl and Sons, a large meat processing company based in Budapest. The Löbl firm's investment also drew the Renner tannery into the Löbls' business networks, made up of extremely dynamic Budapest entrepreneurs who had already made names for themselves (like Samu Stern). It also provided a valuable connection to the Ministry of Agriculture through the adviser Mihály Koós, while the firm's director Adolf Löbl had been a founding board member of the war corporation in charge of raw leather distribution in Hungary.[94]

Wartime prosperity did not necessarily increase consumption by the wealthy since inflation meant that cash payments to shareholders had only moderate value and industrial companies preferred to reinvest their profits in production. The Renner tannery kept its dividends at 8 percent between 1914 and

1918, a decent ratio before the war but a mediocre yield when Transylvania's economy was booming and inflation was running unchecked. The stability of dividends despite the fluctuation in profits also reflected the mentality of contemporary industrialists, that of *rentiers* rather than speculators since they saw their shares in companies as sources of a stable income stream rather than fast enrichment.

For the Renner tannery, the war entailed deskilling and producing less sophisticated leather goods than it had before 1914. The enormous need for military boot soles and straps after 1914 went hand in hand with decreasing consumption of high-end shoes designed for the up-and-coming middle class. Farkas, however, was dedicated to returning to shoe production, in part to support his family's shoe business and to prepare for postwar civilian demand. While the new factory continued to produce shoe soles, its architect made sure that its workshops could easily be switched over to the production of upper leather and machine belts.[95]

Farkas also correctly noticed the Hungarian leather industry's administrative void after the fall of the Tisza government and established his own association, which became the leading Hungarian tanners' organization by 1918.[96] His maneuvering showed how in Hungary, unlike in Germany, even established war industry bodies could be dismantled from the bottom up three years into the Great War. In sharp contrast to Germany, where war corporations subjugated even flagship industrial companies with the help of the military and the government, Hungarian companies retained more of their autonomy and were able to stage a "revolt" against war industry bodies after the political instability that followed the death of Francis Joseph, the Romanian attack, and the resignation of the Tisza government.

When the war broke out, the Hungarian tanning industry was governed by two associations, one focused on production and one focused on the leather trade.[97] Both were headed by older businessmen from Budapest who lacked the agility to remain at the forefront of rapid wartime transformations. Instead, the two associations went into hibernation after August 1914, never convening their members over the next three years. The War Leather Company—or to use its full name, the Leather Industry Center of the Lands of the Holy Crown of Hungary, a war corporation—took over the job of both prewar associations. This corporation was a publicly traded company founded and managed by Budapest's most powerful industrial tanners, including the Mauthners and Wolfners, and there were no Transylvanian tanners on its board of directors.

The War Leather Company was formed in haste in March 1915 to compete with Austrian and German *Kriegszentralen* for military commissions.[98] Its founders aimed to prevent a comparable Austrian association from becoming the sole purveyor of the joint army and marginalizing Hungarian industrialists.[99] While the corporation's main purpose was to obtain leather for military use, it was more autonomous than its German or Austrian counterparts. Unlike the German War Leather Corporation, the Kriegsleder-Aktiengesellschaft (KLAG), the Hungarian firm had no military representation and its management retained the right to override the army's specifications if it did not agree with them.[100]

By the end of the summer of 1917, Farkas had persuaded several tanners to support the creation of a new leather industry association that looked out for the interests of smaller and midsize tanneries. Thirteen of the thirty industrialists on the board of his National Alliance of Hungarian Leather Industrialists were Transylvanians, revealing the growing importance of previously neglected Transylvanian tanners within industry leadership.[101] Farkas also exploited his connections to the Hungarian Bank and the Löbl company, through which he was able to garner the support of the two prewar tanning associations.[102]

As he transformed himself into a leader of the Hungarian leather industry, Farkas spent more time in Budapest. The new association's inaugural meeting took place in the Lloyd Palace, overlooking the royal castle. Farkas echoed the anti-big-business rhetoric of the governments that came to power after 1917 as he called for curtailing war corporations' power over industrial companies and rolling back wartime economic regulations.[103] At the same time, Farkas made full use of the same war economy institutions he castigated. Not only did the Renner tannery manage to acquire a seat on the board of the war corporation that procured raw leather, but in 1917 Farkas also became a member of the board of directors of the War Leather Company, which had originally been the exclusive domain of Budapest's largest tanners.[104] As Farkas's career reached previously unimaginable heights during the First World War, his first marriage with Ilona Rózsa gradually fell apart. Reasons for the divorce are unclear. Records show Farkas's frequent stays away from Kolozsvár; and with the mental illness of the couple's son István, the Farkas family failed to correspond to the ideal of family life as imagined in provincial Hungary at the time, and the marriage failed to produce a viable male heir to Farkas.[105] Some two decades later, Farkas labeled Rózsa in his last will and testament as "morally and financially unfit" to serve as guardian of their two children, and did not bequeath her a penny.[106] "Morally unfit" is an ambiguous term; Farkas may have implied infidelity or a judgement on loose morals, even though he was the one that the tabloid press of the 1920s accused of engaging in extramarital affairs during his second marriage.[107]

In his new capacity as the leader of the Hungarian leather industry, Farkas spent most of his time in Budapest. He dealt directly with the Viennese War

Ministry, which was responsible for supplying the army as well as the KLAG.[108] He also became a regular negotiator at the Viennese War Ministry, where he secured deals for the Renner tannery. As late as October 11, 1918, he managed to organize the shipment of over five thousand pieces of Danish calf leather and sixteen hundred pieces of Norwegian sea calf skin through the Prussian War Office and the KLAG.[109] Farkas's trajectory shows how he benefited from both the economic integration of Germany and Austria-Hungary and Hungary's efforts to shore up domestic industries via economic protectionism and state support of domestic corporations.

Pan-imperial integration in Mitteleuropa and the popularity of territorial autonomy went hand in hand, and territories with a long-standing history of semiautonomy like Hungary were well equipped to defend their interests in the competition for resources. Furthermore, these wartime processes pointed toward both the entrenchment of national boundaries and the territorial fragmentation of national economies into competing regions. A contemporary Hungarian economist noted in 1920 that "the so-called 'unified customs zone' of the [Dual] Monarchy has to be understood in a restricted sense. The transport of a variety of food products, essential goods, and those needed for the military was not at all free between Austria and Hungary"; at times, even individual Hungarian counties blocked the "export" of certain goods from their territories.[110] Thus, what historians have interchangeably labeled as "globalization" or "de-territorialization" in the late nineteenth and early twentieth centuries was coupled with "deglobalization" or "re-territorialization" during the First World War in Central and East-Central Europe. Or, as Glenda Sluga has pointed out regarding the post-1918 era, a "nation-embracing [. . .] version of internationalism was palpably on the rise."[111] In the Central Powers, regional and national boundaries became entrenched even as the integration of the German and Austro-Hungarian economies continued.[112] While commercial and political ties between Austria-Hungary and Germany became more intense, governments, municipalities, regional leaders, and business elites all attempted to retain some degree of autonomy to pursue their separate agendas even as the war gave rise to increasingly similar laws and processes across the two empires.[113]

In this interregional and international competition for resources, Alsace-Lorraine was necessarily left behind, as it was unable to fend for its regional economic interests. The German economy's thoroughgoing centralization and subordination to Prussian interests left few options for even wealthy German industrialists in the Reichsland. Alsace-Lorraine had only gained its limited political autonomy in 1911 and its guarantees proved inadequate to defend the region's economic interest at a time of interregional competition for resources within the German empire and "domestic imperialism" aimed at the integration of Alsace-Lorraine with Prussia during the Great War.

Prosperity and Subordination: Alsace-Lorraine's Industrialists during the Great War

The reorientation of the German and Austro-Hungarian empires toward economic expansion in Eastern Europe left industrialists on the western side of Mitteleuropa in regions like Alsace-Lorraine with a sense of marginalization. The economic integration of Central Europe fueled tensions between the industrialized western regions of Germany and the empire's eastern territories. The Alsatian business leader Ernst Zander castigated the German Reich for treating Alsace-Lorraine as a "stepchild" of Mitteleuropa and as secondary to the "Balkans."[114] Zander wrote, "The growing popularity of the Central European economic ideal has largely shifted Germany's gaze towards the southeast. New commercial roads will spring up from Berlin through Budapest and the Balkans to Asia Minor. . . . As a result, it can be feared that Alsace-Lorraine is being pushed into Germany's blind spot."[115] Alsatian metal industrialist Eugen Jacobi, who otherwise profited tremendously from the war, also viewed Eastern European economic expansion and Austro-Hungarian-German economic integration with a critical eye since he feared it would lead to German products being banned from Western European and colonial markets after the war. Jacobi also pointed to the costliness of rail transport compared with sea routes and the inadequate economic resources of Eastern Europe and Turkey; he noted that "cacao, rubber, skins, timber, [and] plant oils" were lacking, while the modernization of Southeastern European territories would require massive long-term investments that would take years to become profitable.[116] Jacobi's comments revealed the regional differences in the economic impact of the First World War across Mitteleuropa and spoke to the frustration experienced by many industrialists, especially in Alsace-Lorraine, owing to the region's economic decline.[117]

Yet it was not Germany and Austria-Hungary's realignment toward East-Central European expansion that caused the relative economic decline of Alsace-Lorraine. Rather, it was the revocation of its limited political autonomy in 1914 as well as the arbitrary actions of the military administration. The suspension of the limited political autonomy granted to Alsace-Lorraine in 1911 meant that the German bureaucracy was unable to pursue a regional economic policy, while industrialists were unable to further their interests via the regional assembly, the Landtag.[118] Some of the region's difficulties were not specific to

Alsace-Lorraine but affected Germany more generally, including the shortage of raw materials and the increasing grip of military leadership on the civilian government. While Germany's federal states were able to retain some of their independence from the army's encroachment and obtain adequate amounts of raw materials through the war corporations, Alsace-Lorraine's regional interests became secondary to those of the army and other federal states.

Full-blown warfare between the French and German armies in Alsace started in August 1914 as the French army burst into German territory around the Alsatian town of Mulhouse. The solidification of the western front through Upper Alsace put the district around Mulhouse and Colmar operational territory under the direct control of the military, while all industrial activity was halted in the evacuation zones behind the front lines.[119] Lorraine and Lower Alsace were relatively sheltered, although British and US bombers managed to damage steel plants and cause disruptions, particularly during the last two years of the war, as part of air raids that reached as far as the Rhineland.[120] The purely punitive retaliation against enemy businesses in the German Reich was most acutely felt in Alsace-Lorraine, which was home to the highest concentration of French-owned businesses in the Reich. The overeager military leadership made an already difficult situation worse by shuttering businesses it deemed enemy property, even if the majority of their capital was owned by Alsatian businessmen. The premature relocation of entire factories to the interior of Germany starting in 1917 had a particularly severe impact on Alsace's textile industry.[121]

The outbreak of the First World War also put many Alsace-Lorraine families in a bind, given their personal ties to both France and Germany. The industrialist de Dietrichs were no exception in this regard. The family's engineering firm was managed by the septuagenarian Eugene de Dietrich, who had fought against the German states in the Franco-Prussian War of 1870–1871. In 1914, Eugene de Dietrich's oldest son, Frédéric, joined the relatively small numbers of the *Überläufern* who fled to France to join the Allied forces, while his son-in-law Henri Mellon (b. 1880) was an officer in the French army (figure 3.1).[122] His youngest son, Dominique (b. 1892), however, remained in Alsace and fought in the German army on the Russian and Romanian fronts along with the rest of the Alsatians deemed too disloyal to fight against French troops. In order to protect his company from expropriation after his death, Eugene named his "German" son Dominique as his sole heir.[123]

After 1918, official propaganda and collective memory focused on the joyful moment of Alsace-Lorraine's "liberation" from German rule—the discrimination against the region's population by the German administration. What remained silenced is that the First World War led to a series of personal tragedies

FIGURE 3.1. The wedding of Henri Mellon (in French uniform) and Jacqueline de Dietrich, with Eugene de Dietrich (sixth from the left in the last row) and Dominique de Dietrich (third from the left in the first row) and others in attendance. Source: Archive De Dietrich, Reichshoffen.

for Alsace-Lorrainers regardless of who won this total war. Unlike many men who were caught up in the nationalist frenzy of the time on either the French or the German side, women and children in border regions like Alsace-Lorraine dared to express their misgivings and stupefaction about the war that turned this region upside down in the summer of 1914. Jacqueline de Dietrich was one of the Alsatian women who had trouble aligning with either the French or the German war effort as these threatened to claim her husband and her brother, respectively. Jacqueline had married Henri Mellon in 1908, and the newlyweds had moved to the de Dietrichs' Le Riesack mansion on the Alsatian slopes of the Vosges mountains, not far from the Franco-German border. When the war broke out, however, Mellon left for France, leaving his wife behind. In August 1914, as the French army burst into southern Alsace, Jacqueline, now alone in Le Riesack, hastily scribbled a note to her brother Dominique, who was waiting to be deployed to the eastern front; the German-language letter made it through military censorship.[124] In her note, Jacqueline called the war cruel and probably expressed her own uncertainties about the goals of the war effort through her eight-year-old nephew Pierre Ruillier: "How terrible, how cruel this war is. Yesterday I got a letter from Thérèse, she said everyone was well, that the children were playing nicely, and that Pierre doesn't yet understand what the war means."[125]

Despite this difficult start, the de Dietrichs survived the Great War both physically and financially, and both Henri and Dominique managed to return to the Le Riesack estate after the armistice. Alsatian industrialists like the de Dietrichs who managed to become military suppliers also profited economically from the Great War, regardless of whether they were Francophiles or pro-German. The de Dietrich factories profited from selling trench construction material and railway equipment to German war corporations, and the firm also sold products to the Solvay Works, a Germanized chemical company in Belgium.[126]

The region's economic downturn did not leave local German industrialists unaffected, although they had greater opportunities to assert their interests with war corporations and avoid the harassment by military authorities that befell even the de Dietrichs, despite their contributions to the war economy. The wartime trajectory of the Adler and Oppenheimer tannery, owned by Germans who had immigrated to Alsace in the 1870s, shows that Berlin-based war corporations hindered the operations of politically loyal industrialists in the region. On the whole, however, profit figures did not reflect these hardships, as, like other military suppliers, the Adlers and Oppenheimers prospered throughout the war.

The KLAG united Germany's key tanning families, shoe producers, and tradesmen with whom the Adlers and Oppenheimers had worked before the war. This explains why the share of raw leather allocated to Alsace-Lorraine was more than double that of the German empire in terms of size and population, reaching 4.5 percent when Bavaria received 7.5 and Mecklenburg 2 percent.[127] Almost two-thirds of all leather allocated to Alsace-Lorraine by the KLAG landed on the shop floor of the Adlers' and Oppenheimers' tannery.[128]

Unlike textile companies, which suffered from a lack of raw materials owing to the Allied blockade, both German and Austro-Hungarian tanneries were relatively fortunate because the Central Powers had cattle stocks and leather reserves at the beginning of the war.[129] On the eve of the Great War, Hungary imported twice as much as it exported, mostly finished products, but these imports were mainly from Austria and Germany.[130] After domestic stocks ran out, the two empires were successful in outwitting the blockade and securing the import of skins and leather from neutral states.[131] In 1916, after two years of extensive exports, fear of a German invasion led Switzerland to conclude a trade treaty with the Berlin administration that guaranteed thirty-eight thousand cattle annually, while similar political pressure led the Danish government to surrender a large portion of its cattle stocks despite the Allied threat of putting neutral companies that traded with the Central Powers on a "black list."[132]

While one historian has characterized Norway as "one of the only true successes" of the British effort to stop war-related imports to Germany, Norwegian raw leather exporters somehow managed to deliver their products to Central Europe, including to the Renner tannery in Transylvania, which points to the remarkable agency of a few businessmen in neutral and belligerent states as well as the managers of the Central Powers' war economy to subvert the blockade.[133]

The Adler and Oppenheimer tannery's wartime profits totaled more than 20 million marks. Even taking wartime inflation into account, average annual profits of 5 million marks were more than double the average of the three years immediately preceding the war, 1.4 million marks.[134] The tannery made most of its profits during the first year of the war, before leather prices were capped. In 1915, windfall profits in excess of 8 million marks enabled the company to provide a 20 percent return on its shares.[135] This was slightly higher than the German average in the tanning industry that year (19 percent) but significantly surpassed the yields of investments in coal mining (12 percent) and shoe manufacturing (13 percent) and was only slightly lower than the dividends paid out by munitions factories (23 percent) and steel plants (21 percent).[136] Given that states eventually capped the sums that companies could pay out to shareholders from profits, these figures did not reflect the full extent of the prosperity achieved by industrial companies following their often painful transition to wartime production. Gustav Krupp, the managing director of Germany's steel giant, announced as early as 1914 that he "did not intend the company's profits to be any greater than was normal in peace."[137] In fact, Krupp intended to hide the millions his company raked in during the war and avoid paying higher taxes.[138] The Adlers and Oppenheimers also remained uncommunicative on the source of their extraordinary profits in 1915, which were likely generated from sales of leather to the German army before the introduction of price caps. It is no surprise that when a columnist at the otherwise pro-industry *Frankfurter Zeitung* acquired the Adler and Oppenheimer tannery's 1915 annual report, he could not help but notice with disillusionment that "in view of the strong upsurge of profits, one looked forward to the company's annual report and expected a detailed description. In this, he was to be disappointed. Even the presentation of the financial balance is less detailed than in previous years."[139] The journalist thus noticed that the war served as an excuse for corporations to publish superficial annual reports that left even major changes in profits and output unexplained.

Companies had no interest in publicizing their gains as the majority of society struggled with shortages. The fact that their profits depended on the quasi-colonial exploitation of occupied territories and army commissions was kept silent as well. The profitability of the Adler & Oppenheimer and Renner tanneries depended on the support of war corporations that distributed raw leather in Germany and Hungary. These German, Austrian, and Hungarian war corporations increasingly cooperated on the distribution of the leather stocks coercively acquired from occupied Romania, Ukraine, and Belgium as well as leather imports from neutral states. The Renners were more advantageously positioned than the Adlers and Oppenheimers because the tanning sector was considerably smaller in Hungary than in Germany, which allowed its director Mózes Farkas to rise to prominence within the Budapest-based war leather company.[140]

Germany was larger and more fragmented than Hungary, and it was considerably more difficult for any industrialist to assume the amount of power over an industry that Farkas was able to amass.[141] The Adler and Oppenheimer tannery remained subordinate to the War Leather Corporation and the German military, which became especially clear when the army blocked the allocation of raw leather to the company in 1917 owing to fears of an Allied breakthrough to Alsace. The family sought the KLAG's help in relocating part of the company's production from Strasbourg to the firm's Neustadt branch in Mecklenburg, in the German interior. At this juncture, it was especially fortunate that the firm had acquired the Neustadt plant during the escalation of Franco-German diplomatic tensions in the early 1910s. Neustadt was far away from the front lines and so was less affected by the German military's dictatorial measures.[142]

Even within the KLAG, however, the Adlers and Oppenheimers faced competition from several hundred German tanners. In addition, like most war corporations in both empires, the KLAG had turned into a behemoth composed of sprawling subcommittees with overlapping hierarchies that were in charge of the distribution of various types of leather and tanning materials. At first, one of the KLAG's supervisory boards rejected the Strasbourg tannery's request; eventually, however, the Committee for the Distribution of Heavy Livestock Leather acknowledged that the Adler and Oppenheimer tannery "found itself in a difficult situation due to military measures" by 1917.[143] This committee had only two low-ranking army officers and eleven industrialists among its members, which contributed to its favorable treatment of Alsatian industrialists backed by the powerful Deutsche Bank.[144] The committee chair was the industrialist and lobbyist Theodor Adolf von Möller (1840–1925), who had advocated for the interests of companies in the western regions of the German empire as part of the Langnam Association.[145] The committee feared, however, that the reassignment of leather from Alsace to Mecklenburg would increase the already widespread speculation on raw materials. It therefore required the firm to not only process all stocks in Neustadt but also relocate workers from Strasbourg to the new factory, located over five hundred miles northeast of Alsace. This decision showed the KLAG's ambition to substantially reshape the operations of even flagship factories in certain industries.[146] However, wartime shortages of workers' housing and transportation made the relocation of labor a virtually impossible task. Unsurprisingly, very few, if any, workers moved during the war in this failed attempt at wartime labor engineering.[147] As late as 1919, only forty-three tannery employees had relocated from the Alsace factory to Mecklenburg.[148] While it was not until the fall of 1918 that rumors began to circulate about the German military's surrender of Alsace-Lorraine to the French army, the Adlers and Oppenheimers had unknowingly prepared for their postwar survival with their wartime investments in Mecklenburg and divestment from Alsace with the help of the KLAG. The tribulations of one of Alsace's most prominent German industrialists show that even industrialists who were loyal to the German government were subjected to often petty bureaucratic hurdles by war corporations and the army, revealing the inflexibility of the German war economy.

By 1918, despite the hardships they had faced, the Adlers and Oppenheimers emerged considerably wealthier than they had been in 1914, yet they did not engage in conspicuous consumption to show off their prosperity. In contrast to the satirical press's depiction of war profiteers as upstarts who showed off their wealth, in reality industrialists tended to keep a low profile even as they commissioned their own portraits during the Great War. Max Liebermann, for instance, painted the portrait of one of the relatives of the Adlers and Oppenheimers, the industrialist Carl Leopold Netter, who was affiliated with the Wolf, Netter, and Jacobi engineering firm and steel plant in Strasbourg. Although Netter was one of the wealthiest Alsatian industrialists, he preferred a minimalist aesthetic rather than the colorful impressionism of Liebermann's other portraits. Liebermann portrayed him as representative of the industrious *Bürgertum*, seated in a simple chair in front of a modest, rather bleak background (figure 3.2). The only sign of prosperity is the burning cigar in his right hand, a contemporary cliché of masculinity and a solid middle-class existence. Liebermann's painting contrasted sharply with how a contemporary Hungarian satirical paper imagined the portrait of a "war millionaire": as an obese profiteer wearing a coat with a badge and sitting in a large Louis XVI-style armchair in a lavishly decorated lounge while a painter is fitting him onto an oversized canvas (figure 3.3). The inscription below reads, "I received this honorary badge for my merits in legislation. . . . The government modelled the decree against 'sharks' on my activity."

Soon after the paint dried on Carl Netter's portrait, the German and Austro-Hungarian empires collapsed. Wartime profits, however, enabled the industrial-

FIGURE 3.2. *War millionaires.* Max Liebermann's portrait of Carl Leopold Netter (1917). Source: Max Liebermann, *Kommerzienrat Dr. Carl Leopold Netter* (1917), Alamy.

ists of the two empires, even in war-torn Alsace, to emerge with sizable reserves that would allow them to weather the economic consequences of sovereignty change. The reasons for industrialists' wartime prosperity were remarkably similar across the two empires and included low corporate taxes, inefficient state supervision of corporate bookkeeping, and the imperial armies' enormous demand for even low-quality products. In Alsace-Lorraine, the expansion of production took place amid the military administration's growing interference in production, which affected even loyal German industrialists like the Adlers and Oppenheimers. By 1917, Alsace-Lorraine's German business elites realized what their Alsatian colleagues had already learned during the "Grafenstaden affair" of 1912 when the German administration sacrificed the prosperity of a large factory for political reasons: that even loyal industrialists like the Adlers and Oppenheimers had no influence on the German military's questionable measures. In the meantime, on the eastern side of Mitteleuropa, Hungary's autonomy within

Figure 3.3. A caricature of a "war profiteer" in a Hungarian satirical magazine (1917). Source: "The merit of the war millionaire," *Borsszem Jankó*, no. 7 (1917): 9; Arcanum.

the Dual Monarchy did not allow for comparable interference by the imperial army in the affairs of factories, mines, and the civilian population, although such interference was common in Austria.[149] Furthermore, the Hungarian government managed to increase its economic independence from Austria despite wartime economic integration between 1914 and 1918, and backed domestic industrial companies with low taxes and commissions as part of its agenda of anti-Austrian economic nationalism. At the same time, the occupation of Ukraine, Romania, and Serbia gave rise to widespread optimism regarding the future of the postwar Hungarian economy. These false hopes relied on ignoring the increasing subordination of Hungary and the Dual Monarchy to Germany.

Ultimately, solid belief in a favorable outcome of the First World War until the very last months before the armistice prevented most industrialists in the Central Powers from building bridges to the ethnic minorities and workers who would become crucial during the post-armistice transition in 1918. What is more, these social ties deteriorated sharply in the last two years of the war. Unlike in the Second World War, there were no attempts by industrialists or political elites to hide wealth in neutral states or prepare individual escape routes. All that industrialists could rely on was their wartime capital gains that surpassed all expectations. Yet as the war years had already shown, financial capital did not automatically convert to political influence at a time when authoritarian governments and armies could intern even wealthy tycoons and shutter businesses.

CHAPTER 4

The Enemy's Money

Economic Retaliation in the Great War

The outbreak of the First World War changed the relationship between the populations of the Central Powers and their governments, which suddenly received unprecedented prerogatives to intervene in civilian and economic life. Governments and armies could punish, deport, detain, and expropriate their own as well as enemy citizens as a result of wartime legislation, special decrees, and military necessity.[1] The radicalization of state intervention into economic life was gradual, with clear turning points in the summer of 1914, the outbreak of the war, and 1916.[2] July and August 1914 brought about terror and internment for populations adjacent to the front lines, and governments also passed the first measures of economic discrimination against the private property of enemy citizens. In the summer of 1916, a stalemate on the western front and fears of German-Austro-Hungarian economic integration led to the Allies' Paris economic conference, where they ratcheted up economic discrimination against the Central Powers. While in 1914 the Allies pledged to merely guard enemy property until the end of the war, in 1916 they moved toward its liquidation, and the Central Powers soon passed similar legislation.[3] In the meantime, the Romanian attack on Transylvania in August 1916 sent shockwaves throughout the Central Powers and contributed to the radicalization of both German and Hungarian policies on the "home front." The relative success of Romanian troops in penetrating a largely defenseless region and its German and Hungarian-populated towns adjacent to the border contributed to the fall of both Erich von Falkenhayn, chief of the German General Staff, and Hungarian prime minister István Tisza. Falkenhayn was replaced by the joint leadership of Paul von Hindenburg and Erich von Ludendorff, who radicalized Germany's methods of fighting the war and further subordinated the economy to the armaments industry, and the interests of the federal states and Alsace-Lorraine to those of Prussia.[4]

The fate of some territories within the German-Austro-Hungarian alliance also mattered more than others for the outcome of the war effort and in regard to shaping domestic policies. Contested territories like Alsace-Lorraine, the Austrian Littoral, and Transylvania were at the center of attempts at population engineering and became the pivots around which the rest of the two empires and their war efforts turned.[5] The codependence of far-off German and Austro-Hungarian territories generated numerous tensions during the First World War. German industrialists were dismayed that their fate was tied to that of East-Central and Southeastern Europe, and they lamented the shift of their empire's focus to the East.[6] Hungarians also waxed indignant about the impact of Alsace-Lorraine on the prospects of the Hungarian war effort. In the words of one Budapest journalist, who pointed to the undesirably high degree of interdependence among the peoples of Central Europe, "Why should we give our blood for this piece of land, [Alsace-Lorraine], why should millions suffer, and why not give it to the French so as to finally end this thing [the war]?"[7]

Despite the strategic locations of both Alsace-Lorraine and Transylvania and a series of convergences between the Central Powers during the First World War, industrialists and ethnic minorities managed to avoid increasingly radical government interventions into economic life with more success on the eastern than on the western peripheries of the Central Powers. While the German army showcased Alsace-Lorraine as the focus of its retaliation against British and French economic discrimination directed at German property, the Hungarian government attempted to tone down ethnic clashes in Transylvania in 1914 and 1915 and appeal to Allied powers by not retaliating against British and French policies of expropriation of Austro-Hungarian property. In sharp contrast to Austrian practices, Budapest banned the army from actions against civilians on the home front.[8] This was due to the 1867 Austro-Hungarian Compromise, under which "the joint army could not be used in Hungary without the [Budapest] government's permission."[9] The government also curbed widespread antisemitic agitation that targeted industrialists and businessmen. In an act of shortsightedness, however, the Budapest administrations that followed the Tisza government launched a comprehensive campaign of persecution against leaders of Romanian society in Transylvania in 1916, following the Romanian attack on the region. Territorial conquests and government support convinced Transylvania's Hungarian industrialists and politicians that they did not need to build bridges with Romanian elites.

In the meantime, resistance to the German army's dictatorial measures led to the formation of a broad coalition of German and Alsatian industrialists in Alsace-Lorraine, although, coming as it did in the eleventh hour of the First World War, it was ultimately unable to forge class-based solidarity among elites, let alone regionalist solidarity of Alsace-Lorrainers, including Germans who immigrated to the region after 19871. Despite the multinational commercial and personal ties of the Reichsland's industrialists that connected them to both France and Germany before 1914, by 1918 they found themselves coerced to choose between the two states. The First World War had contributed to undermining the security of private property in a capitalist world economy before Lenin and Russia's Bolsheviks started their expropriation campaign, and it also led to nationalist and antisemitic mobilization that raised the question of whether industrialists who thrived on multiethnic and multinational networks of clientele would survive the conflagration.

Germany's Economic Warfare against Domestic "Enemies"

The undermining of liberal property rights during the First World War was a global phenomenon, but belligerents made use of this "opportunity" in different ways, and their impact also concentrated disproportionately on border zones and territories with high levels of enemy investment. Alsace-Lorraine thus emerged as the main target of retaliation against British and French legislation against German property. The United Kingdom passed the first legislation against German property on August 5, 1914.[10] Germany's Reichstag authorized the chancellor to pass any legislation on economic matters that he saw fit on August 4, 1914, but this was a blank check and did not specifically target enemy property. On August 7, 1914, Germany banned enemy citizens and companies from seeking justice through its courts. The Reich's Bundesrat or federal council then passed an ordinance on September 4, 1914, imposing "state supervision" on all enemy property to serve as "an economic defense against the measures taken by England, France and Belgium against German banks."[11] This supervision then served as the grounds for the ordinance on compulsory administration or sequestration by court-appointed managers on October 22, 1914. On November 26, the Federal Council authorized the states and Alsace-Lorraine's Statthalter to proceed with the practice of sequestering (placing under forced administration) companies whose majority shareholders were French or British.[12]

Actual implementation of these seemingly uniform laws against enemy subjects differed. Some states applied exceptions to the law, while others dismissed or restricted the implementation of economic discrimination against enemy subjects, as in the case of Hungary or the Ottoman Empire.[13] Paris exempted native Alsatians and Lorrainers, Poles, Czechs, and their private property from economic discrimination.[14] The property of Bulgarians and Ottomans in France was also exempted in order to safeguard vast French investments in the two countries. As of 1914, Transylvanian Romanians and Tyrol's Italians, however, received no exemptions since Italy and Romania were not Entente allies at the time.[15]

Out of the four thousand enemy companies sequestered by French courts, only ten belonged to Alsace-Lorrainers. Furthermore, only one of these ten companies underwent liquidation, while the rest were allowed to function undisturbed throughout the war, much like French companies.[16] At the same time, Austria-Hungary introduced several exemptions that favored some enemy citizens. The reason was not, as A. J. P. Taylor has speculated, that "only Austria-Hungary stuck to more civilized standards" among "belligerent countries."[17] In fact, the Dual Monarchy's governments only exempted the subjects of Western European Great Powers in the ultimately failed expectation of reciprocation, while they pursued the private property of Serbian and Romanian citizens once at war with these states. There were also disproportionately fewer Allied subjects in the Dual Monarchy than the other way round a further factor in favor of milder treatment. In 1916, Austrian courts even allowed a small business owned by a French woman to win a property dispute that involved five hats for which an Austrian subject had failed to pay.[18] Germany, on the other hand, did not make gestures toward any belligerents and did not attempt to make its rule more attractive to Alsace-Lorrainers either. Even Lorraine's German district president concluded in a memorandum in July 1917 that "it is impossible to make good the consequences of multiple mistakes [that the German administration and military] committed,"[19] which undermined the legitimacy of German rule in Alsace-Lorraine well before the 1918 armistice.

With its extension of economic warfare into the realm of private property, Germany had more to lose than other belligerents, which puts its harsh measures against enemy property in Alsace-Lorraine in a new light. It also shows that economic rationality alone cannot explain the dynamics set in motion by the First World War, even as contemporary German intellectuals like Max Weber argued that "Germans perfected the rational, functional, and specialized bureaucratic organization of all forms of domination from factory to army and public administration. . . . The present world war means the world-wide triumph of this form of life."[20] Economic gain took a back seat to the other war aims of the army and the government.[21]

Direct and indirect German foreign investments amounted to around 28 billion marks in 1914, the majority of which was invested in Entente countries, while British investments in Germany, Bulgaria, and Austria-Hungary totaled only 1.35 billion marks.[22] In 1914, Germany's share of world trade was over 12 percent, while external trade made up more than one-third of its gross national product.[23] French companies and banks held sizable investments in Austria-Hungary, Bulgaria, and the Ottoman Empire.[24] While during the first weeks of the conflict Germany was committed to avoiding all-out economic warfare with the Allies, the increasingly severe blockade of the Central Powers by Great Britain and British measures against German private property overseas pushed the Berlin government to escalate economic warfare even at the cost of substantial harm to its domestic economy.[25]

Throughout Europe, the application of laws attacking the private property of enemy citizens caused considerable upheaval and legal conundrums because legislation did not take into account the extent of economic globalization by 1914 and thus proved inadequate to pursue enemies without causing chaos and uncertainty in commerce. In most countries, the prevailing legal definition of a company's "nationality" was based on the location of its headquarters. There was a growing perception, however, that it was the shareholders' nationalities that determined a company's real allegiance, a shift that attests to the rise of economic nationalism before the war.[26] After August 1914, all belligerents shifted to a definition of a company's nationality as determined by the nationalities of its majority shareholders, which was both more difficult to use and more controversial than that used before the war.[27] Even minority enemy ownership spelled trouble, as companies with a majority of enemy citizens on their boards were sequestered and after 1916 were subject to liquidation, causing harm to domestic shareholders. In Alsace-Lorraine, over one hundred companies, including the largest textile plants and mechanical construction companies, had at least some French or, less frequently, British shareholders.[28] The enforcement of legislation on enemy property thus had a far-reaching impact.[29]

Persecution and Decline: Alsace-Lorraine's "Enemy" Industrialists during the First World War

Within Germany, the primary focus of policies of economic discrimination was Alsace-Lorraine, a region with extensive French investments adjacent to the front lines.[30] The Reichsland industrialists' experience was unique owing to the radicalism of the German administration, which rivaled the treatment reserved for occupied territories and included punishments for using French in public spaces, internment, and plans for population resettlement, among other measures.[31] Furthermore, the tribulations of the region's industrialists started as early as August 1914 and did not end until 1918, while a front ran through Alsatian territory. In sharp contrast to this difficult situation, with the exception of Galicia, which was devastated by Russian troops, the eastern territories of the two empires, including most of Hungary, Austria, and Bohemia, remained islands of relative peace, or suffered from short-lived enemy occupation, as in the case of East Prussia, Transylvania, or Bukovina.

Following the incursion of the French army into a sliver of Alsatian territory in early August 1914, the German army placed Upper Alsace under direct military rule and encroached on the civilian administration in the rest of Alsace-Lorraine. Even though the region was part of the German empire, the army's attitude toward civilian populations and its actions were remarkably similar to its behavior in occupied enemy territory such as northern France or Romania. Similarities included the relentless pursuit of enemy companies, the internment of purportedly anti-German bureaucrats, industrialists, and civilians, and the relocation of part of the region's industrial capacity to the interior of Germany.[32]

German civilian and military authorities placed a total of 101 industrial companies under sequester or forced administration and an additional 104 under surveillance by July 1917.[33] In the aftermath of the war, a Francophile Strasbourg newspaper estimated that German policies of forced administration and other discriminatory measures affected businesses with a total net worth of 1.2 billion marks or 1.5 billion francs ($285 million), an enormous sum amid wartime shortages.[34] According to more moderate postwar estimates by a Francophile Alsatian author, companies worth more than 160 million marks were sequestered or put under surveillance.[35] The majority of firms under forced administration were subject to liquidation between 1916 and 1918. The total value of the firms and assets put up for liquidation in Alsace-Lorraine was 335 million marks, which suggests that the firms targeted by German measures were in large part owned by German subjects, mostly native Alsace-Lorrainers.[36]

The economic downturn and unemployment precipitated by the German civilian and military administrations in Alsace-Lorraine between 1914 and 1918 clearly show how economic policies were guided by military and diplomatic considerations during this period. The persecution and harassment of a substantial portion of the civilian population and the economic elite by the German army in Alsace-Lorraine eroded the results of the preceding three decades of adaptation to German rule, while also failing to make a difference in the war effort. While the French government engaged in a sophisticated and costly propaganda campaign supported by emigré Alsatians and Lorrainers to convince its allies of the legitimacy of French rule in Alsace-Lorraine, Germany did not invest in popularizing its rule among Alsace-Lorrainers or its allies. As a result, the Hungarian press treated Alsace-Lorraine as a bargaining chip in peace negotiations rather than an integral part of the German empire.[37]

The divergent histories of two generations of the Vogt industrialist family illustrate the difference in how the French and German administrations related to Alsace-Lorraine's industrialists and other local elites between 1914 and 1918. The ancestors of the industrialist Joseph Vogt (1847–1921) had come to Alsace from Switzerland, and Vogt emerged as a typical provincial industrialist by 1914; active in regional politics, he developed his father's foundry into a lucrative set of enterprises that included the Kali Sainte Thérèse potash mines, natural gas fields, and a sizable foundry in Masevaux.[38] Potash was a new discovery in Alsace, and its exploitation required sizable initial investments, which the Vogts obtained in part from French businessmen; still, the majority of the mine's shares remained in the family's hands, while a German corporation controlled 97 percent of potash extraction in Alsace.[39]

To the misfortune of the family, the front line that solidified in Upper Alsace put the foundry under French rule while the potash mines remained under German sovereignty. Worse yet, Joseph Vogt was trapped on the French side while his son Fernand remained in German-ruled Alsace. Two weeks after the outbreak of war with France, the army imprisoned then interned Fernand Vogt in inland Germany without any justification. At the same time, the administration placed the family's partially French-owned potash mines under sequester, precipitating its economic decline.[40] In sharp contrast to German measures against the family and its property, France used the Vogt firm to showcase its generosity and the economic benefits of the return to the *patrie*. The army and government helped the foundry prosper on military commissions for shells, while the French administration offered local residents a generous exchange rate for paper marks to francs.[41] President Raymond Poincaré even paid an official visit to the few villages and townships that made up "liberated" Alsace in 1915 and awarded Joseph Vogt the Legion of Honor.[42]

The Vogts were not the only Alsatian industrialist family to suffer from discriminatory German policies during the war. After Great Britain's declaration of war on Germany, German officers knocked on the gate of the Mulhouse villa of Alfred von Glehn, one of the directors and engineers of the Alsatian Mechanical Construction Company (ElMaG), which had drawn intense scrutiny from German nationalists for its alleged Francophile leadership.[43] The officers interned the half-Prussian, half-British manager von Glehn in Bavaria, while the military turned his villa into their headquarters.[44] Even Théodore Schlumberger, a former National Liberal Party deputy at the Reichstag and president of the Alsace-Lorraine industrialists' syndicate, was unable to avoid internment. The septuagenarian Schlumberger died under house arrest in the interior of Germany in 1917.[45]

The tribulations of Vogt, Schlumberger, and von Glehn illustrate the wave of discrimination against enemy subjects and companies that swept through Europe and the colonies despite the contrary stipulations of international law. The escalation of tensions with Alsatian industrialists stemmed from the German army's ignorance of Alsace-Lorraine's society and the uncompromising attitude of the government's top bureaucrats. Germany's federal organization allowed the governor or Statthalter and the Ministry for Alsace-Lorraine to modify or delay enforcement of the laws passed by the Federal Council, but in fact the opposite happened. The state secretary of the Ministry for Alsace-Lorraine, Siegfried von Roedern, ordered the district presidents of the Reichsland to list foreign companies in their districts only a few days after the federal ordinance of September 14, 1914.[46] On the basis of von Roedern's initiative, the Ministry for Alsace-Lorraine began sequestering "enemy" property in mid-September 1914, before the corresponding French measures took effect and preceding comparable measures in the rest of Germany.[47] A Prussian career bureaucrat and finance specialist who had assumed his post in Alsace only a few months before the war, von Roedern had few contacts among local notables and limited knowledge of local society.[48] His ignorance of Alsatian customs and aggressive pursuit of purportedly disloyal industrialists greatly contributed to the plunging of Alsace-Lorraine's economy into a recession by 1916, when he was finally removed from his post.

As early as the fall of 1914, the situation was so fraught with tensions that von Roedern's colleague, Lorraine's district president Karl Freiherr von Gemmingen-Hornberg, characterized it as "mistrust of everyone against everyone else."[49] As a result of Gemmingen-Hornberg's dismissal of denunciations that reached his office, only 1,453 Lorrainers suffered internment during the war, as opposed to 4,820 Alsatians.[50] Even though Alsace's total population was double that of Lorraine's, this was a significant difference.

Furthermore, while there were more French-owned businesses in Alsace than in Lorraine, it is remarkable that the majority of liquidations took place in Alsace under von Roedern's administration, which points to individual top bureaucrats' responsibility for the severity of economic discrimination.

The unnecessary tribulations of one of Alsace-Lorraine's largest banks, the Alsatian General Bank (Allgemeine Elsässische Bankgesellschaft, AEB), are particularly revealing of how the German administration alienated regional business elites without benefiting the war economy or even other German industrialists. The AEB's board included the crème de la crème of Alsace's Lutheran economic elite. Landtag deputy and canning factory owner Leon Ungemach, who also served as vice president of the Strasbourg Chamber of Commerce; the president of the Mulhouse Chamber of Commerce, Albert Schlumberger; Baron Eugene de Dietrich; steel plant owner Karl de Wendel; and tanner Alfred Herrenschmidt were all on its board of directors.[51] An attack on one bank thus created conflicts with a series of businessmen, industrialists, and politicians.

The immediate financial gains from the liquidation of enemy assets in Alsace-Lorraine banks were less than 10.5 million marks, while the 45 million marks in bonds and stocks held by enemy citizens could not be claimed under wartime conditions.[52] In contrast, in the few weeks before it was placed under forced administration, the AEB raised 2.5 million marks in war bonds.[53] Ultimately, the political and economic damage precipitated by the sequestration of regional banks dwarfed the moderate financial gains produced by the German administration's measures.

The government relied on informants to spot its victims, since it lacked detailed lists of French assets. In the first days of the war, the grand duchy of Oldenburg denounced the AEB's "predominantly French character" to the chancellor.[54] In early September 1914, before the chancellor had time to react, von Roedern's Ministry for Alsace-Lorraine had already nominated a supervisor even though it had not yet been informed of this accusation.[55] The AEB issued increasingly aggressive protests against its planned state supervision but won only a few weeks' reprieve through such maneuvering. On September 24, a letter from the bank's lawyer highlighted that only three of the eleven members of the AEB supervisory board were French citizens, and the rest were from the Reichsland.[56] Despite these efforts, on October 6, 1914, von Roedern's ministry appointed a supervisor for the AEB, a loyal administrator who had already worked with the Ministry of Alsace-Lorraine; his monthly salary of 1,000 paper marks was to be paid by the AEB.[57] The bank remained under supervision until the end of the war, although its liquidation was never ordered.[58]

The strictness of German measures against enemy property and the serious damage they did to the home-front economy surfaced in the internal correspondence of the German authorities, although this failed to reverse the course of these policies. Regarding the sequestration of Lorraine's largest bank, the Banque de Metz, it was ironically the supervisory commissioner who pointed out to his superiors that his own job was unnecessary.[59] "I have known this bank for thirty years and never have I heard anything compromising its respectability. Nor do I believe that the bank behaved in a manner hostile to

Germandom (*deutschfeindlich*) in any possible way, even if its character cannot be described as German-friendly (*deutschfreundlich*)."[60] By way of conclusion, the commissioner maintained that "compulsory administration is neither necessary nor recommendable."[61] Still, German authorities sequestered the six major banks that had shareholders from Entente states, including the Banque de Metz, by December 1914.[62]

The de Dietrich engineering company became one of the German army's key suppliers in Alsace since it furnished products to the central railway office and the Solvay Works, a Germanized chemical company in Belgium.[63] Yet even the reorientation of the firm's production to trench supply materials could not save Eugene de Dietrich and his heirs from sequestration and harassment by the authorities, highlighting the inflexibility and inefficiency of the German administration. The German authorities placed the firm under supervision in 1915 on the grounds that 113 of its 2,000 shares were owned by French family members.[64]

Unlike textile companies, mechanical construction companies like the de Dietrich's firm had ample raw materials and were set to be the clear winners of the war economy. Despite the de Dietrich firm's lucrative cooperation with the German railways and other industrial companies, as well as its production of war-related materials, in June 1915 the firm was assigned a supervisor who exercised control over its accounts and payments. While most Alsatian companies came under sequester in 1914, the de Dietrichs remained under more lax supervision until 1917, when the French shares in the company were finally sequestered and the administration's control of the firm tightened. The sequestering agent appointed by the Ministry for Alsace-Lorraine, chaired board meetings and acted as the director of the firm. Starting in 1915, he pressured the firm in vain to change its name to "Von Dietrich" from the French-sounding de Dietrich. After Eugene's death in January 1918, the sequestering agent forced the firm's shareholders' assembly to adjourn for three months in March 1918 since he refused to acknowledge Dominique as Eugene's sole heir and pressed for the liquidation of the shares normally due to French family members. He aimed to use this opportunity to break the de Dietrichs' monopoly over their family firm and turn it into a publicly traded company in which new, German shareholders would constitute the majority.[65] However, Wassmansdorf was inefficient and slow in his maneuvers, which ultimately saved the de Dietrichs from liquidation. The next assembly in May 1918 remained inconclusive, in part because there were no buyers for the de Dietrichs' "French" shares that had been put up for liquidation.

Company liquidations posed numerous challenges to the German administration since they entailed finding a suitable buyer who had enough capital to spare. However, the army and treasury's enormous need for capital also meant that the German authorities had to eventually allow industrialists and businessmen of all stripes to participate in liquidations. Ironically, the German authorities even tried to recruit companies that they had put under sequester and surveillance as buyers. For instance, even the de Dietrichs were encouraged to take part in the liquidation of the French-owned de Wendel steel plants in Lorraine and the ElMaG plant. Eugene de Dietrich turned down the offers for the de Wendel company and the ElMaG, but his firm did purchase part of the liquidated Couleaux iron works.[66] The de Dietrichs were thus both the economic victims and the beneficiaries of forced liquidations initiated by the German wartime administration, which showed that the line between victims, perpetrators, and bystanders of economic discrimination was difficult to draw in wartime Alsace-Lorraine. Native Alsace-Lorrainers were not purely the victims that they cast themselves as after 1918. Similarly, not all German industrialists were beneficiaries of Germany's wartime policies in the region.

Women and the Revival of the Alsatian War Economy

The history of the Alsatian textile industry shows that even Francophile industrialists hit by both the blockade and German discrimination had some agency to keep their businesses going, often with the tacit help of the German-run municipal and regional administration, blurring the sharp ethnic divide that has so often been used as a master key to unlock the region's history. As early as 1914, the effects of the lack of US cotton shipments provided the German regime with a useful excuse for weakening a hostile group of industrialists. The plight of the Alsatian textile industry worsened especially after the Hindenburg Program of 1916 deprioritized industries that were not essential for armaments production.[67] Alsace-Lorraine's light industry, much of which was textile manufacturing, employed ninety thousand people and was based mostly in Alsace.[68] Textile companies were owned almost exclusively by Alsatian industrialists, including the Miegs, Schlumbergers, and Dollfusses, and employed over fifty-seven thousand workers.[69] Because textile production was concentrated in Upper Alsace around the city of Mulhouse, the sequesters threw the entire region and Alsace's third major city into a government-induced recession. Upper Alsace was the most Catholic and traditionally pro-French region of the Reichsland and the home base of Abbé Émile Wetterlé, Daniel Blumenthal, and other Francophile regionalist politicians.[70]

The Upper Alsatian textile industry also faced the most difficult situation of any industry because the Allied blockade had deprived it of US and Indian cotton and because it suffered from French bombardment and the heavy-handed military administration.[71] Wartime hardships forced the wool mills of Mulhouse to fire six hundred workers every month starting in the summer of 1915. By May 1916, all of the city's factories had ground to a halt as the military refused to allocate raw materials to them through the war corporations, even as other textile plants in the federal states continued to receive cotton, wool, and other raw materials, albeit in reduced quantities.[72] The German army also declined to renew its order for thousands of the sacks used in trench warfare, which it had originally placed with Alsatian textile mills in August 1914. By 1917, one in five textile plants had been put up for liquidation (most never found a buyer), while the rest remained idle.[73]

In 1917, the Berlin government facilitated negotiations on the takeover of the major French-owned factories of Alsace between German and Alsatian textile industrialists, but these remained fruitless in part because the Alsatians saw the involvement of German capital as "Germanization" and thus sabotaged deals that would have otherwise been beneficial for the region's economy.[74] Furthermore, the German administration blocked subpar offers by German and Alsatian industrialists, partly because it wanted to use German industrial property as a bargaining chip in peace negotiations.[75]

Many Alsatian textile industrialists decided to move to Germany, but most of them could not afford to build new plants and found themselves subordinated to industry rivals on highly unequal terms. The Bourcart Sons and Partners textile plant loaned its workers and machines to a textile plant near Karlsruhe after it stopped receiving raw materials; in practice, this meant the incorporation of the Bourcart's company into the Baden-based firm.[76] The Latscha brothers' textile plant in Jungholtz was damaged by French bombardments in 1916, after which the German army systematically extracted every last piece of metal from its damaged factory halls, including 2 tons of copper, 5 tons of brass, 40 kilograms of zinc, 122 kilograms of lead, and over 50 tons of cast iron, much as it did in occupied France.[77] The army then relocated 120 workers to factories in Germany and refused to allow their return despite multiple petitions by Paul Latscha, who was both the mayor of their village and their former employer.[78]

While the German regime's measures seriously aggravated the already difficult situation of Alsace-Lorraine's economy, municipalities and those notables who retained their companies still had ample latitude to counter the adverse effects of these measures. Across Central Europe, municipalities and local associations remained important conduits for food supplies, unemployment relief, and welfare, and the Reichsland was no exception.[79] Following the shutdown of the city's textile plants, the Association of Mulhouse Textile Industrialists adopted a unique plan to salvage the industry and employ the thousands of female workers who had lost their jobs in the region. Under the tutelage of the wife of a local notable, Frédéric Lamey, the association helped set up Pagaschuh Ltd. (Paga), a company whose name was the abbreviation for "paper yarn shoes" (*Papiergarnschuhe*) (figure 4.1).[80] The company's shares were partly owned by the Mulhouse municipality, and the factory functioned as a unit of the city's war relief office (Städtische Kriegsfürsorge); as such, it did not count as a regular industrial company.[81]

The camouflaging of textile workers as recipients of municipal aid worked for some time, and the Pagaschuh factory successfully exploited shortages on the domestic shoe market. The factory opened in March 1917, with 8 foremen and managers and 118 female workers. In May of that year it employed 730 workers; by August it employed 1,525, and by February 1918 it employed as many as 2,300, attesting to the increase in shoe production.[82] Four hundred individuals found temporary work in the halls of the Dollfuss-Mieg textile company, which the administration was unable to sell because there were no buyers during the crisis of textile production produced by the blockade.[83] By December 1917, Pagaschuh was producing between 2,000 and 2,400 paper

FIGURE 4.1. Women at a textile plant that has been transformed into a paper shoe factory in Mulhouse. Source: Private collection of author.

shoes daily with no complex machinery. In 1917 alone, the company manufactured 400,000 pairs of shoes, which its sales representatives in Berlin, Stuttgart, and Mulhouse sold to the most neglected civilian populations: women, the elderly, and young children.[84] The venture yielded an income of over 1.5 million marks and saved Mulhouse over 450,000 marks in welfare and unemployment payments.[85] The Paga factory made a profit of over 100,000 marks in 1917, which the city and shareholders donated to charity.[86]

Pagaschuh's success resulted in numerous conflicts with competitors, in both Alsace-Lorraine and the federated states of Germany, especially Saxony, which also had many hard-hit textile plants that had been in competition with their Alsatian counterparts since 1871.[87] The established L. Weyl shoe factory denounced Pagaschuh to the Strasbourg auditor, claiming that the company used schoolteachers in classrooms to advertise its products.[88] The businessman claimed with no evidence that while the company portrayed itself as laboring for "the benefit of mankind," in reality it used POWs as cheap laborers.[89] This incident highlights how industry competitors used the war as an opportunity to bring down their rivals with the help of the German administration.

Pagaschuh's conflicts with German war economy administrators stemmed from the inflexibility of a bureaucracy that was unable to situate a hybrid company founded in response to wartime shortages. The company was equally related to the textile, paper, leather, and shoe industries and retained its independence, at least initially, from the entrenched hierarchies of war corporations as it was part of the municipal welfare system. Furthermore, the company's wartime history illustrated the disadvantages caused by Alsace-Lorraine's subordination to federal states within Germany. As early as July 18, 1917, one of the Bundesrat's economic committees ordered the closure of Pagaschuh on formal grounds: the company violated the ordinance that prohibited the establishment of shoe factories for civilian populations during the war.[90] The head of the economic section of the Bundesrat was a deputy from Saxony, Julius Dehne, who was especially hostile to the Alsatian rivals of Saxon textile industrialists.[91] But thanks to the intervention of the Statthalter of Alsace-Lorraine, Johann Dallwitz, the company was allowed to continue its operations as a nonprofit and charitable undertaking.[92] Yet ultimately it was subordinated to a war corporation for shoe companies with a territorial scope covering Alsace-Lorraine and Pfalz, which meant that the management lost its autonomy to produce and sell shoes as it saw fit.[93]

In response, the Paga company's administrators wielded the language of the moral panic that was to result if its young female workers were left unemployed, pointing to the "demoralizing effects" of the shutdown on the home front.[94] In July 1918, its management complained to the state secretary of the

Reich's office for the economy: "We hoped that . . . the related organs would support our production of ersatz shoes. Unfortunately, the opposite was the case. The Shoe Industry Supervisory Committee and its organs, as well as the War Committee for Textile Ersatz Materials, have thrown greater and greater obstacles in the way of our production."[95] For instance, "we were not allowed to communicate directly or through correspondence with our buyers"; the result was the cancellation of orders amounting to 3 million marks.[96] Moreover, the war corporation capped the company's 20 percent profits at 6 percent. It also increased the difference between the production price and the sales price to 45 percent by forcing Paga to pay various intermediary organs and retailers, making the price of its shoes uncompetitively high.[97]

Apart from the inflexibility of the German war economy, which was unable to handle the resurrection of shuttered textile companies as shoe factories that used paper and not leather for production, it was the administration's general disregard of civilian needs that explained Pagaschuh's decline by the spring of 1918. As Julius Dehne's memorandum explained, if the government allowed the Paga corporation to continue its operations, it would have encouraged other shuttered shoe and textile plants to follow its path, purportedly resulting in the aggravation of the transport situation and labor and coal shortages.[98] In fact, Dehne's obstruction revealed that Alsatian companies that were partially owned by enemy citizens and catered to marginalized civilian populations were extremely low priorities for the government. Despite its directors' efforts, Paga was close to extinction by the end of the war.

While the German economic administration did not see a future for paper shoes, Hungarian companies backed by Budapest exploited the opportunity introduced by the German economic administration's anti-Alsatian stance. A Budapest-based company acquired the license to produce the Paga corporation's paper shoes and distribute them in "Austria-Hungary, Ukraine, and the Balkans" in August 1918.[99] Given the sudden and unexpected armistice, the venture was never profitable; but it illustrates how the First World War enabled Hungarian industrialists to assume the role of regional hegemons in some industries in East-Central Europe, a position previously filled by German, French, and US firms.

Liquidation of Property, Liquidation of Territory

The logic of sequesters, liquidations, and arbitrary seizures and divisions not only did not stop with companies but was transposed to administrative units like Alsace-Lorraine as well. Territories that were unable to assert their regional interests within Germany and its occupied territories were subject to forced integration and administration, as the example of Alsace-Lorraine shows. Prewar developments already pointed to the region's gradual transformation into a federal state, and wartime centralization accelerated discussions of its incorporation into neighboring states. Prussia eventually won out over Bavaria and Baden, and bureaucrats started to plan the merger.[100] The repercussions of the region's incorporation into Prussia went far beyond native Alsace-Lorrainers to threaten the region's German industrialists.[101] The liquidation of Alsace-Lorraine also threatened to further subordinate the port of Strasbourg to Mannheim and Ludwigshafen. One of Strasbourg's leading German magnates, Eugen Jacobi, rightly predicted that war corporations would remain relevant even after the armistice, and he feared the continued subordination of midsize Alsatian family firms like his own or that of the Adlers and Oppenheimers to the gigantic industrial conglomerates of the Rhineland and Westphalia.[102] Faced with these plans for partition, the region's German and native Alsatian industrialists favored the solution the Francophile regionalists had advocated before the war: the elevation of the Reichsland to the status of a federal state with a high level of internal autonomy.

These plans for partition did not ultimately materialize, but they mattered because they indicated that even Alsace-Lorraine's German industrialists who were loyal to the Reich could expect little from the victory of the Central Powers. Moreover, the virtually certain annexation of Lorraine by Prussia served as the grounds for actual social engineering policies that also threatened to marginalize the region's German industrialists. Tycoons like the Krupp family made plans to acquire French mines and steel plants in Lorraine.[103] Furthermore, on December 14, 1917, twenty-four Prussian industrialists and mine owners founded the Westmark corporation in Berlin with initial capital of 7.5 million marks. The Westmark corporation operated under the supervision of the chancellor.[104] Its main purpose was to bring German colonists to French-speaking western Lorraine and subsequently to Alsace, after the army demanded the expulsion of French speakers from the border region.[105]

As with the partition of Alsace-Lorraine, the planned acquisition of twenty-five thousand hectares of land was prevented by the lack of time, and the Westmark corporation also failed to seize real estate destined for German colonists.[106] What it achieved instead was to cement the already entrenched divisions between the German administration, German corporations, and regional elites, preparing the ground for a friendly reception of French troops.[107] The Westmark corporation's excessive economic expansion plans, the disruption of the regional economy caused by the liquidations of enemy companies, the withdrawal of raw materials from Alsatian firms, and the planned partition of Alsace-Lorraine were significant because they expanded the ranks of local industrialists who identified as victims of German rule. More importantly, these measures helped unite Alsace's native and German industrialists for the first time in the Reichsland's almost half-century history.

In April 1917, Ernst Zander, an engineer employed by the de Dietrich firm, founded the Association for the Rebuilding of Alsatian Industries and Businesses as a pressure group to represent regional economic interests. By early 1918, the municipalities of Strasbourg, Colmar, and Mulhouse had joined the organization, alongside the Adlers, Oppenheimers, and Jacobis.[108] Zander was born in Germany and had become the director of the War Office's Upper Alsace machine distribution unit after decades in industrial management, so he had firsthand experience of the transformation of the Reichsland's economy.[109] He had seen how the German army took machines like electric motors as well as raw materials from Alsace-Lorraine, noting that skilled workers tended to follow the machines, and lamented that the military ordered the closure of proportionately more companies in Alsace-Lorraine than in other regions.[110]

Zander castigated the Reich for treating Alsace-Lorraine as Germany's "stepchild." In his memorandum to the region's civilian administration, he warned that many industrialists, even those whose "pro-German conviction was unquestionable before the war," were now contemplating leaving the Reichsland. "Their disheartenment does not stem from political opposition, but from economic concerns about the future."[111] He identified Karl Adler, the Oppenheimer family, and Eugen Jacobi as the German industrialists whose participation was especially important for the *Verband*.[112] Zander hoped that they would "provide encouragement to industrialists, regardless of their place of origin."[113] What Zander did not realize at the time was the extent of the German administration's disintegration by the fall of 1918, when the families of civil servants started to relocate to Germany while Berlin attempted to save the region for the Reich through a series of democratic reforms, including granting Alsace-Lorraine the status of a federal state.[114] This attempt, however, proved short-lived as the German authorities lacked both time and the support of the region's political parties to bring it to fruition.[115]

The harassment of industrialists in Alsace-Lorraine during the First World War by the German administration indicates trends broader than the plight of these companies. The "social question" in most of Alsace-Lorraine centered on the fate of industrial companies and their workers, who suffered from massive unemployment and shortages that the German administration was unable to resolve and in many respects aggravated. Thus, when the French army marched into Alsace at the end of November 1918, it found most of the region's economy in crisis. Yet the wartime blunders of the German administration also meant that the French did not have to deal with nostalgia for German rule, an outcome that was far from foreseeable a decade before.

Belated Social Engineering in Transylvania (1916–1918)

In Hungary, even as the First World War generated a rise in antisemitism and calls to radically limit the economic and political power of ethnic minorities to the same levels as seen in Germany, in contrast to the German administration's militant stance in Alsace-Lorraine, there were no large-scale attempts at social engineering until 1916. Suspect nationalist leaders near the front in regions like the Austrian Littoral, Vojvodina, and northeastern Hungary were interned, but these harsh measures did not amount to a comprehensive policy to remake these regions' societies.[116] Premier István Tisza (1913–1917) even took up the defense of Hungarian laws that restricted the joint army's ability to persecute civilians, protesting to the supreme commander of the Dual Monarchy's army, Archduke Friedrich, when the army court-martialed an ethnic Serbian in Vojvodina without the consent of the Hungarian civilian administration in the first weeks of the war.[117] Tisza was not intervening on behalf of Serbian interests or the rights of Hungarian subjects but attempting to retain the upper hand over the joint army.

On the home front, it was Tisza's Hungarian parliamentary opposition and the press that urged radical actions against "war profiteers," Jews, and ethnic minorities while the conservative Tisza sought to defend the status quo. Hungary had more restricted suffrage than Germany, so ethnic minority parties, social democrats, and radical nationalist and antisemitic deputies who questioned the system established by the 1867 Compromise with Austria were unable to use the war as an opportunity to achieve political change. They had less power than the opposition in Austria, which benefited from general suffrage and a more representative political system. Despite the lack of social-democratic representation in the Parliament, Hungarian trade unions gained importance and the government granted several concessions to workers to stem the tide of strikes and make sure production continued uninterrupted.[118]

Unlike in Alsace-Lorraine, where industrialists emerged as the main targets of social engineering policies, the "social question" in most of agrarian East-Central, Eastern, and Southeastern Europe centered on landownership during the First World War.[119] Owning land embodied political power and social prestige, but it was also a source of social tensions owing to the skewed land distribution that concentrated the majority of estates in the hands of aristocrats, the gentry, and the Catholic Church.[120] In Hungary, for instance, 55 percent of all agricultural workers had either no land at all or a tiny two-acre holding that could not produce even subsistence-level yields.[121] In parliamentary debates, antisemitic criticisms of "war profiteers," large Budapest and German banks, and nationalist critiques of the Romanian gentry by the right-wing opposition of the Tisza government converged on questionable land transfers. Hungarian nationalists claimed with no evidence that Romanian banks and gentry were buying up Hungarian-owned land en masse in Transylvania, a charge that had been at the center of political debates in the early 1910s as well.[122] Debates on landownership did not spare industrialists and bankers, in part because they also owned or leased land, and reflected their increasingly precarious position in Hungarian society between 1914 and 1918, especially when it came to Jewish business elites.

Before 1914, industrial and commercial professions lacked prestige among Hungary's political and social elite, recruited from the ranks of the gentry and aristocracy, even as businessmen like the "Hungarian Krupp" Manfréd Weiss or mine manager Ferenc Chorin acquired fortunes that surpassed those of many aristocratic families. According to Tibor Vadnay, a top-ranking progressive official at the Budapest Ministry of the Interior, businessmen had been met with an "ice-cold attitude" or "belittling shoulder slapping" in elite social circles.[123] Vadnay lamented in 1918 that "the traditional Hungarian middle-class," the descendants of the Christian middle nobility and gentry, "is reluctant to choose commercial occupations. It prefers those jobs that come with social prestige over those that provide a financially beneficial career yet lack corresponding renown, even if the former require more education, more work, and yield a smaller income."[124] "War profiteers" further tarnished the reputations of commercial professions, as the prestige of businessmen sank to an all-time low between 1914 and 1918.[125] Vadnay also noted with alarm that commercial and industry professions were becoming misidentified as Jewish occupations. He observed that the Great War had further broadened the social distance between Christian and Jewish members of the social elite, the middle class, and bourgeoisie as it became common to blame Jews and Jewish army suppliers for every excess and hardship of the war economy.[126] Many prominent Jewish industrialists compensated for the vanishing prestige of their profession by acquiring a landed estate or pushing for ennoblement by the emperor, which in turn fueled further attacks by populist, nationalist, and antisemitic publications and deputies during the First World War.[127] As Péter Bihari has noted, even Manfréd Weiss was attacked in the House of Deputies by Count Tivadar Batthyány, an opposition politician and landowner, for "purchasing a new estate every week."[128] In fact, Weiss bought only one, 5,000-acre estate between 1914 and 1918, a considerably smaller property than those held by aristocratic families.[129]

Political antisemitism was also fueled by a young Catholic bishop, Ottokár Prohászka, whose radicalism nonetheless represented a minority view within the Catholic clergy and among the political elite, while Tisza himself condemned antisemitism and praised the heroism of Jewish front-line soldiers.[130] The campaign against "war profiteers" started in the spring of 1915 when the chaotic organization of army supplies left Hungarian soldiers wearing paper-soled boots and second-rate garments.[131] The opposition Catholic People's Party also started a campaign against large Budapest banks that financed the suppliers that produced faulty military boots and uniforms; many of these suppliers were Jewish merchants from Máramaros.[132] Given that the eastern front stabilized far from Hungary by March 1915, and civilians remained comparatively better provisioned than in Germany and Austria, Tisza managed to silence calls for a more radical treatment of Romanians, bankers, Jews, military suppliers, and other purported enemies of the war effort.

Hungary's relatively sheltered position within Mitteleuropa drastically changed by the summer of 1916, giving rise to the radicalization of policies targeting domestic enemies, especially Romanians, and the palpable rise of antisemitism in Parliament and in the yellow press. In the spring of 1916, Russian general Aleksei Brusilov's offensive broke the Galician front line and exposed Hungary's vulnerability and dependence on the German army. Tisza's position gradually weakened as the country faced the threat of a joint Russian and Romanian attack, while the premier was unable to order the Dual Monarchy's chief of staff Conrad von Hötzendorf to relocate troops to defend Transylvania. Count Mihály Károlyi, the charismatic leader of the anti-Habsburg, "independentist" parliamentary opposition, founded a new party that pushed for peace with the Entente.[133] Food shortages also became prevalent in Budapest, although they were never as severe as in Vienna and Berlin.[134] Civil servants became impoverished, and a 1920 court proceeding claimed that even some high-ranking judges supplemented their salaries, which were hard-hit by inflation, by mending shoes between 1914 and 1918. Although these were exceptional cases, the financial crisis facing civil servants was real, while army suppliers, landholding peasants, and gentry enriched themselves.[135] The Austro-Hungarian crown also inflated rapidly, not only in relation to the Swiss franc or the currencies of other neutral states but even compared with the German paper mark, in part because of German financial policies in occupied territories that disadvantaged Austria-Hungary.[136] Crises on the home front and on the war front were thus interrelated, and the line between the two fronts became blurred.[137] By early 1917, the moderate conservative Tisza had fallen and the governments of Móric Esterházy (1917–1918) and Sándor Wekerle (1918) pursued a more radical line against domestic enemies in light of military victories and conquests in Southeastern Europe.

The summer and fall of 1916 saw the rise of antisemitism across the Central Powers, as Jews became identified with commercial middlemen and shirkers in the antisemitic press. Galician and Russian-Polish refugees who fled to Berlin, Budapest, and the rest of Germany and Austria-Hungary to escape the devastation of warfare and the Russian army's brutal pogroms also received a less than welcoming reception.[138] The unintended consequence of the attempt by Oszkár Jászi's progressive paper *Huszadik Század* (Twentieth Century) to analyze the "Jewish question" using reasoned argument in 1917 provided a further venue for the expression of the antisemitic convictions prevalent among some of the country's intellectual elite.[139] Jenő Cholnoky, a geography professor and antisemitic public intellectual at the University of Kolozsvár, explicitly identified war profiteers with Jewish businessmen. He warned, "The balance is negative for the Jews even if we count their exact percentage among army suppliers, . . . and at a time of reckoning, the people will not count percentages [of Jews among the enriched] but hit wherever they can and that will indeed be a horrible catastrophe."[140]

The leftist press also made use of antisemitic undertones to agitate against "war profiteers" even as social-democratic leaders were wary of explicitly embracing antisemitism.[141] They blamed speculators and large estate owners, the mainstay of the political elite around Tisza, for exploiting the war for their own benefit.[142] In the Hungarian socialist paper *Népszava* (People's Voice), industrialists were portrayed as parasites on society between 1914 and 1916. The newspaper cited the profit margins of German and Hungarian army suppliers and noted that the birth of this new elite was not the sign of a "flourishing" economy but one of "inner rot":[143]

> A swarm of new millionaires is being born in the current shakeup of the world. At the cost of tears and blood new millions are sprouting. From the murky depth of society new men shove to the fore; with hardened fist and hairy heart they carve out a place for themselves among the wealthy. . . . A fat butcher descends from the coach with his wife in front of a rug shop. They pick an expensive Oriental carpet and without the least attempt at haggling they pay 6,000 crowns in cash. . . . A shabby speculator steps into a jewelry store to purchase pearls worth 10,000 crowns for his mistress. . . . Because the rich would pay all the money in the world (100–150 crowns) for a pair of women's shoes, the leather industry has no incentives to produce heavy duty shoes for workers.[144]

By 1917, anger with the enrichment of speculators and military suppliers coalesced into harsh criticism of "war millionaires," or war profiteers, a derogatory umbrella term that denoted upstart military suppliers, the enriched petit bourgeoisie, industrialists, and their wives and mistresses. The use of the expression "war [+ noun]," as in "war millionaire," had become so widespread in the Hungarian language that it prompted the linguist József Balassa to devote an academic article to clarifying how the Great War had altered the Hungarian language. He concluded that the adjective "war" denoted "bad quality," as was frequently the case of products supplied to the military, such as "war coffee" or "war soap."[145] Balassa noted that contemporaries understood "war millionaire" as the synonym of fake millionaire, a pretender, similar to "war waiters" or "war barons," who would not have been able to obtain their jobs or ranks without the labor shortages precipitated by the First World War.[146] Despite press agitation against war profiteers and Jews, the Hungarian government stood firmly on the side of industrialists and resisted antisemitic mobilization even after the fall of the Tisza government.

The situation of Transylvanians, however, took a turn for the worse between 1916 and 1918 and in many respects mirrored the tribulations of Alsace-Lorrainers since 1914. After the successful Brusilov offensive, Romanian troops attacked Transylvania in late August 1916 and occupied the southern part of the region for two months.[147] The economic damage was moderate, however, since the attack had been expected. Transylvanian cities and corporations evacuated at breakneck speed, while the Romanian troops' advance through the mountainous region was slow. Economically, the Romanian seizure of Hungary's largest coal reserves, located in the Jiu valley, presented difficulties in terms of transportation and heating. Miners, including underage children, fled the advancing Romanian troops on foot and in carriages and trains in the chaos produced by the convergence of the war front and the home front.

Fourteen-year-old Lajos Stern, son of a Jewish craftsman and a Calvinist Szekler mother, was a child laborer who had gone to work in the Jiu valley's mines in 1915, at the age of thirteen, after his father was drafted into the army. Stern jotted down his terse memoirs in a French POW camp in 1945 with a pencil on cigarette paper. Notably, even from the perspective of the tribulations of the Second World War, Stern wanted to draw attention to his traumatic war experience in 1916 as a teenaged worker. "In 1916 we had to flee. 100 km on foot until [we reached] Puj, [walking] day and night. I had to take care of my seven small siblings."[148]

The Hungarian administration of southern Transylvania disintegrated after the Romanian attack, while the Romanian military attempted to restore order as the impoverished populations who had stayed behind looted the homes of those who had fled. This modern day Jacquerie or a violent and spontaneous uprising of mostly rural populations united the poor regardless of ethnicity during the invasion and offered a warning sign to industrialists and landowners and prefigured the events of October 1918.[149] In the Szekler village of Barátos, the Hungarian peasants Mária Simon and Miklós Fekete reportedly shouted, "The rule of the Wallachians [Romanians] is much better than the Hungarians, as poor folks have so far been treated as slaves."[150] The presence of Romanian troops sparked hope among Transylvania's Romanian intelligentsia, even as Romanian nationalism was unable to incite an anti-Hungarian insurrection. In fact, most Romanians either fled along with the Hungarians and Germans or remained cautious about expressing their sympathies with the invaders.[151]

The Romanian army acted as the "liberator" of Transylvania, and its actions surpassed the limits on occupying armies defined by the fourth Hague convention, insofar as it attempted to incorporate occupied territories into Romania.[152] An appeal for donations to the occupying army referred to all inhabitants of Transylvania as Romanian "subjects" (*cetățean*), although it had no right to act as sovereign.[153] The Romanian army also ordered street and shop signs to be changed to Romanian, the only language of official correspondence in the occupied territories.[154] Attempts by the Romanian army to block landed property transactions and prevent tampering with land ownership registries was another sign that occupiers had long-term plans in Transylvania that included preparations for land reform, a project that was under discussion in Romania at the time.[155]

The fall of southern Transylvania and the occupying army's attempts to integrate the region into Romania radicalized the governing party and enabled the ultranationalist Transylvanian Alliance political pressure group to realize at least part of its program. The Transylvanian Alliance was a Hungarian political alliance formed on the eve of the First World War by parliamentary deputies and powerful politicians to modernize the region's economy and realize Hungarian "national supremacy."[156] In the spirit of the association's program, the incoming Esterházy administration, which followed the Tisza government, started with the heavy-handed punishment of the Transylvanian Romanian intelligentsia and social elite.[157]

The establishment of a "southeastern cultural border zone" in Transylvania suggested objectives that went beyond retaliation and attempted to achieve the Hungarianization of the Romanian-populated counties of southern Transylvania. The project was eerily similar to the Westmark corporation's Germanization plans in Lorraine.[158] Despite these ambitious plans, the Hungarian government was unable to restore its administration in southern

Transylvania because it lacked both personnel and material resources. When workers like Stern returned to the Jiu valley, they lacked proper housing for months. "There was very little food," wrote Stern, whose plans to study faltered as he had to go back to the mine pits as a teenager and continue to support his family until the war ended.[159] In the same year, the largest mining company in the valley, Ferenc Chorin's Salgótarján Coal Mining Corporation, reassured shareholders of "continuously increasing production" despite shortages of food and equipment and difficulties posed by the Romanian invasion.[160]

The Transylvanian Estate Transactions Committee was formed by a Hungarian government decree in November 1917 to vet land transactions from a "national perspective." It repulsed attempts by ethnic Romanian citizens to acquire land in Transylvania, and land purchases by banks after August 1, 1914, could be invalidated.[161] By 1918, the government had extended restrictions on property transactions to the entire country, showing how Transylvanian measures ended up informing nationwide policies of radicalization.[162]

The Transylvanian Land Relief Action offered generous support for Hungarian landowners at the expense of prosperous Romanian peasants, fusing negative ethnic discrimination with positive class-based discrimination.[163] This policy was modeled on Prussia's discriminatory policies against Poles in Posen and was a continuation of a failed prewar initiative.[164] Minister of Agriculture Béla Mezőssy received 47 million crowns, or 35 million marks ($5.3 million), for the project. This was an enormous sum and dwarfed German expenses earmarked for the Germanization of Lorraine. This discrepancy shows that Hungary could mobilize resources faster than federal Germany, where Lorraine policies were subject to debates among the federal states and Reichstag parties.[165] The allocation of massive funding was an extreme measure given that the monarchy had lost three-quarters of its metallic reserves by 1916 and its capacity to borrow from Germany had also radically decreased.[166] The minister proposed financing the project with funds earmarked for feeding the increasingly destitute urban populations and revenue from the forced labor of POWs, showing the intertwinement of oppression of the disenfranchised poor and ethnic minorities.[167]

The fruitless pursuit of the Transylvanian Romanian Albina Bank was reminiscent of the German administration's harassment of the Alsatian General Bank.[168] The Albina Bank was founded in 1872 with the purpose of supporting the economic interests of Transylvania's Romanians; yet by 1914 it had been thoroughly integrated into the Austro-Hungarian banking system, and its investments, like those of its competitors, were motivated primarily by profit seeking. The bank's achievements in promoting Romanian land purchases and industrial companies were negligible.[169] Given the Albina's association with Romanian nation building in Hungary, after the change of government in 1917 it emerged as a scapegoat accused of precipitating the Romanian invasion by financing Romanian nationalist agitation in Transylvania and engaging in "a secret operation aimed at undermining" Hungarian landowners.[170]

Unlike Germany, which was unable to conquer France and take Alsace-Lorrainer emigres to court, Hungary was able to occupy Romania, giving Hungarian authorities the means to pursue their enemies—Romanian landowners, bankers, businessmen, and intellectuals—across the border. This operation was doomed to fail from the outset, as the basis of the investigation was Hungarian nationalist allegations against Romanian banks and landowners rather than actual business transactions. The vaguely defined mission of the Brassó border police chief Sándor Pietsch was to investigate "the connections between the [Transylvanian Romanian] intelligentsia and banks [in Romania]."[171] Ultimately, Pietsch's mission not only failed but also disproved some of the allegations Hungarians leveled at Romanian banks: after poring over documents in German-occupied Bucharest, the commissioner revealed that the economic elites of the Kingdom of Romania regarded Transylvanian Romanian elites as rivals.[172] He discovered that one of the banks that Budapest suspected of bankrolling Transylvanian Romanians, the Banca Carpaților, was "poorly managed" and did not provide significant support to the Romanian national movement.[173] While civilian authorities accepted Pietsch's report, the military continued to pursue Transylvania's Romanians, whom it suspected of precipitating the attack. As early as December 6, 1916, the military court of the Hungarian *honvéd* army was in operation in Kolozsvár.[174] One official of the Albina Bank, Romulus Popescu, received an eight-month prison sentence for undermining Hungary's security.[175]

The paradox of Hungary's small war (against Transylvania's Romanians) within the Great War was that it took place while Hungarian interests were being marginalized in Germany's emerging "empire in the East."[176] What Pietsch and Hungarian industrialists encountered in occupied Romania was not a cross-border Romanian subversion effort affecting Transylvania but the suppression of their economic interests by the German military government in Bucharest. The German government treated Hungarian economic interests in Romania with an arrogance comparable to the treatment of the interests of Alsace-Lorraine industrialists closer to home. Hungarians complained that the German-run Reimbursement Office (Entschädigungsamt für Rumänien)[177] did not adequately compensate the 175 damaged Hungarian companies for the liquidation of their assets by the Romanian Kingdom, even though these were worth over 150 million crowns; the German military also frequently denied visa applications by Hungarian industrialists eager to reclaim their assets in occupied territory. At the same time, despite ambitious plans for economic expansion in Southeastern Europe, the Hungarian government was unable to appoint judges who could speak both Romanian and German in the occupied territories since the judicial corps lacked experts with the necessary language skills.[178] A young student at the Cluj faculty of law noted sarcastically that the planned chair in Balkan Studies would have to teach students who had no prior knowledge of Southeastern Europe and "cannot even name five Bulgarian cities" as they were more interested in learning about France and England.[179]

While the Mitteleuropa concept had fewer and fewer Hungarian advocates by 1917, it galvanized pan-German nationalism throughout East-Central Europe and boosted German and Saxon nation building in Transylvania, which was further enhanced by German emperor Wilhelm II's visit to Transylvania in September 1917 (figure 4.2).[180] Even General August von Mackensen became involved in Hungarian German nationalist activism.[181] Mackensen directed military operations from his base in Temesvár in the fall of 1915. Upon leaving the city, he asked the city's mayor, Josef Geml (who had learned Hungarian at the age of twelve but identified as Hungarian), why Hungarians oppressed Transylvania's Germans. The incident even reached Prime Minister Tisza, who judged it wise not to irritate the German military by contradicting Mackensen.[182] In the

FIGURE 4.2. Patron Wilhelm II meets the Hungarian elite cavalry regiment of the "Kaiser Wilhelm Hussars" in Transylvania (1917). Source: *Vasárnapi Újság* 64, no. 40 (1917): 645; Arcanum.

meantime, the leaders of Transylvania's wealthy Saxon community of 240,000 used Germany's hegemony over Hungary to initiate an aggressive land purchase program aimed at buying up Hungarian estates to consolidate and extend their holdings.[183] While the Romanian attack on Transylvania eventually put a stop to the project, it was a clear illustration of the increased latitude of Saxon banks and community leaders during the First World War.

While Hungarian industrialists dreamed of economic expansion in the Balkans, German industrial companies and banks like the Deutsche Bank acquired key positions in Hungarian industry. The country's dependence on Germany increased after the fall of southern Transylvania because Falkenhayn's troops were crucial in recovering the territory. In 1916, the German Petrol Corporation acquired Transylvania's natural gas fields through the Deutsche Bank.[184] While the Budapest government and Hungarian banks had invested 7 million crowns in the project by that point, the German bank paid just 4 million crowns for the exploitation rights and did not promise further investments in local industries, let alone in the pipelines that were to transport natural gas from Transylvania to the rest of Austria-Hungary. The opposition, including the civic radical and Anglophile Oszkár Jászi's journal, denounced economic "colonization" as it traded in Orientalist stereotypes and hierarchies among European and colonial peoples. The paper *Huszadik Század* indignantly compared the deal to economic practices in Asia and Africa and charged the government with allowing a foreign power to colonize Hungarian national space. The paper pondered "why the government gave such a 'sweet gift' to this foreign, *alldeutsch* bank, and why it rescinded the country's irreplaceable natural resources on conditions as if they were the resources of unpopulated territories in the Kongo, Mongolia or Northern Siberia. We cannot justify this decision in a poor but already capitalist and civilized country (*kulturország*)."[185] The article reflected the deep rift between civic radicals and social democrats on the question of Mitteleuropa. In the same issue of the journal, Jászi hailed the increasing integration of Hungary and Germany, while the socialist Zsigmond Kunfi doubted that German capital in Hungary would usher in a more progressive approach to labor relations. Kunfi noted the connection between the idealism of Central European integration and Germany's lurking economic imperialism. He pointed out that "the 'legendary' German industrialist . . . would not bring about modern administration, education, and agriculture" as free gifts for Hungarians.[186] His views were remarkably similar to those of Romanian national liberals and Transylvanian regionalists with regard to French and German economic expansion after 1918. Central European integration under an economically developed Great Power left East-Central

European elites, Hungarian and Romanian alike and on both the Left and the nationalist Right, deeply divided in the early twentieth century.

The First World War simultaneously ushered in the economic and military integration of the Central Powers and their increasing fragmentation into territories that attempted to shield their economic interests and protect their resources. Hungary was among the territories within the Central Powers' alliance that was able to exploit the benefits of its autonomy to further the interests of domestic industrialists, including those of Transylvania, while Alsace-Lorraine was the least able to do so. The First World War showed that even the potential victory of the Central Powers posed many difficulties for the bourgeoisie of the German and Austro-Hungarian empires. The war set in motion radical population engineering and expropriation policies, the rising power of military administrations, and above all, processes of economic and political integration led by the German government, army, and corporations that hurt numerous local interests from Alsace-Lorraine to Transylvania. Furthermore, the Great War left home-front societies deeply divided, particularly in the case of the contested territories that were at the center of population engineering efforts. In Alsace-Lorraine, German industrialists became closely identified with the unpopular military and civilian administration, while antisemitic mobilization against "war millionaires" in Hungary imperiled the wealth that industrialists and bankers had acquired between 1914 and 1918.

Population engineering in turn alienated ethnic minorities in contested territories. This "war" within the Great War, the Central Powers' quest for the wealth of their domestic and foreign enemies, was soon buried under more radical attempts to reshape property ownership during the socialist revolutions of 1918–1919, in the Soviet Union of the 1920s and 1930s, and most importantly, during the Second World War and its aftermath. Yet the state's willingness to intervene in the composition of private property based on the citizenship, ethnicity, and ancestry of industrialists, landowners, and shareholders was one of the most decisive legacies of the First World War. These costly efforts ultimately remained unsuccessful since both Germany and Austria-Hungary lacked the time and resources to remake their societies while fighting an all-consuming war, but their wartime attempts to remake economic hierarchies created precedents and models for their successors after 1918. The widespread disillusionment and bitterness that surrounded the actions of the German and Hungarian administrations in Alsace-Lorraine and Transylvania, respectively, enabled successor states to pursue even more radical policies of mass expulsions and expropriations, riding the waves of anti-imperial sentiments, antisemitism, and populism. Despite the enrichment of many industrialists and the bourgeoisie more generally between 1914 and 1918, the continued economic and political influence of economic elites that had emerged in the German and Austro-Hungarian empires was not a foregone conclusion by the end of the First World War. Ironically, the largest threat to businessmen was not the workers' movement but competing nationalizing states that advocated a changing of the guard in the ranks of the bourgeoisie.

CHAPTER 5

Profiting from Victory

Property Transfers in the Shadow of the 1918 Armistices

Fighting in most of Europe ended abruptly by November 1918, followed by the even more abrupt collapse of Austria-Hungary and Germany, which ushered in a power vacuum in the middle of Europe. Workers' and national councils took over the administration of major cities, but in many cases they were not powerful enough to extend their control to the countryside or initiate sweeping economic changes. While the Allies gradually occupied the territories they claimed from the Central Powers, it was far from clear whether the peace treaties would endorse the annexation of these territories and if so under what conditions, which gave further reason for caution for states that were eying German and Austro-Hungarian territory. In the meantime, as the Entente did not fully occupy the defeated Central Powers in November 1918, Germans, Austrians, and Hungarians did not immediately experience defeat. Instead, the left-of-center revolutionary governments that came into power in the fall of 1918 positioned themselves as the opponents and victims of the defunct German and Austro-Hungarian governments, and cast themselves as sympathetic to the Allies and especially to Woodrow Wilson's peace plans. Wilson's urge to respect the rights of ethnic minorities further increased uncertainties regarding whether France, Italy, Great Britain, Romania, and Serbia would be able to exploit victory to their advantage by sidelining the national self-determination of Germans, Austrians, and Hungarians.[1]

Rather than victorious Entente troops, it was local societies that spearheaded the transformation of the former German and Austro-Hungarian empires in the fall of 1918. Social and national revolutions became intertwined, especially in multiethnic territories of Central and East-Central Europe. As most territory of the former Central Powers descended into chaos, the people of villages and towns used the opportunity to seize food and assets left behind by "lords," fleeing imperial administrations, and shopkeepers, with enormous brutality.[2] The twelve rooms of Budapest sugar baron Rezső Schosberger's mansion in Transylvania were among the first victims of imperial collapse, along with castles and estates plundered by peasants and returning soldiers.[3] In Alsace-Lorraine, the Strasbourg municipality put up posters in an effort to prevent widespread looting. Transformation in East-Central Europe affected considerably larger swathes of territory than in continental Western Europe, where Alsace-Lorraine was the only major region to change hands. Furthermore, East-Central Europe was plagued by a series of wars, paramilitary violence, and pogroms. Still, by 1921, the leading industrialists and businessmen in the region were the same as those before 1918, while those of Alsace-Lorraine changed substantially with the near-complete elimination of industrialists and businessmen categorized as German. While "bourgeois" Europe was "recast" after the wars and revolutions of the second half of the 1910s, the composition of the bourgeoisie changed substantially in Alsace-Lorraine.[4] The divergence between the fates of industrialists in Alsace-Lorraine and those in East-Central Europe is intriguing as France influenced the fates of both territories yet pursued different policies: massive expropriation of Germans in the former, and the protection of the German, Hungarian, and Jewish property in the successor states of Austria-Hungary. The Paris administration wanted to preserve its position as arbiter and seize key assets before successor states of Austria-Hungary nationalized them, and also prevent further chaos in an already chaotic region crucial for the French "crusade" against Russia's Bolsheviks.[5]

Actors in local societies had unique leverage because successor states were slow to become established on new territories, the League of Nations did not yet exist, and the peace treaties were still in the making. Seemingly petty deals struck far from capital cities were in fact important for the making of postwar borders and economic hierarchies as the peace conference primarily reacted to events on the ground even as it tried to influence or reverse the outcome of often enormous changes in East-Central Europe. We thus need to direct our attention away from the well-documented gathering of diplomats in the leafy suburbs of Paris and the equally well-documented nationalist rallies in Central Europe that are the customary focal point of histories of postwar transition; instead, we must engage with the "power vacuum" that Hannah

Arendt and historians in her wake have identified as the hallmark of the post-armistice period and see how armies, industrialists, diplomats, and ordinary people exploited it.[6] A closer look at behind-the-scenes deals and property transfers helps explore how strongmen of local societies and speculators beat states in the post-armistice "primitive accumulation" of property and reaped the economic fruits of victory, while the insurrection of peasants, workers, and soldiers that followed the 1918 armistices was contained.

France was the most powerful Allied state with sizable territorial claims on Germany, and it was the first state to "nudge" Central Europe out of the post-armistice power vacuum by marching into Alsace-Lorraine and concluding an armistice with the Hungarian revolutionary government as early as November 1918. The Paris government created a fait accompli by occupying the departments it had lost in 1871, as it thereby upended any realistic talk of a plebiscite or interference in the region's reconstruction by the United States and Great Britain. The French administration, however, created a new set of problems by not having an efficient administration in the region, which allowed for speculators and agile Alsatian and French businessmen to amass fortunes after sovereignty change. East-Central European successor states possessed even fewer resources and deployable administrative personnel than France, and they depended on industrialists to sustain their occupying armies and production, which gave more maneuvering power to the defunct empires' business elites.

French troops encountered an exuberant reception as populations of Alsace-Lorraine fostered outsize expectations regarding the new administration; the first speeches and orders by French politicians and army commanders added fuel to the fire as they promised to sideline everything German, from people to currency, yet neither had clear-cut plans or personnel to follow through with this objective. Families wanted apartments, food, and coal for heating, along with jobs for returning soldiers. Middle classes and civil servants needed money to augment their inflated salaries, while the traditional mainstay of the region's political and economic life, Alsace's industrialists, wanted political power and material compensation for their marginalization by the German military during the war.

Agile businessmen and industrialists from both Alsace and the rest of France realized this power vacuum and swung into action to seize German property for themselves on the cheap, sidelining French courts that had been in charge of enemy property in France between 1914 and 1918.[7] They pointed to and exploited the fierce anti-German rhetoric of the new administration to coerce Germans into unfavorable deals and to justify their actions as serving the national interest. By the time the French administration gathered enough momentum to curb such profiteering, many of these transactions became difficult to reverse without embarrassing France at the League of Nations and the Allies, as the case of the Maison Rouge, Strasbourg's most prominent hotel and other prime real estate, showed.

The Maison Rouge Affair: Changing of the Guard and Corruption in Alsace after the Great War

Visitors to the Alsatian city of Strasbourg can hardly avoid the Maison Rouge, a modernist shopping mall reminiscent of the former Eastern Bloc. Located in the heart of the city's Kléber Square, the mall contrasts sharply with the eighteenth-century garrison next door and the surrounding medieval timber-framed houses. Before its demolition in the 1970s, a grand hotel had occupied the enviable spot where the mall now stands. The Hotel Maison Rouge reflected the extent to which the Alsatian bourgeoisie had acclimated to German rule by 1900. It was the fruit of cooperation between German investor Otto Back and Alsatian architects Jacques Albert Brion and Eugene Haug.[8] The building's architectural aesthetic combined a French-style neoclassical facade with motifs taken from contemporary Central European apartment buildings, and the hotel prided itself on an art nouveau winter garden. According to a contemporary guidebook, the luxurious Palast Hotel Rotes Haus, as Germans called it, was "first class" and located "in a most open situation," with 130 bedrooms equipped with bathrooms (figure 5.1).[9]

This hotel was one of the many assets that changed hands during the "troubled times" after French troops entered the city, when it became clear that the new administration intended to expropriate Germans' private property and expel them.[10] A Parisian speculator, previously unknown in Alsace, seized the hotel from its German owner by means of extortion involving local police, a judge, and a prosecutor. According to a French investigation in the early 1920s, the nascent French administration's involvement in extortion and corruption was widespread and included the sale of the Pechelbronn potash mines and Lorraine's mines and plants, costing the French treasury hundreds of millions of francs. The case of the Maison Rouge offers a revealing and in-depth illustration of how the French state privatized the economic benefits of victory over Germany and condoned the actions of well-placed industrialists and magistrates as they found ways to profit at the expense of both the ninety-five thousand expelled Germans and the French treasury.[11]

In November 1918, amid the uncertainty about the details of reconstruction in Alsace and Lorraine, Parisian businessmen bet on the impending expropria-

FIGURE 5.1. Birthday mass for Wilhelm II in front of the Rotes Haus in Strasbourg in 1916. Source: Strasbourg Municipal Archives, AVES, 112 Z 10.

tion of German property, while Germans were eager to sell their assets quickly before the French state took them by force.[12] Deputies and senators had special prerogatives to enter "liberated" Alsace-Lorraine without a permit, although the region remained closed to civilian travel. Some politicians sought to turn this into a financial advantage by taking investors who were keen to cruise the region looking for suitable German assets with them for a fee. Abraham Adelson, a relatively unknown Parisian businessman, entered Strasbourg in the company of the Radical Left deputy, the reserve captain Alfred Le Roy (1875–1944); Adelson intended to seize the Maison Rouge hotel and prominent department stores in downtown Strasbourg from their owner, Wilhelm Wiesmayer.[13] The extortion scheme surrounding this prominent hotel illustrates that many Frenchmen were lured to Alsace-Lorraine by the hope of rapid enrichment rather than pure patriotic fervor. Yet no investigation was launched until 1922, well after the fall of the Clemenceau government in 1919, in line with other probes by the chamber of deputies and the senate that aimed to learn why the reintegration of Alsace and Lorraine had cost the French treasury the enormous sum of 3.3 billion francs ($230 million).[14]

Germans like Wiesmayer had ample reason for concern in the last days of November 1918. Behind the facade of the official rhetoric of Franco-Alsatian unity, the French administration had good reasons to doubt the loyalty of many Alsatians to the French cause and feared that they would interfere with a potential plebiscite and undermine French democracy more generally.[15] These French doubts manifested in the vetting and ethnic categorization of the region's population with the intention of removing Germans and the most notoriously Germanophile Alsatians and Lorrainers from public life—and in the case of Germans, expelling them from the territory of reannexed regions. As soon as the French army occupied Strasbourg and the rest of Alsace and Lorraine on November 22, it started to categorize the two regions' populations by origin. Those whose ancestors had lived in the region before 1871, who numbered over one million people (approximately 59 percent of Alsatians and Lorrainers), received identity card A.[16] Those born in Germany and their children, along with citizens of enemy states and POWs, who numbered more than one hundred thousand, received the least desirable card, D, and their expulsion began immediately.[17] People with mixed German and Alsatian ancestry received cards B or C.[18] The introduction of the card system resulted in widespread discontent and uncertainty among the local population, since many families had members who received an inferior card and yet were pro-French.

Because of personnel shortages during demobilization, the incoming French bureaucracy never compiled a list of German property in Alsace and Lorraine, which proved to be a recipe for unchecked and overlooked property transfers. Furthermore, with industrialists like Reconstruction Minister Louis Loucheur informing the government's economic policy, taking German assets into state ownership was never considered. Lack of oversight also signaled to French speculators that Paris was not there to profit economically from expropriations but to use them as a collective punishment for Germans.

In the case of large, German-owned industrial companies like the Adler and Oppenheimer tannery or the Wolf, Netter, Jacobi (WNJ) engineering firm, it was the French state's scarce financial resources and a drive to maintain production that prompted local tribunals to authorize negotiations between German owners and French investors, thus allowing the state to rid itself of the financial obligations of managing German assets. The Maison Rouge affair, on the other hand, reveals blatant corruption and extortion that surpassed even German pressures on Francophile Alsatian industrialists like the de Dietrichs between 1914 and 1918.

A 1922 French investigation noted, "Adelson and his associate realized from the beginning how easy it was to acquire the property of Germans at risk of expulsion at bargain prices. Starting on December 5, 1918, they bought up the Tensfeldt store . . . for 525,000 paper marks, the Odéon café for 140,000 marks, and the Maison Rouge palace hotel . . . along with several other businesses,"[19] including the Kauffmann clothing factory and the Palais des Nouveautés, a five-story department store next to the Maison Rouge on Place Kléber. At 11 o'clock on the morning of Sunday, December 15, 1918, detective Grombach appeared at the Maison Rouge hotel and told Wiesmayer, "I have been sent to purchase your hotel, but first I have to tell you something that grieves me deeply. Today the French government passed a decree stating that all German property is to be liquidated. That decree is already in the hands of the Strasbourg authorities, but at the insistence of the people who sent me, and on my own behalf, we are holding it back to enable the sale of your property. If you want to save any of your fortune, you need to sell now. The decree is here. As your friend, I have persuaded high commissioner Maringer to leave it in his drawer until the sale of the Maison Rouge is closed."[20]

Wiesmayer had only four hours to decide whether to sell. Grombach returned in the afternoon accompanied by the police chief Jules Lévy, the French deputy Le Roy in his French officer's uniform, and Adelson; Lévy had already been appointed vice president of the Strasbourg tribunal, effective the following Monday, which lent his presence additional weight.[21] These well-connected men confirmed to Wiesmayer that if he did not sell the hotel for 300,000 francs, about one-tenth of its price, it would be expropriated without compensation by the French state. Wiesmayer caved, and the five men rushed to a notary named Bär and concluded the transaction at six in the evening on the same Sunday.

The deputy Le Roy had sat in the chamber between 1914 and 1916 as it legislated on the liquidation of German assets, so he was aware that their actions pushed the limits of the law.[22] Even in the interior of France, enemy property could be purchased only after a tribunal had sequestered it and appointed a sequestering agent, who in turn managed and initiated the liquidation of the assets after public bidding. Yet Lévy's endorsement of the transaction lent credibility to the sale; both Lévy and Grombach received 50,000 francs for their services.[23] Wiesmayer, however, ended up without a sou. After Adelson deposited the purchase price with the notary Bär, the latter refused to hand it over to

Wiesmayer; citing French law, he deposited the sum in a Strasbourg bank, where it was duly confiscated as German property.[24] Just a few months later, Adelson sold the hotel for 2.4 million francs.[25]

Jules Lévy exercised similar pressures during the liquidation of the WNJ foundry and engineering company. His and Grombach's actions after 1918 illustrate the opportunities that the French takeover of Alsace provided for some low-ranking Alsatian bureaucrats who had already been active in the Reichsland period. Lévy had worked on the Strasbourg war tribunal during the war and seized the vacant position of police chief when its German occupant was forced to retire during the brief period of the socialist National Council, between November 10 and 22, 1918.[26] Before the French troops marched in, however, he had recast himself as a Francophile and ensured his own prominence by initiating the removal of the red flag from the Strasbourg cathedral and replacing it with the French tricolor.[27] This move earned him a position as vice president of the Regional Tribunal of Strasbourg as early as December 1918, even though he had previously received the Iron Cross from the German army.[28] Grombach, who had worked as a furniture salesman during the war, was appointed acting police commissioner by Lévy during the rule of the revolutionary National Council.

Regionalism and International Accords in the Service of German Businessmen

Until 1922, it seemed that Adelson's plan had worked, since neither the French courts nor the French municipality had any interest in reopening the troubled files on post-armistice property transfers, and local courts sabotaged even the prime minister's call for the cancellation of the Maison Rouge transaction.[29] According to an annex to the Versailles Treaty, crimes committed during the liquidation of German private property were to be prosecuted by the victorious powers. Wiesmayer had therefore filed a report with the state prosecutor of Strasbourg in 1920, charging Adelson and Le Roy with coercion, but the French authorities did not open an investigation.[30] The general commissioner, the chief magistrate of Alsace and Lorraine, also disregarded a second call to examine the transaction, this one submitted by the German Foreign Ministry in June 1920.[31] The French prosecutor who eventually dismissed German diplomats' petitions about corruption and coercion defended himself during an investigation by the Chamber of Deputies by arguing that all Germans were "liars" and their testimonies were worthless.[32]

It took a Frenchman in a position of power, yet an outsider to Parisian and Alsatian circles of notables, bureaucrats, and politicians, to prosecute the culprits in the Maison Rouge transaction. Jules-Othon Jaeger (1864–1935) was a relatively unknown lawyer from a rural Alsatian family. After finishing law school in the 1880s, the Francophile Jaeger, a critic of the German administration, was only able to secure the low-ranking position of village notary in provincial Alsace-Lorraine before 1914. Upon the start of the First World War, the German army deported Jaeger to Bavaria along with hundreds of other political enemies of the regime.[33]

German internment gave Jaeger sizable political capital and credibility after the French occupation of Alsace. In line with the democratic turn in French politics after the war, Jaeger was one of the numerous newly elected deputies with no experience in national politics. He ran on the ticket of the National Bloc, the leading center right governing party, and soon secured the role of vice president of the speculation commission, headed by the seasoned politician Louis Marin.[34] The commission embarked on the investigation of Aristide Briand's and Georges Clemenceau's governments. Jaeger, who was pushing sixty, had nothing to lose by gaining enemies among the Parisian establishment.

An amateur politician, Jaeger was driven by his convictions rather than a thirst for power; his cousin described him as "more of a clean conscience than a leader, more of an honest man than a politician."[35] He was a man of "old Alsace" and "an enemy of snobbery," who never felt at home amid the intrigues of Paris politicians; and he was either too naive or too inexperienced to understand the multiple political agendas of the government and his own party in Alsace and Lorraine, including the goal of covering up the existence and mistreatment of German minorities in the former Reichsland.[36] Instead, Jaeger was determined to hold the French regime to its own stated ideals, even if doing so exposed the administration's corruption to Germany and the League of Nations. His cooperation with Wiesmayer shows that French rule in Alsace produced situations in which Germans and native Alsatians found allies in each other as early as the post-armistice period.

In March 1921, Jaeger pressed the government to reexamine the sale of the Maison Rouge, although he had to have realized that the French judicial system and bureaucracy had sabotaged the investigation. Later in June, he openly protested in the chamber against the administration's dilatory practices, and his fiery speeches printed in the *Journal Officiel* eventually earned him an audience with Prime Minister Briand and Théodore Tissier, the undersecretary of state responsible for Alsace-Lorraine.[37] Even the French president, Alexandre Millerand, who had headed the General Commissariat in 1919, sent a telegram ordering his successor to look into the Maison Rouge affair.[38] These interventions from the highest circles of government produced no results, however, because the regional French administration was relatively autonomous until it was disbanded by the government in 1926, and it refused to act on a delicate matter that compromised several of its top bureaucrats.

Tensions between Paris and its regional representatives reveal that the first French administration in Alsace and Lorraine was a makeshift organization that failed to oversee economic transactions in the recovered departments. At the time of Adelson and Le Roy's purchases in Strasbourg, it was Jules Jeanneney, a staunch advocate of centralization and anticlericalism, who held the highest office in matters related to the recovered provinces.[39] Jeanneney was a poor fit for a region with strong religious currents in its political life and a penchant for autonomy.[40] His administration consisted of three government commissioners coordinated by a high commissioner in Strasbourg, a position he filled with his brother-in-law Georges Maringer. Alsatian legal scholar Frédéric Eccard sarcastically described Maringer as a "jovial fellow, a gourmet, and a heavy smoker" who nonetheless had "no sense of the administration" and who spoke no German, the mother tongue of over four-fifths of Alsatians and the region's administrative language.[41]

As Jaeger was making his case in Paris, his colleague at the head of the illicit speculations commission, the centrist Republican deputy Louis Marin, decided to travel to Alsace to launch his own investigation despite the discouragement of undersecretary of state Tissier, who claimed that there was no Maison Rouge affair.[42] When Marin exited the train in Strasbourg, he was met by the director of justice, who immediately told him, "There is nothing in this affair; you won't find anything."[43] The local administration refused to allow Marin to interview witnesses and screened his contacts. When Marin finally met with Lévy, the judge was condescending and demanded to have his name cleared. It became clear to Marin that Lévy had passed the French vetting examination for Reichsland officials with the collusion of Prosecutor Cura, who had cleared him of accusations of bribery, in part because Cura himself was also implicated in a coercive business transaction involving Grombach. Before coming to Alsace with his large family, Cura had been a colonial official in Algeria.[44] Upon his arrival in Alsace, Cura urgently needed housing, so he prompted detective Grombach to evict two elderly Alsatian women from their Strasbourg villa in 1919.[45] Under pressure from Cura, Lévy's examining magistrate omitted questions about the Maison Rouge during the vetting process and confirmed him in his position. Lévy spoke openly about the affair to Marin because he was convinced that by transferring his commission to the treasury, he had already saved his job:

DEPUTY LOUIS MARIN: Do you think it natural for a magistrate to be able to retain his position after receiving a 50,000-franc commission under these circumstances?

JUDGE JULES LÉVY: What do you want from me? It was right after the armistice, and I lost my mind for a minute, just like everyone else, I was seized with the urge to make money. . . . After I had been summoned to testify, I visited public prosecutor Cura and told him the facts [about the Maison Rouge]. . . . He and I came to an agreement that I wouldn't say anything about it [during the vetting of Alsatian officials]. . . . We also agreed that Cura would meet with the examining magistrate [to prime him about my case.][46]

The subsequent months revealed that not only Cura, the examining magistrate, and Lévy but also the entire leadership of the judicial apparatus in Strasbourg were all involved in covering up the affair. The investigation also caused trouble for the commissioner general, since the sale of the hotel revealed that he headed a corrupt bureaucracy that had rehired "bad apples" from the previous German administration. When Prime Minister Briand eventually instructed Commissioner General Alapetite to nullify the sale of the Maison Rouge, he prevaricated and instead proposed launching an investigation, intending to force Adelson to pay the "fair price" of the hotel and Lévy and Grombach to repay their commissions.[47]

Adelson remained in Strasbourg for several years after the transaction and was eventually a candidate for the Legion of Honor.[48] The French government demoted the most exposed figures involved in the scheme but refused to reopen the case in order to avoid inquiries into its expropriation policies by Germany and the League of Nations. The justice minister reassigned Prosecutor Cura to Tizi-Ouzou in rural Algeria; Lévy and Grombach lost their jobs in Strasbourg; Jaeger retired soon after the affair but remained in touch with Wiesmayer and continued to help him seek justice, mostly in vain; Marin continued to pursue the corruption of left-wing governments, most notably the irregularities during the conversion of paper marks to francs, and emerged as an advocate of cooperation between France and Romania against the global Left, the Bolsheviks.[49]

The Maison Rouge affair was far from the only, or even the largest, coercive business transaction in Alsace. Alsatians at the time cast the affair in a regionalist mold as proof of their region's economic exploitation by businessmen from the French interior. Alsatian regionalism also had considerable antisemitic undertones. The region was not exempt from the rise of wartime antisemitism in the German empire, a trend that French sovereignty was unable to eradicate. The

Maison Rouge affair gained notoriety in part because both the buyer and the magistrate were Jewish, which allowed Alsatian elites to play up regionalism without criticizing non-Jewish Frenchmen or French rule more generally.[50] It also offered a convenient way to avoid facing Alsatian industrialists' widespread involvement in the expropriation of Germans, which deputies from the French interior pointed out during debates on the Maison Rouge affair.[51]

Yet even the city's established business elite engaged in similarly dubious efforts to extort their German neighbors. For instance, in November 1918, a group of Alsatian businessmen led by Léon Ungemach, president of the Strasbourg Chamber of Commerce and an agrifood industry "war millionaire," approached the businessman Engelhorn, the owner of the largest Alsatian daily, the *Strassburger Neueste Nachrichten*. Ungemach and his business partners pressured Engelhorn to sell nearly three-quarters of the newspaper's shares at a below-market price.[52] While Adelson used Le Roy as a cover to camouflage his profiteering, Ungemach and his partners, two Alsatian bank directors and a mill owner, invited Aristide Quillet and Henry Emil, Legion of Honor recipients from the interior of France, to serve as editors of the newspaper and thus legitimate the transaction in the eyes of Paris.[53]

Helping to Solidify French Rule: German Companies in Alsace after 1918

The Maison Rouge affair was not the only questionable transfer of German property to French hands that passed through the offices of Prosecutor Cura and Judge Lévy; the two officials were also involved in the expropriation of German-owned industrial companies. Unlike the Maison Rouge, industrial enterprises like the WNJ engineering company and steel plant or the Adler and Oppenheimer tannery affected the lives of thousands of families. The lack of means of transportation, credit, and coal and other raw materials that firms in these regions had imported from Germany ushered in a severe crisis of industrial production that led to mass layoffs starting in November 1918. The French administration scrambled to sell off these firms as fast as possible to prevent an economic crisis that could compromise the popularity of French rule over Alsace and Lorraine.[54] Alsatian and Mosellan trade unions saw their membership rise from the prewar 25,000 to 120,000 by 1919.[55] Despite their increased power, they followed a shortsighted policy of supporting the expulsion of German workers in the false hope of alleviating the effects of the economic crisis on Alsatian labor.[56] Moderate Francophile socialists such as Strasbourg's powerful mayor Jacques Peirotes did nothing to stop the expulsions and sought to cooperate with Alsatian bourgeois politicians since the beginning of French rule.[57]

It was during the crucial weeks of labor unrest at the WNJ factories that Marcel Dumuis, the general director of the Firminy steel plant in central France, approached Commissioner Cura and Judge Lévy with the news that he was to take over the company. Dumuis said that after he had gained the approval of the Commissariat General's Foundries Department he had struck a deal with the German owner, Eugen Jacobi, who was slated to be expelled, as well as the Alsatian engineer Edmund Schisselé, who acted as the firm's sequestering agent.[58] Given his own doubts about the legality of the transaction, Dumuis asked the two officials how to proceed without "exposing Firminy to any criticism"; but to his surprise both the sequestering agent Schisselé and Jacobi endorsed the deal.[59] Unlike uncompromising German and French expropriation measures before 1918, the post-armistice period thus allowed for cooperation and negotiations between expelled industrialists and new owners that eased the harshness of Paris's expropriation decree. At the time, Jacobi could not know that the Versailles Treaty would make the Weimar Republic pay compensation for the expropriated assets of Alsace-Lorraine industrialists.[60] The sale was officially concluded on January 22, 1919.[61] Firminy paid 7 million francs, or close to $1 million, for the company, and an additional 6.5 million francs for its installations.[62] Given that the company's wartime profits amounted to 8 million marks (around 7 million prewar francs), the deal was very advantageous for the French buyer. The purchase price went to the French treasury; it is unknown how much money Jacobi received for his cooperation.

About a week later, however, Reconstruction Minister Loucheur delivered a fiery speech to the Chamber of Deputies in which he condemned premature liquidations and exploratory trips by French firms to Alsace-Lorraine, as he realized that the French budget would have to write off enormous losses. After the speech, the rather naive Dumuis immediately headed to Loucheur's Paris office without an appointment. He honestly explained his intention to purchase the WNJ firm and told the minister about the endorsement he had received from regional officials.[63] Loucheur was dismayed to learn that the Firminy steel plant in central France had already sent its engineers to assess the value of the WNJ firm in December 1918.[64] The minister preferred to deal directly with the head of the Comité des Forges, Robert Pinot, rather than with Firminy, a relatively insignificant and underfinanced member of the industrialist alliance that was increasingly mired in fierce competition for the former Reichsland's industrial property.[65]

The fact that the prosecutor, the judge, and the sequestering agent had cooperated with Dumuis in defiance of government decrees alarmed Loucheur, who immediately wrote to undersecretary Jeanneney to cancel the transaction. Loucheur also criticized Jeanneney's Alsatian staff for disregarding the ban on visits to sequestered plants by French industrialists: "Everybody is telling me that foreign and French negotiators are trying to create rights [for themselves over German property in Alsace and Lorraine]."[66] In a moment of indiscretion, Loucheur even went so far as to criticize the French tribunal and the local administration in a letter to Dumuis. His harsh censure of the director was wrapped in diplomatic politesse that nonetheless failed to hide the rupture between the bureaucracies in Paris and the "liberated regions": "I have the honor of informing you that the investigations revealed that the Government Commissioner committed an enormous error of interpretation. . . . I hereby confirm that this acquisition [of the WNJ] will not under any circumstances be approved by the French government."[67] Dumuis, however, contested Loucheur's assessment of the situation. The affair took months to resolve, and during this time workers of the firm went on strike. Firminy was eventually forced to share ownership of WNJ with other French and Alsatian industrialists, and the conglomerate was rebaptized the Forges de Strasbourg in 1919.[68] The ultimate beneficiaries of Loucheur's intervention were thus the industrialists of Alsace and Lorraine because they also received a share of this important firm, although it was also in the government's interest to distribute the benefits of expropriations among Alsace's and Lorraine's notables, who were the key supporters of French rule in the region.

Maneuvering and Resistance to Expropriations

Dumuis's unsuccessful attempt to swallow a much larger firm on his own drew the ire of both Loucheur and industry competitors. As the fate of the Adler and Oppenheimer tannery showed, when industrialists from France and Alsace formed a consortium to take over German assets, property transfers went more smoothly than when they acted alone, because lone wolves drew denunciation and envy. The Adlers and Oppenheimers, owners of the largest and most modern tannery in Alsace, continued to operate their factory even after the takeover of Strasbourg by French troops. In part, this was because the new administration struggled to find a sequestering agent for this large company, which employed over two thousand workers and made up an entire neighborhood in the Strasbourg suburb of Lingolsheim. Disrupting the plant's production by removing its management threatened to throw the entire neighborhood into unemployment at a time when the French administration was highly sensitive to the threat of revolutionary turmoil and wanted to retain its popularity among Alsatians. The meeting of the Adler and Oppenheimer shareholders took place as planned three days after the sovereignty change. What the shareholders did not know at the time was that the meeting in November 1918 was to be their final session in Alsace.

After a three-year hiatus, the next business report, dated 1921, rendered the intensity of the changes of November 1918 in the usual terse style of annual reports, masking the enormous losses the company had to write down as a result of the French administration's decision to expropriate and expel the two families. "A few days after the shareholders' meeting [in November 1918], the French military administration requisitioned our entire leather stock. We were forced to transport huge quantities of leather into Northern France. Then, on January 2, 1919, the French army placed our entire Alsatian property under forced administration. . . . In January of the following year the French justice administration sold our factory to a group of French investors."[69] This report confirmed the victimhood narratives that were characteristic of memoirs by expellees from all over Central Europe, including Alsace and Transylvania.[70] Left out of the account, however, were the two families' activities between January 1919 and January 1920 and their attempts to obtain special favors from the French administration.

How did the Adlers and Oppenheimers manage to remain in the Alsatian capital when most Germans had already been expelled? While the company's decimated archives remain silent on this question, the files of the interim French administration in Alsace, the Commissariat General, show the intense negotiations between French investors and the Adlers and Oppenheimers, who had actively assisted in the transfer of their tannery to French hands. The two families were ultimately able to remain in Alsace for more than a year after the armistice, before they were finally expelled under more favorable conditions than the majority of Germans in March 1920. By that time, the Franco-German agreement on the personal belongings and furniture of expellees had come into force, allowing them to take with them all their movable assets, including a collection of paintings by Dutch masters. This was in sharp contrast with the majority of Germans, who had to make do with a single package weighing a maximum of ninety pounds.[71]

The expropriation of the Adler and Oppenheimer tannery started with a broad alliance of investors who formed a partnership in order to seize the tannery. The partnership was initiated by Ulysse Roux (1879–1957), a young tanner from a family of provincial industrialists and notables in the environs of Lyon.[72] Roux realized that the Adlers' and Oppenheimers' major Alsatian industry rivals, the Francophile Herrenschmidts, had to be included, along with the Weil family, which had been active in the leather business in both the Reichsland and France before 1914. Financing came from Strasbourg's Staehling and Valentin banking house.[73] The vice president of the city's chamber of commerce, the automobile manufacturer Émile Mathis, served as a connection to regional business elites and the administration; Mathis was a war profiteer who had helped the German administration procure foreign currency exchanges in Switzerland between 1916 and 1918.[74] Backed by this consortium, Roux approached High Commissioner Maringer and the sequestering agent Georges Schmoll, both of whom supported the transaction.[75]

The Adlers and Oppenheimers had considerable latitude in shaping their exit from Alsace, especially since they had known not only the Herrenschmidts but also Mathis and Schmoll for decades. Despite the religious and political differences between mostly Francophile Alsatian Jews and Germanophile immigrant Jews in the Reichsland period, the Adlers and Oppenheimers had worked with Schmoll to finance the Jewish Vocational School of Strasbourg in the 1900s.[76] Schmoll, a lawyer, had also been the head of the Lower Alsace Jewish Congregation before and during the First World War.

Despite his prominence during the Reichsland period, Schmoll developed good relations with the new sovereigns in part because he gave an enthusiastic speech to French troops in November 1918. He confirmed what the French wanted to hear when he exclaimed that "our Mother, France, has come for us. . . . The four years that we have spent in a bloody nightmare are thus over."[77] As Vicki Caron noted, however, "for all the jubilant rhetoric of Franco-Jewish patriotism in 1918 and 1919, the transition back to French rule was not entirely without obstacles."[78] Schmoll, for instance, had to actively assist in the purge of all prominent rabbis from the Reichsland period from Jewish consistories and witnessed the expulsion of four thousand German Jews, which reduced the numbers of the Strasbourg community alone by nine hundred.[79]

Eventually, the consortium led by Roux agreed to pay 32 million francs—less than two-thirds of its actual value—for the firm, which it renamed Tanneries de France. The firm's prewar assets totaled 46 million francs, while its wartime profits alone amounted to 26 million francs.[80] It is unknown how much, if anything, the consortium paid the Adlers and Oppenheimers.

The scant photographic and archival evidence on how expulsions took place in Alsace attests to the rapidity of the process: families carrying small bundles were loaded onto military trucks or marched to train stations by uniformed French soldiers (figure 5.2). The agency of the expelled rarely comes to the fore, let alone the participation of native Alsatians in the process of expropriation. Wealth often moderated the effect of ethnic discrimination, however, as German industrialists wielded more leverage than working- and middle-class Germans, and their presence in Alsace and Lorraine was deemed less problematic than that of "unruly" German workers and labor organizers.[81] The

FIGURE 5.2. French troops escort Strasbourg Germans to the Kehl train station, November 22, 1918. Source: Strasbourg Municipal Archives, AVES, 1 Fi 251.

local administration needed the Jacobis' and Adlers' cooperation in handing over their firms, and any delays or sabotage threatened production stoppages and the loss of the incoming administration's legitimacy. Paradoxically, these controversial business transactions surrounding the partition of German industrial property created bonds of complicity between the French regime and native Alsatian and French businessmen that ultimately contributed to the consolidation of the Third Republic in the region; unsurprisingly, as the Maison Rouge affair reveals, few of the parties showed any interest in a judicious examination of this "dubious era" of Alsatian history.

Transylvania's Hungarian and German Industrialists Face Transition

While the Maison Rouge affair and the expropriation of the Adlers and Oppenheimers were ongoing, the owners of Transylvania's largest tannery, the

Renners, were planning their firm's expansion despite the collapse of Austria-Hungary and the onset of Romanian rule.[82] Furthermore, a full year after the Romanian annexation of Transylvania, the headquarters of the Renner tannery, one of the larger factories in the region, could still remain in Budapest, Hungary. The Budapest banker Pál Engel, who continued to sit on the tannery's board of directors, noted in August 1919 from the comfort of his Budapest office that "we do not think that any change in the composition of the directorial and supervisory boards is necessary. If the political situation in Cluj makes it pressing, however, we do not object to filling the directorial position with an adequate [ethnic Romanian] person."[83] Yet, as Engel predicted, no such change was necessary until 1921, and even then it amounted to token representation. The Renner family's success in retaining its wealth was not unique to their business or to Transylvania but stood for the continuity of Austro-Hungarian industrialists and bankers in successor states.[84] The period between October 1918 and August 1919 produced disruptions in production and trade and ushered in the Romanian takeover of the region, yet Transylvania's business elites remained the same.

The reasons for their remarkable endurance stemmed from the sheer demographic and economic weight of ethnic minorities in the region, the interethnic solidarity of the Romanian and Hungarian middle class and bourgeoisie against an increasingly powerful labor movement and Romanian "intruders" from pre-1914 Romania. Transylvania's uncertain future also prevented the Romanian government from initiating sweeping changes between 1918 and 1920, as France and the peace conference warned against large-scale ethnic discrimination. While the French army assisted in the expropriation and expulsion of German minorities in the former Reichsland, it struggled to maintain the economic status quo in East-Central Europe as the region descended into chaos in October and November 1918.

In Transylvania, the period of chaotic looting in October and November 1918 was followed by fragile stabilization via the competition but also cooperation of Hungarian and Romanian local executive units, the national councils that had a shared interest in restoring order despite their sharply divergent politics. The rule of national councils gave way to a Romanian regional administration, the Directing Council, after the Romanian army gradually occupied most of the region by December 1918, upending the Budapest government's remaining hold over Transylvania and the rule of the Hungarian national councils. The population of the territories that Romania annexed from Hungary alone amounted to over five million people, rivaling prewar Romania's population of seven million, a fact that gave Transylvania and its industrialists considerable leverage within the new, primarily agrarian state. The sheer number of non-Romanians in the region, over two million people, also made mass expulsions like those in Alsace and Lorraine extremely difficult. Hungarians, Germans, and Jews made up four out of five town dwellers in the region and owned around 90 percent of stock-exchange, mining, and industrial companies, making compromises between the new sovereign and propertied elites all the more appealing.[85] Rather than a "changing of the guard," imperial collapse and sovereignty change led to the integration of the Romanian political and banking elite with the pre-1918 Austro-Hungarian networks of bankers and industrialists who had preserved their assets and importance despite the collapse of the Dual Monarchy.[86]

The prolonged period of transition and uncertainty from Austro-Hungarian rule to that of successor states in East-Central Europe also meant that a quick military "solution" to tilt the ownership of private property from Hungarians, Germans, and Jews to Czechs, Romanians, and South-Slavs was not a viable option. The French Eastern Army marched north from Salonica in 1918, and by the time the Central Powers collapsed, France was the only major power with a military force in Southeastern and East-Central Europe, as East-Central and Southeastern European states scrambled to organize or reorganize their armies.[87] The French army's presence thus preceded and surpassed the deployment of Czechoslovak and Romanian troops against Hungarian territories, giving the French unique leverage, even as the upcoming month showed that the French army was unable to influence the considerably more powerful armies of successor states; only eight out of forty-five divisions active in Southeastern Europe were French, and even these were looking forward to demobilization.[88] At this stage, however, the weakness of the French army remained hidden from the Hungarian and Romanian leadership.

As both Hungary and Romania expected France to draw a fair border in Transylvania, the presence of the French army ushered in a period of Francophilia as intellectuals and politicians tried to forge connections between France and Transylvania and "translate" their territorial demands to French references, claiming, for instance, that the "Tisza river is our Rhine" as justification for the westward extension of Romania's borders.[89] References to Alsace-Lorraine proliferated as a means of undergirding a variety of Hungarian and German territorial ambitions. These demands included the autonomy of the Banat, or Hungarian sovereignty over Transylvania. One particular map "explained" that the Szekler Land in Transylvania was comparable in size to Alsace-Lorraine, implying that the Szekler Land also had the right to belong to its "mother country," which was Hungary and not Romania. Another memorandum that reached the peace conference from self-proclaimed representatives of Banat Germans, who were in fact part of the regional Hungarian elite before 1918, referred to these populations as "Alsace-Lorrainer inhabitants" of the Banat and Vojvodina. The signatories demanded the formation of a Banat Republic and noted that the "Alsace-Lorraine emigrants" of the Banat "put all their trust in the justness of the Allies and hope that the great and generous France will not forget her children who had emigrated to far-off Hungary as the pioneers of civilization"; this new republic was also to serve as the granary of the Austrian republic, thus boosting Austria's economic viability and preventing an Anschluss to Germany (figure 5.3).[90] The Hungarian government commissioner to Oradea, Péter Ágoston, also tried to convince French general Henri Mathias Berthelot of the inherent connection between France and Transylvania by pointing to his own mother, whose family had immigrated to the Banat from Lorraine a century earlier. In the meantime, Ágoston's wife, the noted feminist Auguszta Buzárovits, organized a lecture series with writer Béla Zsolt on the Gallic [French] spirit; Zsolt also told a newspaper that the new Hungarian generation was Francophile and anti-German.[91] The wealthiest city in the Banat, Timișoara, came under French occupation by early 1919, prompting its chamber of commerce to organize a shopping trip to France with help

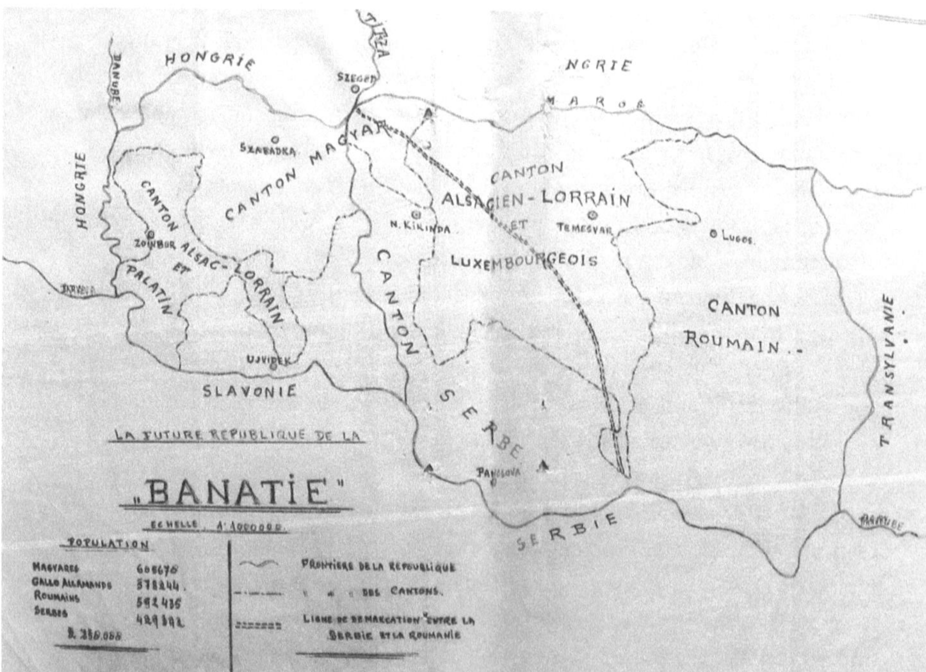

FIGURE 5.3. The proposed "Alsatian-Lorraine canton" of Banat. Source: Bódy, "A semleges, független Bánát," c. Momentum Trianon 100.

from the French military in order to procure industrial equipment and sell local goods. Although the trip did not ultimately materialize (the Serbian troops who were temporarily occupying the city looted merchants' stocks before the delegation set out), it reveals the extent to which the French military presence in East-Central Europe went hand in hand with market expansion.[92] The time thus seemed ripe to supplant Austria's and Germany's long-standing economic domination of the region.

As regards Transylvania and the rest of Hungary, Clemenceau's goal for the peace conference was to obtain a free hand for France to draw the final borders as it saw fit, an idea that rested on the assumption that Romania would accept France's plans for reconstruction.[93] However, the actions of the French army and government in East-Central Europe generated mistrust in the Romanian administration and prompted it to act on its own, especially as France was reluctant to confirm the Allies' 1916 territorial promises to Romania given the country's separate peace with the Central Powers in 1918, which released the Allies from their 1916 obligations.[94] The French general Louis Franchet d'Espèrey made the revolutionary government of the Hungarian count Mihály Károlyi sign an ad hoc armistice on November 13, 1918, that disregarded ethnic boundaries and left most of Transylvania and its Romanian population under the rule of Budapest. Unbeknownst to d'Espèrey, Romania had rejoined the Allies only three days earlier and was not invited to the armistice negotiations.[95] Little wonder, then, that Bucharest did not acknowledge the Belgrade armistice and applied the same tactic that France was pursuing in Alsace and Lorraine as it aimed to make the occupation of Transylvania a fait accompli by the time the peace conference started.[96]

In the meantime, d'Espèrey designated the Strasbourg-born optant to France after the Franco-Prussian War, Lieutenant Colonel Fernand Vix, to prepare for the French occupation of Budapest and serve as the French government's liaison to the Hungarian government. The Alsatian connection proved useful as Vix spoke German and could thus communicate directly with the germanophone Hungarian administration.[97] While the French army ultimately lacked the forces needed to occupy Budapest, let alone Transylvania, Vix remained the main channel of communication between the peace conference and the Hungarian government until March 1919. Károlyi was unaware of French and American reluctance to intervene militarily in East-Central Europe to defend the principle of national self-determination, and so complied with the increasingly radical territorial demands of the peace conference, including withdrawal of the disintegrated Hungarian army from Transylvania, in hopes that these measures would be temporary and Hungary would eventually receive Wilsonian peace terms.[98]

The period between mid-November 1918 and August 1919 brought about a series of conflicts among the French, Hungarian, and Romanian governments in which the French generals Paul Henry, d'Espèrey, and even Clemenceau tacitly sided with the Károlyi government as Romanian troops violated d'Espèrey's armistice terms and gradually occupied Transylvania despite repeated French protests,[99] while General Berthelot emerged as the major supporter of Romanian aspirations in Transylvania. Berthelot's activity showed the disunity of the French military, the civilian-military split, and the inability of the French government to effectively control and micromanage events and its own troops in East-Central Europe.

Apart from his personal sympathy toward Romanian politicians like Premier Ion I. C. Brătianu, whom he had developed as the adviser to the Romanian army between 1916 and 1918, Berthelot had two main motivations.[100] As commander of the French Danube Army in charge of aiding the Whites against the Bolsheviks, he knew all too well that the recovery of French investments in Bolshevik Russia was only possible with the aid of Romania, a formerly small state on the periphery of three defunct empires that had suddenly acquired key strategic importance on the southern front of the Russian civil war. Berthelot also wanted to make Greater Romania indebted to France for the annexation of Transylvania, and to simultaneously economically exploit the Romanian alliance. As he explained in January 1919, "In Greater Romania we could have the nicest French colony in the world."[101] Berthelot personally spearheaded economic "colonization" as he took over the Transylvanian castle of the onetime aspirant to the Albanian throne and noted paleontologist, Baron Ferenc Nopcsa, who had relocated to Hungary.[102]

To the dismay of Henrys, d'Espèrey, and Clemenceau, Berthelot allowed the Transylvania-born Romanian general Traian Moșoiu to violate the Belgrade armistice line and push toward the center of the region on December 12, 1918, occupying Cluj on Christmas Eve.[103] Cluj had emerged as the hub of the Károlyi government at the end of October 1918 even as the rule of the Budapest administration had gradually shrunk to the city limits as the administration collapsed in the Transylvanian countryside. Hungarian and Romanian national councils sprung up in most localities; in this period of political and economic crisis, national councils attempted to rein in chaos and provide food supplies, often in cooperation with each other despite their divergent views on the future of Transylvania.[104] The director of the Renner tannery, Mózes Farkas, became the Cluj leader of the Civic Radical Party of Oszkár Jászi, the Left-liberal nationalities minister of the Károlyi regime, and worked closely with trade unions to ensure the continuity of commerce. By December 1918, hostility between Hungarian and Romanian national councils and violent clashes between the Romanian army and Hungarian troops were common.[105] This rising tide of conflict stemmed from uncertainty over the future of the region and the inability of the French government to curb the advancing Romanian army.

On December 1, 1918, the Alba Iulia assembly of Transylvania's Romanians declared the region's unification with Romania. The Alba Iulia assembly also nominated a regional government for Transylvania, the Directing Council, composed of the leaders of the Romanian National Party and three Transylvanian Romanian social democrats.[106] Three of its members, Alexandru Vaida-Voevod, Ștefan Cicio-Pop, and Vasile Goldiș, also became part of the Romanian government in Bucharest. This ended the period of compromises between various national councils, ushering in a year of protracted transition.[107]

Unlike the reception of French troops in Alsace and Lorraine, the Romanian administration encountered sizable resistance in Transylvania's mostly Hungarian- and German-populated towns and among their business communities. Romanian occupying forces also had to remain cautious because Bucharest had failed to secure Allied approval of its territorial demands.[108] Large-scale discrimination against Hungarians, Germans, and Jews in the form of expulsions would have imperiled the efforts of the Romanian peace delegation in Paris, which presented Romanian sovereignty as an alternative to the purportedly oppressive rule of Hungarians over Transylvania; while the regional police prefect of Cluj did issue mass expulsion orders, these were never implemented.[109]

There were practical reasons as well that enabled Transylvania's ethnic minority business elites to retain their possessions. Apart from the lack of Romanian capital, concerns about stopping industrial production and the threat of massive unemployment cautioned the new administration against embarking on sweeping changes, similar to the pressures on the French administration in Alsace and Lorraine to maintain production even at the cost of condoning deals with Germans. Massive strikes in the Jiu valley also called for caution. In January 1919, the firing of office workers and the forced appointment of Romanians led to a wave of strikes that also slowed down the movement of Romanian troops, which depended on the availability of coal and railway personnel.[110] Miners resented censorship and curfews and disobeyed inexperienced new managers; they were also afraid that the autocratic Romanian monarchy would roll back the rights they had gained during the First World War and the revolutionary period.[111] The Romanian army's brutal retaliation against strikers backfired as it led to a general strike in Transylvania of eighty thousand workers, including railway operators.[112]

Resistance to Romanianization by the workers' movement and repeated warnings by the peace conference put an end to attempts to seize control of large industrial companies and prompted the Romanian occupying authorities to seek a compromise with the Budapest firms and banks that owned them.[113] Furthermore, as the example of the Renner tannery showed, the new administration attempted to recruit ethnic minority firms to supply Transylvania without asking for any participation in these companies in return. As an early sign of cooperation between prewar trade experts and the new administration, the Directing Council allowed the Cluj Chamber of Commerce to delegate industrialists to accompany its officials to Austria in order to purchase raw materials. The Hungarian István Tamási, one of the leaders of the chamber, was immediately hired as the representative of industry affairs in the new Romanian administration.[114] While the Renner tannery was still supplying leather to the Austro-Hungarian army in the fall of 1918, by July 1919, the Romanian Directing Council had commissioned the company to organize all of Transylvania's supply of tannin, a substance used for leather production, prompting Farkas to reactivate the tannery's wartime supply chains in Austria and Switzerland.[115]

Between December 1918 and November 1919, cooperation between the Romanian administration and Hungarian industrialists like Farkas went relatively smoothly despite their political differences and interethnic strife. Unlike in Alsace and Lorraine, where the top administrators sent from France and their German predecessors had nothing in common except decades of enmity, in Transylvania the Directing Council was recruited from the region's prewar Romanian political elite, which had personal ties to the former Hungarian administration, chamber of commerce, and industrialists.[116]

The Romanian government's conscious policy of conquering Transylvania despite warnings by the peace conference was effective but precipitated the Bolsheviks' rise to power in Hungary, which was yet another indication that Transylvania's fate deeply influenced the fate of post-1918 Hungary. The peace conference was reduced to the role of a mere spectator as events unfolded, and its priority was to prevent a local war. When on March 20, 1919, Vix ordered the obedient Károlyi to evacuate Hungarian-populated territories west of Transylvania in light of yet another advance by the Romanian army, Károlyi's pro-Allied stance lost its legitimacy. The count resigned, leaving the communists around the Transylvanian clerk turned ambitious revolutionary Béla Kun the only political force capable of filling the political vacuum and standing up to the invaders. Many men signed up to the Bolshevik army for patriotic reasons, in defense of Hungary's territorial integrity rather than as an expression of leftist political convictions. Yet the panic sparked by the "Bolshevik menace" in Paris allowed Romania to come in from the cold and rekindle its ties with France by posing as Hungary's liberator from communism, thus legitimating the Romanian army's occupation of Transylvania and other Hungarian territories.[117] Kun's takeover also persuaded the peace conference to grant Romania the north–south railway line between Timișoara and Satu Mare, which was of strategic importance in the anti-Bolshevik fight in Poland and Ukraine, even though these cities had a majority non-Romanian population.[118]

After a brief Romanian-Hungarian war between April and August 1919, Romanian troops defeated Kun's Red Army and occupied Budapest. Because the solidification of Romanian rule in Transylvania now seemed inevitable, Hungarian and German industrialists sought to strike long-term deals with the Romanian Directing Council. The protracted transition period and war undermined the security of private property in the region, and it was not a foregone conclusion that Transylvania's business elite would be spared by the Romanian government in light of popular mobilization against the bourgeoisie by the Kun regime and the impatience of the general population with "war profiteers." Millions of returning soldiers had expectations of a more equitable distribution of land. In Transylvania, in order to cement Romanian legitimacy at the expense of ethnic minority landowners, Bucharest instead carried out one of the most thorough expropriations of agricultural estates in postwar Europe.[119] On the territory of prewar Romania, these expropriations undermined the political base of the pro-German conservative party, which drew its support from owners of large estates.[120] In Transylvania, it was Hungarian aristocrats, gentry, and churches as well as Saxon communities that lost the most owing to the land expropriations, although the actual distribution of land took years and many landowners managed to retain at least part of their assets.[121]

The Romanian national liberals who dominated governments after 1918 were unwilling to provide blanket guarantees of private property rights as these limited the scope of their long-term plans to create a self-sufficient economy run by Romanians without the participation of foreign investors and domestic ethnic minorities.[122] Premier Brătianu noted that "this principle [of private property] should not on any account be stipulated in the [new] Constitution, and be in contradiction with the interests of social development."[123] Eventually, article 17 maintained that private property rights were "guaranteed" but nevertheless sanctioned the lawfulness of "expropriation" for "public utility," effectively undermining these guarantees.[124]

In the aftermath of the 1918 armistice, the Directing Council and the Bucharest government pursued two strategies for industrial property in the annexed territories. First, they attempted to take natural resources, especially oil, into state ownership; and second, they promoted loyal bankers and politicians to the boards of foreign companies and those owned by ethnic minorities in annexed territories.[125] The first strategy encountered opposition as early as

1919 from France, which wanted a share in German-owned oil wealth. Viennese and Budapest business elites who were reluctant to surrender their assets also mobilized their connections in Western European states; the result was a compromise that allowed Western European states to take over German oil interests in Romania in conjunction with Romanian businessmen while allowing Budapest firms to dominate Transylvania's factories through newly formed Romanian corporations. Highlighting France's influence over Romania, the Bucharest minister of industry and commerce's 1919 order on the forced state administration of all foreign stock-exchange companies was never implemented owing to repeated French protests against such initiatives. French diplomats feared that French bankers and corporations would be left out of the redistribution of enemy assets if Romania proceeded to sequester foreign companies.[126]

The second attempt to gain control over Transylvanian industrial companies was subtler than expropriation and involved concerted pressure on industrialists to "nationalize" their companies. Unlike after 1945, in the aftermath of the First World War nationalization did not denote taking private property into state ownership. Instead, it referred to the incorporation of Austrian and Hungarian firms as Romanian ones and the inclusion of Romanian politicians or banks on the boards of directors of the region's corporations. "Nationalization" was used interchangeably with "Romanianization," although the latter term only became widespread during the 1930s and 1940s in campaigns against Jewish presence in economic and social life.[127] The ambiguity of the meaning of nationalization also stemmed from the uncertain boundaries of Romanianness in Transylvania. Official correspondence used the term "foreigner" (*străin*) to denote both foreign citizens and domestic minorities, while some politicians from prewar Romania, such as Nicolae Iorga, regarded even Transylvania's Greek Catholic Romanian elite, led by Iuliu Maniu, as profoundly Magyarized.[128]

After the solidification of Romanian rule over the region, municipal, regional, and national administrators and politicians approached key firms and tried to promote themselves to lucrative positions within these companies. Nationalization involved coercion that was difficult to document since officials rarely left a paper trail. In the Banat, however, the local national liberal leader, Iancu Conciatu, provided numerous traces.[129] Born in the small Romanian-populated village of Bozovici in the Banat, Conciatu graduated from a commercial school in Brașov, where he picked up German. Soon after graduation and before the outbreak of the First World War, he left for Romania to work as a bank accountant and returned to Transylvania in Romanian uniform in 1916 as an agent in the army's counterintelligence service.[130] Despite the fact that the Romanian troops were pushed back in a matter of months, his wartime merits earned him the position of government commissioner to the Banat in 1918. As the Ministry of Commerce and Industry's delegate to the Timișoara German- and Hungarian-dominated Chamber of Commerce, he warned industrialists to "adapt" to the new circumstances and reorient their companies from Hungarian to Romanian markets. He openly warned the city's industrialists not to lose this "trust extended by [the administration]." Industrialists got his message, and soon after at least three banks and corporations employed Conciatu himself on their boards.[131]

Romanian lobbyists well versed in the complex hierarchies of the regional, municipal, and national administrations offered more help to Transylvanian companies than did national courts or petitions at the League of Nations. Nearly every part of the production process required passes from the administration, each of which in turn required interventions from well-placed lobbyists. For instance, the transportation of raw materials and finished products depended on the availability of passes from the Directing Council, the army, and the ministry; the shareholders' meeting had to be approved by the commander of the local garrison; capital increases, a routine exercise for shareholders' meetings before 1914, required the approval of the Ministry of Commerce and Industry in Bucharest (which involved a lengthy train trip to the capital that took at least a day).[132] It took a brief telegram or letter from the mayor of the town—the prefect, who was the top government official of cities and counties—or a parliamentary deputy to obtain these passes. The admissions of lawyer Dénes Popp and bank director German Laurean to the board of the Cluj Chamber of Commerce helped the chamber avoid requisition by the army and provided direct access to the Romanian administration.[133] Cooperation between business elites and politicians thus lowered transaction costs and bought autonomy from state interference, even as the need to bribe officials and satisfy rent-seeking state institutions decreased companies' profitability.

By the early 1920s, nationalization had become an official Romanian government policy under the supervision of a commissioner.[134] Yet a contemporary investors' handbook from 1924, which offered a comprehensive overview of more than seventy key industrial companies, showed that Hungarian investors, banks, and executives remained dominant in Transylvania.[135] This handbook was not exhaustive, since it omitted heavy industries and mines and other companies whose formal ties to Budapest had ceased; yet even so, the prewar business elites of Hungary and Transylvania remained dominant. These omissions reflected the complex and confusing changes of headquarters, board members, and shareholders that perplexed even contemporary economists. Otherwise, the list accurately mapped the financial and social networks of business elites as it listed even small companies, breweries, mills, and electrical companies as well as large cement works, tanneries, and textile works with over one thousand employees.[136]

Some common trends emerge. Between 1919 and the early 1920s, most Transylvanian firms were legally incorporated as Romanian entities, took a Romanian name, and moved their headquarters from Budapest to Transylvania. Furthermore, three out of four companies had at least one newly appointed Romanian politician or banker on their boards of directors or their supervisory boards. Similar patterns characterized the transformation of the boards of Hungarian companies in Czechoslovakia and Yugoslavia, pointing to comparable patterns of "nationalization" after 1918.[137] Finally, Romanian banks close to the National Liberal Party, primarily the Banca Marmorosch and Blank (BMMB), emerged as minor shareholders or creditors, supplanting Budapest banks. Yet the BMMB itself was partially owned by the Pest Hungarian Commercial Bank, and thus its increased participation in the Transylvanian economy did not amount to Romanianization.

While nationalization was a success on paper, its real outcome was a compromise that benefited ethnic minority industrialists, Romanian elites, and the nationalizing state alike. The situation of ethnic minority business elites was explicitly favorable when compared with the expropriation of German industrialists in Alsace and Lorraine, or that of German optants who had left Poland after 1918, let alone that of expropriated landowners in East-Central Europe more generally.[138] The management of banks and industrial companies remained exclusively in the hands of the region's prewar business elites, and Romanian politicians gained only token representation and a modest number of shares. In the meantime, the new investment banks funded by the Transylvanian Romanian bourgeoisie after 1919 had a smaller network of affiliated companies than historical Budapest banks like the Anglo-Hungarian Bank.

Transylvanian industrialists emerged from the change in sovereignty relatively unscathed and rarely took the fate of their firms in Romania to domestic or international courts. This was in sharp contrast to the confrontational strategy of expropriated landowners, who spent fortunes on litigation and petitions to the Romanian-Hungarian Mixed Arbitral Tribunal or the minorities section of the League of Nations seeking compensation for their estates until the Second World War.[139] The coercive transactions that accompanied the inclusion of Romanian members on the boards of these companies were more difficult to prove and document than land seizures, which also explains why such incidents did not reach the public or courts.[140] In addition, a modus vivendi between Transylvanian industrialists and the new state administration was fostered by the fact that the two parties were locked in "a situation of mutual hostages."[141] The Romanian political elite needed the extra income from industrial companies and was unable to initiate a full overhaul owing to the lack of Romanian capital or a class of Romanian professionals to replace technocrats recruited from among ethnic minorities, while the prewar business elites had to rely on the services of Romanian officials and lobbyists. Pre-1918 ties between the Hungarian and Romanian elites and the middle class also survived the violent period of transition with remarkable success, and this class-based interethnic solidarity also enabled continuities in business life. The outcome was a compromise that left most industrialists of the former Austria-Hungary in place. The inclusion of Romanian politicians like Conciatu, Emil Hațieganu, and Gheorghe Tătărescu on the boards of banks and corporations owned by Transylvania's German, Hungarian, and Jewish businesses exemplified a coercive state-business relationship in Greater Romania. But after "giving to Caesar what belonged to Caesar" in the new state, businesses enjoyed relative autonomy to operate as they saw fit. While the Romanian state pursued nationalization more thoroughly than its predecessor, the Hungarian kingdom, the inclusion of politicians on the boards of industrial companies was already widespread before 1918 and thus did not represent a rupture in terms of how these companies operated.[142]

Official discrimination and coercive business transactions in "liberated" territories in the shadow of the peace treaties showed that successor states were unable to stop the erosion of private property rights unleashed by belligerents between 1914 and 1918. Unlike during the wave of nationalizations that followed the Second World War, it was not primarily state treasuries and the public that benefited but local elites who were able to act with relative autonomy and with impunity to seize assets and lucrative corporate positions on the cheap. While women were crucial players in the war economy as workers, shop managers, and labor organizers—and in Alsace, even as factory founders—this post-armistice maneuvering was almost exclusively the province of men, reflecting the reversal of even the modest advances women had enjoyed during the First World War.[143]

Given that the minority rights treaties were often sabotaged on the ground and that the nationalist and antisemitic rhetoric of East-Central European states often surpassed that of France, it is more fruitful to look at what successor states did rather than what they said when comparing the fates of ethnic minorities in Western Europe with those in East-Central Europe. East-Central Europe's ethnic minorities fared better than their counterparts in France, yet this was hardly proof of conciliatory attitudes on the part of successor states.

Because the relationship between the Allied Great Powers and their East-Central European allies remained massively hierarchical, states such as Greater Romania, Poland, or the Kingdom of Serbs, Croats, and Slovenes grudgingly accepted the minority rights treaties, although this did not prevent them from engaging in policies that discriminated against ethnic minorities or wielding nationalist rhetoric on par with or even more strident than anti-German mobilization in France. Furthermore, in East-Central Europe, hostile practices that targeted ethnic minorities moved from national policies to the level of local societies, where they flew under the radar of the League of Nations.[144] In other cases, they were camouflaged as economic policies pertaining to all citizens that nonetheless overwhelmingly targeted ethnic minorities, such as the land reform, the valorization of war bonds, or the nationalization of church and state schools and universities.[145]

Ethnic minorities and especially industrialists in East-Central Europe did far better for themselves than their Alsatian and Lorrainer counterparts after 1918 primarily for reasons other than protection by international law, which only became operational in the early 1920s. Rather, the protracted process of sovereignty change and the limited resources of successor states in the region played a major part as they allowed pre-1918 business elites to maneuver and retain their positions. The industrialists of the defunct Austria-Hungary simply had greater latitude to salvage their assets since governments like that of Greater Romania depended on their services. The sheer demographic and economic weight of ethnic minorities in East-Central Europe was also a factor in their continuity.[146] Unlike in Alsace and Lorraine, where wealthy local and French investors "queued up" to take over German property, there was neither capital nor an alternative business class in Greater Romania. Bohemia was a partial exception given that the powerful Czech banks of Prague managed to "nostrify" many Austro-German assets; yet in Slovakia, the prewar owners of industrial companies managed to retain their positions after the armistice, not unlike the situation in Vojvodina.[147]

While entire societies shouldered the burden of the First World War, it was not the treasuries of victorious states or their citizenry in general but a small circle of individuals who profited at the end of the conflagration, as states privatized the fruits of their victory. Even though ethnic minorities often appear as collective victims of the Versailles settlement, class and wealth often moderated the negative impact of sovereignty change; and especially in the former Dual Monarchy, the defunct empire's business elite paradoxically became key for the stabilization of new states, complicating the binary of minorities and majorities, oppressors and the oppressed. Industrialists like Farkas were coerced into cooperation with new regimes in Greater Romania in order to retain their factories, which led them into a no-man's-land as they became both the beneficiaries and the victims of new regimes that were otherwise far from popular. Continuities in the social positions of ethnic minorities in East-Central Europe went hand in hand with the ossification of hierarchical societies despite expectations to the contrary during and after the First World War, as "national" governments shied away from and were unable to initiate large-scale social and economic transformations. Necessarily, this bred enormous discontent among ordinary Romanians, whose sentiments were increasingly captured by the nascent extreme right. Yet instead of targeting the Romanian political elite that sabotaged the social mission of unification, the anger of the "new generation" of the ultraright was directed at Jews, Hungarians, and Germans.

Chapter 6

France's East-Central European "Empire" after Versailles

The Hotel National was one of Geneva's most luxurious hotels in the early twentieth century, with a "fine view of the Lake and the Mont Blanc."[1] It was a natural choice for Eric Drummond and Jean Monnet, who designated it as the headquarters of the Secretariat of the League of Nations, which started operations in November 1920 and handled numerous property disputes involving the former Central Powers over the next two decades. Ironically, the hotel had already served as a venue for negotiations on the fate of German and Austro-Hungarian property before the league was formed, playing host to meetings between industrialists and bankers from the former Austro-Hungarian Monarchy and their French and Swiss counterparts. The Budapest banker Henrik Fellner established his temporary office in the Hotel National in September 1919 as he attempted to sell the Transylvanian mines financed by the Pest Hungarian Commercial Bank (PHCB), one of the defunct Austro-Hungarian empire's largest investment banks. Fellner rightly feared that many of his bank's mines, railroads, municipal loans, and other assets in successor states would be subject to expropriation.[2] The ease with which Fellner conducted his negotiations contrasted sharply with the plight of the German heavy industrialists in Lorraine, who had been expropriated and expelled by the French army a few months after the November 1918 armistice; at home, meanwhile, they faced the ire of workers' councils that subjected even one of the wealthiest of their number, August Thyssen, to an unpleasant interrogation.[3]

French investors and the Paris government were active in Alsace, Lorraine, and East-Central Europe in order to replace the Russian alliance and investments in Russia with military, diplomatic, and economic ties that were designed to keep Germany in check on its eastern and western borders. Contrasting these two different settings for French economic expansion reveals why the political context of expansion mattered, leaving Alsatian and Lorrainer German industrialists less room to maneuver to counter French expansion than their Eastern European counterparts. As the French government involved regional industrialists in the distribution of German property in Alsace and Lorraine, there was no serious pushback against French economic policies after 1918 in the former Reichsland, even as these measures fueled regionalism from the mid-1920s onward.[4]

Like in the French mandates of Syria and Lebanon, the Paris government's policies in Eastern Europe were "schizophrenic" and contradictory.[5] Unlike Germany's unveiled economic imperialism in the region during the First World War, French governments had to tread more carefully in East-Central Europe as they wielded less power in the former Austro-Hungarian empire than in their mandates and the colonies. France resorted to the language of alliance between equal parties while simultaneously promoting French economic interests, which led to an ambivalent reception by the Little Entente, France's regional allies. The Paris government's reliance on capital from French industrialists rather than its own coffers to further economic imperialism also plagued its Eastern European plans from the outset because it was often corporations rather than diplomats that gained the upper hand.[6] What the Paris government was able to do in East-Central Europe, however, was to frustrate attempts by successor states to copy its policies of expropriation and expulsion of Germans in Alsace and Lorraine. In Transylvania, rival French and Romanian economic imperialisms created a deadlock that allowed for maneuvering by the industrialists of the former Austria-Hungary to defend their property. While these patterns are visible in retrospect, contemporaries, including industrialists themselves, experienced the years between 1918 and 1920 as an era of profound uncertainty, which left even Keynes pondering whether the aftermath of the Great War would destroy the bourgeoisie of the German and Austro-Hungarian empires.[7]

With all its contradictions, the saga of French economic expansion in Central and East-Central Europe opens a window on the "economic consequences of the peace": it shows that moving borders did not automatically obliterate Austro-Hungarian and German financial networks, supply chains, and commercial routes even as the two empires vanished from the map; replacing them with alternative French air routes, railway lines, and corporations proved a difficult challenge. The scramble for steel plants and coal mines also attests to the long shadow of the First World War in terms of the importance states placed on securing resources for national defense.

While the expropriations initiated by the Bolsheviks in Russia and Hungary are well known, synchronous attempts by capitalist states such as France or Greater Romania that succeeded Germany and Austria-Hungary are less commonly explored, yet they point to the continuing erosion of property rights and the exposure of economic elites to state policies after 1918.[8] Between 1914 and 1918, governments learned that the ownership of strategic natural resources like coal, steel, and oil was better left in the hands of loyal economic elites than in the hands of free markets. In East-Central Europe, states reached similar conclusions regarding landed property as land expropriation and redistribution became a tool in the stabilization of popular support behind new regimes.[9] Assets of strategic importance received more attention from France and other successor states than smaller and midsize industrial companies, which either were seized by apt speculators, as in Alsace and Lorraine, or remained in the hands of their pre-1918 owners, as in the case of most East-Central European businesses owned by ethnic minorities.[10]

France unexpectedly emerged as a hegemon over Central Europe in November 1918, a role for which it was financially unprepared.[11] Its position as a great power after 1918 was the inverse of that of the United States. While the US administration had the economic means to establish hegemony over Europe, President Woodrow Wilson was unable to exploit this advantage to force a Wilsonian peace on the continent and also left unexploited the opportunity to create an "irresistible" US "market empire" in Europe.[12] France, meanwhile, embraced an imperialist agenda of hegemony over Central and Eastern Europe even as its economy was roiled by a profound crisis and its banks remained cash-strapped.[13] Despite its economic woes, Paris was able to act as a hegemon because its industrial companies (like the Schneider-Creusot metallurgy conglomerate) emerged enriched and enlarged from the First World War, while none of the other victorious powers were interested in competing with its plans for peaceful economic expansion in Central Europe.[14] The United Kingdom focused its imperial ambitions on the naval clauses of the peace treaties and its colonial empire, weakened by mutiny, civil war, and calls for colonial autonomy during the Great War, and it was interested in the stabilization of the region, including vanquished states, rather than favoring former Entente allies.[15] Italy had no standing army in the region and no team of experts dedicated to preparing East-Central European peace terms. It was unable to provide substantial economic and diplomatic support to successor states, and the fascist regime that eventually rose to power sided with the vanquished instead of building an East-Central European economic "empire."[16]

France, meanwhile, presided over the Allied forces in Southeastern Europe and acted as the convener of and most active power at the Paris peace conference; it continued to assume the preeminent role among the Western Powers in the region throughout the 1920s.[17] At the same time, the reluctance of the United States and Great Britain to continue to prop up France economically and maintain the wartime agenda of Allied economic cooperation after 1919 also prompted Paris to tighten its economic relations with new states in Central and East-Central Europe.[18]

France had several reasons to focus its agenda of economic and political expansion on the former Mitteleuropa. In many respects, the region's geopolitical and economic potential for France surpassed that of the French colonies in the aftermath of the 1918 armistices.[19] Especially until 1920, French diplomats attempted to support states such as Greater Romania, Poland, and Czechoslovakia in order to recruit them to fight Bolshevik Russia.[20] Later, Paris supported their territorial ambitions with the goal of forming a cordon sanitaire of allied states in order to keep Germany in check from the east and isolate it from the Soviet Union.[21] Diplomatic hegemony over Europe also bolstered French national identity after a war that had almost crushed it, painfully revealing its dependence on the United Kingdom, the United States, and its colonies.[22] Cultural ties between East-Central European states and France also flourished through an extensive network of language teachers and French institutes that facilitated exchanges of students and professors, serving as reminders of France's presence in the region.[23] Ties between France and Romania were especially strong; frequent references to "Romance" solidarity against German expansion and similarities in languages and cultures helped bridge political differences between the democratic French republic and the Romanian monarchy.[24]

While the duty of a *mission civilisatrice* in Europe's east and the drive to keep Germany in check with the Little Entente of successor states mattered to French policymakers, none of France's motives for opening up toward Central and East-Central Europe was more pressing than its need to re-create its foreign investments.[25] France had lost a steady flow of interest payments when the Bolsheviks repudiated Russia's foreign debts and expropriated industrial companies, necessitating what David Harvey has termed a "spatial fix"—resolving an economic crisis by creating new markets and outlets for French corporations.[26]

In the three decades preceding the Great War, the French state and French companies had invested approximately 30 billion francs in the Russian empire, representing around 24 percent of all French foreign investments and surpassing even investments in the French colonies.[27] While France ran a trade deficit every year between 1875 and 1914, yields from foreign, mostly Russian,

Table 6.1 French imports and exports in 1913 and 1919 (in millions of French francs)

YEAR	VALUE OF IMPORTS	VALUE OF EXPORTS
1913	8,421	6,880
1919	29,778	8,713

Source: The minister of commerce and industry, Auguste Isaac, to President Alexandre Millerand, December 10, 1920, ANF F 12 9174.

bonds and investments had helped fill this trade gap since the 1890s.[28] The German army's systematic exploitation of the industrialized French northeast between 1914 and 1918 and the negative impact of wartime restrictions on European commerce after the armistice exacerbated the impact of Bolshevik expropriations on the national economy; by 1919, France's imports were more than triple its exports (table 6.1).

Little wonder, then, that Minister of Commerce and Industry Auguste Isaac sent an alarming memo to Premier Alexandre Millerand in December 1920 warning that "this situation [of trade imbalance] cannot persist without leading to extremely grave consequences for our commerce and finances. If we do not manage to diminish the difference between the two sides of our commercial balance as quickly as possible, we will encounter the greatest of difficulties as regards both our purchases of raw materials indispensable for our industrialists and our grain supply."[29] Russian investments had to be replaced with shares in lucrative companies in the former Central Powers.[30]

Concerns with the viability and profitability of France's expanded industrial capacity explained why the highest circles of the French government, including Reconstruction Minister Louis Loucheur and Secretary of the Foreign Ministry Maurice Paléologue, were involved in in-depth negotiations on the fate of specific companies and mines in Lorraine, Hungary, and Romania.[31] They used the crisis of Bolshevik expropriations as an opportunity to build a new and more consolidated portfolio of interlinked investments in Alsace, Lorraine, the Saar, the Rhineland, and East-Central Europe in lieu of "haphazard" and disconnected ventures in Russia before 1917.

The biggest prize was the seizure of several of the world's finest steel plants in Lorraine as early as November 1918, followed by a series of direct and indirect investments in key factories, mines, oil drilling, and steel plants in East-Central and Southeastern Europe, including Transylvania. The Banque de Paris et des Pays-Bas (Paribas) bank's takeover of Romanian oil companies from the Deutsche Bank, the Schneider group's acquisition of majority shares in the Škoda metallurgy conglomerate in Czechoslovakia, and French participation in the Danzig ship industry were among the successes of French economic penetration in Central and Southeastern Europe.[32] In Lorraine, the rapid expropriation of German steel plants exposed the extent to which French governments depended on business elites, foreshadowing its problems in East-Central Europe.

After Expropriation: Running and Selling Lorraine's German Steel Plants

While local women and men dressed in regional costumes greeted French troops with makeshift arches as soldiers marched into Alsace and Lorraine, the French government went ahead with one of the largest and fastest transfers of private property in postwar Europe. According to the contemporary American business scholar Abraham Berglund, Lorraine was home to "the finest iron-ore basin in Europe, and one of the finest in the world."[33] Iron ore mines in German Lorraine provided one-fifth of Europe's output before the war, fueling the region's steel plants; this represented almost a third of the German empire's steel production on the eve of the Great War.[34] While the Allies approved of France's annexation of Alsace and Lorraine, the specifics of their reintegration were far from clear. Paris thus needed to act rapidly to present its allies with a status quo favorable to France before the opening of the peace conference.

Starting in November 1918, the French army rounded up and expelled the Germans who had moved to the region after 1871 and their descendants. The impounding and forced administration of German-owned companies followed the script practiced during the Great War, pointing to legal and administrative continuities between the wartime and post-armistice periods.[35] The army nominated military officers as sequestering agents, who functioned as interim directors of these businesses. Yet the new administration had to face the sobering fact that the operating costs of large factories and mines amounted to millions of francs every month. Unless the government could obtain these funds, production would stop and mass unemployment would follow in a region adjacent to Germany, which was rocked by revolutionary turmoil. Fears of Germans merged with fears of communism and organized labor among the French occupying administration in a region with a strong labor movement. The interception of Hungarian and German communist agents at the new Franco-German border further stoked fears of imminent "communard-Bolshevik" subversion coming from the east.[36]

The French budget was almost completely depleted and therefore unable to inject capital into Lorraine's economy, while French banks were also short of reserves, so much so that France had to ban even its East-Central European allies from raising funds on Parisian markets.[37] Only French industrial companies possessed surplus capital, which gave them the upper hand over the administration and ensured that Minister of Commerce Étienne Clémentel's plans to control French heavy industrial production would fail.[38] As early as 1918, the remaking of Lorraine's economy showed that recovery from the Great War would benefit industrialists rather than empower ambitious economic planners, as states scaled back the scope of economic planning and redirected their resources to benefit loyal corporations in the hope of using them to roll back German influence in Central and Eastern Europe.[39] The transfer of Lorraine's steel plants painfully revealed Paris's inability to rein in its own industrialists, even in a region under French military occupation. The scarcity of state funds set in motion a spiral of dependence in which large banks from Alsace, Lorraine, and the French interior and powerful French steel plants were in a position to blackmail the government for concessions while promising to save the French administration from the humiliation of strikes and unrest on "liberated" territories. Nonetheless, by the early 1920s it became clear that subsidizing French corporations was a costly yet ineffective means to achieve stability in Alsace and Lorraine.

After the expropriation of German owners, French military personnel acted as the interim administration of Lorraine's steel plants; however, without the necessary financial capacity, they scrambled to keep the plants in operation. High maintenance costs prompted the French government to hastily transfer these precious assets to French industrialists at a fraction of their market price, with no regard for the resulting losses for the treasury. The expulsion of German workers offered only a temporary solution to the steel plants' depleted coffers, while the lack of experts and workers hindered recovery once the economy got back on its feet in the early 1920s.

Industrialists soon gained the upper hand over Reconstruction Minister Louis Loucheur, who had initially forbidden them to travel to explore German assets in "liberated regions."[40] After the region's top administrator, the general commissioner, proved unable to come up with the necessary financing for the steel plants, the French regional administration attempted to end the crisis locally by using Alsatian bankers. Subsequently, on a national level, Loucheur personally approved a loan of 40 million francs to troubled steel corporations, but the Senate's budgetary commission "clearly refused" to support the initiative—after all, it meant extending credit from French taxpayers to companies that were still technically German.[41] Loucheur's inability to secure financing from his own government and the limited resources of Alsatian banks, suffering from the financial transition themselves, meant that he had to give enormous concessions to French metallurgists to shore up French rule in the region. The interests of French and Lorrainer forge masters were, however, contradictory, which spelled trouble for the region's workers and steel plants.

Already during the Great War there were warning signs that French and Lorrainer metallurgists were locked in a competition, which foreshadowed the economic crisis that would engulf Lorraine after its reintegration into France.[42] Yet this did not prevent Paris from handing German-owned steel mills over to their French competitors, who subsequently subordinated them to their own production needs. The anti-Lorraine lobby was so strong in the Chamber of Deputies that Loucheur had to explicitly deny the rumor that the French army had deliberately spared Lorraine's steel plants from bombings between 1914 and 1918 in order to safeguard the French de Wendel family's property in Lorraine.[43] In the meantime, Jean Schneider, owner of the Schneider-Creusot steel plant in Central France, unsuccessfully lobbied the government for a punitive export tax on Lorraine's steel exports to Germany in order to even out the competitiveness of steel manufacturing across France. Schneider continued his campaign until the government granted the company a share in Lorraine's steel plants.[44]

French forge masters believed that the former Reichsland's heavy industry would undermine their own plants. Robert Pinot, the head of the French metallurgist organization the Comité des Forges, warned that the "badly situated" and less efficient "factories of Central France, precisely those that allowed us to score a victory," would "disappear" if not protected from Lorraine's competition.[45] Pinot pointed out that the annexation of Alsace-Lorraine would double France's iron ore output, increase cast iron production by 75 percent and steel production by 50 percent, and aggravate the country's prewar oil and coke deficit.[46] Unsurprisingly, the Comité was instrumental in pushing for the duty-free entry of Alsace-Lorraine products into Germany for five years at the Paris peace conference.[47]

The administration's concerns centered on four German-owned steel plants in Lorraine, located in the industrial towns of Knutange, Uckange, Rombas, and Hagondange. Equipped with blast furnaces, rolling mills, and steel producing units, these plants employed tens of thousands of workers.[48] The prewar net worth of three of the four major steel plants—those in Rombas, Hagondange, and Knutange—amounted to 1.4 billion gold marks, or approximately 4 billion French francs, in 1919.[49] French exports totaled less than 9 billion francs in 1919, while the country's total material losses in the Great War amounted to 55 billion francs, figures that highlight the enormous value of the steel plants in German Lorraine.[50]

The transfer of Lorraine's most modern steel plant, the plant in Hagondange, to French ownership is a particularly excellent illustration of how some industrialists increased their wealth at the end of the Great War with minimal risk and investment at the expense of the French treasury and German owners. In the 1910s, Hagondange was a key hub of European heavy industry in the border region of France, Belgium, Luxembourg, and Germany and attracted workers from as far away as Italy and Poland.[51] In 1911 in this town on the Moselle River, the Thyssen corporation built one of Europe's most advanced steel plants, with six modern blast furnaces on 1,250 acres of land and adjoining iron ore concessions on 14,000 acres. Because the Thyssen family was close to the imperial government, the plant received thousands of Russian POW workers during the war and production declined by just 10–15 percent despite Allied bombing, which killed mostly Russians and caused only minor damage to the plant.[52] Soon after the armistice, however, the fate of the Thyssens, one of Europe's wealthiest industrial families, took a turn for the worse.[53] The family patriarch, August Thyssen, was unable to avoid French expropriation measures and was barely able to secure his personal safety.[54] Business elites had quickly become targets of postwar retribution in Germany, often initiated by workers' and soldiers' councils.[55] The workers' and soldiers' council of Mühlheim in the Ruhrland arrested the septuagenarian Thyssen along with his son Fritz in early December 1918. Although they were soon released, the family spent the next months in hiding.[56]

On October 17, 1919, the regional tribunal of Metz rubber-stamped the decision of the consultative commission of sequesters, the government organ that decided on the composition of French ownership. It allocated the Thyssen corporation's plant in Hagondange to a motley assortment of French industrialists united as the *Union des Consommateurs de Produits Métallurgiques et Industriels* (Union of Consumers of Metal Products and Industrialists). Within this consortium, priority was given to companies that used steel to produce finished products such as cars, machines, or train carriages.[57] In addition to the two leading automotive manufacturers, Peugeot and Renault, the Alsatian de Dietrichs also acquired a stake in the new company.[58]

Allowing engineering and automotive companies to take over a steel plant was like letting a wolf mind the sheep.[59] The subordination of Lorraine's steel plants to the interests of their French owners was especially glaring in the case of Hagondange. The new management had to completely reorient production to smaller and midsize products to serve the interests of car manufacturers, leading to underuse of its capacity—so much so that the plant ran at just 30 percent of its production capacity after the French takeover.[60] The Union des Consommateurs kept the prices of Hagondange products at an artificially low level so that their own companies, mostly car manufacturers, could supply themselves at below-market prices. The price cuts were especially pronounced since even under normal circumstances, the Hagondange plant's prices were 50 percent lower than those of foundries in central France.[61]

In the meantime, Renault and other members of the consortium were unconcerned with the decline of Lorraine's industrial heartland even though permanent labor unrest undermined not only support for the governing party but also French rule in the region. Tensions ran so high that some workers even tried to assassinate the middle-aged engineer Étienne Orfila, the first French director of the Hagondange plant, in March 1920 by blowing up his villa. Because the perpetrators had received their training in bomb production in the German army, the Francophile press cast it as a nationalist conflict, when in reality this act of terrorism underscored class tensions and dissatisfaction with the region's decline.[62]

Louis Renault, the leading car manufacturer behind the formation of the Union of Consumers, explained frankly to members of the group in an internal corporate memo, "We have chosen to acquire the Hagondange plant because under normal circumstances this foundry can produce at the lowest possible price."[63] As a consequence, he added, "we will be able to set the prices of our own products so low as to defy all competition (which will allow us to recover the capital we have invested)."[64] This practice was not uncommon or unique to the Union des Consommateurs. The de Dietrich engineering company—a former supplier of the German army—borrowed 5 million francs to buy one of its technologically superior competitors and suppliers, the Dingler-Karcher steel plant in the Saar,[65] subsequently using this purchase to drive down prices and corner the market.[66]

By 1921 and 1922, the Hagondange plant's losses had skyrocketed, reaching 25 million francs in both years, a situation detrimental not only to workers but also to small shareholders.[67] The French administration was unable to force the Union of Consumers to invest capital in the steel plants and set their purchase prices at extremely low levels. While the 1914 value of the Thyssen complex in Lorraine was 850 million gold marks, the Union of Consumers had the option of purchasing the company for 150 million francs in 1919, even though 850 million gold marks amounted to approximately 2.5 billion francs at the time.[68] The Union of Consumers thus purchased the company for approximately 6 percent of its actual value. Furthermore, the consortium paid only a fraction of this price up front. It transferred only 37 million francs to the French state (about 1.5 percent of the plant's prewar value) in 1919, while it intended to raise the remaining 113 million francs from the annual profits of the newly acquired company.[69]

The sale of Hagondange at a bargain price was not an exception. In the case of the Rombas plants, the winning consortium of French industrialists, 85 percent of whom were *sinistrés* (who incurred war damages), acquired the plant for the low price of 125 million francs but paid only 63 million up front, with the remainder due in March 1922.[70] It is also remarkable that in both cases, the buyers financed the purchase and operations of these plants with long-term state loans. The Union des Consommateurs de Produits received a loan of 115 million francs due in 1974, while the Rombas plant's owners were awarded 100 million francs, due in 1952.[71]

The new owners subsequently petitioned for the suspension of loan payments, their lawyers wielding the anti-German rhetoric of the French government as the grounds for their request. As the Rombas steel plant's representative noted, it was "absolutely unheard of" that the French administration should be more lenient with Germany, which had received extensions on reparations payments, than with its own citizens.[72] A 1924 arbitration between the state and French investors reduced the Rombas plant's debt to the state by more than 42 million francs, and that of the Knutange and Hagondange plants by 42 and 75 million francs, respectively.[73] Ultimately, shareholders paid only half of the nominal value of their shares to the company, which automatically and immediately doubled their investments.[74]

Altogether, the French socialist deputy Louis Cluzel estimated in 1928 that the state had lost 315 million francs on the liquidation of the Rombas, Hagondange, and Knutange steel plants alone.[75] The actual losses were likely higher. The buyers had paid only 165 million francs by 1927, amounting to 2 percent of the plants' prewar net worth, which had been estimated at 1.4 billion German gold marks or 8.6 billion French francs as of 1927.[76] The inflation of the French franc further reduced the income of the French treasury.[77]

The lack of capital to operate Lorraine's formerly German-owned steel plants pushed the government to hand them over to French firms on the cheap in a relatively short time. As a result, large French corporations rather than the French treasury were the real winners in this market expansion, as successive governments helped domestic corporations acquire prime industrial property, often at a fraction of its real value. The proliferation of labor unrest and the short-term economic decline of Lorraine also showed that French corporations were unable to cement French rule in the region, despite enormous financial incentives from the Paris government. Some of the firms active in the former Reichsland also participated in French expansion plans in East-Central and Southeastern Europe. Schneider-Creusot, for instance, made plans to take control of the port of Budapest.[78] Market expansion was, however, considerably more difficult to implement abroad, where both successor states and former enemy businessmen wielded considerable power—unlike in Lorraine, where German industrialists were temporarily powerless.

The French and the Survival of Austro-Hungarian Business Elites after 1918

The scramble for East-Central Europe's coal mines, oil reserves, steel plants, and heavy industrial property started as soon as Austria-Hungary collapsed. The economic expansion of French banks and companies was a methodical effort that rested on the cooperation of French banks, industrial companies, and diplomats.[79] It proceeded through the Paribas and other French banks' acquisition of shares in key investment banks of the former Austria-Hungary, such as the Viennese Länderbank or the Hungarian General Credit Bank (GCB), which in turn gave French capital access to a series of heavy industry firms and mines.[80] French bankers and diplomats would then push for the participation of French corporations in these firms. French investors allowed for the continued participation of Austro-Hungarian capital in these ventures in order to minimize their own risk and exposure; furthermore, they also had personal ties and business connections with the former Dual Monarchy's bankers and industrialists that not even the Great War could sever, which also fostered the survival of Austro-Hungarian business elites.[81] Ultimately, however, the French government cooperated with its recent enemies and prevented mass expropriations in East-Central Europe because it was easier to gain a market share through the frightened business elite of the former Austria-Hungary than through the heavily nationalist successor states that sought to limit foreign capital in their economies. Austrian and Hungarian industrialists and businessmen, on the other hand, were eager to "internationalize" their assets by selling a portion of them to French investors.

Yet this pressure was not clear to most contemporaries. Despite French diplomatic intervention against expropriations, successor states continued to threaten ethnic minorities with the complete or partial seizure of their industrial companies and banks, while French governments also supported the Little Entente's anti-Hungarian rhetoric, sending a mixed message.[82] It was also more advantageous for French banks to pressure Czechoslovak or Romanian banks to pay for participation in industrial companies on their newly acquired territories, because credit for these purchases came mostly from French banks. Unlike prewar state loans, these and other credits came with more strings attached, such as mandatory purchases in France, and had to be regularly renegotiated, which enabled the French government to put pressure on its East-Central European allies.[83]

Clemenceau's right-hand man at the peace conference, Minister of Liberated Regions André Tardieu, noted with alarm that France's eastern allies continued to compare their cause to that of Alsace even after 1918, which implied that they claimed the same prerogatives that the French government had claimed over the former Reichsland, including the expropriation of property owned by ethnic minorities.[84] Yet the Paris government had no intention of extending the liberties it exercised with regard to German minorities to East-Central Europe. While contemporaries were thinking about Central European regions in comparative terms by the time of the Paris peace conference, it was essential for France to cast the case of Alsace-Lorraine as unique, similar to how France was unique among nation-states.

Transylvania's coal reserves were among the key East-Central European assets that sparked the same intense interest as Lorraine's steel plants and natural resources among successor states and international investors. The scramble for the Jiu valley's "black gold," which was actually brown lignite, strongly resembled the "war of succession" over Romania's oil reserves, the second largest in Europe after Russia's at the time, or the disputes concerning the Chorzów nitrogen factory in Upper Silesia and the conflict over the nationalization of the German-owned munitions factory in Bratislava.[85]

Transylvania's coal made up four-fifths of Romania's reserves, and two-thirds of the region's coal deposits were located in the Jiu valley, lending it both economic and military weight.[86] Before 1918, the valley's coal heated stoves in Budapest apartments and fueled the locomotives of the Hungarian state railways. During the Great War, the output of the Salgótarján Coal Mining Corporation (SCMC), the valley's largest mine owner, was key for moving Austro-Hungarian troops, while after the armistice, Serbia, Romania, and Hungary felt equally entitled to coal shipments from the region that played a key role in the gradual advance of Romanian troops into Hungarian territory as well.

A close look at the fate of Transylvania's coal mines in the Jiu valley attests to the deft maneuvering of the former Austria-Hungary's business elites, who built new ties and mended old ones with Western European investors to keep the Romanian authorities in check and prevent the expropriation of their Transylvanian assets. The ultimate outcome was a compromise between Hungarian and Romanian industrialists, which would not have been possible without French and other Western European firms that competed for Eastern Europe's natural resources; the SCMC's Jiu valley holdings were eventually transformed into a Romanian company, and a stake in the company was ceded to Romanian banks. This "nationalization," as the creation of a Romanian corporation from a Hungarian one was known, was thus a partial success for the Romanian administration, which managed to subvert the minority rights provisions of both the Austrian and Hungarian peace treaties a mere few months after they were signed, even as Romanian investors had to pay a high price, literally, for co-ownership of these mines. According to the minority rights treaties, ethnic minorities and optants in Austria and Hungary were allowed to retain their assets in successor states, but since this was a negotiated, if coercive, settlement, representatives of the SCMC never pressed charges against the Romanian administration at international tribunals.

The Romanian administration's first steps against enemy property were remarkably similar to the French government's contemporaneous expropriations in Lorraine in terms of their radicalism. Less than a month after the November 13 Belgrade armistice between the Allies and Hungary, on December 7, 1918, the Romanian army expropriated the few mining pits owned by the Hungarian state in the Jiu valley.[87] It also liquidated German-owned coal mines and companies, including those owned by the puppet bank of the German occupying forces, the Banca Generala.[88] However, Bucharest soon discovered the limits of its power.

The interim regional administration of Transylvanian Romanians, the Directing Council, sent delegates to supervise all private mines in Transylvania, including the largest one, which was owned by the Budapest-based firm SCMC. Yet these delegates had little power and the Austro-Hungarian management remained in place, especially after the strikes that broke out in the Jiu valley, paralyzing all of Transylvania and blocking the advance of Romanian troops.[89] Sovereignty in Transylvania remained unclear until the spring of 1919, and radical measures by the Romanian occupying forces threatened to undermine the country's claim to sovereignty. Furthermore, French banks were indirectly financing Transylvania's coal mines, which was another argument in support of moderation at a time when the region's fate depended on the goodwill of French diplomats. Paris closely monitored Romanian economic legislation and directly intervened to have legislation on the expropriation of foreign property withdrawn in the spring of 1919.[90] In humiliating negotiations in Paris, Brătianu himself had to engage directly with representatives of the Royal Dutch Shell company, which also protested the expropriation of its shares in the Steaua Română oil company; these successful interventions by the French government and international corporations revealed the limits of Romanian sovereignty over the country's natural resources.[91]

Like France, Romania lacked capital to purchase and operate mines and heavy industries. This explains why the informal offer made by the SCMC's general director, Johann Winklehner, to the head of the Directing Council's commerce department, Victor Bontescu, to sell his firm's Jiu valley holdings for 100 million crowns or 50 million lei as early as December 1918 was eventually turned down by Brătianu himself, who admitted that the treasury lacked the necessary funds.[92] The closest the Romanian state came to acquiring the Jiu valley's coal reserves on the cheap was during the Hungarian dictatorship of the proletariat in the spring of 1919, which sent the SCMC's managers, Ferenc Chorin Sr. and Jr, into internal exile while expropriating their firm. In dire straits, Chorin Jr. agreed to sell majority ownership of the company's possessions in Transylvania for 18 million Swiss francs. The price was a good deal for the buyers, yet the Romanian government was unable to come up with the funds.[93]

By the time these negotiations ended, Bucharest had run out of time to transfer the valley's coal to Romanian ownership at a coerced bargain price, since the gradual solidification of states and the finalization of the Austrian and Hungarian peace treaties by the fall of 1919 had drastically limited its latitude to maneuver. The Treaty of Saint Germain was signed in September 1919 and explicitly forbade the expropriation of Austrian nationals and ethnic minorities in successor states, with similar provisions expected in the Hungarian peace treaty. Asymmetries of information were key; while the Romanian government did not know that the peace conference was unable to use force to compel Eastern European states to protect the rights of ethnic minorities, Hungarian industrialists and Allied diplomats were unaware of the Romanian administration's dilemmas and uncertainties with regard to the expropriation of industrial property in Transylvania. Industrialists like Chorin had good reason to believe that if they did not act fast, their assets would share the fate of the landed estates, which were slated to be expropriated with no compensation in sight.

While postwar French governments were united in their views and policies on the expropriation of German property, the period between 1918 and 1921 saw two general elections and three governments in Greater Romania. While the National Liberal Party around Brătianu and the Populists around General Alexandru Averescu favored the nationalization of companies owned by foreigners and ethnic minorities, the coalition government of Transylvanian regionalists and peasantists under Alexandru Vaida-Voevod (September 1919–March 1920) was more open to negotiation with business elites.[94] Regardless of these internal differences among the Romanian political elite, by September 1919 the field of play looked more favorable than at any point since October 1918 for the former Austria-Hungary's industrialists. In an ironic twist of history, it was the Romanian army's defeat of Hungarian Bolsheviks in August 1919 that freed Budapest tycoons Fellner and Chorin and enabled them to rekindle their ties to Allied industrialists in the following month.

Despite his eventual success in retaining his position and wealth, Chorin Jr., who was threatened with the loss of most of his company's coal mines, experienced a turbulent 1918 and 1919. Since November 1918, when Romanian troops occupied the Jiu valley, he had been unable to contact or access the SCMC's mines by phone, telegram, or rail; this was shortly after he had given up his law practice in order to devote all his time to the SCMC.[95] As a portent of even more troubles to come and a sign of the general breakdown of public order and property rights, a burglar entered his Budapest apartment in February 1919 and stole his winter coat.[96] A month later, Béla Kun's Bolsheviks turned the family's villa above Budapest into an open-air school for proletarian children at the peak of the Spanish flu epidemic, and a journalist mockingly depicted Chorin Sr. as a cross-dresser, showing that Bolshevik critique of the bourgeoisie resorted to homophobic clichés to slander opponents.[97] The Bolsheviks targeted the Chorins with expropriation for being bourgeois, while counterrevolutionaries following the demise of Kun's regime attacked them for being Jewish in a wave of pogroms that swept through the former Austria-Hungary and Eastern Europe.[98] These momentous and traumatizing changes in 1919 prompted Chorin to shed Judaism, convert to Christianity, and reconfigure his company's future.[99]

As Hungary was unable to defend Chorin's assets at home and in occupied territories, he needed another state or a powerful corporation that could guarantee the security of his investments. He was not alone in this endeavor, as the fall of 1919 saw a veritable "pilgrimage" of Austro-Hungarian industrialists and bankers to the financial centers of Western Europe seeking to hand over their holdings under Czechoslovak, Romanian, and Serbian occupation to powerful corporations with strong networks among Allied heads of state.[100] For instance, Adolf Ullmann, the director of the Electric Trust Company and the GCB, used his prewar business ties to the French reconstruction minister Loucheur to receive an entry visa to France; Ullmann's bank financed the Urikány and Jiu Valley Hungarian Coal Mining Corporation (UZMC), the second-largest coal mine in the Jiu, which was partially owned by the Crédit Lyonnais and other French investors.[101]

As soon as Fellner arrived at the Hotel National in Geneva, he contacted his Swiss connection, the private banker Émile Darier, who put him in touch with representatives of a Newcastle-based coal mine as well as Swiss and French investors.[102] The Jiu valley's mines had been well known to French investors since the 1880s, which helped his case. The SCMC's stock prices also regularly appeared in the French specialized press.[103] Furthermore, French business papers had already started to promote these mines to French investors while Fellner and Chorin were still held captive by the Hungarian communists. According to these reports, Petroșani, the region's major mining town, was supposed to "have the most compact reserves of black lignite, an excellent industrial combustible. . . . One does not find such high-quality lignite in Moldavia and Wallachia."[104]

Members of the Budapest stock exchange saw an opportunity in the political crisis brought about by imperial collapse and sovereignty change; the formation of joint companies incorporated in successor states with the participation of Allied businesses sparked particularly keen interest and drove up stock prices. A journalist at a Budapest stock-exchange newspaper optimistically concluded four months before the signing of the Treaty of Trianon that "after economic and political consolidation, Budapest would [once more] assume its prominent role" in the economic life of East-Central Europe.[105] Even though the loss of Transylvania to Romania had eventually become the foundational "trauma" of Hungarian identity under Miklós Horthy's regime, the experience of the Hungarian bourgeoisie in 1919 and 1920 pointed beyond an identity of victimhood and showed how at least some Austro-Hungarian industrialists economically exploited Romanian sovereignty over Transylvania and realized that the political crisis of state collapse would result in gains for some of their investments.

Even the introduction of the Romanian currency, the leu, in Transylvania was in the short-term interest of the Hungarian industrialists negotiating deals in Western Europe because the leu was inflating less rapidly than the crown of politically unstable Hungary.[106] Fellner circulated a memorandum among the company's Swiss and Entente negotiating partners that emphasized the economic advantages of Transylvania's annexation by Romania. The memo argued that the annexation was highly advantageous for Entente investors, since "Romania will develop its agriculture, along with the expansion of industries. Both agriculture and industry will need the Jiu valley's coal in large quantities; the valley is Romania's only coal reserve."[107] Fellner and Chorin did not switch their allegiances from the Hungarian to the Romanian nation-building project. Rather, much like Košice's Hungarian and German bourgeoisie that invited Czech troops to reestablish order in the city in 1919, or Fiume's Slavic populations that sided with Italy instead of a Slavic successor state, Fellner's stance showed that nationalism was not in fact the sole, or even the most important, compass for East-Central European populations during the years of transition that followed the collapse of Austria-Hungary. In the case of Hungarian industrialists, concern for prosperity and political stability trumped the pursuit of Hungary's territorial integrity.[108]

Fellner and Chorin broadly publicized their trips to Western Europe in order to put pressure on the Romanian administration and boost the company's stock price. Budapest tabloids and stock-exchange papers inflated these Western European trips, trumpeting them as imminent business deals, which contributed to the doubling of the SCMC's stock price between August and November 1919.[109] High stock prices that far surpassed the level of inflation helped Chorin and Fellner negotiate a better deal. In the meantime, the Jiu valley mines' sequestering agent urged Chorin more and more impatiently to "nationalize" the SCMC's possessions in Romania.[110] On January 11, 1920, the supervising manager appointed by the Directing Council sent a coercive note to the SCMC stating that "at this point the nationalization of your mines on Romanian territory can suffer no further delays. This note is private and I am only sending it to save you from the nuisance of the consequences."[111] Chorin was undeterred and embarked on yet another trip to Switzerland in February 1920 while also opening negotiations with "the Romanian group," an association of banks and companies similar to the Union of Consumers that took over the Thyssen steel plants in Hagondange.[112]

Chorin and Fellner lacked detailed and convincing documentation on the Jiu valley's mines, which prevented them from concluding a deal with Western investors. What really mattered, however, was that such a deal seemed entirely possible in the "gold rush" toward East-Central Europe's mines, factories, and oil concessions that swept through France and the rest of Western Europe after 1918.[113] Both the UZMC and Chorin's SCMC had ties to French capital through the PHCB, which financed the mines.

The threat of being outbid by powerful Western investors and the longstanding presence of French capital in the Jiu valley's mines eventually helped Chorin reach a favorable agreement with Romanian investors. The SCMC's holdings in Romanian-occupied territory were transformed into a company headquartered in Romania, the Petroșani corporation. On paper, it was a separate Romanian company with no ties to Hungary, which pleased Romanian nationalists. In reality, however, the SCMC and the investment bank that financed it, Fellner's PHCB, retained half of the shares in this new Romanian company and the corresponding representation on its supervisory board; French investors also retained their indirect participation through the same bank. Like the buyers of Lorraine's steel plants, Romanian investors paid only a fraction of the purchase price up front. But the Romanian group pledged to pay the enormous sum of 18 million Swiss francs, or $3 million, in exchange for 50 percent of the Petroșani corporation's shares by 1924 or else the transaction would become void; the Romanian party was thus unable to obtain the majority of shares. Given the rapid inflation of the Romanian leu almost immediately after the transaction was concluded, the requirement to pay in Swiss francs became extremely difficult to fulfill. In the meantime, the Romanian group also had to pay 5 percent interest to the SCMC on the unpaid portion of the 18 million francs.[114]

The purchase price of 18 million Swiss francs was equivalent to 15 million prewar gold crowns and suggested that the parties took the plant's book value as the basis of their negotiations, disregarding wartime damage, yet another advantage for the Hungarian group. In addition, the buyers paid an immediate lump sum of 23.75 million lei, or $420,000. Chorin was also able to have the Romanian state railways compensate the SCMC for the coal it had used since November 1918 to move troops and keep the economy going under Romanian rule.[115] The SCMC's Budapest shareholders also retroactively received their interest payments from the Jiu valley for the transition period, a sum of 8 million lei.[116] Chorin managed to conclude a deal that was so advantageous that it resembled an agreement between two equal parties.

Romanian prime minister Alexandru Averescu approved the transaction in June 1920, because the Romanian investors included the core supporters of his government and its national liberal allies. These investors were the major prewar financial institutions of Bucharest such as the Banca Românească and the Berkovitz Bank, as well as new banks such as the Franco-Romanian, Chrissoveloni, Romanian Credit, and External Credit banks. French capital was thus present among both Hungarian and Romanian shareholders, although that meant only indirect control over the mines, which continued to be managed by Chorin's representative. Notably, however, Transylvanian Romanian investors subscribed to only 5 percent of the Petroșani company's shares, while Bucharest-based banks and corporations took 45 percent, reflecting the enormous leverage of Bucharest's capitalists. The Albina, Transylvania's oldest Romanian bank, which had close ties to the opposition regionalist National Party, subscribed to only a token number of shares (2 percent).[117] Credits for these purchases came from Western European banks, mostly French ones, which shows that the Allies indirectly made successor states in East-Central Europe pay for their territorial enlargement or independence. As regards vanquished Hungary, some French diplomats openly advocated granting territory from French allies like Greater Romania to Hungary in exchange for economic concessions in favor of France by Budapest.

Trains for Territory: French Diplomacy in Service of French Firms

Negotiations on revising the territorial clauses of the Treaty of Trianon started after the ousting of the Clemenceau government in January 1920 and the promotion of Maurice Paléologue, who attempted to include Hungary in the system of French alliances in the Danubian region, as secretary general of the Foreign Ministry.[118] The Hungarian government, in the meantime, wanted to reestablish its army by importing French armaments via Romania, which pushed it toward the planned Franco-Romanian bloc; this rapprochement was the continuation of aborted plans in 1919 to establish a personal union between Hungary and Romania by the ascension of the Romanian king to the Hungarian throne, thus preventing the complete severance of Transylvania from Hungary.[119]

By the spring of 1920, it was clear that the diplomatic route to reversing Hungary's territorial losses had failed. In his references to Hungarian cultural supremacy, the conservative leader of the Hungarian peace delegation, Albert Apponyi, was unsuccessful in his efforts to persuade Lloyd George and Clemenceau to preserve the economic unity of the Carpathian basin under Budapest's authority.[120] Unlike Romanian politicians and industrialists, who were mainly newcomers to European big business, their counterparts from the Hungarian "empire" had fostered personal and commercial ties to major French businesses dating back to the last quarter of the nineteenth century. These relationships survived the enmities of the Great War; the investment bank behind the SCMC, Fellner's PHCB, had cooperated with the Paribas bank on Balkan investments before 1914. The director of the Paribas, Horace Finaly, was born in Buda to a Hungarian Jewish family and had family ties to the Viennese Rothschilds and the Credistanstalt bank, while Paribas was also a long-standing partner of a Hungarian bank with investments in Transylvania, the Hungarian Société de Crédit Foncier Bank, which had also been listed on the Parisian stock exchange before 1914.[121] Not only Clemenceau, whose daughter married the son of a Hungarian judge, but also several French diplomats such as Louis de Robien had family ties to Hungary.[122] Hungarian lawyer Károly Halmos, who led the initiative, had concluded lucrative deals in the Ottoman Empire and the Balkans with Reconstruction Minister Loucheur before the war.[123] Little wonder, then, that Loucheur took his initiative seriously. He and Count Armand de Saint-Souveur, the director of the Schneider-Creusot metallurgy firm, introduced Halmos and bank director Ullmann to Paléologue. Adolf Ullmann was one of the directors of the Hungarian GCB. Both Loucheur and Saint-Souveur were active in transferring German steel plants to French ownership in Lorraine, showing that French economic elites connected the different parts of the former Mitteleuropa when planning the future of the French economy.[124]

Among other stipulations, the unofficial peace delegation led by Halmos demanded the return of the Hungarian majority and prosperous cities adjacent to the border, and autonomy for Transylvania on April 13, 1920.[125] In his response, Paléologue proposed that Hungary take control of the Maramureș salt mines, which were located in territory annexed by Romania, in a move similar to the French seizure of the Saar coal mines in Germany. Echoing Halmos's note, the French proposal suggested a free-trade agreement between Hungary and Romania, much like the French solution for ensuring the prosperity of Alsace-Lorraine via customs-free trade arrangements between France and Germany.[126] Most importantly, French industrialists wanted a long-term lease of the Hungarian state railways, control over Hungarian industrial companies via Ullmann's bank, and an option to build a river port in Budapest.[127]

Paléologue, however, was unable to make his proposals official French policy and was more interested in gaining immediate economic concessions in exchange for potential diplomatic rewards to Hungary in the future. Both the president and the army opposed upsetting the balance of France's relationship with Hungary and Czechoslovakia. Paléologue therefore kept the Hungarian negotiations secret from Marshal Ferdinand Foch and others. In the meantime, on May 5, 1920, the Hungarian delegation received the final peace terms, accompanied by a cover letter from Millerand that only vaguely alluded to possible modifications to the treaty.[128] The original article 47 was amended with a paragraph that oddly combined Romania's obligation to protect its minorities with the requirement to "protect [the] freedom of transit and equitable treatment for the commerce of other nations."[129]

For Hungarian industrialists, landowners, and businessmen, the most significant modification was one that affected the fate of their property on former Austro-Hungarian territory. Not only did article 250 order the restoration of Hungarian ownership of assets nationalized or expropriated by Romania between the 1918 armistice and the peace treaty, it also provided for a so-called Mixed Arbitral Tribunal that would serve as an international court of appeal for these cases.[130] The affairs of prewar Hungarian industrialists and landowners thus ceased to be the problem of the Hungarian state, becoming instead a fixture of international law.[131]

While the delegation of Hungarian industrialists was ultimately unable to achieve its desired border changes, it achieved more than the official Hungarian peace delegation. Lobbying by Halmos, Ullmann, and others contributed to safeguarding Hungarian-owned assets in successor states and enabled Chorin to make the Western European investors' takeover of the Jiu valley's coal mines a credible threat. The maneuvering in which Hungarian industrialists engaged after the collapse of Austria-Hungary is proof of their remarkable social and business networks, which transcended the divisions between the former Central Powers and Allied states and survived the collapse of the monarchy. Ultimately these negotiations showed that economic considerations continued to make East-Central Europe key for France even after the failed Russian intervention reduced the region's military importance by 1920.

Riding the Simplon-Orient Express, Flying the Paris-Bucharest Route

Several French industrialists pushed for more moderate forms of economic expansion in East-Central Europe than that promoted by Paléologue. The businessmen and diplomats behind the National Committee for Economic Expansion in Eastern Europe advocated combining cultural cooperation with economic expansion. This association was founded in the spring of 1919 with the intent of "regaining" a "market of 600 million francs" from France's "Austro-*Boches* [German]" rivals.[132] It was the first organization to unite French and Eastern European bankers, businessmen, and politicians with the aim of boosting French commercial ties in the former German, Russian, Austro-Hungarian, and Ottoman economic spheres of influence in Europe. Paul d'Estournelle de Constant, the former French diplomat in Montenegro who compiled the Carnegie Commission's report on the Balkan Wars, French senator Edouard Herriot, Romanian premier Ion Brătianu, Romanian foreign minister Take Ionescu, Greek premier Eleftherios Venizelos, former "Yugoslave" prime minister Nikola Pašić, and Czechoslovak foreign minister Eduard Beneš were among the committee's honorary members. Aristide Blank, Bucharest's Romanian Jewish banker and the financier of the national liberals, acted as one of the four vice presidents. Louis Marin, who supervised expropriation of German assets in Alsace and Lorraine, was an honorary member of the committee. The Bank of Mulhouse in Alsace was one of the fifteen inaugural subscribers to the association's publications.[133] These connections suggest that French "economic expansion" efforts in Alsace, Lorraine, and East-Central Europe were interrelated.[134]

Whereas in Lorraine French companies faced no competition and were able to sacrifice the region's prosperity for their own interests, in East-Central Europe they faced higher expectations and competition in addition to paying a higher price for extending their participation in these markets. The economist Henri Hauser had already warned during the Great War that France had to "imitate" Germany to impress foreign consumers. "Exportation is not a joke that one can improvise. It is an art. The example of Germany shows us that it is also a science, a technique. . . . We have to 'organize' exportation in the same way that we had to organize war."[135] E. V. Letzgus, an expert on colonial trade who had retrained himself as an Eastern Europe specialist after 1918, chided the "inertia" of French businessmen and compared them to their German counterparts who had "carefully studied the market," "employed a true army of consuls and commercial attachés," and "flooded the Romanian market with luxurious catalogues written in Romanian or French."[136] It was notable that French commercial experts saw Eastern European trade as an area in which France was Germany's less modern, if not backward, counterpart.

Instead of wielding the crude language of economic imperialism used by wartime advocates of Mitteleuropa, the publications of the National Committee for Economic Expansion cast French economic expansion as a natural result of globalization, modernization, and the continent's integration, which had been interrupted by the Great War. The Simplon-Orient Express and the Paris-Istanbul flight route via Strasbourg and Bucharest became the most visible manifestations of the shrinking distance, both metaphorical and actual, between Western and Eastern Europe and the benevolent nature of French hegemony over continental Europe; French economic expansion thus equaled modernization. At the same time, both projects allowed the elites of Greater Romania to parade themselves as the equals of any industrialized nation. It was Queen Marie of Romania who inaugurated the Simplon-Orient Express in April 1919, while Aristide Blank avowedly supported the unprofitable aviation company so that the "Romanian flag" could fly at every major European city where the company had offices.[137]

Even though the Simplon-Orient Express was advertised as a major breakthrough in interwar European transport infrastructure, this new train line that connected France with Turkey through Southeastern Europe came with numerous limitations. "Mademoiselle, the Orient Express leaves Stamboul every day of the week. Even if you had missed the connection it would only have been a matter of twenty-four hours' delay," detective Hercule Poirot reminded a fellow passenger in Agatha Christie's 1934 best-selling mystery novel, *Murder on the Orient Express*.[138] In reality, however, travel through Europe on this new east–west route was far from smooth because it had to defy geography and resort to zigzagging side tracks in order to avoid traveling through vanquished states; both France and the former Austro-Hungary had centrifugal lines centered on their capital cities, and it would take years to build the missing tracks in France and Yugoslavia.[139] The train had to make an inconvenient detour through the Simplon tunnel in the Alps to avoid the faster and shorter prewar route through Germany and the Danube valley. The Simplon-Orient effectively came to a halt in Trieste, where it turned into a local train to Belgrade and Bucharest, deliberately bypassing Austria and Hungary. Ironically, as there was no train connection between the two capital cities, the carriages of the Simplon-Orient Express ultimately had to pass though the Hungarian city of Szeged to reach the Romanian capital.[140]

A further paradox of the Simplon-Orient line was that it actually increased the distance between Eastern and Western Europe even though it was supposed to bring France closer to its Eastern European allies. As the French geographer Auguste Jardé noted in 1922, Romanians "complained" that the distance between London and Bucharest had increased from 2,830 to 3,156 kilometers and "demanded that just like before [the First World War] the direct train services pass through Vienna . . . via Budapest and Bucharest."[141] Transylvanians were also less enthusiastic about the Simplon-Orient Express, since the discontinuation of the prewar east–west route via Budapest deprived them of a direct connection to Central and Western Europe. It therefore seems ironic that one of the major slogans of French economic expansion was "bringing the peoples of Europe" closer to each other by land and air (figures 6.1–6.3).

The Franco-Romanian Aviation Company was yet another sign of France's imperial ambitions in Southeastern Europe (figure 6.2). French businessmen

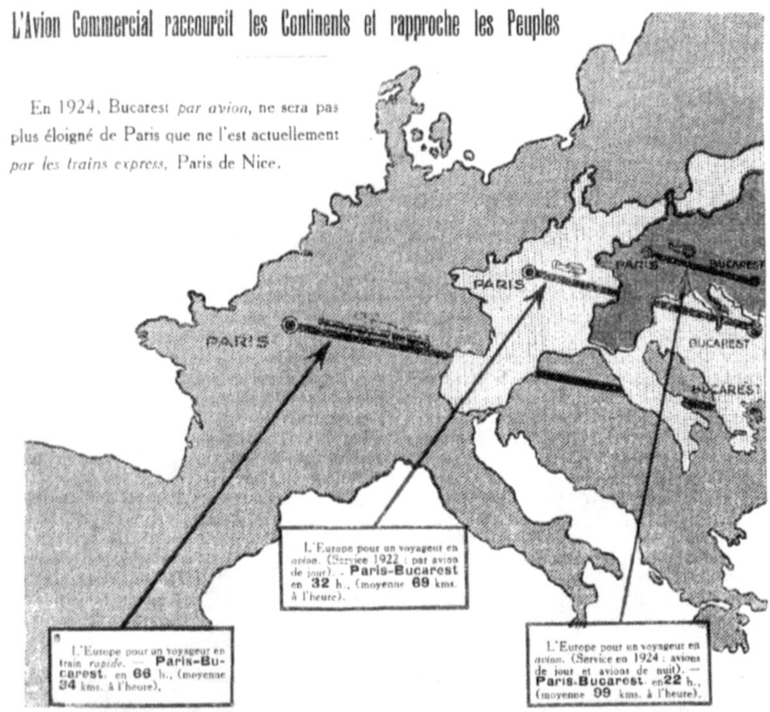

FIGURE 6.1. Franco-Romanian Aviation Co. advertisement (1924). Source: *Bulletin de Renseignements*, January 1, 1924, 1, BNF.

FIGURE 6.2. The targeted territories of the National Committee on Economic Expansion and the route of the Simplon-Orient express. Dotted lines indicate tracks to be built. Source: Charles Seignobos, "Notre champ d'action," *France-Europe Orientale*, April 1, 1919, 3, BNF.

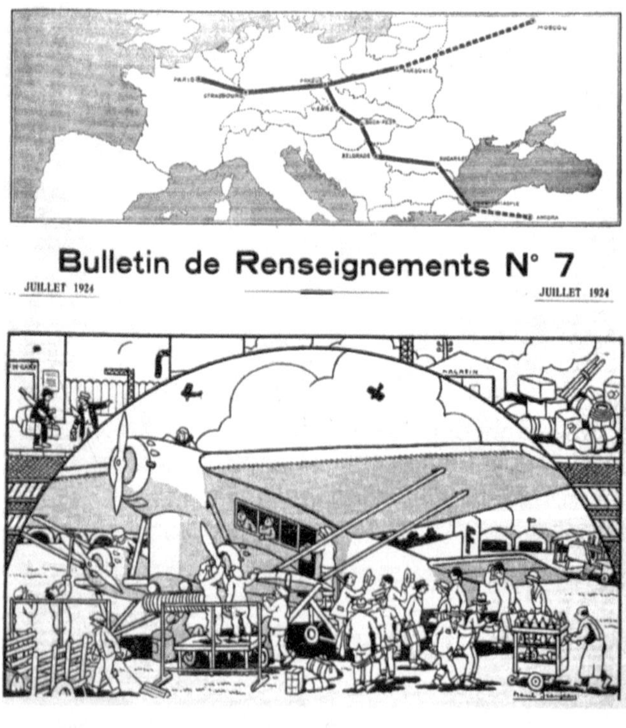

FIGURE 6.3. Empire in the Air; advertisement of the Franco-Romanian Aviation Company. Source: *Bulletin de Renseignements*, July 1924, 1, BNF.

founded the company in 1920, largely on the basis of a promise by the Romanian government that pledged 6.5 million lei ($116,000) in annual support for twenty years in exchange for operating its Paris-Strasbourg-Prague-Vienna-Budapest-Belgrade-Istanbul route via Bucharest.[142] The company was a questionable item on the Romanian budget as it flew fewer than one hundred passengers a year and mainly functioned as an express mail service. Given contemporary flight technology, which required frequent refueling, the company was unable to avoid Austria and Hungary as the Simplon-Orient Express could and was even forced to make several emergency landings in Germany between 1920 and 1924.[143] In 1923, the company found itself in trouble when the Romanian government stopped payments of its annual contributions while the Bavarian administration denied it access to its airspace, a situation that showcased the fragility of France's relationships with East-Central Europe.[144]

A comparison of French economic expansion in Alsace and Lorraine and in Transylvania and East-Central Europe more generally reveals the importance of sovereignty or direct rule for its success. Ultimately, French economic expansion in the former Mitteleuropa was most successful in regions directly controlled by Paris, such as Alsace, Lorraine, and the Saar, while in East-Central Europe it ran headlong into the nascent economic nationalism of successor states and the resilience of the former Dual Monarchy's industrialists. Comparisons also reveal just how similar the aspirations of France and Greater Romania were in terms of promoting the interests of loyal industrialists and sidelining foreign participation on annexed territories, which also explains why the Franco-Romanian alliance was fraught with conflict from 1918 onward. Furthermore, even as France was a victorious Western European state while Romania emerged from two years of military occupation on the eastern periphery of the continent, both states struggled with a lack of capital and were dependent on industrialists and bankers in their new territories in order to run their economies, which also explains why neither country's government considered taking key mines and steel plants into state ownership. While victory celebrations in Paris, Metz, and Strasbourg attracted vast crowds, it was powerful French industrialists and bankers who reaped the economic fruits of war and victory and the French economic expansion that followed. In Greater Romania, it was the Bucharest bankers with close ties to the governing National Liberal Party that benefited, along with those of the former Austria-Hungary who played a key role in the economic stabilization of Greater Romania.

The period between 1918 and the early 1920s was riddled with uncertainties for the industrialists and bankers of Austria-Hungary and Germany who were not privy to the agenda of the French government and the peace conference but had to negotiate a compromise with menacing government officials and armies. Ultimately, the former Austria-Hungary's industrialists who became ethnic minorities or had investments in successor states were better off than their German counterparts. While the Versailles Treaty was generous to Germany insofar as it was allowed to retain most of its European territory, the settlement meted out harsh punishment to German minorities and corporations of the Wilhelmine empire, which were subject to expropriation worldwide.[145] By contrast, the peace conference condoned the dissolution of the Dual Monarchy and punished both of its constituent states with severe territorial losses that turned millions of Austro-Germans and Hungarians into ethnic minorities.[146] Nonetheless, thanks to concerns about East-Central Europe's political stability and Western attempts to gain participation in the region's natural resources and key industries, the "orphans" of Austria-Hungary received considerably greater protection of their rights than did Germany's minorities, including the right to retain their assets in successor states.[147]

The relative success of the Dual Monarchy's tycoons in retaining their wealth and influence was overlooked by contemporaries, who focused on revolutionary turmoil and those ethnic minorities that suffered from overt and covert forms of discrimination in schools and at work.[148] Yet these observers failed to notice that behind the chaotic and rapidly changing political situation in East-Central Europe, the industrial capacity of the former Austria-Hungary remained intact during the Great War as did the power and wealth of the empire's industrialists. The unintended consequence of minority rights treaties was thus the ossification of ingrained class hierarchies and the continued influence of the prewar bourgeoisie, which was composed mostly of ethnic minorities in territories ceded by Hungary, such as the Banat, Transylvania, Slovakia, and Vojvodina.

Chapter 7

Imperial Currencies after the Fall of Empires

The Conversion of the German Paper Mark and the Austro-Hungarian Crown at the End of the First World War

Currency smuggling was all the rage in Europe after the First World War ended. The profiles of many smugglers can be found in archives from France to Romania: the two Bolshevik agents who smuggled more than one million Austro-Hungarian crowns into Romanian territory, hidden among pamphlets by Béla Kun; Miriam Haber, a woman from Poland who smuggled paper marks into French-occupied Alsace to support her family; and the man from Alba Iulia who hid 8,000 lei in a padded envelope sewn into his overcoat when he crossed the Hungarian-Romanian border.[1] As different as these people were, they shared one important characteristic: they were all caught by the authorities. Yet tens of thousands of other people and institutions like banks and industrial companies also engaged in currency smuggling and speculation, and their activities have remained unrecorded. Those who were caught tended to be on the margins of society as ethnic minorities, communist revolutionaries, women, or all of these at once. That even ordinary people were able to regularly smuggle currency shows just how difficult it was to police the flows of elusive paper money as empires collapsed and borders remained porous. In addition to strategic assets like mines and industrial companies, the successor states of Germany and Austria-Hungary also nationalized currency, which proved to be the most expensive part of the integration of new territories.

Businessmen and industrialists had outsize leverage to increase their fortunes when states scrambled to establish new borders and possessed little information on the financial situations of annexed territories. Successor states of Germany and Austria-Hungary faced enormous challenges when they decided to convert imperial currencies because they had no idea of the exact amount of "enemy" currency in circulation in new territories and lacked the funds to convert it. This also foreshadowed the setbacks faced by incoming administrations from the very beginning as they attempted to implement ambitious plans to reshape societies in annexed territories.

While successor states all tried to favor ethnic majorities over minorities in their new territories, they ran into unforeseen challenges when it came to currency. Unlike nationalist conflicts, which were easy to generate and then solve via propaganda and press campaigns—such as the one aimed at inciting hatred against Germans in French-occupied Alsace in order to prepare their expulsion in 1918—the currency problem constituted a real crisis that called for a series of carefully planned and costly measures. The currency crisis after the Great War had far-reaching social and political consequences that prevented a technocratic solution such as taking the last available exchange rate as a yardstick or letting markets decide on the conversion rate.[2] Given the rapid wartime and postwar inflation of the German and Austro-Hungarian currencies, adopting the market rate hurt the interests of broad sections of the population, as did the option of offering a lower rate for new populations to save on the cost of conversion. Incoming administrations rightly feared, as the case of Greater Romania would demonstrate, that offering a low conversion rate to people in new territories would erode the administrations' popularity and lead to nostalgia for the era of the Austro-Hungarian and German empires. Alternatively, successor states could provide a better conversion rate for new citizens to cement their loyalty. Yet this required sacrifices from taxpayers on the home front. The preferential treatment of populations in newly incorporated territories raised several paradoxes and moral dilemmas because people in some of these regions had fought against the motherland in the First World War, as in the case of Alsace-Lorraine, Eupen-Malmédy, Transylvania, Vojvodina, the Banat, the Austrian Littoral, or western Thrace.

The juxtaposition of the first and one of the last currency conversions in the aftermath of the First World War, by France in Alsace and Lorraine and by Greater Romania in Transylvania, respectively, yields surprising results. The comparison reveals that a major Western European power, France, pursued more radical policies of ethnic and financial discrimination against ethnic minorities than did Greater Romania. Compared with the market exchange rate between the French franc and the German paper mark, Paris offered a premium to Alsatians and Lorrainers whose families had lived in the region before its annexation by the German empire in 1871. In sharp contrast to this generosity, the incoming government offered no such safety net for Germans who had immigrated to the region after that date. They had to resort to the rapidly declining rates available on the market while being forced to pay their debts in French francs.

Despite the Bucharest government's nationalist and antisemitic agendas, it was in no position to remake social hierarchies in annexed territories by favoring Romanians "liberated" from Hungarian rule, as it scrambled to end the chaos in Transylvania after the collapse of the Hungarian administration.[3] Furthermore, like other successor states in East-Central Europe, Greater Romania did not have solid borders, as these were slowly established by war and the peace conference between 1918 and 1920. Lacking a well-defined national territory meant currency conversion had to be put on hold as well. The Romanian administration also lacked the financial means to follow French practices and offer a higher exchange rate to the over five million Romanians of Transylvania, the Banat, Bessarabia, and Bukovina. Instead, the governments of Greater Romania discriminated among people by giving preference to the economic interests of prewar populations over those of the populations of annexed territories such as Transylvania, where ethnic minorities made up half of the population. Ironically, however, this also meant that they discriminated against Transylvania's Romanian populations as well.

One of the first measures of the incoming Romanian administration in Transylvania was to offer a temporary exchange rate that halved the value of the Austro-Hungarian crown compared with the Romanian leu in the fall of 1918 but left the crown in circulation as well. The Romanian administration waited almost two years to phase out the crown. Thus, by the time of the final conversion in September 1920, even this lower exchange rate proved to be a generous subsidy to the mostly Hungarian, Jewish, and German bourgeoisie of Transylvania owing to the rapid inflation of the crown, which sank below one-fifth of its prewar value in the two years after the First World War. While successor states like Greater Romania waited for the peace conference to solve the currency problem, bankers and industrialists in Transylvania showed remarkable adaptability in profiting from the financial crisis and political uncertainty. They operated using several crisis scenarios, diversified their currency portfolios, profited from the fluctuating value of paper monies, and exploited differences in the exchange rates of multiple currencies across cities and regions. In a situation that echoed the scramble for German and Austro-Hungarian industrial companies, well-connected politicians and speculators were able to outmaneuver slow-moving bureaucracies. Those who failed to sell in time or lock in a favorable exchange rate risked sharing the (somewhat exaggerated) fate of the writer Gregor von Rezzori, whose "legendary [family] fortune" in Austro-Hungarian crowns was reduced to "nothing more than its zeros" in Greater Romania.[4]

In successor states at the end of the war, widespread uncertainty about whether the peace conference would compel vanquished states and their banks to cover the cost of converting imperial currencies was another reason new administrations waited to implement currency conversion. Only the French administration took it for granted that the peace conference would be able to compel Germany to pay for the cost of phasing out paper marks in Alsace and Lorraine. With this confidence, it offered unheard-of subsidies to the non-German populations in Alsace and Lorraine. That decision proved to be so costly that it almost bankrupted the French treasury, while its effect of solidifying the loyalty of local populations proved to be ephemeral. The Romanian government adapted the less risky strategy of postponing the financial integration of its new territories, which jump-started inflation and eventually left Bucharest exposed to French creditors throughout the 1920s.[5] Yet the tardiness of the currency conversion also meant that the industrialists, bankers, and prewar bourgeoisie in Transylvania had ample time to maneuver and diminish the losses generated by the inflation of the Austro-Hungarian crown.

Similar blunders accompanied the process in both France and Greater Romania. The two regions also had a number of similar leading players in their monetary transitions, including economically incompetent military leadership that claimed the right to introduce temporary conversion rates and override experts; a central government that sought to regulate the issue in line with its own noneconomic interests; regional business elites whose social status and economic positions hinged on the outcome of the monetary transition; and bankers, entrepreneurs, and wealthy peasants who all maneuvered to reap profits.

Information about Western currency conversions only selectively filtered into East-Central Europe. France's hegemony over the region and its Prime Minister Georges Clemenceau's image as the most powerful actor at the peace conference blinded Romanian observers to the fact that the Paris government was faced with dilemmas similar to their own. Instead, they regarded Western European currency conversions as the models on which postwar financial stabilization would rest. This warrants a comparative investigation.[6] Transylvanian Romanian economist and Peasant Party politician Horia Maniu contrasted Romanian conversion practices with their French and Italian counterparts, lamenting that "in Alsace and in the Italian Trento region, the motherlands considered it a national obligation not to let their new co-nationals suffer the consequences of the devaluation of their former currencies. [By contrast] in our Transylvania, not only were we not protected, but on the contrary, the new country created a worse situation."[7] In reality, the phaseout of the paper mark in Alsace and Lorraine was among the costliest and least efficient monetary transitions in Europe.[8] Its results were especially staggering given that it was Europe's best-prepared currency conversion and had been the subject of a series of studies by French experts since 1914.

The Genesis of French Policies on the Paper Mark

The French bureaucracy first encountered the conundrum posed by the paper mark in August 1914, when French soldiers reached the westernmost villages of Alsace and entrenched themselves in a small territory around the township of Thann.[9] In December 1914, the commander of the French occupation force, the Lorraine-born general Gabriel Putz (1859–1925), wanted to extend "an act of extreme benevolence" to the local population when he established a favorable exchange rate for gold marks and paper marks, at 1.23 and 1.02 francs for 1 mark, respectively. Putz's exchange rate was very close to the prewar ratio (1.25 French francs to 1 gold mark) and thus disregarded the sharp decline in the value of paper marks since the outbreak of the war—a decline that was due to massive currency emission coupled with reduced German exports.[10] During the war, the issue affected only the inhabitants of a handful of towns under French occupation.[11] The conversion of German money at a favorable rate thus provided a venue for the French administration and army to make this small sliver of land the poster child for French reconstruction at a relatively low cost, offering an attractive alternative to the situation facing Alsace-Lorrainers still under German rule (figure 7.1).

The French government also gathered a group of experts on Alsace-Lorraine's economy and society who provided a series of technocratic suggestions to handle the conversion of German paper marks, taking French colonial administrative practices, the constraints of the French budget, the inflation of the paper mark, and the expectations of the regional population into account. The president of this advisory board, the Conference of Alsace-Lorraine (Conférence d'Alsace-Lorraine), was former prime minister Louis Barthou, and its members included Jules Cambon, the head of the political section of the French Foreign Ministry, and other diplomats, émigré Alsatian politicians, and top-ranking military officers.[12] On November 19, 1918, French troops marched into Strasbourg and occupied the entire territory of Alsace-Lorraine. The sudden end of the war

FIGURE 7.1. The "redemption" of Alsace-Lorrainers from German rule by the French army. Poster of a theater performance (1918). Source: Le Contemporaine, "Tracts français concernant l'Alsace-Lorraine," 4 Δ 1511.

and the surprisingly smooth and rapid reconquest of Alsace-Lorraine put regional elites and experts on the sidelines as they had played no direct role in the defeat of Germany and posed challenges to the government's plans to reintegrate the region on its own terms. By early January 1919, the government dissolved the Conference of Alsace-Lorraine.

On November 26, Prime Minister Georges Clemenceau ordered the conversion of paper marks at the rate in force during the war: 1 paper mark to 1.25 French francs.[13] Clemenceau's decree dismissed not only the conference's suggestions but also French legislative practices, since it bypassed the Chamber of Deputies, thus circumventing any debate on its provisions even though the conversion required funds from the French budget. The prime minister's main goal was to secure French sovereignty over Alsace and Lorraine as soon as possible, since there was no consensus among the Allies in November 1918 that the region would automatically return to France without a plebiscite.[14] A rapid currency conversion was the most effective means to establish French sovereignty over the region, as it gave Alsace-Lorraine's population an immediate financial interest in the permanence of French rule. This was especially important because discontent among the local population could have imperiled the legitimacy of French rule in the eyes of Allied diplomats and the international press.[15] Furthermore, the measure also attempted to cement the loyalty of Alsace and Lorraine's Francophile bourgeoisie, who lost out politically after Paris abolished the restricted administrative autonomy that the Reichsland had enjoyed within the German empire and appointed bureaucrats from the French interior to key administrative positions. Finally, the favorable conversion rate and top-down policymaking fit well with French traditions of paternalism toward Alsace-Lorrainers. Since 1871, French propaganda tracts had depicted Alsatians and Lorrainers as the orphaned children of the French nation, forcefully torn away from the *famille française* by Germany in 1871 (figure 7.2).

There was one important exception to the French government's financial generosity in Alsace and Lorraine: the favorable exchange rate was available only to around 1 million of the region's population of 1.8 million.[16] Clemenceau's decree confirmed that only "Alsatians and Lorrainers" and citizens

FIGURE 7.2. Celebration by the Interallied Parliament and the Friendly Union of Alsace-Lorraine in front of the statue of Strasbourg on May 6, 1917, in Paris. Alsace-Lorraine is represented by two young girls wearing the traditional Alsatian and Lorrainer headdresses, surrounded by Maurice Barrès (*second left*), Abbé Émile Wetterlé (*center right*), and others. Source: Le contemporaine, "Tracts français concernant l'Alsace-Lorraine," 4 Δ 1510.

of allied and neutral states who had lived in the region before 1914 were eligible to benefit from the phaseout of paper marks. Subsequent measures of the French administration made it clear that the region's Germans did not count as "Alsatians and Lorrainers" and that they were not eligible for this generous exchange rate. As Laird Boswell has pointed out, "French bureaucrats and military officials came armed with an ethnic vision of the borderland."[17]

Despite the rapidly depreciating paper mark, French politicians from President Raymond Poincaré to his political rival Prime Minister Clemenceau believed that Allied loans to France would continue to flow and eventually German reparations would prop up the French treasury.[18] The Clemenceau government's finance minister, Louis-Lucien Klotz, proposed an election budget for 1919 that refused to raise taxes and expected Great Britain and the United States to finance French expenditures until German reparation payments were transferred.[19] As Klotz explained to the Finance Committee of the Senate and to the Chamber of Deputies on January 30, 1919, "The government estimates that Germany should reimburse, at a rate of 1.25, [the cost of] the monetary reform."[20] At a time when France's allies were reluctant to extend any more loans, the Bolsheviks had repudiated their debt to French creditors, and Germany was sabotaging its reparation payments, Klotz's expectations were unfounded.[21]

Unlike in 1871, when the French government had paid the extraordinarily high 5 billion franc indemnity imposed by Germany to the last sou (because reparations were the precondition for ending the German occupation of northeastern France), Paris had no comparable leverage over Germany after the Compiègne armistice because the Entente decided not to occupy Germany in November 1918.[22] The French government never used the expropriation and expulsion of Germans from France as leverage to receive reparations from Germany, as it prioritized policies of ethnic discrimination over economic benefits.[23] Clemenceau himself regarded finances as secondary to his major goal of reintegrating Alsace and Lorraine on French terms as soon as possible.[24] Voices of resistance within the government were soon sidelined—or possibly never even reached the ministers responsible, Clemenceau and Klotz. It was the Foreign Ministry of Stephen Pichon that attempted to marshal expert opinion in favor of a lower exchange rate. A highly critical memo that reached Pichon's desk on November 23, 1918, claimed that the intended exchange rate reflected "a more than benevolent decision that no one has asked for, one that Alsace-Lorrainers did not even expect," accused the administration of giving a "gift" to the region's "400,000 Germans," and noted that "in reality Germany will not be able to pay [for the cost conversion] or even if it could, its other obligations would suffer."[25] The Foreign Ministry had, however, lost its authority over the former Reichsland after the armistice, and the region was thereafter administered as core French territory in an effort to transform an international issue into a matter of French domestic politics.

In Klotz's defense, it should be noted that Belgium also adopted the same high ratio when it ordered that 1.25 Belgian francs were to be exchanged for 1 paper mark. This measure shows how deep-seated the belief was in Paris and Brussels that Germany would fully compensate the victors for the costs of monetary transition.[26] The French radical socialist senator Raphaël Milliès-Lacroix summarized the government's dilemma, which led to the sidelining of concerns similar to those of the Foreign Ministry: "Can one leave this loss on the accounts of Alsatians and Lorrainers in possession of German currency? The government did not consider that option at all: it deemed it an injustice to make our Alsatian-Lorrainer compatriots bear the burden of this depreciation [of the paper mark]. It wanted to avoid the development of the feeling that Alsatian and Lorrainer populations have to bear the burden of the German defeat and that they must pay for their reintegration into French unity with a [financial] loss."[27]

In a similar vein, Georges Delahache, a contemporary Francophile chronicler of Alsace's postwar transition, reasoned that the unrealistic exchange rate in the decree "stemmed from France's moral obligation to take back German bills from Alsatians and Lorrainers."[28] The conversion of the paper mark, however, also gave rise to other political and moral issues: Should the government favor Alsatians and Lorrainers, who had fought on the side of Germany against France, at the expense of French taxpayers?

Critics and Beneficiaries of the French "Gift" to Alsatians and Lorrainers

French currency conversion measures benefited the majority of Alsace-Lorrainers, but industrialists, bankers, and wealthy farmers were among the biggest winners.[29] Currency conversion came at the right time for the region's business elites. In the fall of 1918, insecurity about the financial consequences of a French takeover was rampant among the industrialists and bankers who had reaped profits during the First World War but were unsure of the financial consequences of French sovereignty, which they otherwise favored over German rule in the region. The first annual report of the largest Alsatian-owned bank, the Alsatian General Bank (Allgemeine Elsässische Bankgesellschaft [AEB]), shows how economic elites viewed the favorable exchange rate of the paper mark as a key component of preserving their business positions:

"Indeed, we faced some difficult problems after the conclusion of the armistice. The most important question that we asked ourselves was the following: how will it be possible to extend the necessary financial support to our customers, businessmen and industrialists after this change in circumstances? The French government ended this uncertainty in a generous manner. . . . From one moment to the next, our financial life was fully harmonized with that of France. The farsightedness and generosity of the measure are among the most generous in world history."[30]

The managerial board exhorted shareholders, "Given the plight that would have been caused by not exchanging the mark [at a favorable rate], we recognize it as our duty to ask you to express your gratitude to the French government along with us."[31]

The years 1918 and 1919 were indeed a time of thanksgiving for the AEB and other financial, commercial, and industrial companies. The AEB was the poster child for what the favorable exchange rate, continued access to German markets, and cash flows from Paris could do for an Alsatian or Lorrainer company after the French takeover. The bank increased its turnover from 376 million paper marks (470 million francs) in 1918 to 870 million francs in 1919 while reopening its branches in major urban centers of Weimar Germany.[32] In exchange, it had to subsidize the operating costs of German-owned steel plants that the French government had seized after the armistice, like Thyssen's Hagondange plants. The management of these steel plants benefited from the favorable conversion rate of the paper mark, but the measure still caused short-term problems. Because European commerce had not yet recovered, the plants had to pay their workers a higher wage. The result was the mass firing of Germans, followed by layoffs of Italian and Polish guest workers, and inevitably even the letting go of native Alsatians and Lorrainers. Since the economy was slow to recover, the region remained a hotbed of strikes and social unrest throughout the early 1920s.[33] The situation of German-owned firms that remained under forced administration for an extended period of time was even more desperate. The artillery commandant in charge of the German-owned Adler and Oppenheimer tannery in Strasbourg alerted the French regional administration that the firm was heading toward insolvency. This was because workers' wages had to be paid on the basis of the higher rate, and management was only able to convert the company's cash flow in paper marks at the low rate reserved for Germans; as a result, the factory had to fire forty to fifty workers daily.[34]

Politicians in the French interior were not pleased with Clemenceau's currency conversion policies. The economist Henri Hauser, who worked closely with the French government and advised it on the new economic administrations of Alsace and Lorraine, lamented that the measure only benefited rentiers, the bourgeoisie that owned and "rented apartment buildings," as well as "farmers, who have already become tremendously rich [during the war]," while "small business owners and consumers have become its victims,"[35] owing to price hikes, rising wages, and the concomitant layoffs. With French industrial production stagnating at 55 percent of 1913 levels, the enormous increase in real wages precipitated by the currency conversion was at best unrealistic and contributed to the mass firing of miners and steel workers, with a large wave of strikes following in 1919 and 1920.[36] Hauser himself had proposed an exchange rate of 0.65 French francs to 1 paper mark, nearly half the rate that the French government ultimately offered native Alsace-Lorrainers.[37]

As for the region's population, the ethnic discrimination that accompanied the monetary transition alienated many families given that its effects could not be neatly limited to Alsace-Lorraine's ethnic Germans.[38] Even the French propagandist Delahache noted that the coupling of ethnic discrimination with currency conversion slowed down monetary transition and created problems. Many Alsatians and Lorrainers contested their ethnic categorization or were unable to prove their ancestry by the time they had to declare the amounts to be converted. There were fifteen thousand contested cases, representing around 70 million paper marks or 8 percent of the 900 million paper marks reported for exchange by December 1918.[39] The sheer number of these problematic cases prompted the French administration to set up a special commission to process them.[40]

As a result of the shortage of French francs, the region's banks resorted to blocking deposits and savings and extended credit at a high rate of 6 percent, as opposed to the prewar rates of 3 and 4 percent.[41] The lack of cheap credit considerably slowed the economic recovery of Alsace and Lorraine at a time when industrial companies needed capital to readjust to French markets. As in the case of bank imbalances and credit defaults by Germans, the French treasury had to step in to resolve the issue.[42] The Senate and the Chamber of Deputies had no other choice but to approve a law that injected capital into Alsace's and Lorraine's banks and provided for the expenses of currency conversion on April 23, 1919.[43]

Only during the debate leading up to the law of April 23 did the enormity of these expenses become clear to the deputies.[44] The withdrawal of the paper mark from Alsace and Lorraine at a generous exchange rate cost close to 2 billion francs ($250 million)[45] (table 7.1)—a figure comparable to the income from the extraordinary war profit taxes levied across France in 1918, which brought in 1.780 billion francs.[46] Furthermore, two weeks after the law was passed, the final peace terms offered to Germany made it clear that the former enemy

Table 7.1 The cost of Alsace's and Lorraine's reintegration

TYPE OF EXPENSE	EXPENSES (IN 1,000 FRENCH FRANCS)
Exchange of the paper mark	1,822,539 [final sum: 2,250,000]
War damages in Alsace and Lorraine	1,215,483
Total cost of reintegration of Alsace and Lorraine (incl. currency exchange)	**3,387,393**

Source: Commissaire Général to the Garde des Sceaux, November 26, 1923, ANF, AJ 30, 180.

would not be forced to pay for the cost of currency conversion in Alsace and Lorraine.[47] Article 72 of the Versailles Treaty maintained that for prewar debts, the "rate of exchange . . . shall be the average rate quoted on the Geneva Exchange" in the month before the armistice: 0.8134 instead of 1.25, or 35 percent less than the rate desired by the French government.[48]

André Tardieu, one of France's chief diplomats at the peace conference, explained in his memoirs why the French and Belgian governments were unable to persuade their allies to make Germany pay for the cost of converting paper marks to French francs in Alsace and Lorraine. According to Tardieu, the reason was that the Allies wanted "to avoid the contingent effect of such a principle in Central and East-Central Europe, where Germany had abused the compulsory circulation of her currency to an even greater extent."[49] In other words, France was unable to demand that Germany pay for the cost of converting paper marks in Alsace and Lorraine because comparable Eastern European claims on Germany would have bankrupted the Weimar Republic and channeled reparation payments from France to East-Central Europe. Tardieu and Clemenceau were thus unable to persuade their Entente allies to make Germany pay for the generous exchange rate that Clemenceau had already made available to most Alsatians and Lorrainers.

The practice of pairing ethnic discrimination with monetary policy came with an enormous price tag that pushed the French budget to the brink of insolvency. Thus, it is not surprising that senators and deputies from the interior of France, regardless of party preference, were angry at the government. They realized that it was their constituents who were to foot the bill, even though the former Reichsland's population had fought against the Allies in the war and the region was economically better off than much of France—especially the northeast, which Germany had exploited for four years.[50]

The first currency conversion in postwar Europe thus proved to be a financial disaster, and yet most international observers, like the Transylvanian Maniu, saw only the benefits extended to some Alsatians and Lorrainers and thus cast it as a model to emulate. It is true that many ordinary Alsatians and Lorrainers also benefited, but the controversial ethnic categorization of the region's society, the appointment of bureaucrats from the interior of France to key positions, and the radical recasting of Alsace's and Lorraine's administration resulted in considerable malaise that canceled out the effects of the favorable conversion rate.[51]

The Afterlife of Austro-Hungarian Crowns in Greater Romania

As in Alsace and Lorraine, the conversion of Austro-Hungarian crowns to Romanian lei in Greater Romania produced several social conflicts and left broad swathes of the population dissatisfied, even though the process cost the Romanian treasury dearly. Unlike in Alsace and Lorraine, where most people welcomed French troops, in Transylvania even the region's Romanian politicians feared the economic and even the political consequences of incorporation into the impoverished Romanian Kingdom. Like Alsace and Lorraine, Transylvania was economically better off than its "liberator" and also possessed more food reserves than pre-1914 Romanian territories that the Central Powers had systematically exploited. It had more cattle, grain, coal, and industrial and food supplies in general, and Transylvanians feared that currency conversion would be used as a tool to create an artificial equilibrium between old and new territories.[52] Unlike Bukovina or prewar Romania, Transylvania did not suffer from prolonged enemy occupation and had adequate stocks of food and raw materials when the First World War ended. Furthermore, the region's level of economic development surpassed that of prewar Romania, with Transylvania becoming the industrialized core of the new state. By contrast, prewar Romania suffered a military defeat in 1916 followed by two years of occupation and economic exploitation by the Central Powers. On top of that, the Romanian treasury was in dire straits after the Bolsheviks expropriated Romanian gold reserves deposited in imperial Russia in 1916.[53] The sheer size of the territories the Romanian government had to integrate, the prolonged stabilization of borders, and the continued emission of crowns by the Austro-Hungarian Central Bank even after the collapse of the Dual Monarchy posed additional challenges, resulting in massive delays in currency conversion.[54] Consequently, Greater Romania lacked a sufficient base to stabilize the leu after the war, to say nothing of financially integrating the new territories.

While the Austro-Hungarian crown was the most important foreign paper money in the enlarged state, three other currencies presented further obstacles for the government. The so-called General Bank leu was issued by the German occupying army between 1916 and 1918, while the rubles of the tsarist regime and the Russian revolutionary governments were legal tender in Bessarabia, a territory that Romania annexed from the defunct Russian empire.[55] Before the war, the Romanian and Austro-Hungarian currencies were almost on par, since 100 crowns were worth 106 Romanian lei. In early 1919, the Romanian army artificially reduced the value of the crown by 50 percent, and this rate served as the official, albeit temporary, exchange rate until the final phaseout of the crown in September 1920. When the measure was first introduced, it created discontent in Transylvania. But by 1920 this temporary rate had become a generous premium for the region's inhabitants owing to the inflation of the crown.[56]

Following in the footsteps of Czechoslovakia and the Kingdom of Serbs, Croats, and Slovenes, Bucharest stamped the crowns in circulation in Transylvania in the summer of 1919 in order to differentiate domestic currency from the inflow of crowns from other successor states.[57] The Romanian administration's decision to reduce the value of the crown by 50 percent was not considered an extreme measure at the time; rather, it represented a middle ground between the practices applied by Prague and Belgrade.[58] In Czechoslovakia, the exchange rate between the old and new currencies was 1 to 1, but the state withheld half of the converted amount as a forced loan that yielded a meager 1 percent and was irredeemable by citizens. In Yugoslavia, the exchange rate of the crown and the dinar was officially 4 to 1, and in practice 5 to 1.[59] Because Romania's two western neighbors started conversions in 1919, their treasuries were less exposed to the inflation of the crown than was Romania's, which finally completed the conversion process in September 1920. By then, the Romanian administration found itself unwillingly subsidizing populations in Transylvania and southern Bukovina, territories that were the least ethnically Romanian and had fought on the other side of the trenches in the First World War, not unlike the predicament faced by the French government in Alsace and Lorraine.

The Great Postwar Crown Speculation

The Romanian army and administration's temporary halving of the crown's value in November 1918 triggered enormous discontent among Transylvanians.[60] Every time Transylvanian businesses wanted to purchase goods from Bucharest, they needed to buy lei, which generated a demand for that currency and prompted a flight from the crown and the flow of assets from Transylvania to pre-1914 Romania. Banks and speculators from the territory of prewar Romania acquired an advantageous position on Transylvanian markets since they were able to acquire goods at a cheaper price than at home. "As we have a highly depreciated currency when compared to the leu, it is normal that all the speculators of prewar Romania will swoop down on everything that is for sale in Transylvania and transport these goods to the Old Kingdom. The consequence: Transylvania will be stripped of all commodities, which we will then have to procure for expensive leu in Bucharest," warned one of the leading officials of Transylvania's Romanian regional administration, the Directing Council (1918–1920).[61] Nonetheless, the council's temporary ban on free trade between Transylvania and prewar Romania could not stop the depreciation of the crown.[62]

A group of Transylvanian Romanians started a grassroots propaganda campaign for the conversion of the crown and the leu at par and distributed anonymous pamphlets on the Făgăraș–Sibiu train, replete with complex economic arguments set in small type, likely aimed at Romanian notaries, wealthy farmers, teachers, and members of the provincial intelligentsia. The flyer used the language of Transylvania's "equalization" (*egalizarea*) and "liberation," common demands of the Romanian national movement before 1918, and tailored it to the situation of Transylvanian Romanians, who were purportedly suffering under "criminal exploitation" owing to the inferior exchange rate of the crown due to the policies of the Bucharest government.[63]

The Austrian peace treaty signed at Saint-Germain-en-Laye offered a warning sign in September 1919 that Greater Romania would receive no aid for the conversion of crowns in Transylvania, yet this did not prompt Bucharest to act. Article 206 of the treaty stipulated that the government had to convert crowns in circulation in Bukovina, a territory annexed by Romania from Austria, and that the Romanian government would assume a portion of the Austrian state debt.[64] The conversion of sharply depreciating German paper marks in Pomerelia to inflated Polish marks in November 1919 also showcased how belated currency conversion could impoverish populations in annexed territories, while the simultaneous circulation of prewar and postwar currencies in Upper Silesia led to speculation and ultimately proved untenable after the hyperinflation of the German paper mark.[65] The Transylvanian economist and politician Ion I. Lapedatu delivered a long speech in the Bucharest Chamber of Deputies on February 16, 1920, and pressed for an immediate conversion of crowns to leu. Lapedatu warned against unfounded claims that Romania would enjoy the same economic privileges that France had received with regard to Alsace and Lorraine in the Versailles peace treaty. He called attention to the "decisive sway of France at the peace conference" as opposed to Romania's minor influence and highlighted the circumstances that "enabled France to pursue [policies] that other states did not have the power to pursue."[66]

The Treaty of Trianon, finally concluded between the Entente and Hungary in June 1920, copied verbatim the provisions of the Austrian peace treaty on the stamping and exchange of crowns in Transylvania. Article 189 even referred directly to the Austrian treaty in stating that "within twelve months of the coming into force of the Treaty with Austria, each one of the States to which territory of the former Austro-Hungarian Monarchy is transferred, . . . shall replace, as it may think fit, the stamped notes referred to above by its own or a new currency."[67] The final conversion did not take place until September 1920, and as the government did not announce the conversion rate until then, currency speculation flourished throughout Greater Romania.

Currency was easily transported, smuggled, and transferred between cities, counties, and regions, unlike other commodities or labor. Given the breakdown of state administration and transportation and the travel restrictions exacerbated by the Romanian-Hungarian war, between November 1918 and September 1920 the crown's unofficial exchange rate varied from city to city, enabling speculators to amass fortunes from this arbitrage or exploit the very different exchange rates for the same currency in different localities. It is no wonder that Transylvania's financial life had been chaotic since November 1918.[68] While historiography has correctly emphasized the protracted solidification of the new state administration in Transylvania and the numerous legacies of the Austro-Hungarian empire in the region and East-Central Europe more generally, when it comes to finance, Transylvania and prewar Romania became intertwined relatively early, starting in November 1918.[69] The leu thus became the most visible and tangible manifestation of Romanian sovereignty over the region, at a time when resistance by the pre-1918 civil service and the presence of Hungarian street signs and Austro-Hungarian imperial insignia on public buildings continued to challenge Romanian sovereignty in Transylvania.[70]

Profits from arbitrage trading attracted an unlikely combination of speculators, established banks, and politicians, regardless of ethnicity.[71] On top of that, well-informed speculators from prewar Romania had scared farmers with the threat of a low final exchange rate and bought up their crowns at 20–30 percent of the value at which they were ultimately redeemed in 1920. While the crown was not even official legal tender in the territory of prewar Romania, one in six crowns was presented for conversion in Bucharest.[72] Apart from speculation, this also indicates the flow of Transylvanian commodities to prewar Romania between 1918 and 1920.

The circle of speculators from prewar Romania was broad, and many of them were close to the government and its financial policy director, Take Ionescu. Ionescu was nominally the foreign minister but he influenced the government's financial policies through his friend and protégé, finance minister

Nicolae Titulescu. Ionescu offered misleading clues about the final exchange rate during the summer of 1920, which further increased speculative purchases of crowns.[73] While he claimed in the Chamber of Deputies less than two months before the final conversion, "I cannot tell you the final exchange rate until the day has come," he added that "since June [1920] we have been paying the salaries of Transylvanian civil servants on the basis of three crowns for a leu," suggesting that the final rate of exchange would be 3 to 1 instead of the army's rate of 2 to 1.

Ionescu also served as a board member of private banks, such as the Bucharest-based Marmorosch, Blank & Co. Bank, which presented considerable amounts of crowns for exchange. Alexandru Marghiloman, the ousted wartime prime minister, had returned to Romania on the day of the conversion following a spa holiday in Karlovy Vary. He was taken aback by crown speculation among Romania's political elite. "Everyone is in the utmost excitement about the fantastic crown transactions," wrote the "Germanophile" Marghiloman in his French-language diary.[74] "One would buy them at twenty and thirty centimes [*sic*]; some well-informed journals predicted further falling rates. . . . The young Xenopol, chief of Take Ionescu's staff—in utmost secrecy—changed 13 million crowns for himself alone and another 3 million for his family."[75]

The former prime minister thus implied that corruption had permeated even the highest government circles, including the "father" of the conversion, Ionescu. Marghiloman did not limit his stupefaction to his diary. "It is an open secret today," he exclaimed in the Bucharest Chamber of Deputies on August 14, 1920, "that everybody is speculating; people keep asking each other: and you, how many crowns have you heaped up?"[76] Ionescu did not refute these accusations, but he did block the establishment of a committee that was to investigate speculative crown purchases by multiple banks, including the Marmorosch, Blank & Co. Bank, which was close to the governing political elite.[77] Ionescu's role in the conversion process suggests that the phaseout of the crown entrenched the positions of the prewar doyens of Bucharest's political and financial life, while providing a secondary role for the Transylvanian middle class and business elites when it came to profiting from the formation of Greater Romania.

Ironically, the region's mostly Hungarian- and German-owned banks also profited from the extension of one piece of the Hungarian government's wartime legislation—namely, the provision that individuals were allowed to withdraw only a limited amount of their deposits, capped at 2,000 crowns[78]—into the post-armistice period by the incoming Romanian administration, the Directing Council. Banks thus possessed enormous surpluses of capital and cash as it was relatively easy to reap profits from the exploitation of currency fluctuations. The limitation of currency exchange licenses to banks that had operated before the First World War aimed to curb speculation, but it also inadvertently helped well-established Hungarian and German banks, as well as Romanian-owned banks with close ties to the Directing Council, such as Banca Albina.[79] As a result, cash-rich banks with branches in multiple Transylvanian cities, such as the Budapest-based Pest Hungarian Commercial Bank (PHCB), easily exploited these differentials to stockpile goods and currencies in one location and sell them at a profit in another.[80] While the Romanian administration accused Hungarian banks of bankrolling Hungarian nationalist organizations, an improvised audit of the PHCB's books by the Directing Council revealed that the bank's various Transylvanian branches were fighting an internecine battle over exploiting exchange rate differentials. What is more, the bone of contention between the Brașov and Sibiu branches of this Hungarian bank was not even the exchange of crowns but that of the "General Bank lei" introduced by the German army in occupied prewar Romania.[81]

At the same time, the PHCB's former director Henrik Fellner pushed for a rapid transition from crown to leu in Transylvania by phasing out the crown in order to cut his losses due to inflation. As he confided in private correspondence to Transylvanian mine owner Ferenc Chorin Jr., if Chorin needed to sell his mines to French and British investors to protect these assets from Romanian nationalization, "it would be more advantageous—in fact decisive—if I could assure [Western investors] that Transylvania's future currency would be the Romanian leu."[82] Some Hungarian business elites with investments in the region thus preferred stability under Romanian sovereignty over the rule of a postrevolutionary Hungary mired in high inflation and political instability, pointing to the limits of national loyalty when it came to personal and corporate financial interest.

Most of Transylvania's more than four million peasants, pensioners, and especially civil servants were on the losing side of the currency exchange process as they had neither the geographic mobility nor the information needed to exploit the fluctuating value of the crown. Shortages of small denomination leu notes also disproportionately burdened the poor.[83] Pensioners and civil servants lost out on the currency conversion because the army's exchange rate reduced their payments by half.

The disadvantaged parties of the crown conversion found an ally to plead their cause: the low-level officials of the Directing Council. One official amplified his claim for an increase in pensions by referring to the plight of "orphans" and "war widows," these "most faithful populations of the fatherland," reduced to an "extreme plight" by currency conversion.[84] The official did not specify which fatherland he meant, since it was likely that he, together with the families on whose behalf he had intervened, had fought for the Austro-Hungarian "homeland" against Romania between 1916 and 1918. His petition showed that the unfavorable exchange rate undermined the legitimacy of the Romanian administration, which had no means of winning over Transylvanian populations with a favorable rate, unlike comparable French practices in Alsace and Lorraine.

After waiting in vain for the peace conference to force Austria and Hungary to compensate other successor states for the cost of converting the former empire's crowns, the Romanian government's official publication, the *Monitorul Oficial*, announced the date of the upcoming exchange of the crown on August 14, 1920, but did not publish the final exchange rate until September 1, 1920. The decree confirmed the army's 1918 conversion rate. Two crowns were thus exchanged for one leu, representing enormous losses for Transylvanian companies and capitalists compared with their 1918 financial positions. However, by 1920, one leu was worth three to six crowns on Romanian markets. The inflation of the crown in 1919 and 1920 thus considerably reduced the negative impact of the government's exchange rate.

Satirical papers in the Romanian capital were quick to react to the financial upheaval produced by the phaseout of the crown (figure 7.3). The cover of *Veselia* showed Ionescu as a doctor administering the "drug" of "ruble and crown conversion" to his emaciated patient, the Romanian leu. While the skeletal patient is at death's door, the doctor seems optimistic and says that "the pulse seems to be alright."[85] This caricature pointed to the hypocrisy of a government that denied its involvement in currency speculation and downplayed the country's severe financial crisis.

By early 1921, soon after the conversion ended, the government ran into the same problem that the French administration had experienced during the conversion of paper marks in Alsace and Lorraine: the amount presented for exchange surpassed all expectations.[86] The Romanian government was responsible for exchanging almost 9 billion crowns (table 7.2), more than any other successor state of the former monarchy, including Hungary, which came in second with 8.5 billion.[87] The incorporation of Transylvania and Bukovina into Greater Romania thus burdened the cash-strapped Bucharest government with a 4 billion lei ($50 million) debt by the end of the conversion process in 1920.[88] The 41 million gold crowns that Romania eventually received in the 1920s after the dissolution of the Austro-Hungarian Bank hardly compensated for the expenses of phasing out the bank's bills of exchange.[89]

FIGURE 7.3. The impact of the conversion of Austro-Hungarian, German, and Russian currencies on the Romanian leu. Source: "Doctor and Patient," *Veselia, Revista Umoristica* 26, no. 29 (August 24, 1920): 1.

Table 7.2 The cost of currency exchange in Greater Romania

EXCHANGED CURRENCY	FOREIGN-ISSUED CURRENCY (MILLION)	COST OF EXCHANGE IN LEU (MILLION)
Austro-Hungarian crown	8,720	4,355
German-issued leu	1,460	1,460
Total cost of crown, German-issued leu, and ruble exchange	**x**	**7,026**

Source: Costin C. Kirițescu, *Sistemul bănesc al leului și precursorii lui* vol. 2 (Bucharest: Editura Academiei Republicii Populare Romîne, 1964).

While the Romanian government was unable to copy France's discriminatory measures against the German minority during currency conversion, it did resort to covert forms of ethnic discrimination. For instance, unlike Czechoslovakia, Bucharest refused to convert the Austro-Hungarian war loans contracted in crowns by mostly Hungarian, Jewish, and German Transylvanians between 1914 and 1918.[90] The value of these war loans amounted to more than 2.2 billion crowns, roughly equivalent to the amount of crowns in circulation at the time of the armistice in Transylvania.[91]

Transylvanian industrialists initially suffered from the low temporary exchange rate of the crown to the leu in early 1919, but as the Austro-Hungarian currency depreciated below this rate, they eventually welcomed the final conversion with relief. As in Alsace and Lorraine, however, the favorable exchange rate also ratcheted up wages; and as in Lorraine, businesses reacted with wage cuts and layoffs. In 1921, for instance, the Renner tannery in Transylvania reduced the salaries of its workers in two steps, a 15 percent cut followed by a 10 percent cut.[92] Given that the final conversion rate technically halved the value of the Austro-Hungarian crown, the measure fueled Hungarian nationalist and regionalist grievances. The phaseout of the Austro-Hungarian crown rekindled prewar discussions among Transylvania's Romanian middle classes and elites about the economic "exploitation" of the region by outsiders. This time, however, Bucharest was the target of these accusations.[93]

Disillusionment led to the revival of the interethnic political networks and lobbying among the region's Hungarian and Romanian middle classes that had been prevalent before 1914, when they were overshadowed by the ethnic discrimination enacted by the wartime Hungarian and the postwar Romanian administrations.[94] Transylvania's chambers of commerce, represented mostly by Hungarian Jews and Germans, and representatives of the Romanian Directing Council sent a joint delegation to Bucharest to protest what they perceived as the low conversion rate of the crown.[95] The existence of the delegation highlighted what Gábor Egry has described as "the importance of a [shared] pre-1918 middle-class social background, socialization and traditions" among Transylvania's Hungarian and Romanian elites that fueled political mobilization against the Bucharest government.[96] "With the exchange of currencies, prewar Romania has gained the upper hand in the financial life of Transylvania and the Banat,"[97] noted Transylvanian Hungarian politicians Elemér Jakabffy and György Páll in the interwar period. The Romanian Maniu warned in the same vein that "this ever-intensifying operation [of currency conversion] will establish the permanent monetary inferiority of the new provinces within their own state." A Banat-based economist, the Romanian Traian Nichici, argued that "the new provinces had the impression that they were being exploited (*secătuit*)" by the unfavorable exchange rate.[98] The Banat German politician Gaspar Muth claimed in the Bucharest Chamber of Deputies that "we, the populations of Banat and Transylvania, have been rendered underlings of Bucharest's and Galați's financiers. Given the artificial and unfavorable exchange rate of the crown and the leu, millions [of crowns] have left Transylvania for the Old [prewar] Kingdom of Romania."[99]

Given that inflation and the solidification of borders were in part beyond the control of the Romanian administration, it would be a mistake to attribute excessive powers and agency to the Bucharest government in the manipulation of the crown's gradually depreciating value. The intentionalist interpretation that concentrates on how Bucharest followed through on a plan to systematically discriminate against Transylvania and especially ethnic minorities, as contemporary regionalists believed, is far from the full picture. Rather, it is remarkable how the Romanian government was just one, albeit the most important one, of the many actors that tried to influence the process. Because of rapid inflation, extensive currency smuggling, war with Hungary, and speculation, the government lost control over the process by early 1919 and ultimately ran out of options by September 1920, when it had to stick to its own temporary exchange rate even though it represented a premium over the market value of the sharply depreciated crown.

Ultimately, Transylvanians who could afford to wait until the final conversion were among the beneficiaries of the process by 1920, as the government paid a higher rate than that available earlier on the open market. Greater Romania was thus saddled with deep financial problems and unfulfilled expectations of social mobility for Romanian populations, which contributed to its unstable domestic politics and the rise of antisystem, ultranationalist movements around A. C. Cuza and Corneliu Zelea Codreanu as early as the 1920s.[100]

Imperial Currencies—Interwar Legacies

When viewed in terms of the "age of extremes," which started in 1914, the conversions of imperial currencies were important steps in state-led attempts to manipulate the social hierarchies of European societies.[101] After the First World War, inflation and currency conversions nearly broke the Austro-Hungarian and German bourgeoisie in successor states.[102] Ironically, while states were committed to a return to the gold standard, it was the suspension of fixed exchange rates that enabled their social engineering policies, since diverging from the set exchange rates dictated by the "golden fetters" of the prewar period was now a possibility.[103] The French government's conversion of paper marks in Alsace and Lorraine was also the first and overlooked warnings after the end of the First World War that the return to the exchange rates of the prewar gold standard era came at a steep price.[104]

The saga of phasing out imperial currencies showed that the process exceeded the capacities of individual successor states; however, a pan-European solution was painfully lacking at the time, and France was initially reluctant and unable to oversee and finance the process in the successor states of Germany and Austria-Hungary. Yet Greater Romania was on the brink of financial collapse after it converted imperial currencies in September 1920, and Paris had to exert pressure on French banks to step in as lenders of last resort.[105] The stakes were high as France had to sustain its nascent East-Central European "empire" and lend credibility to the Versailles system that Hungarian and German observers and even critics like John Maynard Keynes or Montagu Norman, governor of the Bank of England, castigated for creating economically unviable states built on the ruins of empires.[106] The governments of Greater Romania had unique leverage in negotiating with the Great Powers, especially France, as the country was a key market for Western products and its oil remained a sought-after commodity. The Paris government thus cooperated with the Paribas bank, which issued 150 million francs in long-term loans to Greater Romania, similar to the loan of 300 million francs that Czechoslovakia received from a consortium of French banks in 1920.[107] In the meantime, Bucharest threatened the Weimar Republic with the expropriation of German assets in Greater Romania unless Germany paid compensation for issuing a paper currency between 1916 and 1918; these negotiations led to the first postwar trade treaty between the two states.[108]

French financial assistance to East-Central European allies after the conversion of imperial currencies was not a onetime measure but had to be extended to the stabilization of the leu in the second half of the 1920s. France had to sustain its financial hegemony in the region in an increasingly competitive environment. Paris needed to demonstrate its financial prowess yet again by extending loans in light of competition from the League of Nations and the Bank of England; thus, according to Kenneth Mouré, the "stabilization of the Romanian leu turned into a test case for French political influence in the region" between 1926 and 1931.[109] Ironically, the same French "money doctors" Charles Rist and Pierre Quesnay orchestrated the stabilization of both the French franc and the Romanian leu.[110] While France devalued its currency by 80 percent to stabilize it, Greater Romania resorted to French loans.[111]

Financial cooperation between the two states came with an enormous price tag for the French government, casting doubts on General Henri Mathias Berthelot's assumption in 1919 that France would be able to turn Greater Romanian into an economic "colony" and profit financially from the process.[112] On the one hand, in East-Central Europe, the devaluation of Austro-Hungarian, German, and Russian currencies and inflation served as a backdrop to Western European, US, and most importantly French economic expansion. As it would in the aftermath of other political crises and ruptures, such as in 1945 or 1989, East-Central Europe became cheap for Western investors in the aftermath of the First World War.[113] On the other hand, even as French banks and industrial companies gained ground in East-Central Europe and seized some key German and Austro-Hungarian assets, they also had to invest heavily in the region in order to sustain cooperation.[114]

A similarity in the fate of imperial currencies after the fall of the German and Austro-Hungarian empires was the inefficiency and collateral damage produced by state apparatuses in their handling of currency conversions not only in Eastern Europe but also in Western Europe. Successor states treated currency conversion as a political issue rather than a financial one, which shielded populations from losing out financially from integration into new states but came with a huge price tag for governments. The failure of technocrats to impose their will on administrations is remarkable, as the interwar period is usually identified as the heyday of ambitious economic planners and technocrats such as Louis Loucheur, Étienne Clémentel, Ernest Mercier, and Ludwig van Mises.[115]

While the victorious powers regarded the withdrawal of imperial currencies as key to the breakup of defunct empires and the economic unification of successor states, currency conversion measures ironically reproduced the geographical fragmentation normally associated with empires and amplified the legal, economic, and ethnic differences among the populations in successor states.[116] Apart from the financial integration of annexed territories, the introduction of new currencies often brought about new layers of differences among the populations of postwar states, whether based on ethnicity, as in France, or on geography, as in Greater Romania. The end result of the process was that both France and Greater Romania came to resemble the ethnic and economic diversity of the empires they had successfully defeated.[117]

Chapter 8

Return Home? Alsatian Industrialists in France and Germany after 1918

Alsace-Lorraine underwent a series of well-documented political crises in the 1920s that have so far served as guideposts to understand the region's economy. Such an approach is partially understandable since commerce and industrial production were deeply entwined with politics. For instance, the expulsion of Germans negatively affected many industrial companies, while incorporation into the French customs zone posed challenges to the region's agriculture and textile industries. Anticlerical laws passed by the left-wing Édouard Herriot government led to turbulence in the Alsatian countryside and among the religious middle class starting in 1924, while the dismantlement of the Commissariat Générale, Alsace-Lorraine's regional administration, in 1925 recalled German centralization.[1] From 1922 until 1926, the inflation of the French franc reduced the capital of Alsatian industrialists and the middle class, while the creation of an overvalued franc by Raymond Poincaré led to declining production and exports across French industry.[2]

Despite these difficulties, the former Reichsland's economy was in much better shape in the 1920s than its troubled political situation, not so much because of reintegration into the French economy but because of the retention and expansion of commercial ties to Germany and East-Central Europe.[3] The prospects of industrialists and their companies were profoundly different and markedly more positive after the First World War than they had been after the

Franco-Prussian War. Alsace and Lorraine found themselves at the geographical center of a French-dominated Central and East-Central European zone of economic expansion after 1918. This location made the two regions the French economy's "port of entry" to the markets of the former Mitteleuropa, a position that was advantageous for France's cherished ambitions to create a zone of influence in East-Central Europe. Furthermore, in sharp contrast to the situation under the Wilhelmine empire or under the rule of Napoleon III, customs agreements favored Alsatian and Lorrainer companies over other regions of Germany or France.

In an era of economic protectionism, Alsatian and Lorrainer corporations were able to trade with both France and Germany duty-free since the Paris government's military hegemony in Central Europe effectively forced Germany to receive products duty-free from the former Reichsland. This measure went into effect on January 30, 1919, a few weeks after the Paris peace conference reopened.[4] Article 68 of the Treaty of Versailles between the Allies and defeated Germany granted five years of exemption from customs duties to Alsace-Lorraine products exported to Germany, proof of the French government's uncontested power to regulate the region's economy as it saw fit.[5] Furthermore, the Saar region of Germany, which was an industrial hub and the source of the coal that fueled Lorraine's steel plants, remained part of the French customs zone until 1935. Little wonder, then, that a French government memorandum noted as early as 1919 that "the Alsatian market is a favored market if one compares it with the rest of France."[6]

The peace treaty's economic clauses on Alsace-Lorraine and the commercial accords signed by Germany and France in Baden-Baden were among the successful parts of the postwar economic settlement, as they regulated to the minutest detail economic issues that affected the lives of millions of people along both sides of the Rhine. Regardless of continued diplomatic tensions between France and Germany and nationalist mobilization, Alsatians and Germans could resort to these mutual treaties to resolve personal and commercial issues raised by border changes and expulsions. This contrasted sharply with the situation in East-Central Europe, where peace treaties included no such provisions, leading to the economic decline of border regions and their dependence on politicians and industrialists who maneuvered to revive pre-1918 commercial routes in the absence of interstate commercial accords.[7] On the French-German borderland, even after the expiry of duty-free exports from France in 1925, a commercial treaty regulated trade starting in 1927.[8] The inability of these treaties to prevent economic difficulties for some Alsatian industries stemmed from the inflation of the paper mark, which rendered French products expensive and threw the German economy into a recession. As a result, textile industrialists were unable to export as much as the quota attributed to them.[9]

Ironically, the conclusion of treaties on the economy by French and German technocrats began at the same time as the brutal expulsion and expropriation of Germans in Alsace and Lorraine. On November 15, 1919, the Franco-German mixed committee on furniture, for instance, agreed that Germany would pay 25 million francs to compensate the Alsatians and Lorrainers interned in Germany during the First World War; in exchange, the French government agreed that expelled Germans would be allowed to take the furniture they had been forced to leave behind in Alsace and Lorraine.[10] While the expropriation of Germans was not motivated by economic considerations, it went hand in hand with measures that made Alsatian industrialists not just bystanders but profiteers from these expropriations. Alexandre Millerand, who was the general commissioner of Alsace and Lorraine, the top French official in the region, extended the Faillot law of January 21, 1918, to the former Reichsland, which enabled businesses to rescind prewar contracts with former enemy citizens and lay claim to their property to cover debts. This law helped the region's businessmen further profit from the expropriation and expulsion of their German business partners and competitors.[11]

Unlike the situation after 1871, when Germany, and even France after the onset of economic protectionism in 1890, showed little interest in actively supporting the Reichsland's economy, French governments had carefully engineered Alsace-Lorraine's economic reintegration into the *mère patrie* in the aftermath of the First World War. The attempt at reintegration brought with it numerous challenges, and the self-assured yet often uninformed Parisian bureaucracy hurt regional interests in the process. Even an interwar Alsatian administrator sympathetic to French rule in Alsace admitted that the Reichsland had been thoroughly integrated into the German economy before 1918 and that its commercial ties to Switzerland and Belgium had become more important than those with France: "This [the economic reintegration of Alsace into France] was a delicate situation. False prophets even called it catastrophic."[12]

The French government's top-down policies to reintegrate Alsace-Lorraine were contradictory from the outset, which explains their mixed reception in the recovered regions: they covered the creation of markets, support for industrialists, and expansion of pro-worker labor laws. The Paris government wanted to reintegrate the two regions into the French economy while keeping some of their products out of the French interior to avoid creating competition for industries that had supported the French war effort. Such considerations undergirded attempts to retain German markets and conquer East-Central Europe for Alsace's and Lorraine's products as well as the less successful attempts to integrate

Alsace and Lorraine, among the most landlocked regions of France, into the country's waning colonial empire.[13] France's industries were less competitive on international markets, which called for economic protectionism. But some industrialized regions of the country, like Alsace and Lorraine, also produced excess capacity, which called for economic expansion that necessitated low tariffs and free trade elsewhere.

The continued orientation of Lorraine's steel plants and Alsace's economy in general toward Germany was the wish not only of the powerful French industry organization the Comité des Forges but also of Alsace's leading industrialists and even Alsace's socialist politician and Strasbourg's mayor Jacques Peirotes. The Parisian ministry official approvingly noted the turn of the region's firms to Germany just a few months after the end of the First World War: "The cooperation with Germany has been further supported with the very frequently repeated assertion that it is in fact in France's interest to reestablish commercial relations with Germany, and to turn towards yesterday's enemies rather than towards the Allies. It is better to buy our cutlery in Germany at low prices, than to buy English products since the English sell them to us at high prices."[14]

Peirotes's view of the region's postwar economic development revealed many similarities to the wartime visions of the Reichsland's economic reconstruction advanced by the liberal Alsatian Germans Eugen Jacobi and Ernst Zander.[15] Both Francophile socialists and Germans in Alsace-Lorraine saw federal states in southern Germany as the region's main economic competitors.[16] In order to boost Strasbourg's economic potential, Peirotes advocated the annexation of the port of Kehl from Baden to Alsace.[17] Kehl was a rival port to Strasbourg during the prewar period, and its annexation was intended to make Alsace's capital the most important hub of Rhine trade.[18] Accordingly, in 1926 the French government invested over 100 million francs in the expansion of the port of Strasbourg, making it the leading Rhine port in the former southwestern Germany and trumping its prewar competitor Ludwigshafen.[19] Peirotes's vision showed that economic competition among regions continued to matter in a Europe dominated by nation-states, while the redrawing of national borders did not immediately change the "mental maps" and economic orientation of business managers who adopted a regional next to a national mind-set.

Finally, French rule in Alsace and Lorraine relied on direct subsidies to business elites, including the major industrial companies of the two regions that profited from the expropriation of Germans and banks that reaped the fruits of an advantageous conversion rate for paper marks. However, Paris's introduction of more democratic labor laws that expanded workers' rights led to a series of strikes after 1919 that caused business elites considerable chagrin. The French labor act of March 25, 1919, empowered workers' organizations by allowing unionization in all factories—including the de Dietrich firm, which had previously tried to prevent it by relying on industrial paternalism.[20] The law of April 23, 1919, introduced the eight-hour workday throughout France, including Alsace and Lorraine.[21] The formation of a union required the firm owner's consent, but as the example of the de Dietrich mechanical construction company's labor disputes shows, industrialists were no longer able to force their decisions on their workers. The de Dietrichs tried to resist the formation of labor unions, which in turn incited the ire of the communist labor organizer Charles Huber, who organized a two-month strike at the factory from May to July 1919.[22] This was the first strike in the firm's history and was followed by others in the 1920s, highlighting how the First World War and the revolutions that occurred in its aftermath rendered the industrialists' traditional paternalism inadequate to placate their workers.

Strikes did not undercut the profitability of the de Dietrich firm. The firm reported profits that ranged from 1.5 million francs ($114,000) in 1921 to 4.5 million in 1923 ($237,000) and 8 million in 1926 ($224,000). Even so, in absolute terms, the company's profits decreased between 1923 and 1926 owing to the inflation of the French currency.[23] In the 1920s, the de Dietrich firm also drew revenues from new markets that the French government had created for Alsatian firms in East-Central Europe on formerly German territory. Yet France's inability to remain a diplomatic and economic hegemon in the former Mitteleuropa in the 1930s undercut the value of these investments. One such investment was the takeover of the German-owned Danzig Shipyard and Ironworks corporation, a vast industry complex on the Baltic Sea, by the de Dietrich firm and a majority of French investors. The new Franco-British-Polish company was known as the International Shipbuilding and Engineering Company, and the de Dietrich firm's Paris-based manager, Henri Schloesing, became one of its administrators. Despite its English name and new shareholders, this originally German corporation remained much the same after the Great War. Its first director, ironically, was one of the most successful corporate managers of the German war industry, the Saar-born Ludwig Noé, who had directed an engineering company between 1914 and 1918. Noé's directorship attests to the continuity of German business elites in East-Central Europe.[24]

The de Dietrich firm's management noted that "we believe that with this transaction, which is excellent in itself, we will be able to secure new orders in Eastern Europe";[25] this hope was not unfounded as the Polish state was required to order railway carts from the de Dietrich firm and other Danzig shipyard investors in exchange for their investments.[26] Yet the Great Depression and the rise of the Nazi Party in Germany in the early 1930s shattered ambitious plans to economically conquer the markets of the former eastern territories of the German empire under the aegis of French economic "empire" building in East-Central Europe after 1918. The main trading partners of Alsatian firms remained the firms of southwestern Germany; while the economic importance of the interior of France had risen, neither East-Central European expansion plans nor plans to forge lasting relations with French colonies came to fruition in the 1920s.

The Alsatian "Discovery" of the Colonies

Some Alsatian companies managed to export to French colonies. One such company was the Alsatian Mechanical Construction Company, which sold railway construction materials in Indochina and concluded a contract with the Franco-Ethiopian railways.[27] In 1922, the de Dietrich company shipped one hundred bathtubs a day to Algeria.[28] Yet these contracts did not constitute a permanent commercial link or a substantial portion of exports; rather, they were considered a last resort, especially for troubled industries like textiles. Alsatian textile products were too expensive for Germany and countries like Greater Romania, while the textile industry in the French interior did not need Alsatian products, especially since it was grappling with British competition. Even many French colonies had made separate arrangements with Japan and Great Britain and did not need Alsace-Lorraine's textiles.[29]

In 1918, Alsatians and Lorrainers joined a country that was considerably different from the France they had left in 1871. The campaign for secularization, the Dreyfus affair, and the creation of a colonial empire had substantially altered France while Alsace-Lorraine was under German rule.[30] The First World War further united French society and raised awareness of the extent to which France's existence depended on workers and soldiers from its colonies. As one flier for a French colonial exhibition maintained, "The war has proven how much we can expect in manpower, food, and all kinds of resources from our colonies; we can conclude that their contribution to the defense of our Nation was one of the essential factors in our victory."[31]

France's increased colonization drive in Southeast Asia and Africa in the late nineteenth century was in part a reaction to the loss of Alsace-Lorraine to Germany and the diplomatic humiliation it produced.[32] Yet France's colonies remained dispersed and impoverished, and their population hardly surpassed that of the metropole, which undercut their potential as a market for Alsace's expensive textile products, even as they undergirded French ambitions of remaining a great power.[33] In 1918, fifty million people lived in the French colonies, the most populous of which was Indochina, with a population of seventeen million.[34]

The organizers of the 1922 national colonial exhibition in Marseille overemphasized the economic relevance of French colonies with far-reaching repercussions for Alsace. The economist Henri Hauser, who advocated French commercial expansion both overseas and in East-Central Europe, suggested that "an effort must be made to see all the territories" of "Greater France as one unit."[35] Not unlike how Friedrich Naumann and other advocates of Mitteleuropa had glossed over sharp internal differences in Central Europe, Hauser downplayed these as regards the French empire.[36] Alsatian industrialists and chambers of commerce followed the Marseille exhibition closely since Strasbourg was slated to organize the 1924 edition (figure 8.1). The Marseille exhibition centered on the demonstration of France's unity with its colonial possessions.[37] Organizers of the exhibition stressed the viability of the French empire after it had almost perished under the duress of the First World War and was threatened by revolts in Indochina and demands for decolonization.[38] Much like wartime German visions of a cohesive economic union of Mitteleuropa, this colonial exhibition portrayed France and its colonies as a united "bloc in which all of the parts are in solidarity with each other" and constitute a "harmonious ensemble."[39]

The government explored possibilities for Alsatian textile exports to Indochina by sending Camille Simonin, a deputy of Bas-Rhin, on a trip to Southeast Asia with his son, but the voyage did not lead to any tangible economic results.[40] Finally, in an atmosphere of growing interest in France's colonial empire in the metropole, the Paris government also established a colonial institute in Strasbourg, headed by law professor Maurice Moncharville, who was also a member of the French Colonial Union lobby group.[41] With the colonial fairs and the network of colonial institutes in Strasbourg, Nancy, and other cities, Alsatian and Lorrainer business elites who "had not had the chance to follow French colonial policies in detail" before 1918 suddenly found themselves flooded with information on colonial commerce, even as actual trade between the former Reichsland and French colonies remained modest.[42]

As it turned out, Moncharville fueled turmoil instead of commercial ties between Alsace and France's colonial empire. In September 1921, Moncharville, in part to foreground his role as an expert on colonial markets, alerted all Alsatian chambers of commerce about planned legislation in Indochina that would allow the entry of Japanese textiles with minimal customs duties.[43] This poured oil on the fire of the grievances of the region's struggling textile

FIGURE 8.1. Poster for the 1924 Strasbourg colonial fair, featuring the Strasbourg cathedral. Source: AVES.

industrialists, who feared that losing colonial markets would spell serious trouble after the free entry of Alsatian products into Germany expired. The uproar among Alsatian notables against Japanese textile imports to Indochina showed how ignorance of the colonies' economic relations and profound fears of losing markets led to xenophobic mobilization in the former Reichsland.[44] The fear generated by Japanese textiles in Alsace also showed that France's colonial empire and economic globalization posed challenges rather than a clear-cut opportunity for regional business elites. The situation of Alsatian textile industrialists was comparable to that of textile industrialists in the new states of East-Central Europe, who prompted their governments to protect their interests with tariffs.

The Chamber of Commerce of Colmar, the main textile town in Alsace, put the issue of Japanese imports to Indochina on its October 31, 1921, agenda and noted to the regional administration that it "saw with regret that at the time when the Alsatian textile industry is in the process of creating commercial relations with our magnificent colonial world, it finds a competitor that benefits from its more advantageous geographical and economic position; as such, [Japan] is able to export to our colonies under considerably more favorable conditions than are we."[45] According to the chamber, the economic "crisis" in Alsace also warranted bringing the issue to the attention of the Washington Naval Conference.[46]

Gabriel Alapetite, the politically weightless general commissioner of Alsace and Lorraine, sided with the region's chambers of commerce. He conjured up the image of a nationwide economic crisis to the prime minister and the minister of colonies if Alsace's and Lorraine's economic interests did not receive adequate protection in the colonies. Alapetite tried to appeal to the fears of industrialists in the French interior as he noted that "if France does not secure outlets for textile industries on reconquered territories, Alsatian producers will be obliged to flood the French market with their products; this will result in a very serious crisis for each center of the textile industry in the country."[47] Yet this petition and several others in a similar vein received no response from Paris.[48]

Salvaging the Alsatian economy posed more challenges than that of Lorraine. In Lorraine, the distribution of German steel plants and mines among French and Alsatian companies remedied the firms' economic crisis even as it failed to solve the region's economic problems. German industrialists had made only minimal investments in textiles before 1918. As a result, the incorporation of textile plants into French firms was not a politically viable option as it would have hurt the economic interests of Alsatian industrialists. Instead, Alsatian textile industrialists expected France's colonies to be economically subordinated to the needs of their family firms.[49] While Alsatian business elites were not involved in the creation of France's or Germany's colonial empires in the late nineteenth century, some of them, including troubled textile producers, emerged as advocates of the most radical forms of economic colonization in the 1930s.

The syndicate of Alsatian textile printers, for instance, proposed canceling the 1898 Franco-British treaty on Niger that allowed English products to enter the colony.[50] In 1938, the Alsatian industrialist association suggested turning French West Africa into a territory where Alsatian textiles received preferential treatment over imports from other French regions.[51] While these radical plans of economic colonialism by Alsatian textile producers never became official French policy, they revealed tensions and territorial competition within the interwar French empire.

Ambitious Alsatian plans to conquer the colonies ran into serious trouble from the outset, not unlike French plans to expand economically in East-Central Europe. The French Foreign Ministry attempted to side with Alsatian industrialists but had few tools to support them. There were political and legal differences in the level of autonomy wielded by various colonial possessions, and Paris was unable to unilaterally impose its products without generating uproar among both natives and foreign competitors. Furthermore, Alsatian firms' major competitors in colonial markets were British companies that produced cheaper goods than their Alsatian competitors and had decades of commercial relations with most French colonies, unlike Alsace.[52]

The French government's efforts to influence the composition of textile imports to Morocco were directly related to the plight of the Alsatian textile industry.[53] Morocco was a case in point for the discrepancy between France's political power and Britain's economic power, which prevented a "colonial fix" for the problem of Alsatian textiles.[54] While most of Morocco was firmly under the influence of the French colonial administration, France had lost ground to British cotton and textile importers during the First World War; its share of cotton imports to Morocco had dropped from 12 to 5 percent between 1913 and 1917 while Great Britain's had increased from 85 to 93 percent.[55] Alsatian products were too expensive for colonial markets, and industrialists made few efforts to adapt to changing demand. Ultimately, none of these ambitious colonial expansion plans came to fruition, and in the 1920s France returned to its usual recipe to solve the problem of Alsatian textile industries: exports to Germany.[56] As a result, even in the late 1920s, three-fourths of Alsatian textile exports ended up in Germany, which showed that despite border changes, Alsace remained part of the economic zone of the former southwestern Germany, a region that survived the First World War without significant damages to its economic life.[57]

A Long Wait for Weimar: Alsatian German Industrialists in Interwar Germany

When the French administration expelled the Adlers and Oppenheimers in March 1920, they had to leave their factory behind.[58] Surprisingly, however, by the late 1920s the two families had managed to re-create a network of factories that rivaled their Alsatian colleagues who were not subject to expulsions and even received numerous perks from the French administration, such as the family firm of the de Dietrichs. Since companies owned by expelled German industrialists like the Adlers and Oppenheimers had to wait years to receive compensation from the Weimar Republic, it appears that the key to the firm's success lay elsewhere. The Weimar Republic provided several economic opportunities for German industrialists expelled by the French from Alsace and Lorraine but remained hostile to ordinary expellees. Federal states refused to accommodate German refugees, who lingered as quasi-homeless populations for many months, not unlike Transylvanian Hungarian refugees who were temporarily housed in railway carts in Budapest. In Karlsruhe, for instance, the expellees were put up in wooden barracks in the middle of a noisy city square. Many towns and cities "welcomed" refugees with warning signs that read "Beware of Moving Here." These instances painfully revealed how Alsace-Lorraine's incomplete integration into the German Reich backfired on even ethnic German settlers after 1918.[59]

Of all the territories Germany was forced to cede at Versailles, the German industrialists of Alsace-Lorraine fared the worst, while Polish Upper Silesia's tycoons were in the most advantageous position. Polish Upper Silesia, however, was a small territory with few German investments.[60] In this region, the Permanent Court of International Justice eventually voided the expropriation orders of Polish courts.[61] The territory of Polish Posen constituted an intermediary case between Alsace-Lorraine and Polish Upper Silesia. The fate of German property in Polish Posen was comparable to that of German private property in the rest of East-Central Europe. In these regions, the minority rights treaty and international courts offered some protection. Even so, the Polish government's approach to German property was more radical than states that did not annex territories from the German empire, like Greater Romania. The Polish government expropriated German state property in Posen and created an insecure economic and political environment that prompted over two-thirds of the region's 1.2 million Germans to emigrate by 1931.[62]

German businessmen who had invested in Austria, Romania, Hungary, and Czechoslovakia before 1918 were more likely to retain their wealth than those who had invested in Alsace and Lorraine, even though comparable stipulations applied to German property in all these lands. East-Central European states had a vested interest in retaining their commercial ties to Germany, and German property emerged as a bargaining chip in commercial negotiations.[63] Greater Romania's governments, for instance, expropriated large German oil concessions in part to prevent the Entente powers from seizing them but left less strategic assets undisturbed.[64] After a commercial agreement between the two states in the late 1920s, the Bucharest government formally renounced its right to expropriate German assets.[65] In the meantime, Transylvania's German businessmen emerged as key bridgeheads for German economic expansion in Southeastern Europe.[66]

Keynes waxed indignant in 1919 about the devastating consequences of expropriating the private property of Germans. "So far as I know, there is no precedent in any peace treaty of recent history for the treatment of private property set forth below, and the German representative urged that the precedent now established strikes a dangerous and immoral blow at the security of private property everywhere."[67] Yet the Versailles Treaty was not alone in undermining the social status and economic positions of German business elites on lost territories and in defeated states. Article 297 and its related annex stated that "Germany undertakes to compensate her nationals in respect of the sale or retention of their property, rights or interests in Allied or Associated States."[68]

The treaty, however, neither set a deadline for reimbursements nor specified the amount of compensation or sanctions for Germany in case it failed to satisfy the demands of its own nationals. This gave the Weimar administration considerable wiggle room at the expense of the defunct Wilhelmine empire's business elites. Similar to its attitude toward reparation payments to the Allies, the Weimar government's strategy was to buy time as its currency underwent rapid inflation.[69] It was thus not only the peace treaty that imperiled the financial standing of German business elites through expropriations but also the dilatory reimbursement practices of the Weimar administration. A series of complex laws on war damages regulated the issue until the "final law on war damages" (*Kriegsschädenschlussgesetz*) went into force on April 1, 1928.[70] Yet even this law covered just a fraction of actual losses to companies. Unsurprisingly, the management of the Adler and Oppenheimer firm noted with a hint of irony that "despite its name, we hope that this law will not be the final one" on reimbursements.[71]

The Adler and Oppenheimer corporation received its first installment of compensation in 1922, before the peak of hyperinflation. This payment of 173 million marks was worth 1.1 million prewar marks ($270,000)—less than 10 percent of the company's share value.[72] The company's Strasbourg assets alone were worth more than 10 million marks in 1913, and its profits in the last year of peace totaled 1.7 million marks.[73] Given that even one of the largest

German investment banks, the Deutsche Bank, lobbied the government on behalf of the firm, the amount of compensation was moderate. Despite repeated interventions by the firm and its financier, the treasury accorded only a minor addition. After the stabilization of the mark, the Adler and Oppenheimer tannery received 140,000 Reichsmark, or $33,000, the equivalent of around 135,000 prewar marks.[74] Yet this compensation came in the form of unredeemable treasury bills that yielded meager annuities and covered only a fraction of the tannery's losses.

The Adler and Oppenheimer families' inability to gain immediate and adequate compensation from the Weimar Republic for their expropriated assets showed glaringly that the Versailles settlement was unable to guarantee both the sanctity of private property and the right of victorious states to profit from the expropriation of Germans. The Adlers' and Oppenheimers' ability to rebuild their company with minimal help from the Weimar Republic also reveals the limits of state-centered accounts of European reconstruction. Laws and peace treaties may have insisted on compensation of expropriated businessmen, yet postwar states managed to forgo or substantially reduce obligations that stemmed from the conversion of currencies, war bonds, and compensation for material losses suffered by conationals on lost territories.

The Adlers and Oppenheimers and the rest of the expropriated businessmen from formerly German territories could not count on the young Weimar Republic for reimbursement of their assets, so they turned to speculators eager to lend to risky businesses in the short-lived boom that characterized the Weimar economy between 1920 and 1922.[75] To regain their status as leading German industrialists, the Adlers and Oppenheimers employed a strategy of leveraging their firm with tens of millions of marks to expand the small tannery that remained in the firm's possession in Neumünster into a large factory. The firm had acquired the Neumünster chrome leather factory before the war with loans from the Deutsche Bank. It had started to develop it after 1916 when the German army's withdrawal of raw materials from Alsace rendered the Strasbourg headquarters temporarily idle, but the war did not allow for a significant expansion.[76]

The firm's management also realized that even tanning, an industry that had been dominated by family firms, had undergone substantial concentration during the war while midsize businesses that did not join cartels had become insolvent. On credit, the firm bought three tanneries in Cologne, Berlin, and Munich, as well as the Dutch Amsterdamsche Leder Maatschappij and the Wiltz tannery in Luxembourg. The firm also increased its capital from 12 to 60 million marks in 1921 and up to 100 million in 1922 before the onset of hyperinflation. By 1923, the Adlers and Oppenheimers were on track to lose control of their family business to the creditors, banks, and shareholders who financed reconstruction and expansion in Weimar Germany. By 1922, the firm had accumulated debts in excess of a half-billion marks, or $800,000, amounting to 60 percent of its turnover and over fifteen times its annual profit.[77]

The evaluation of German hyperinflation has divided historians. On the positive side, inflation helped create jobs, prevent an economic downturn, and stabilize the fledgling Weimar government.[78] Yet, as Italian economist Bresciani-Turroni emphasized at the time, inflation led to "the vastest expropriation of some classes of society . . . it annihilated thrift. . . . It destroyed . . . moral and intellectual values."[79] Stefan Zweig, as well as others after him, drew a direct line between inflation and the rise of Nazism, noting that "the inflation served only to make [Germany] feel soiled, cheated, and humiliated; a whole generation never forgot or forgave the German Republic for those years and preferred to reinstate its butchers."[80] Hyperinflation also hindered investment, production, and international trade.[81]

The experience of the Adlers and Oppenheimers shows that inflation and hyperinflation had mixed effects on industrial corporations. The tannery benefited from inflation more than most firms because it was extremely indebted at the onset of hyperinflation. The financial burden on the Adlers and Oppenheimers evaporated in a matter of a few months as the mark became worthless. By 1924, the firm had repaid its creditors, and its debts hovered around 15 percent of the company's turnover and one-third of its share capital in the second half of the 1920s.[82] As in most companies, production came to a complete halt by 1923 when the firm was unable to trade with its foreign partners during hyperinflation.[83] Yet this was a small price to pay for rebuilding the Adler and Oppenheimer empire after the expropriation of the firm's headquarters and most important factory complex in Strasbourg.

On the whole, the Adlers and Oppenheimers failed to become as prosperous in the Weimar Republic as they had been in imperial Germany despite surviving hyperinflation with lower losses than other firms. Out of the six business years after hyperinflation and the onset of the Great Depression, the firm declined to pay dividends in three of those years, and the maximum return on its shares was 6 percent, far less than the prewar average. The firm had forty-six years of prosperity in the Reichsland, while its twelve years in the Weimar Republic were marred by economic turbulence caused by hyperinflation and the Great Depression.

The Adlers and Oppenheimers, whose economic prosperity was originally connected to the presence of German garrisons in Alsace that required large amounts of leather products in the 1880s, learned the hard way between 1919 and the 1930s what it was like to manage a company not only without government support but in an environment in which states turned against particular industrial companies. Their ability to rebuild their factory in Weimar Germany was an exception reserved for Alsatian German business elites with extensive networks among bankers and industrialists. While the Weimar Republic eventually supported the company, state support came belatedly and proved inadequate to guarantee the families' continued prosperity. The fate of the expropriated Germans of Alsace and Lorraine thus closely resembled that of German and Hungarian landowners in the successor states of Austria-Hungary, who received only a modicum of compensation after years of litigation and petitions to the League of Nations.[84]

While the Adlers and Oppenheimers were negatively affected by the French takeover of Alsace and castigated the expropriation of their Strasbourg factory in their first annual report published in Weimar Germany, there were some Germans who were less affected by sovereignty change.[85] Like the Adlers and Oppenheimers, Werner Wittich was an Alsatian German whose fate and politics diverged sharply from the majority of the region's Germans expelled by the French administration after 1918. Wittich was a former professor at the German University of Strasbourg, yet he praised the achievements of the Alsatian economy after the region's reintegration into France. Writing in Strasbourg in 1933, Wittich noted that "the entry of the regional economy into that of France was followed by a general [economic] boom." Looking back to the period since the French Revolution, Wittich also wondered whether Alsatian industrialists simply managed to survive and prosper regardless of political and technological changes. Wittich's positive view of Alsace's prosperity after the region's reintegration into France was grounded in both the continued industrialization of Alsace and his positive personal experiences in French Alsace.[86] Wittich was the only German university professor whom French authorities allowed to stay in Strasbourg after 1918, an unusual generosity for which Wittich could thank his Alsatian wife and well-placed Alsatian friends who lobbied in his behalf.[87] Both his personal life and the fate of Alsatian industrialists after 1918 showed the importance of government policies for continuities and ruptures among social and economic elites. Alsace's and Lorraine's economies opened up to Central and East-Central Europe in the 1880s, and the two regions entered France in 1918 with minimal commercial ties to the *mère patrie*. When the French administration tried to separate the region from the former Mitteleuropa, whether through the expulsion and expropriation of Germans or the conversion of German currency, it encountered financial losses and social turbulence in Alsace and Lorraine. It comes as no surprise that the main economic goal of the French administration was therefore to retain Central

European markets for Alsace and Lorraine, even as this aim was often masked by hostile anti-German rhetoric. The Alsatian economy's continued dependence on the German economy after 1918 was also clear to Wittich, who attempted to counter this with a narrative on national character that set Alsatians apart from Germans, despite Alsace's close economic ties with Germany. According to Wittich, the Alsatian bourgeoisie preserved its "rural character" and retained its ties to the countryside, just like the French and unlike German city elites, cut off from their rural roots.[88]

The French political elite needed to build up the reconquest of Alsace-Lorraine from Germany, a marginal issue in French political life in 1914, into a tangible war aim to justify the horrendously bloody war effort that eventually claimed as many French lives as the entire population of the "lost provinces."[89] Yet once the moment of return arrived, it became clear that the French national economy would have trouble accommodating the three departments. While individual French corporations that seized lucrative firms in Alsace and Lorraine profited amply from sovereignty change, the region struggled to find outlets for its products in an already industrialized French state eager to find export markets for its own products. In this regard, the situation of Alsatian industrialists was less advantageous than that of industrialists from Transylvania, Vojvodina, or Polish Upper Silesia, who were integrated into less industrialized, more agrarian states, Greater Romania, the Kingdom of Serbs, Croats, and Slovenes, and Poland. As Alsatian textile industrialists painfully realized, French colonies had no demand, had no purchasing power, or were already serving as outlets for British, Japanese, and French firms. Unsuccessful calls to subordinate French colonies to Alsatian economic interests attested to the jingoism, desperation, and ignorance of France's complex commercial relations with its colonies among some Alsatian industrialists who first encountered France's colonial empire after 1918.

In practice, the French solution to the problem of the borderland economies of Alsace and Lorraine was to turn them "quietly" toward their former ruler, Germany, as early as 1919 and use France's nascent East-Central European alliance to absorb some of Alsace's and Lorraine's industrial capacity. The first effort succeeded but the second failed, in part because East-Central European states were eager to support their own industrial capacity and were busy erecting tariff barriers to protect domestic industries, and were also more prone to purchase cheap German products in an era of German inflation than expensive French ones. Unlike Transylvanian and other East-European industrialists in the successor states of Austria-Hungary, who were incentivized to cut ties with the core territories of the former Dual Monarchy, Alsace-Lorraine's industrialists and bankers were able to continue to cultivate connections with their pre-1918 German markets, and French laws even encouraged them to do so. Ultimately, the French solution to the region's economic plight was very similar to that proposed by the founders of the European Coal and Steel Commission after the Second World War. Both rested on regional economic cooperation and the free trade of certain commodities. Yet after the First World War, this cooperation was forced on Germany as a massively hierarchical relationship that favored France. As a result, its achievements also vanished when France's Central European political ambitions collapsed in the early 1930s.

CHAPTER 9

A Marriage of Convenience? Austro-Hungarian Industrialists in Greater Romania

The debate on the economic viability of East-Central European successor states after the Great War began even before these states were born and was closely linked to the prospects of the bourgeoisie they inherited from the Austro-Hungarian, German, and Russian empires. Contemporaries wondered how the mostly German, Jewish, and Hungarian cities and their bourgeoisie would fare under the domination of Slavs and Romanians in an age of heightened nationalism and antisemitism, confined behind the heavily guarded borders of states considerably smaller than Austria-Hungary. Over the intervening century, historians have tended to view East-Central Europe's economic life through an ethnic filter despite the fact that the actual economic processes showed a remarkable accommodation of old and new elites and the birth of a new business elite that was not organized on the basis of ethnicity alone.[1] In 1919, John Maynard Keynes and many of his contemporaries were convinced that the destruction of the Austro-Hungarian Monarchy would bring about the economic decline of East-Central Europe. Keynes called Poland "an economic impossibility with no industry but Jew-baiting"[2] and believed that French plans to replace Germany's economic hegemony in the region would fail as successor states would discover that "the seductive policy of France is pure rhodomontade and that there is no money in it whatever, nor glory either."[3] This former member of the British peace delegation labeled the creation of Greater Romania "a scatterbrained conception" and called the country unworthy of a recovery loan as "the ruling classes of Roumania [*sic*] will divide up the booty among themselves."[4] Keynes's views were not far from the arguments articulated by the German and Hungarian peace delegations at Versailles. Albert Apponyi, the conservative politician who headed the Hungarian delegation, warned Lloyd George and Clemenceau that the separation of Transylvania from the rest of Hungary would precipitate a sharp economic downturn as "Roumania [*sic*] could only maintain its unnatural dominion by using every means in her power to hinder the economic development of the Magyar and German elements and thereby of the country [Transylvania] as a whole."[5]

Despite the pessimistic expectations of Keynes, Apponyi, and others, the Romanian annexation of formerly Austro-Hungarian territories created a new, multiethnic, and multinational business elite in which Hungarians, including culturally assimilated Hungarian Jews, Germans, and Romanians, learned to cooperate on corporate boards and exploit each other's political and social networks to further their own economic interests. This marriage of convenience between elites old and new has been overlooked by historians as neither ethnic minorities nor Romanian politicians and businessmen at the time trumpeted business deals that connected people on different sides of the political and ethnic barricades of Greater Romania.

The continued prosperity of ethnic minority industrialists in interwar East-Central Europe also challenges the established tenets of national histories, centered on ethnic strife and state building, because these transactions highlight continuities and connections between the social hierarchies of Austria-Hungary and its successor states and showcase the prevalence of class next to ethnicity as the organizing principle of interwar East-Central European states. The lure of narratives that stress ethnicity as the organizing principle of successor states is that they are remarkably simple and persuasive. Accordingly, 1918 either signaled a "trauma" for vanquished peoples like Hungarians and Germans or was a harbinger of "new beginnings" and "unification" of national territories for the French, Romanians, Poles, Czechs, Slovaks, and southern Slavs. Ironically, these narratives of national trauma and national rebirth closely resembled each other. Both histories written from the perspective of victorious states and those from the perspective of vanquished states or specific ethnic minorities would agree that 1918 constituted a break in history and that the successor states of the German and Austro-Hungarian empires engaged in a changing of the guard among the propertied elite, and that as a final outcome, Romanian, French, Polish, and Czech businessmen gradually replaced those of the prewar era. Yet the stated goals of governments and nationalist public intellectuals more often echoed intentions and predictions rather than actual economic processes on the ground, which showed that massive changes in borders did not result in the elimination of the Austro-Hungarian bourgeoisie.

Given the importance of economic life for successor states and the importance of economic viability for their political legitimacy, there is surprisingly little information on how their economies actually worked. Posterior assessments of the interwar period focused on individual states and national economies as units of analysis and have fluctuated between wholesale rejection and one-sided nostalgia, preventing a nuanced analysis. Works written during the communist period cast the era in a negative light, focusing on the "capitalist exploitation" of workers by industrialists, and viewed the period from the perspective of its fascist culmination.[6] In contrast, following Romania's gradual transformation into a capitalist state after 1989, as Cornel Ban has noted, issues of social inequality and "class smacked of communism."[7] Little wonder, then, that the way was open for the rehabilitation of interwar Romania and its bourgeois world, which were gradually surrounded with a certain "period charm" as the country searched for a usable past while it transitioned back to a capitalist economy.[8] The era thus became identified with national unification, territorial expansion, and cultural effervescence and multiculturalism that were eventually destroyed by outside forces such as Nazis, communists, and their coterie of local acolytes.[9] Finally, the revival of research into the Hungarian, German, and Jewish communities in the spirit of nationalism and identity politics starting in the 1990s often relegated their integration into the economic and political life of Greater Romania and their fluid boundaries to the background and focused on community building and victimization.[10]

More recently, however, "interwar nostalgia" has been subject to criticism. Lucian Boia emphasized that the "interwar period [as a] golden age is a product of post-1989 myth-making . . . [and] despite some partial accomplishments, the era was neither really bright economically nor politically."[11] Economic historian Bogdan Murgescu, in agreement with Boia, noted Greater Romania's "contradictory responses to modernity and its economic, political, and moral failure."[12] After all, the country's attempt to catch up to industrialized states between 1922 and 1928 while limiting foreign capital and imposing a 40 percent tax on industry imports failed, despite producing a remarkable industrialization drive and postwar recovery comparable to Yugoslavia's.[13] Greater Romania's economy also suffered from low agricultural prices in both the 1920s and 1930s, the disastrous impact of the Great Depression, and an unsuccessful oil export policy that increased exports during times of global oil market saturation.[14] Pogroms occurred regularly in both the 1920s and 1930s and were condoned by the government, while the country subjected its Turkish, Jewish, and other minorities to a series of discriminatory laws in the second half of the

1930s before Greater Romania's gradual disintegration under pressure from Nazi Germany, Italy, Hungary, and the Soviet Union after 1940.[15]

Surprisingly, however, even myth-busting accounts tend to leave the purported ethnic divisions in Greater Romania's economy unquestioned, often relying on statistics from the late 1930s or the 1930 census authored by antisemitic experts invested in upholding and reifying these ethnic divisions, especially when it came to foregrounding the "Jewish" role in economic life.[16] Transformed into captivating narrative history, even problematic statistics take on a uniquely convincing charm of their own:

> Minorities formed rather powerful blocs, especially in urban areas and multiple sectors of [Greater Romania's] economic life. . . . Above all, many Romanians were disturbed by the fact that, in a self-proclaimed nation-state, most of the economy was in "non-Romanian" hands. The official statistics from 1938 show the ownership of individual commercial and industrial companies. Out of the total of 229,042 companies, 48.49 percent were [in the hands of] Romanians, while 31.14 percent had Jewish owners, and 20.37 percent belonged to other minorities. . . . The Romanian share was 36.15 percent in Transylvania, 47.36 percent in the Banat and 21.22 percent in Crișana-Maramureș.[17]

Antisemitic statisticians such as Sabin Manuilă had a vested interest in portraying Jews and Hungarians as powerful "blocs," separate from Romanians. Statistical overviews like the one above suggest that Greater Romania's economy was dominated by a cohesive "bloc" of businessmen and industrialists from the former Austria-Hungary, with ethnic Romanians relegated to a secondary role in their own country. Such "groupism," or "the tendency to take discrete, bounded groups as basic constituents of social life, chief protagonists of social conflicts, and fundamental units of social analysis," is misleading, as it diverts attention from actual social and economic alliances that often united businessmen from a variety of ethnic backgrounds.[18] Once ethnic groups are reified "as substantial entities," or "blocs," agency can be attributed to them. This was the case in Romania, despite the fact that, in practice, interwar Romania's economic life did not break down neatly along ethnic lines and that it was impossible to separate capital on the basis of ethnicity; state administrations had learned this the hard way during campaigns against enemy property between 1914 and 1918 and, subsequently, between 1940 and 1944 when Hungary annexed northern Transylvania.[19]

Given that successor states and their loyal business elite had no capital to buy out ethnic minorities from industrial companies and banks, they had to make do with window-dressing measures. In Transylvania, as a compromise, all companies had to be incorporated as Romanian entities headquartered in

Greater Romania, a process called "nationalization" or "nostrification" at the time. Unlike after 1948 in Eastern Europe, nationalizations after the First World War thus did not include taking privately owned entities into state ownership. In Greater Romania, a special government office was in charge of "nationalizing" the firms owned by ethnic minorities, which included exerting pressure on formerly Austro-Hungarian industrialists to include Romanian politicians on corporate boards and have Romanian shareholders. In exchange for access to state resources, including loans, permits, and labor laws favorable to corporate interests, Austro-Hungarian industrialists surrendered some positions to Romanian politicians and banks.

By 1922, just over fifteen hundred Transylvanian industrial companies with total capital of 6 billion lei, or $41 million, had been nationalized.[20] Most of these companies hired Romanian lawyers, accountants, and clerks, while Romanian banks assumed a portion of the companies' finances, often by channeling capital from French banks to them. Was the outcome of this process that "the former Magyar hegemony was replaced with Romanian hegemony in which the Romanian elite dominated both the political and the economic sectors"?[21] To the contrary, evidence suggests that state-business coercion and the subjugation of Hungarian industrialists was far less successful than nationalist newspapers, politicians, and government policies suggested. Instead, numerous mutually beneficial partnerships emerged, to be met with dismay by contemporary nationalists. On paper, the biggest losers in this transformation were the big banks of Vienna and Budapest, which were forced to cede their branches and investments in Transylvanian industrial companies. In practice, however, they passed on their interests in Greater Romania to their prewar partners, like the Marmorosch and Blank Bank, or Transylvanian trustees like Mózes Farkas or Zsigmond Szana, and thus did not suffer major losses from the change in sovereignty. Apart from key oil companies, French participation also remained indirect since French investors had to "hide" behind Romanian banks.

Nationalizations were thus not always top-down processes that locked nationalizing governments and ethnic minorities in newly annexed territories in conflict. Instead, regional elites, including those active in pre-1918 Hungary, were able to subvert and redefine nationalization policies to serve their own interests. This was all the more possible since laws did not explicitly forbid the participation of Transylvania's Hungarian and German industrialists in nationalizing companies headquartered outside Greater Romania or firms that had previously been funded by Budapest banks. The result of nationalizations was thus often the concentration of Transylvania's industrial wealth in the hands of ethnic minority industrialists, such as Farkas and Szana.

Romanians' partnerships with "domestic foreigners" were the subject of heated debates and criticism by national liberals, ultranationalist Romanians, and even Hungarian observers, as these business practices did not conform to nationalist ideals.[22] Victor Slăvescu noted in reference to a particular business partnership between a Bucharest bank and the Timișoara banker Zsigmond Szana, a Hungarian Jew, that "it is very painful to realize . . . that there are individuals who lend their Romanian name for shares in the bank's profit and act as lobbyists towards the administration with the aim of gaining advantages."[23] As Slăvescu highlighted, such transactions were far from exceptional. Thus, ironically, Transylvania's Hungarian, German, and Jewish business elite contributed to the economic unification of Greater Romania by forging ties among economically disjointed regions like northern Transylvania, Bukovina, and prewar Romania.[24] One revealing example of the extent of the economic ties between Transylvania and the rest of the country is that by 1940, two-thirds of the Cluj-based Renner tannery's thirty-two branches, including stores, were located outside Transylvania in the rest of Greater Romania, from Cernăuți in Bukovina to Bucharest.[25] By expanding their networks among Romanian politicians, prewar tycoons became part of the new establishment, not only prospering economically but also supporting political parties and newspapers and lobbying for favorable legislation.

From Ethnic Minorities to Business Elites

The reemergence of Austro-Hungarian industrialists as the business elite of successor states was not a straightforward process. Czechoslovakia, Greater Romania, and the Kingdom of Serbs, Croats, and Slovenes were born out of the crucible of the First World War, which left its mark on their militant attitudes toward national economies and interventionist social and educational policies that negatively affected ethnic minorities.[26] In the 1920s, all East-Central European states adopted economic policies that aimed to create or prop up a national bourgeoisie. The bourgeoisie inherited from Austria-Hungary did not fit into this agenda. The refusal to convert war loans (or a policy of converting them at a disadvantageous rate), the conversion of billions of Austro-Hungarian crowns below the prewar ratio, land reforms, and administrative centralization all disadvantaged Hungarians, Germans, and Jews in successor states more than they did Slovaks, Serbs, and Romanians.[27] The prospects of collective resistance against these measures via political organization or Hungarian or German economic nationalism were especially dim in the Kingdom of Serbs, Croats, and

Slovenes and led to visible but modest results in Greater Romania and Czechoslovakia, where political parties of all stripes could function despite having no hope of achieving power.[28]

If successor states of empires learned from the First World War, so did industrialists. While the former learned to engage in ethnic categorization of populations and came to believe that the economy should be domestically owned, preferably by ethnic majority businessmen, the latter learned how to prosper and function in a volatile business environment and how to profit from economic crises and the breakdown of state administration. Postwar states were far from "robust" and appeared "fragile," while Central European companies learned how to thrive and profit from uncertainty between 1914 and 1918.[29] False accounting, the creative use of substitute materials, and falsification of products were a few of the tools that corporations could rely on in the post-armistice period, as they had during the war, to maintain their influence.

Not all successor states were created equal in terms of economic prospects for the industrialists of the former Austria-Hungary. Transylvania's industrialists were better placed to benefit economically from new borders than other territories of pre-1918 Hungary, such as Slovakia or Vojvodina. The prosperity of annexed territories depended on the makeup and size of their new national economies, the relative weight of annexed territories in their new national economies, and the economic policies of successor states. Transylvania was the largest territory lost by Hungary after 1918—larger, in fact, than postwar Hungary itself—and its population amounted to over two-thirds of Hungary's. Transylvania's territory and population provided unique economic advantages for its industrialists. Unlike the disjointed fringe territories that Yugoslavia, Austria, and to a lesser extent Czechoslovakia annexed from Hungary, Transylvania had a distinct regional identity, its own political elite, and commercial ties that linked its various subregions.[30] The region's sheer economic and demographic leverage within Greater Romania proved to be yet another asset. With 5.5 million inhabitants, Transylvania was home to 31 percent of Greater Romania's population, made up 35 percent of its territory, and provided an even larger share of the new state's industrial potential. It had almost as many large industrial companies as prewar Romania, and according to Romanian statistics, its firms' motor power surpassed that of prewar Romania.[31] Since prewar Romania's industries centered mostly on oil production, Transylvania's role in light industries, food processing, and mining was even more pronounced than its share in the country's total industrial potential indicates.[32] The region's industries also benefited from the Jiu valley's coal and the widespread use of the natural gas discovered in the vicinity of Cluj—

the new, Romanian name of the region's "capital" Kolozsvár.[33] The business elites of Cluj and other Transylvanian cities also benefited from the new borders that cut them off from the industrial core of East-Central Europe, reaping the rewards of Romania's protectionist economic policies of the 1920s. This was hardly a secret at the time, as these companies even advertised the benefits they received from the Romanian government to prospective Hungarian shareholders.[34]

Because Transylvania was more industrialized than the rest of the country, its corporations did not face competition from prewar Romania, Bessarabia, or Bukovina. On the contrary, Transylvanian companies that had previously been located on the periphery of the Hungarian kingdom became the industrial core of Greater Romania, which provided new and unsaturated markets for their products. While the economic policies of the 1920s tended to favor prewar core territories in Greater Romania, Czechoslovakia, and Yugoslavia, Transylvania's economic interests within Greater Romania were considerably more difficult to ignore than those of Vojvodina in Yugoslavia or of Slovakia within the Czechoslovak Republic.[35] Vojvodina was Yugoslavia's second most industrialized region, behind Slovenia, but made up just 15 percent of the new state's population and attracted a mere 10 percent of industrial investments throughout the interwar period; it suffered from disproportionately high taxes compared with prewar Serbian territories.[36] Slovak firms, in the meantime, faced fierce competition from the larger, more efficient, and more numerous Bohemian and Moravian industrial companies.[37]

It is little wonder that, coupled with the effects of protective tariffs that shielded Transylvanian companies from Czechoslovak and Hungarian competition, some industries developed more quickly after 1914. The Romanian tanning industry's production doubled between 1919 and 1921 and increased an additional 33 percent by 1923, while the ban on cattle exports decreased the industry's dependence on raw material imports.[38] Annual per capita leather consumption increased from 1.4 to 1.7 pounds in the early 1920s.[39] In the era of protectionism, the state acted as a buyer of last resort for many industrial companies; the Romanian state railway company, for instance, purchased two-thirds of the Jiu valley's coal at advantageous prices, much like the Hungarian Royal Railways before 1918.[40]

Gradually loosening economic ties between Hungary and Transylvania gave way to the revival of regionalism among Hungarian economists of the region; ironically, this regionalism turned against both Hungarian and Romanian attempts at the economic "exploitation" of Transylvania. Regionalism in Transylvania, or "Transylvanism," showcased deep rifts within Hungarian nationhood as it revealed that the Hungarian nationalism of Transylvanian elites differed from the "imagined community" of a homogenous Hungarian nation projected by the Budapest government.[41] Some Transylvanian Hungarian public intellectuals even came under the influence of what Roland Clark has identified as a "postcolonial mentality" among interwar Romanian political elites, which reduced economic relations among Ottoman, Hungarian, and Austrian imperial "centers" and Transylvania as a simple economic exploitation.[42] They rejected the "imperialist" Austro-Hungarian economic policies that purportedly subordinated Transylvania to the interests of Budapest banks, even as, ironically, this regional elite emerged as a result of the modernization projects of the Hungarian state before 1918.[43] The Transylvanian Hungarian Party's finance specialist Elemér Gyárfás, educated in law in Budapest, went so far as to compare the Hungarian capital's prewar financial ties with Transylvania to relations between the colonizing metropole and the colonized periphery.[44] As he explained, "Such a system of economic life [that had characterized the relationship of Budapest banks and Transylvania before 1918] and such use of capital showed an eerie similarity to the capital policies of western maritime powers, which they pursue when economically exploiting their overseas colonies."[45] Gyárfás's views attested to the influence of fiercely anti-Hungarian economist Victor Slăvescu, whose work on nationalization and banking he had translated from Romanian into Hungarian.[46]

Slăvescu was close to the governing National Liberal Party, which dominated Romanian economic policymaking intermittently from the armistice to the late 1920s. While Austrian liberal economists wanted to free global markets from "tariff walls," Romania's national liberals dreamed of a "closed Romania, living by its own means of production."[47] Despite the divergences between the Austrian liberals who gathered around Ludwig von Mises in the 1920s and Bucharest's national liberals, the two groups of thinkers agreed that postwar states had to actively intervene in the economy to protect corporate interests.[48] As Ștefan Zeletin, an interwar intellectual close to the national liberal government, put it, "Liberalism needs to surpass its former attitude of passivity and start the work of social reconstruction."[49] The Viennese Ludwig von Mises served as the economic adviser of the young Otto von Habsburg, and his endeavor to re-create a tariff-less "world economy" echoed the longing for the economic unity of the defunct Austro-Hungarian empire seen among many contemporary Central European intellectuals like Oszkár Jászi. After all, the Dual Monarchy had come the closest to the liberal ideal of unified customs and industrial promotion ever seen in Central Europe.[50] Where Austrian liberals had lost an empire in 1918, one that they attempted to re-create on a global scale during the interwar period, their Romanian counterparts gained a "little empire" at the end of the Great War and attempted to shield its fledgling domestic industries from the threat of global competition.[51] While classical liberalism as well as its early twentieth-century Central European iterations endorsed international trade as beneficial for all parties involved, Romanian national liberals viewed economic transactions as a zero-sum game, which explained their resistance to French, and later German, investments.[52]

The future foreign minister Mihail Manoilescu argued that "the advantage of international exchange exists only for industrial countries which export industrial goods, and it does not exist for agricultural countries which export agricultural produce."[53] Thus, the Romanian political elite of the 1920s was far from economically liberal: it embraced a protectionist and nationalist ideology, while authoritarian elements dominated its political practice. The German- and French-educated sociologist Ștefan Zeletin, who baptized the national liberal tenets of the 1920s "neoliberalism," argued that Romania would only be able to pursue classical liberal trade policies after an autochthonous industry and bourgeoisie had been created.[54] Until such a class came into being, "closed gates [should await] foreign products."[55] The National Liberal Party's main political rivals, the fusion of Transylvania's regionalist National Party and prewar Romania's Peasantist Party, which held power between 1928 and 1931, proved more open to foreign capital, but their political rhetoric on ethnic minority businesses echoed that of the national liberals.

National liberals advocated the policy of industrialization "by ourselves" (*prin noi inșine*), under ethnic Romanian leadership and excluding foreign capital. While this policy was impossible to implement in its entirety, it led to the bankruptcy of numerous Transylvanian firms that were unable to obtain loans to finance operational expenses or the costs of modernizing their plants. The otherwise prosperous Dorma textile works in Cluj was among the victims of this national liberal policy; the firm was only able to compete by taking out expensive loans from banks that it was unable to repay.[56] The Romanian economy's weakness became especially clear during the Great Depression, when the lack of both foreign and domestic capital bankrupted several, mostly smaller and midsize, Transylvanian companies and several regional banks.[57]

The attempted exclusion of ethnic minorities from economic life was in sharp contrast to the country's need for both foreign and minority capital for industrialization. Apart from French and Italian banks, the main source of foreign capital came from Austrian and Hungarian banks, often channeled through corporations owned by Transylvania's ethnic minorities. It was simply impossible to implement industrialization with the exclusive backing of ethnic Romanian banks and industrialists. The rhetoric of the national liberals and Romanian nationalists in general on the Romanianization of the economy is thus inadequate to understand how the economy worked on the ground.

Ironically, even Romanian government policies contradicted the doctrine of exclusive economic nationalism. For instance, despite their fierce antiminority rhetoric, national liberals soon realized that they were unable to carry out their program of industrialization without actual industrialists, most of whom came from the ranks of non-Romanians. Even the Banca Centrală, an investment bank set up by the Directing Council to create a strong Romanian industrialist class in Transylvania, ended up financing minority-owned companies owing to the paucity of Romanian ones.[58] The Renner tannery, an oil and soap factory in Timișoara, the Corvin engineering company in Cluj, the Alfa chemical company, and various construction companies were among the businesses financed by the Banca Centrală, and all were under Hungarian or Hungarian Jewish ownership.[59] Even companies financed or owned by Budapest banks and corporations received aid through the Romanian government's industrialization drive, despite an explicitly hostile relationship between the two states. Cluj, Timișoara, the Jiu valley, and the Saxon towns around Brașov were especially well placed to reap the economic fruits of incorporation into Greater Romania since they were less dependent economically on the core territories of prewar Hungary.

Businesses along the new Hungarian-Romanian border were particularly hard-hit by the lack of commercial cooperation between the two states. Diplomatic representation between Hungary and Romania was not established until 1921, and interstate trade took place on the basis of ad hoc agreements, while Budapest industrialist Ferenc Chorin only managed to form a joint Hungarian-Romanian chamber of commerce in 1931 and even contemporary statisticians had no clear estimates of trade volume between the two states.[60] Unlike in the case of Alsace, Lorraine, and Germany, the Versailles Settlement did not contain detailed stipulations on commercial exchanges between Transylvania and Hungary. This increased the importance of individual arrangements by industrialists, bankers, and merchants to facilitate interstate commerce and financial transfers. In the absence of such deals, border region firms lost easy access to the markets and products of the Hungarian Great Plains and Budapest since customs agents frequently hindered the cross-border flow of goods.[61] Cities adjacent to the Hungarian border, like Arad, Oradea, and Satu-Mare, stagnated or declined despite their stellar trajectories as part of the industrializing growth zone of the prewar urban network.[62] Geography was a common destiny that ethnic minorities shared with Romanians in these regions, even if new Romanian banks and the state attempted to support Romanian-owned corporations.[63] Still, many Romanians shared the feelings of the Banat economist Horia Maniu, who noted that "the new state created a worse situation" economically than these cities and subregions had enjoyed within Hungary before 1918.[64]

The Integration of Prewar and Postwar Business Elites

By the early 1920s, Transylvania's Hungarian, German, and Jewish industrialists had reemerged as part of the establishment of Greater Romania, becoming integral members of the new state's business elite. Some Transylvanian corporate boards featured a remarkable combination of old and new elites, as well as people connected to both Hungary's and Greater Romania's leading politicians, thereby serving as bridges between the two hostile states at a time when diplomatic and commercial treaties to regulate trade were lacking. The brother-in-law of Hungarian prime minister István Bethlen, Ármin Mikes, served on the board of a major Transylvanian timber company along with Ion. I. C. Brătianu's confidant, Arthur Văitoianu.[65] The board of directors of the Turul shoe factory in Timișoara included the city's wartime mayor, German and Hungarian Josef (József) Geml; a Jewish "war millionaire" from Bukovina, Max von Anhauch; and Budapest banker Pál Engel.[66] Yet Constantin Argetoianu, a postwar Romanian minister in Alexandru Averescu's government and a major proponent of the nationalization of industrial companies, also sat on the company's board, along with minor Romanian officials from the new administration.[67] The largest bank in the Banat also featured a highly diverse pool of board members in terms of class, ethnicity, and political ideology.[68] The national liberal financiers the Blanks, the Transylvanian Romanian National Party deputy Sever Bocu, and the city's major Hungarian Jewish banker and industrialist Zsigmond Szana, who had been designated as "English Vice Consul," were all on the bank's board of directors. Other board members included recently expropriated Hungarian landowner György Beniczky, the prewar secretary of state Iván Ottlik of Budapest, and several executives from the Budapest-based Anglo-Hungarian Bank, as well as the head of the Bucharest Chamber of Commerce, the city's mayor, and the director of the local high school.[69]

This diverse pool of board members reveals not only cooperation between Transylvanian and Bucharest Romanians but also the ability of some landowners and even members of the prewar Hungarian political elite to turn their pre-1918 political influence into economic capital despite Romania's annexation of Transylvania. During the sovereignty change period between November 1918 and the early 1920s, over 100,000 of Transylvania's Hungarian population of 1.7 million left permanently or temporarily for Hungary.[70] This wave of emigration centered disproportionately on civil servants and employees of state-owned companies like the railways and postal services, which makes it even more remarkable that some top members of the prewar administration managed to remain in Transylvania, replacing their Hungarian state salaries and land yields with income from the private sector.[71]

The continued influence of Ottlik, Geml, Beniczky, and other members of the pre-1918 Hungarian elite on corporate boards in Transylvania was not an exception. Even landowner Kálmán Tisza (a relative of Hungary's wartime prime minister István Tisza), the prewar minister László Beöthy, and Oradea's prewar prefect Kálmán Cziffra were members of the board of a Transylvanian bank, years after the region's incorporation into Greater Romania.[72] They shared this lucrative position with representatives of a French tobacco company incorporated in Vienna and a Romanian city official.[73] Furthermore, Hungarian and Austrian corporations, as well as Hungarian and German minorities of Transylvania, also served as agents of German companies in Greater Romania at a time when open economic penetration by the Weimar republic was not a possibility.[74]

The success of the Renner tannery and its director Mózes Farkas is an excellent illustration of how many businesses were able to prosper in a state that otherwise advocated the marginalization of Jews and Hungarians. The making of Farkas's social network offers a glimpse into how Greater Romania's economy worked on the ground, beyond nationalist rhetoric. The firm's success shows that integration into the social fabric of local society mattered for economic success, which remained inseparable from political connections. This "bubble" around Farkas was so strong that it shielded him and most Transylvanian businessmen from ethnic discrimination, ultimately lulling them in the face of the radical antisemitism of the late 1930s.

Much like Budapest industrialist Ferenc Chorin, owner of the Jiu valley coal mines, who changed his religion and transformed his economic empire between 1918 and 1920, Farkas had to reinvent himself three times after the collapse of the monarchy. In October 1918, Farkas headed one of the most prominent associations of Austro-Hungarian tanners and spent most of his time in Budapest, where he became affiliated with a suburban real-estate development project and was elected to the boards of several industrial companies.[75] But later that month, he took one of the last trains back to Kolozsvár, Transylvania, where he was one of the local leaders of the Civic Radicals, a progressive governing party in Mihály Károlyi's revolutionary government. Following the Romanian takeover of Transylvania two months later, his factory started to supply the Directing Council with raw materials.[76] With its tight connections to the Romanian administration, the tannery, like other corporations, benefited from the looting of Hungary by the Romanian army in 1919 and 1920, receiving factory equipment as well as a share of the booty that German general August von Mackensen's retreating army had left behind.[77] The deindustrialization of Hungary was a violation of international law reminiscent of German measures in occupied France between 1914 and 1918, yet it was not simply a transfer of wealth from Hungarians to Romanians since it paradoxically helped the postwar transition of Transylvania's Hungarian businesses as well.[78] Apart from unleashing a wave of ethnic violence and state-sponsored looting, the Romanian occupation of Hungary also resulted in the redistribution of some industrial assets from the core to the peripheral regions of pre-1918 Hungary.

By 1919, the Renner tannery had become the leading employer in Cluj. It amassed tens of millions of lei in annual profits in the 1920s and paid average dividends of 35 percent, making its shares a stellar investment, especially after 1922 and the relative stabilization of the lei owing to deflationary government policies.[79] The company increased its capital from 2.5 million to 40 million lei in 1922 and built a fine leather factory, a shoe factory, and a dedicated shoe sole production unit. In other words, it followed through on the plan that Farkas had prepared in 1917, implementing it despite the collapse of the empire and the change of sovereignty. This may appear surprising since Romanian rule caused several ruptures in Transylvania's political and economic life. Ultimately, however, business operations showed remarkable similarities between pre-1918 Hungary and Greater Romania; close ties between industrialists and politicians, cronyism, and the close interaction of political and business elites on corporate boards were essential for economic success in both states.

Given the relative destitution of societies, state treasuries, and even incoming political elites throughout Central Europe after 1918, financial capital took on increasing importance for social mobility compared with the more hierarchical societies of the prewar era, in which education and symbolic and cultural capital were key to elite status, especially in Romania. The Renner tannery's prosperity thus allowed Farkas to rapidly form alliances with municipal, regional, and national political leaders, including Romanian national liberals, peasantists, Zionists, socialists, and the left wing of the National Hungarian Party. In 1921, Farkas took part in the establishment of the political organization Hungarian Alliance. The next year, he became president of the Foundation Fund (Keren Hayesod), a Zionist organization that promoted Jewish immigration to Palestine.[80] He was elected vice president of the Cluj Chamber of Commerce in 1925 and also became one of the regional directors of the Alliance of Romanian Industrialists, along with two other Hungarian Jews, Zsigmond Szana and Albert Bürger.[81] Farkas openly rejected ethnicity and nationalism as guiding principles of business alliances. As he noted in an essay in the literary journal *East* (*Napkelet*), which he helped finance in 1921, "Nowadays, one has to face the situation that the government, the administration, and workers are all guided by ethnic, racial, religious, and political considerations, instead of looking out for the interests of production."[82]

The Renner tannery became an indispensable source of support and income for a variety of local elites and the middle class in Transylvania soon after the change in sovereignty. Some Hungarians in Cluj even expected the Renner tannery to expand the city's tram network at its own expense in 1919, highlighting how the public expected corporations to assume state functions in a political vacuum.[83] When the Romanian administration fired Hungarian civil servants who refused to take the oath of loyalty to King Ferdinand, the Renner tannery took them on as laborers and white-collar employees, a move that earned Farkas respect among Hungarian elites. Ironically, these bureaucrats, recruited from among the Christian middle class, had to work under the socialist manager Sándor Kun, the brother of Bolshevik revolutionary Béla Kun, whom Farkas retained even after the fall of the Hungarian Soviet Republic, along with the communist lawyer Hillel Kohn, as a gesture to the Left.[84] The family of the Transylvanian Béla Kun was composed of provincial lawyers, pharmacists, and white-collar workers who continued to enjoy a comfortable middle-class existence as the local elite of their Transylvanian small town, despite Kun's failed efforts to beat back Romanian troops in the Hungarian-Romanian war of 1919 and despite the family's Jewish ancestry.[85] Greater Romania outlawed the Communist Party in 1924, yet much like Czechoslovakia, it offered a more welcoming home to Hungarian socialists and liberals than Miklós Horthy's Hungary because they helped erode the base of the Hungarian minority party and attacked its aristocratic and gentry wing.[86]

Farkas purchased the biggest printing house in town, the Newspaper Press Company, in order to influence the bad press garnered by the chamber of commerce and the Renner tannery during the recurrent strikes of the 1920s. Investing in the press also allowed him to support intellectuals and writers who in turn included him in their works, bringing him fame and renown. He also supported the moderate left-wing and liberal daily *Keleti Újság* (*Eastern Paper*), which helped filter out news unfavorable to the company. Within five years of the change in sovereignty, Farkas had achieved equivalent, if not higher, status in Greater Romania's social and business life than he had enjoyed as the leader of the Hungarian leather industry in 1918.

His strong position in the company was further supported by the sudden death of the Renner tannery's founding father, the onetime immigrant from Germany Johann Renner. According to family lore passed on through an oral history interview with his grandson, when the first shipment of skins from China arrived after the First World War, Renner rushed to examine them; coupled with a shaving accident, he caught anthrax and died within weeks.[87] Farkas subsequently became a veritable "dictator" within the firm. He headed a cartel of the three families—the Renners, Hechts, and Farkases—that founded the company in 1912, and forbade members to sell their shares or make decisions without his consent. Johann Renner's sons were reduced to the status of technical directors, even as they continued to draw substantial incomes, allowances, and social capital from the tannery.[88]

Cronyism, Bribes, and Prosperity: Greater Romania's Economy from the Bottom Up

Emil Hațieganu emerged as Farkas's key partner in his firm's expansion. Hațieganu spoke Hungarian fluently and had developed long-standing ties to the region's Hungarian political elite through his work as a jurist in the royal Hungarian administration before 1918; he even shared an office with the would-be leader of the minority Hungarian Party of Transylvania, the judge Emil Grandpierre.[89] Hațieganu became one of the chief administrators of the Transylvanian regional administration, the Directing Council, between 1918 and 1920 and remained one of the leaders of the Peasantist-Regionalist Party, the strongest Romanian political organization in Transylvania (figure 9.1). Along with former prime minister Alexandru Vaida-Voevod, former minister of commerce and industry Mihail Manoilescu, and the deputy Dan Sever, Hațieganu became a key lobbyist for the firm. The relationship between Farkas and Hațieganu was so close that the industrialist made him the executor of his will.[90]

Farkas and Hațieganu also cooperated to foster the Renner tannery's expansion, often disguised as nationalization, as in the case of the incorporation of the Korber hat factory into the Renner tannery. Ultimately, nationalization also became a tool wielded by Hungarian industrialists like Farkas to increase their hold over small or less-connected businesses and offer a token representation to the new, Romanian administration in the process.

Mihály Korber was a craftsman who had founded a small hat factory with Hungarian state support in 1892. By 1920, the factory employed eighty workers, most of whom were women, in the small village of Perjámos/Periam.[91] In partnership with the Anglo-Austrian Bank, Farkas transformed the factory into a publicly traded company in which he owned the majority of shares and the founder, Korber, was a minority shareholder. Emil Hațieganu became a member of the board of directors. The Romanian Liviu Luțai, a minor administrator in the village, played only a perfunctory role in the process. Yet all parties, including Farkas, insisted on using nationalist language to describe a

FIGURE 9.1. Emil Haţieganu (center left) with the political elite of Greater Romania, including King Carol II (bottom right), 1930s. Source: ANR, https://www.centenar-romania.ro/en/.

transaction that had nothing to do with "Romanian interests" or "nationalization." The minutes of the transaction show how Farkas wielded the "newspeak" of Romanian nationalism in order to seize the firm:

FARKAS: I am convinced that the company will work most effectively if it transforms itself into a Romanian company and supports the economic interests of Romania. I have high expectations for the future of this corporation and I hope it will turn into a significant Romanian factory.

EXECUTIVE BOARD MEMBER PÁL DÉNES TO LUŢAI: I ask you, the representative and head of administration, to protect the company's interests within the limits of the law.

LUŢAI: I support the company because I've gotten to know director Korber as a good citizen; the company will be in good hands under his leadership.[92]

Farkas's role as an agent of Romanianization is all the stranger because, under a 1924 law that tied citizenship to continuous residence on Greater Romania's territory, he did not even possess Romanian citizenship at the time of the Korber transaction. The law did not mention Jews, but in practice it served as a bureaucratic means to withdraw citizenship from Jewish residents, many of whom had moved to Greater Romanian territory from Galicia and the Russian empire during or after the Great War.[93] Farkas was born in northern Maramureș, which had become part of Czechoslovakia after 1918, and thus he did not automatically receive Romanian citizenship; his name subsequently appeared on a long list of petitioners seeking to regain their Romanian passports.[94] The incident further highlighted the physical and metaphorical distance between Bucharest, the seat of the Romanian government, and Transylvania and its regional elites since even a major piece of national legislation had few practical consequences on the annexed territories, at least for wealthy industrialists who were able to remain influential despite their uncertain citizenship status.

There were times, however, when even former ministers and prime ministers of Greater Romania, like Vaida-Voevod or Hațieganu, were unable to remove the roadblocks erected by bureaucrats, revealing that the Romanian administration was far from unified. Farkas's strategy involved co-opting top politicians, yet this did not automatically smooth his path when it came to the Commerce Inspection Authority in Cluj. In 1921, the Renner tannery decided to increase its capital from 2.5 to 20 million lei to expand during the postwar economic boom. At the time, the laws and decrees of the Hungarian government continued to govern Transylvania's economy despite the change in sovereignty.

Wartime Hungarian decrees, however, contradicted prewar Hungarian laws, which ironically led to legal debates on the judicial heritage of a defunct monarchy in the Romania of the 1920s. According to a decree passed by the Hungarian administration of Sándor Wekerle in the final weeks of the Great War, companies had to request the approval of the Budapest government to increase their capital.[95] Ironically, by 1921 this decree meant that the Renner tannery had to seek the approval of the Ministry of Industry and Commerce in Bucharest. The Renner tannery, however, argued that this contradicted an 1875 Hungarian industry law that also remained in force in Transylvania. The Renner tannery's lawyers argued that since the war had ended, wartime Hungarian decrees were no longer in force in the region. A Cluj bureaucrat, however, saw an opportunity in retaining this wartime Hungarian legislation and noted that "it is the laws of Austria-Hungary that provide us an opportunity to nationalize Transylvanian industrial companies. That state [the Dual Monarchy] knew how to support national capital as opposed to foreign interests."[96]

When laws clashed with each other in Greater Romania, bribes and personal connections helped companies get their way. The Renner tannery sent one of its Romanian lawyers, Titu Popescu, to Bucharest to obtain authorization for its capital increase in July 1921. Popescu came armed with Emil Hațieganu's letter of reference that he was to hand over to Hațieganu's ally in the Romanian National Party, Petru Groza, who was then a minister in the Alexandru Averescu government.[97] When Popescu arrived, Theodor Deleanu, the chief secretary in charge of Transylvanian companies at the Ministry of Industry and Commerce, was vacationing in the royal resort town of Sinaia along with most of the top bureaucracy, and the Renner company's request had been awaiting processing for weeks.[98] Nonetheless, after paying 2,000 lei ($22 at the time, a significant amount of money) in bribes to a ministry clerk, Popescu obtained access to the entire Renner file submitted to the ministry, including a lengthy denunciation of the firm by the Cluj Commerce Inspection Authority that urged the government to "nationalize" the company.[99] Popescu took the carbon copies of this memorandum from the minister's desk and sent them to Farkas immediately.[100]

The memo pointed out that 65 percent of the company's shares were in the hands of the Anglo-Austrian Bank of Vienna, while the shares of the Renners, the Hechts, and Mózes Farkas, the original founders, "can hardly be called Romanian capital as these families are of a foreign nationality (*naționalitate străină*). . . . The raising of capital offers a perfect opportunity for the nationalization of a company without considerable difficulties."[101] The official proposed that only ethnic Romanians subscribe to new shares but did not name any possible investors or offer any proof that Romanian capital was available. Given that the Renner tannery supplied the Romanian military, he further suggested that the state take control of part of its production process, as had been done during the First World War.[102] The inspection authority correctly predicted that the tannery aimed to recruit four influential Romanian politicians to join its board of directors in order to avoid surrendering part of its shares and key managerial positions to Romanians. The Renner tannery thus found a formidable opponent in the Commerce Inspection Authority dedicated to implementing nationalization even as it hurt the interests of industrialists and Romanian politicians in Transylvania.

Bribes helped the Renner tannery divert the ministry from following the course of action that the Commerce Inspection Authority suggested. After Popescu's initial meeting at the Ministry of Commerce, the well-connected lawyer managed to meet a mystery official over the weekend, whose name he did not divulge to Farkas in writing. It was either Deleanu, Manoilescu, or a top official at the Ministry of Industry and Commerce who offered to have the Renner firm's request to raise its capital approved for 10,000 lei ($112), around two-thirds of Farkas's annual base salary as company director.[103] The following Monday, both Deleanu and Manoilescu had returned to Bucharest from Sinaia and the capital increase was approved.[104] Manoilescu, the future founder of the antisemitic Romanian Front in the 1930s, joined Farkas on the Renner tannery's board of directors, which suggests that he was among those who contributed to the approval of the capital increase.[105]

The incident offers a glimpse of the tensions and disunity within the Romanian administration regarding nationalization of private companies and shows that a low-level, regional bureau could almost outmaneuver the Bucharest authorities by pursuing a more radical line than the central administration. It also contradicted the widespread perception among Transylvanians in the 1920s, Hungarian and Romanian alike, that Bucharest politicians enforced policies in disregard of the region's local realities—for instance, by ordering the compulsory teaching of the Romanian language despite the lack of teachers or by requiring ethnic minority officials to take a Romanian language exam.[106] Furthermore, the incident shows that the goal of creating an economy run by Romanians alone and excluding foreigners and ethnic minorities was not merely an elite ideology promoted by the national liberals but permeated the lower levels of the Transylvanian bureaucracy as well. While some used the "newspeak" of Romanian economic nationalism to cover up favorable business deals, as in the case of the Korber hat factory, others, like the Cluj Commerce Inspection Authority, took this rhetoric seriously.

It was the minister of industry and commerce who eventually called for moderation as he patronizingly told off his Cluj subordinate and warned him to "avoid the mistakes [of economic nationalism] that the Hungarian administration had committed" and refrain from "arbitrary" measures against the Renner tannery. Somewhat hypocritically in light of the massive nationalization campaign, he pointed out that there were no laws in Greater Romania that compelled corporations to include ethnic Romanians as shareholders, and suggested that the authority "convince" and "persuade" rather than force or "hinder" companies.[107] The ministry's opinion was likely influenced by bribes, but it was also motivated by the national liberals' economic policy, which aimed to cut imports and support the expansion of domestic industries. This approach explains why it was the ministry's "foreign currency" section that dealt with companies like the Renner tannery.

There were clear limits on what ethnic minority industrialists could achieve through special deals with the Romanian administration. They gradually had to replace shareholders from Hungary with Romanian citizens and bring in a few ethnic Romanian board members, but this did not mean the replacement of ethnic minority shareholders with Romanians, as it was Hungarians, Germans, and Jews based in Greater Romania who replaced Budapest capitalists. In 1922, the firm's expansion required another 20 million lei capital increase, once again requiring approval from the ministry. This time, bribes alone were not enough. As a compromise, the Renner tannery offered three seats on its executive board to Romanian politicians of the ministry's choosing in exchange for putting the question of "nationalization" to rest. Although the government threatened the company with the nomination of a government-appointed administrator during the negotiations, in the end Farkas managed to retain complete control of the company. Subsequently, a former secretary at the Ministry of Labor, Nicolae Maxim, former prime minister Alexandru Vaida-Voevod, and Virgil Dessila, who served as the director of the Banca Românească, joined the Renner tannery's governing board.

The Banca Românească was close to the National Liberal Party and played a key role in the transformation of the Jiu valley coal mines, owned by Budapest's Salgótarján Coal Mining Corporation, into a Romanian company.[108] These positions were sinecures, and new board members did not even attempt to influence the tannery's day-to-day operations, apart from occasionally intervening on the company's behalf with the administration, much like Hungarian politicians on corporate boards before 1918. Paradoxically, the Romanian administration's insistence on purging Viennese and Budapest banks also inadvertently helped Mózes Farkas because it achieved what Transylvanian Hungarian regionalists had been unable to achieve under the Dual Monarchy: shifting, at least nominally, the balance toward Transylvanian banks. Much like in the company's early days before expansion during the First World War, Farkas and the Renners enjoyed unquestioned supremacy among the shareholders; the ratio of their shares increased from one-third to two-thirds. By 1923, the Farkas, Renner, and Hecht families owned more than two-thirds of the shares, similar to their position in 1914 (table 9.1).

The Anglo-Hungarian Bank continued to covertly finance the tannery, and it likely passed on some of its shares to Romanian entities while retaining ownership. Banat Hungarian banks (23 percent) increased their participation, suggesting that the Timișoara banker Zsigmond Szana helped nationalize the Anglo-Austrian Bank's participation in the Renner tannery. Romanian banks (6 percent) acquired new but small positions among shareholders. Yet the Renner tannery was unable to ignore the Romanian state and the interests of Romanian banks and companies and remain within the bubble of a purported ethnic economy.

In 1922, the Romanian authorities, much like their postwar French counterparts in Alsace and Lorraine, compelled industrial companies like the Renner tannery to submit data on the ethnic composition of their employees. These data show that the Renner tannery was far from being the reserve of "foreigners" or ethnic minorities since its employees mirrored an increasingly multiethnic Cluj, where the Romanian share of the population increased from

Table 9.1 Shareholders at the Renner tannery, 1914–1923

	$N = 273$ [$T = 400$]	$N = 3,952$ [$T = 4,000$]	$N = 25,000$ [$T = 25,000$]	$N = 102,115$ [$T = 200,000$]
SHAREHOLDERS	1914	1918	1919	1923
Transylvanians				
Original founders (Farkas, Renner, Hecht families)	75%	32%	32%	66%
Other Transylvanian shareholders	18%	0%	2%	28%
Budapest shareholders	0%	68%	66%	0%
Bucharest banks, Romanian politicians	0%	0%	0%	6%
Total (*n*)	**100%**	**100%**	**100%**	**100%**

Source: DJAN Cluj, Fond Combinatul de pielărie și încălțăminte "Clujana," 1/1914, 1/1919, 1/1923.

Note: *n* = number of shares presented at shareholders' meeting; *t* = total amount of shares issued.

12 percent in 1910 to 33 percent a decade later.[109] Romanian employees clustered in the best-paid and highest-status positions, making up a quarter of its CEOs and all of the company's four lawyers, but also constituted one-fourth of its workers in 1921. Altogether, Romanians made up 11 percent of the Renner tannery's white-collar employees but pocketed at least 13 percent of salaries through above-average representation among the highest-paid positions.[110] Romanian and Hungarian employees mingled not only in the workplace but also at home, since the Renner tannery built two modern apartment buildings for its two hundred white-collar workers and several housing units for the over one thousand workers. Company housing was a unique perk amid the general shortage of urban housing in postwar Europe, a shortage that hit Cluj especially hard because rural-to-urban immigration and the incoming Romanian civil service had caused the city to expand.[111] While Hungarians and Germans constituted a majority of the firm's managers, employees, and workers, this reflected general demographic trends in Transylvanian cities rather than a conscious policy of limiting the number of Romanian employees.

Industrialists in the Era of Populism: Farkas between Workers and Ultranationalists

In the 1920s, a tight circle of Hungarian, Romanian, German, and Jewish middle-aged men ran Transylvania's economic life in close cooperation with each other and in coordination with Bucharest's changing governments. While this business elite never formed a unified group, and political differences persisted among its members, shared experiences in Austria-Hungary, such as studies at the Budapest and Cluj law schools and *gimnáziums* or prestigious high schools, knowledge of Hungarian and German, and joint business partnerships, forged connections among them.[112] Under the national liberal governments led by Ion Brătianu between 1922 and 1927, policies promoting domestic industrialization channeled capital and credit to at least a few Transylvanian companies, while lax labor laws and protective tariffs also aided companies. But the prosperity of this new elite emerged against a backdrop of the impoverishment of the middle class, the curtailment of workers' rights, housing shortages, and the continued plight of the peasantry, which destabilized the country's political system.

Greater Romania's press laws were laxer than those of both prewar and interwar Hungary, and the press emerged as a major critic of wealthy industrialists. The extramarital affairs, questionable business transactions, and other dirty laundry of industrialists reached a broad readership, while Hungarian and Romanian nationalist papers also attacked the enrichment of Jewish industrialists like Farkas. These attacks highlighted the remarkable continuity of antisemitic mobilization against "war profiteers" between 1914 and 1918 and prefigured the late 1930s and 1940s when businessmen, especially Jews, found themselves mired in a political no-man's-land as both the economic beneficiaries of Romanian rule in Transylvania and the victims of ethnic discrimination in Greater Romania.[113] The 1920s thus brought numerous new challenges to the social status and wealth of ethnic minorities, which complicated their clear success in increasing their fortunes.

Mózes Farkas's ambiguous coverage in the press and contemporary literature attested to the challenges that industrialists faced in the 1920s despite their material prosperity. Farkas came to embody the new-rich millionaire of the times, and his prosperity generated considerable attention among Cluj's traditionalist, mostly Calvinist middle class. Hungarian writers and journalists used his figure to address the remarkable economic boom of some of the region's companies. As the son of a small-town Jewish cobbler in rural Maramureș, Farkas embodied a US-style rags-to-riches story that ran counter to the hardships endured by former Hungarian civil servants and the region's workers in the interwar period.

While for Romanian intellectuals like Mircea Eliade it was Christian mysticism that offered an escape from disillusionment in Greater Romania, for some Transylvanian Hungarian writers the transformative potential of US-style industrial capitalism served a similar purpose.[114] For them, capitalism erased the boundaries between "national and international" and rendered the petty ethnic discrimination that minorities often faced in Greater Romania a mere side story to the grand narrative of development.[115] Accordingly, in a contemporary sci-fi novel, *Methania Co.*—the writer Károly Molter's satire on the way natural resources transform society and human characters—people are obsessed with stock speculation and the newly discovered resource of natural gas; banks rather than politicians rule society; and the church, the factory, and bourgeois apartment buildings all revolve around an enriched Transylvanian bank with an English name, Bank of Mezőség, denoting the region where natural gas was discovered in the 1900s (figures 9.2 and 9.3).

In *Methania Co.*, the entrepreneur Mózes Hegyi's trajectory closely resembles Mózes Farkas's gradual takeover of the Cluj tannery from the Renner brothers. Molter was drawn to social democracy and Transylvanian regionalism, so it comes as no surprise that his satire castigated a society in which "a bank is more important than church, savviness trumps honesty, and credit is more important than credibility."[116] *Methania Co.* tells the story of the miraculous prosperity that gases from a smelly underworld kingdom of "Konstantin Gazolni," a metaphor for Romania, bring to Transylvania. These gases in turn efface the "smell" of "races" and create a mass society in which ethnic, racial, and religious differences become nonexistent.[117]

Yet Molter, who was a Banat German assimilated into Hungarian culture, had little warmth for the capitalists behind this transformation, and the novel was especially critical of Jewish characters. Fictitious director Mózes Hegyi "did not give much for sentimentality, all he cared for was power over the matter," vacationed in Biarritz, France, and mocked both Judaism, his old religion, and Christianity, to which he converted out of opportunism. Molter was not alone in this criticism of capitalism that verged on antisemitism. Mózes Farkas inspired several leftist Hungarian writers at the time, who portrayed him with antisemitic undertones. Writers depicted him as a calculating figure who managed to survive the change in sovereignty thanks to dubious deals. In *The Sieve*, a 1931 novel by Emil Kolozsvári Grandpierre, a young Transylvanian writer and son of the Hungarian Minority Party's onetime leader Emil Grandpierre, the downward social mobility of the Hungarian gentry after the First World War contrasts sharply with the prosperity of the Hungarian Jewish "Mr. Berger."[118] In this realist novel, the characters reflect real-life individuals: Mr. Berger closely resembles Mózes Farkas or Zsigmond Szana, while the protagonist resembles the writer's father, Grandpierre Sr., a former Austro-Hungarian judge who is trying to make a fresh start in minority journalism and politics after Transylvania's integration into Greater Romania. Mr. Berger is the self-congratulatory tycoon of Cluj who offers patronizing assistance to former Hungarian civil servants and their families, including the judge. Mr. Berger explains to the judge that his factory is able to weather any politi-

FIGURE 9.2. Depiction of the transformative potential of modernization in Károly Molter's novel *Metania R.t.* Source: Molter, *Metania R.t.*

FIGURE 9.3. Depiction of the power of banks in Károly Molter's novel *Metania R.t.* Source: Molter, *Metania R.t.*

cal transformation. The judge eventually concludes that "the Berger factory possesses huge amounts of capital that can withstand the gravest of crises"[119] and decides to send his son to be a factory worker there instead of law school in Pécs, Hungary.

A character resembling Farkas also appears in Hungarian Jewish writer Ernő Ligeti's 1925 novel *Up into the Saddle*.[120] Krompacher, the leather merchant turned bank director, survives the failure of his institution. He speaks Hungarian with a foreign accent and feels uneasy among the bank's employees, who were recruited from the ranks of the prewar middle class, the Hungarian gentry. When the dismissed civil servant Elekes, who had helped Krompacher avoid imprisonment before 1918, applies for a job at the Union Bank, the director is condescending. Although he eventually gives Elekes a job, he also lets him know that his skills are worthless in modern bank administration.[121] The novel thus offers a critical perspective on the Renner tannery's "generosity" in employing civil servants laid off after the Romanian takeover of Transylvania.

The bank's lawyer and vice director Grosz, a lascivious womanizer and well-fed man, is another unappealing Jewish character in Ligeti's novel. Dressed in a tuxedo, Grosz is contrasted sharply with the former civil servant Elekes, who was forced to sell his books and dress coats in order to support his family. The distinction between the Hungarian Elekes and Hungarian Jews Grosz and Krompacher is also conveyed by the drawings of Hungarian writer and politician Károly Kós, who illustrated the novel. The unemployed former civil servant and his wife are shown as gaunt, unhappy figures whose distressed demeanor and modest clothing contrast with the portly banker's fashionable oxford shoes and calm but haughty expression (see figures 9.4 and 9.5). Ligeti was Jewish, Grandpierre and Molter were not, yet all of their novels represented the growing social distance between the bourgeoisie and former civil servants, despite their shared past in Austria-Hungary and attachment to Hungarian culture. As Gábor Gaál, editor of the leftist journal *Korunk*, noted, the decisive conflicts in society were not between Hungarians and Romanians but between "landowner and peasant, Jew and gentry, political conservatives and radicals."[122] Gaál's formulation also showed that it was not only ultranationalist Romanians but also the Hungarian Left of Transylvania that wielded the language of antisemitism against the economic elite of the former Austro-Hungarian empire.

In the meantime, both the yellow press and anonymous critics attacked the owners of the Renner tannery. Accusations centered on the frivolous use of automobiles, lovers, and the families' unconventional lifestyles. The family papers reveal that Farkas transgressed the conservative social conventions of Cluj insofar as he divorced his first wife, Ilona Rózsa, when his business was expanding during the First World War. In the early 1920s, Farkas's new wife,

Figure 9.4. The unemployed civil servant. Source: Drawings by Károly Kós in Ligeti, *Föl a bakra*, 17.

Figure 9.5. The banker. Source: Drawings by Károly Kós in Ligeti, *Föl a bakra*, 83.

Rachel Sennensieb, received an anonymous letter stating that the CEO of the firm ferried a young, married female clerk to work every morning, implying that they were having an affair. Another typed denunciation pleaded with Farkas to stop the affairs that the Renner brothers' wives indulged in with young company employees. Around the same time, a tabloid journalist claimed to have seen the Renner directors street racing in downtown Oradea in the company of a popular actress; the writer cast it as a sign of the "new rich" from Hóstát, in the lowly working-class outskirts of Cluj, taking over the urban space of Oradea's refined bourgeoisie, suggesting a reversal of the class hierarchy.[123] Another paper noted that director Richárd Hecht "never took a step on foot, and only raced through the streets with his big black car."[124]

Given the low standards of accuracy in the contemporary press and the fact that editors and owners often used papers to discredit political rivals, it is likely that these reports were exaggerated or unfounded and reflected social tensions rather than the freer lifestyles of these families. While tabloids portrayed industrialists' female companions purely as objects of male desire, we know much less about their wives, who had an active role in family life, and some of whom pursued their own careers. Gusztáv Renner's wife, Baba Halász, was an actress (figure 9.6). While the Renners' promotion of the Cluj theater scene likely played a part in her early success, she remained a popular actress even

FIGURE 9.6. Actress Baba Halász, wife of Gusztáv Renner. Source: *Szinház és Társaság* 10, no. 2 (1926): 5; Arcanum.

after her husband, who had started a new business, went bankrupt, which suggests that her success was independent of her husband's fortune.[125]

Farkas's last will and testament showed a high level of trust between him and his new wife, Rachel Sennensieb, a Jewish woman in her early twenties when the two married, making her just ten years older than Farkas's first daughter, Ella, and seventeen years Farkas's junior.[126] Not only did Farkas make generous provisions for Sennensieb in his will, but he also designated her as the guardian of István, his son from his first marriage.[127] Farkas also made his wife the beneficiary of his British and Swiss insurance fortune in the early 1930s.[128] The couple lived comfortably in a large apartment in downtown Cluj; Sennensieb's work as a homemaker and mother was aided by a "German governess," a maid, and a live-in cook.[129] Sennensieb gave birth to two daughters, Zsófia and Hedvig, in 1921 and 1922, respectively, whom Farkas designated as heirs to part of his fortune, while severely limiting the claims of his two other children from his first marriage.[130]

Farkas's last will centered on the future of the Renner tannery, the passion and major achievement of his life; he excluded his own family from the leadership of the company after his death and entrusted his two male colleagues, lawyer Emil Hațieganu and vice director Ervin Gurisatti, with the execution of his last will and testament. Unlike the Renners, Farkas renounced any ambition of building a business dynasty, in part because he lacked a suitable male heir. Farkas obtained a medical certificate stating that his son from his first marriage, István, was an "imbecile,"[131] a reason to prolong István's status as a minor. At the time, female heirs participated in family businesses through their husbands, if they were married, or by exerting their influence informally through family networks. Farkas's two daughters from his second marriage were underage and single when he prepared his final will.[132] Farkas wrote his last will and testament in 1934, amid political uncertainty and the rise of ultranationalists in Greater Romania and Hungary and the Nazis in Germany. While he made generous provisions to some of the firm's workers in his will, he shied away from preparing his wife or daughters to work for the company, owing to the general uncertainty of the era.

When Deals Broke Down: The Transylvanian Student Riots of 1927

By the late 1920s, Transylvania's ethnic minority industrialists' strategy of making deals with mainstream Romanian parties and politicians, including the governing national liberals and the Hungarian Party, proved inadequate to defend their interests. Apart from the workers' movement, it was primarily the nascent ultranationalist Right that posed challenges to businesses. Transylvanian industrialists benefited from the pro-business environment in Greater Romania and rolled back the gains that workers had achieved between 1914 and 1918. Attesting to the political leverage of workers and craftsmen during the Great War, in the final days of the Hungarian administration, the city's police captain canceled the Renner tannery's plans for a new factory because the building did not conform to workplace comfort and safety standards.[133] The Romanian administration proved laxer and gave the project the green light. In the following years, workers saw their wages and bargaining power decline. The practices of Farkas the industrialist stood in sharp contrast to the stated beliefs of Farkas the onetime politician and strongman of Transylvanian society. In the revolutionary days of October 1918, he had worked closely with socialists and workers to manage the transition from war to peace in Cluj.[134] Within a few years, however, the relationship between the management of the Renner tannery and the trade unions turned sour. In order to reduce its losses from the conversion of Austro-Hungarian crowns to Romanian lei, the Renner tannery cut workers' salaries by 10 percent and then again by 15 percent within six months. In light of the firm's expansion at the time and the generous tax breaks and industrialization subsidies it received from Bucharest, the measure was excessive and triggered a wave of strikes.[135] Overall, however, the working class had disproportionately little political leverage, and the Romanian police proved apt at defending ethnic minority industrialists from mostly Hungarian workers.

Ultranationalist Romanians proved to be more formidable opponents of both ethnic minority industrialists and the national liberals. The difference between the ideology of young ultranationalists and that of national liberals was slight and pertained to the speed and method of Romanianization rather than its content.[136] The ultranationalists' ideas "reflected in a raw and exaggerated way many of the main concerns of mainstream nationalists," as Irina Livezeanu has emphasized.[137] Ultranationalists labeled themselves "nationalists" and "antisemites," ideologies shared by "the majority of politicians."[138] In order to contain the ultranationalists, the Romanian governments of the 1920s adopted some of their ideas as government policy and condoned occasional pogroms to let off steam among ultranationalists and demonstrate the need for parties of "law and order."

The waves of antisemitic violence that swept through Transylvanian cities in the 1920s, peaking in 1927, showed the limits of the business deals concluded by Farkas and other Hungarian, Jewish, and German industrialists in Greater Romania and shed light on both the inability and the unwillingness of traditional political elites to defend their business partners against the ultranationalist "new generation" of young Romanians.[139] In early December 1927, a disorganized police force surrounded three thousand angry university student from the Old Kingdom of Romania at the Cluj train station. However, two hundred of these students broke through the flimsy police lines and stormed into the city center, where they broke shop windows, tore signs off foreign-sounding businesses, and destroyed the interiors of synagogues (figures 9.7 and 9.8). In a matter of two hours, they caused damage that some papers estimated at 60 million lei, or $360,000.[140] Students smashed the windows of the Renner shareholder and creditor Marmorosch Blank Bank, the financier of the national liberals, which occupied the offices of the Pest Hungarian Commercial Bank.[141] Retailers that carried Renner products, such as the Stern and Kohn shoe store and the Bergner leather goods shop, suffered as well.[142] These students had come of age during the Great War and the "unification" of Greater Romania and felt that the national liberals had betrayed the promise of 1918 by leaving ethnic minorities (Jews in particular) in key middle-class positions and in charge of business life.[143] Instead of turning against national liberals, who held actual power, students directed their anger at politically powerless ethnic minorities—first and foremost, Jews.

The 1927 student riots made Transylvania's exposure to power struggles in Bucharest brutally clear. The deaths of both King Ferdinand (1914–1927) and the national liberal prime minister Ion Brătianu that year ushered in a power

FIGURE 9.7. Student riots in Oradea in 1927. Source: MNL-OL, K 66, 1928/I/5/a./1.

FIGURE 9.8. The destroyed office of the Hungarian paper *Nagyvárad*. Source: MNL-OL, K 66, 1928/I/5/a./2.

vacuum in Greater Romania that gave ultranationalist students tremendous leverage. Vintilă Brătianu, the late prime minister's politically weak brother who took over the government, needed the support of university students to push through the underage Mihai I's ascension to the throne. At the same time, a pogrom served the short-term interests of the administration as it directed anger toward Jews and ethnic minorities and away from dissatisfaction with the national liberals, who were especially unpopular in Transylvania. As the 1928 elections showed, the National Liberal Party had very little support, dropping from 63 percent to 7 percent of deputies in the space of a year, a disillusionment exacerbated by the fraudulent electoral system.[144]

What implicated the government internationally was that it did not take any steps to prevent the riots even though Jewish deputies had pointed out the threat of pogroms weeks before they occured. The meeting occurred on the fifth anniversary of a student congress that had ended in a pogrom, but while the national liberal government had banned the Transylvanian election rally of its chief opponent, the National Peasant Party, it approved the student congress.[145] The destruction in Cluj came a day after a considerably larger pogrom by the same group of students in Oradea, which claimed 390 victims.[146] A Jewish politician of the Hungarian Party, Nándor Hegedűs, concluded decades later that until the 1927 student congress "we had believed that the frequent disasters in the lives of eastern Jewry . . . did not pertain to us, Western Jews. . . . For the first time, [rioters] showed us that there is no difference between Jews in Berdychiv and Oradea,"[147] blurring the often orientalizing lines between Central and Eastern European Jewish identity. Yet Hegedűs's statement reflects retroactive thinking, seeing the 1920s through the prism of the Holocaust. For most Jewish and other minority businessmen, life seemed to return to normal after the student riots. The international uproar that followed the pogroms did not lead to any sanctions against Greater Romania despite the protest of US ambassador William S. Culbertson to foreign minister Nicolae Titulescu. Notably, Culbertson protested because an American citizen Wilfred Nedson Keller was hurt in the riots, but he did not raise the issue of antisemitic violence.[148] Protests by Jewish organizations like the French Alliance Israélite Universelle, the Anglo-Jewish Association, and Jewish papers like *Paix et Droit* had even less impact on Bucharest, although bad international press around the atrocities did play a part in the allocation of modest compensation to victims, totaling 6 million lei ($37,000), or less than $100 per business.[149] Keller accepted a settlement that granted him $2,500.[150] Notably, with the exception of the American victim, the government did not pay any compensation for physical abuse by students.[151]

In East-Central Europe, the peace treaties were far less specific on economic matters than the Versailles Treaty on Alsace-Lorraine and Franco-German trade more generally. In the absence of commercial treaties among successor states, it was up to the industrialists and bankers of the former Austria-Hungary to work out the specifics of commerce across the new borders and reorganize their supply chains. In the case of Hungary and Greater Romania, hostility between the two states over the sovereignty of Transylvania prevented the passage of an interstate commercial treaty, which compelled industrial companies to reactivate pre-1918 business networks and informal ties with Budapest banks that ensured the continuity of financial and trade flows. Yet the lack of a stable business environment also meant that Transylvanian industrial companies decreased the volume of transactions with Hungary; the reorganization of train schedules, the hassle of border control and customs duties, and general uncertainty prompted Transylvanian industrialists to conquer Greater Romania's markets instead. While the Treaty of Trianon turned Transylvanian industrialists into ethnic minorities, it also "gave" them a new, agrarian market in which they faced less competition than they did before 1918 in Austria-Hungary, where Austria's, Bohemia's, and Budapest's businesses dominated the market. Romanian policies of nationalization further undermined the already uncertain business environment in Transylvania as the administration threatened ethnic minority industrialists with drastic measures in order to put pressure on corporations and achieve concessions. By the early 1920s, however, it became clear that the Romanian administration had neither the power nor the capital to "Romanianize" ethnic minority businesses. Instead, strongmen in the regional and national administrations used nationalization to acquire well-remunerated sinecures on the corporate boards of these businesses, thus sabotaging Romanianization and leaving the existing management intact.

While nationalization was an annoyance for Transylvania's industrialists, it also indirectly benefited them since Budapest and Viennese banks had to camouflage their investments in Transylvanian companies by handing them over to the companies in which they had invested before 1918. The 1920s turned out to be a prosperous decade for Transylvania's pre-1918 business elite, which successfully reinvented itself as a member of the oligarchy that ran Greater Romania. "Middle-class" solidarity among Transylvanian Romanian and non-Romanian professionals and politicians going back to the era of Austria-Hungary helped ease the shock of transition to Romanian rule for Transylvania's industrialists.[152] Although their businesses prospered, the 1927 pogroms and the radicalization of Romanian politics cast a shadow over this economic success, even as the tragedies of the 1940s were difficult to foresee from the perspective of general prosperity that unexpectedly developed for many Hungarian, German, and Jewish industrialists in Greater Romania after 1918. Firms like the Renner tannery in Cluj refused to strike a deal with ultranationalists, while ultranationalists and the "new generation" of Romanian elites that came of age after 1918 no longer needed the cooperation of ethnic minority business elites by the 1930s. It seems, however, that at least some of these industrialists tried to achieve a compromise with workers.

The Great Depression and Romania's increasing turn to fascism in the second half of the 1930s prompted the Renner firm's director Farkas to reconsider his approach to workers in the Renner tannery, which had since been given the less foreign-sounding name Dermata Works. His solution to the social tensions of his time also pointed far beyond the industrial paternalism practiced by the Adlers, Oppenheimers, de Dietrichs, and other Central and Western European family businesses of the time. Instead, he returned to the radical ideals of the Aster Revolution in the fall of 1918.[153] Just as the then prime minister Mihály Károlyi started the land reform by distributing his own aristocratic estates among peasants in 1919, so too did Farkas attempt to share his factory with workers, managers, and the company's officials after his death. Farkas's 1934 will bequeathed his shares to a future foundation representing the workers and managers of the Renner tannery and shoe factory.[154] He specified that the workers and the company's managing officials were to elect delegates to the company's executive board.[155] Farkas personally selected the first delegates, including deputy directors, two drivers, a turner, a machine operator, and a locksmith. He also specified that in order to be eligible, workers and managers had to have worked at the Renner factory for more than ten years. Even periods of strikes, noted Farkas, counted as periods of employment.[156]

He also left part of his estate to build a holiday resort in the mountains around Cluj, in the middle of a twenty-acre forest.[157] Farkas resigned from active management of the firm in 1937 owing to heart problems that required treatment in Budapest sanatoria. He died in the Hungarian capital four years later, when both Cluj and northern Transylvania had been returned to Hungary.[158] While Farkas was convalescing, Hungary passed three anti-Jewish laws, entered the Second World War, and harbored hostile relations with its nominal Axis ally, Romania.[159] If this alone was not enough to block the execution of his last will and testament, one of his daughters also contested the will, while the Renner family had no interest in the massive transformation of the tannery into a quasi-socialist corporation.[160]

Successful accommodation to both Hungarian and then Romanian rule and belief in the power of informal deals with changing political elites contributed to the lack of a mass exodus of Hungarian Jewish industrialists who had fewer and fewer options of emigration by the late 1930s. Unlike industrialists in French Alsace (like the de Dietrichs) close to the German border, or German Jewish business families who were actively planning their emigration since the 1930s, most Jewish industrialists and bankers of Hungary did not emigrate, which resulted in tragic consequences during the Second World War. Still, the tragedy of the Holocaust was not foreseeable in the Greater Romania of the 1920s. New borders, often drawn with military considerations in mind, posed several challenges to industrialists across East-Central Europe, along with laws and administrative practices that discriminated against Jews, Hungarians, and Germans despite the Minority Treaties forced on successor states by the Paris Peace Conference in 1919. Yet informal arrangements among Budapest business elites and industrialists from former imperial peripheries like Transylvania often rendered new borders porous with goods and people crossing them unchecked, while institutionalized corruption, informal connections of businessmen with customs officials, and police prefects often eased the shock of sovereignty change. Informal connections of businessmen with customs officials, police prefects, and other administrators mattered just as much as the cacophony of Hungarian, Austrian, and Romanian commercial laws regulating trade in the Hungarian-Romanian border regions. Continuities among business elites despite the First World War and the collapse of Austria-Hungary contradict still-dominant historical narratives that emphasize the undifferentiated victimhood of ethnic minorities, the "trauma" of vanquished states like Hungary, and the rhetoric that the successor states of empires ushered in a substantially new era for Romanians, Czechs, Slovaks, and other populations "liberated" from imperial sovereignty.[161] It is thus more fruitful to look at what successor states did rather than what they said when examining the "balance sheets" of interwar East-Central European economies and the fate of ethnic minorities, especially as regards the chaotic and turbulent years between the 1918 armistices and the Great Depression.

Epilogue

The trajectories of the business families studied in this book attest to just how important a handful of industrialists were for regional, national, and even imperial economies in early twentieth-century Europe, so much so that even seismic political changes could not diminish their prospects. This may sound strange today, in an era when institutional shareholders and a revolving cast of professional CEOs dominate corporations in the United States and around the world. Yet family capitalism, the domination of key companies by old moneyed families, persists even today, not only in developing states like Mexico and Argentina but also in Israel, Singapore, Hong Kong, Germany, Sweden, and other states typically identified with the vanguard of capitalist development.[1] While the era of the Great War is usually associated with state capitalism and economic planning, the growing power of states did not diminish that of business families, and the wartime expansion of production even catapulted some of them to new heights. At a time of chaotic changes, war, and the dissolution of empires, economic life rested far less on abstract institutions than on personal connections and certain key actors who proved crucial for keeping European economies in motion.

Comparisons across the defunct Iron Curtain help us move beyond sterile juxtapositions of "developed" Western Europe and "backward" Eastern Europe. They show that some regions in the latter could surpass industrialized

Western European territories in terms of their attractiveness to investors. The trajectories of Alsace-Lorraine's industrialists also show that being located in the heartland of European industrialization did not necessarily mean continuous and guaranteed economic prosperity. Industrialists in Western European regions like Alsace-Lorraine, who have hitherto been identified as the engines of European capitalism, experienced a series of tribulations; both industrialists and workers in these regions were often subjected to more ordeals than their peers in East-Central Europe. Comparisons also point to parallels and similarities that suggest common European experiences in the era of the Great War, even as some of these, such as the rise of ethnic nationalism, have been repeatedly ascribed to Europe's East. Other commonalities include the economic opportunities that resulted from the crisis of the Great War for most industries and army suppliers, and the simultaneous erosion of property rights in most capitalist economies in Europe and worldwide.

The comparison of Western and East-Central European business families has shown the meteoric rise of the latter from circles of social outsiders, Jews, or immigrants, while business families were much more closed in Western Europe; the long-standing industrialist families of Alsace-Lorraine, for instance, made sure that outsiders did not enter their circles via marriage or lasting business partnerships. War between France and Germany, and subsequent anti-German passive resistance, made the social integration of immigrant industrialists like the Adlers and Oppenheimers nearly impossible. In resource-rich yet altogether more rural Transylvania, both large banks and corporations from the imperial centers of Vienna and Budapest, as well as immigrant craftsmen like Johann Renner or the cobbler's son Mózes Farkas, had better prospects for making a fortune than those in the saturated markets of Western Europe. Austria-Hungary was a welcoming place for skilled immigrants and offered prospects of rapid enrichment for businessmen regardless of religion and ethnicity, even as the monarchy had few opportunities for its own class of landless peasants who headed in droves to Ellis Island.[2]

Unlike in Alsace-Lorraine, where the narrative of this book followed entrepreneurs from established business dynasties, in Transylvania, as well as in Hungary and Greater Romania more generally, the most decisive players were newcomers to business life who emerged as powerful players owing to state subsidies, government connections, or both.[3] As a result, the achievements of multiple business generations were condensed into a single lifetime, attesting to the general dynamism of state-fueled economic development in East-Central Europe during the late nineteenth and early twentieth centuries. This timeline was collapsed still further in the case of the many industrialists studied in this book who had already made a career before turning to business;

the Chorins and Farkas had established careers in law and politics before turning to business, while Johann Renner was a craftsman.

While new businesses can flourish in a matter of a few years, establishing business *dynasties* takes time, and time was cut short for most of the region's industrialists by the rise of Nazi Germany, the Second World War, and the subsequent turn to state socialism in the region. The Chorins came closest to establishing a business dynasty, especially after Ferenc Chorin Jr. married Daisy Weiss, the daughter of Hungary's wealthiest arms manufacturer, Manfréd Weiss. Farkas's less strategic marital choices and divorce point to the importance of marital ties and heirs more generally for the resilience of business dynasties.

Taken as a whole, the trajectories of industrialists gesture toward a new history of modern Europe, one that is less centered on ethnic divisions and the force of nationalism.[4] The study of business life serves as a fruitful departure to showcase the limits of nationalist mobilization and point to social class, regional loyalties, and above all material interest as factors that shaped the trajectory of late nineteenth- and early twentieth-century Europe, a period customarily identified with the pervasiveness of ethnic strife as a guiding principle of domestic and foreign policies. Despite their fiery nationalist rhetoric, successor states of Germany and Austria-Hungary were more eager to cooperate with the business families of the "world of yesterday" than to eliminate them, and this was especially true in East-Central Europe. Industrial companies were just too essential for stabilizing economic production, plus they offered lucrative sinecures to placate officials of successor states; expropriating them would have required capital and expertise that successor states in the region were sorely lacking. This is why Greater Romania was eager to cement its alliance with the industrialists of defunct Austro-Hungary and even Germany rather than expropriate them, which would have threatened to both throw the country further into chaos between 1918 and 1920 and risk marginalization by France and Great Britain, countries that were otherwise keen to gain markets in Greater Romania. The minority rights treaties certainly helped to deter expropriations; yet, as the land reforms that disproportionately affected ethnic minorities indicate, international law and pressures from Great Powers alone failed to protect the existing social hierarchy in East-Central Europe, as successor states had numerous, clandestine ways to engage in ethnic discrimination that flew under the radar of the League of Nations and the provisions of the peace treaties.

In the meantime, both the pre-1918 German and postwar French administrations adopted a rigid and ideological approach to business life, as compared with the pragmatism of the Hungarian and Romanian governments with regard to industrial companies, which led to far more disruptions in the economy of Alsace-Lorraine than in Transylvania during the 1910s and 1920s, especially due to the expropriation of Germans in Alsace-Lorraine. Even so, the French government also turned to pragmatism when it took the half century of "loyalty" of Alsatians and Lorrainers to France at face value and did not investigate the embeddedness of these regions' economies in that of Germany, or the role of Alsatian companies in the German war effort against France.

Subnational regions like Alsace-Lorraine or Transylvania, and supranational entities such as Mitteleuropa, also appear as drivers of political change in addition to the familiar imperial and national frameworks. Yet decentering the nation-state as a unit of analysis does not mean belittling the importance of borders and governments, resulting in the jubilant "globalization talk" of an earlier historiography.[5] Economic integration went well with and even fueled the increased popularity of tariff boundaries and projects to shore up regional or national autonomy in a realigned European order undergoing political and economic convergence. While business elites are commonly associated with the privilege of transcending borders as cosmopolitan globe-trotters or advocates of market expansion, industrialists large and small often thrived economically owing to imperial, national, or regional borders and tariff walls that protected them from competition. Ironically, they often benefited economically from state and customs barriers, or even the territorial reshuffling that they otherwise lamented on grounds of national sentiment. This was the case with the Franco-German border after 1871, which ultimately protected French industrialists from Alsatian competition, or the post-1918 Hungarian-Romanian border that shielded Transylvania's Hungarian industrialists from Hungarian and Austrian rivals.

The multifaceted connections of France and French businesses to Germany and East-Central Europe offer a useful addition to the study of colonial-metropolitan relations, immigration, and decolonization. In fact, as the history of Alsatian businesses in the post-1918 French economy shows, East-Central Europe and French colonies could simultaneously appear as "spatial fixes" to problems of the Alsatian economy by offering venues for market expansion.[6] Even as France's multifaceted ties to East-Central Europe have remained less studied in anglophone and francophone histories, case studies in this book also offer a prehistory to the current, intensive economic relations between the formerly socialist countries of Eastern Europe and France, at a time when French foreign direct investment to these regions far surpasses all capital invested in France's former colonies, not unlike in the late nineteenth and early twentieth centuries.[7]

It is also remarkable that social change did not move in lockstep with politics and shifting borders, and that the composition of societies remained relatively stable, despite historiographical fixation on key turning points and "new beginnings," such as 1918. Continuities undermine the force of narratives centered on 1918 as a clear rupture or "blank slate," even as such narratives became key for the foundation myths of interwar European states and have since been recycled to serve similar purposes after 1989.[8] Long-term, postimperial continuities in social hierarchies also offer a comfortable distance from the triumphalist or self-pitying narratives of states formed as a result of the Versailles settlement, as it turns out that new borders may have had fewer immediate consequences for the remaking of societies and the prosperity of economies.[9] A close look at geographical peripheries in chaotic times helps us learn about the limits of national or imperial power and the limits of modern states' ability to change societies. At times, even key decisions that included the fate of strategic assets and territories could be decided on the ground by improbable historical actors like businessmen or makeshift army units, while the fate of ethnic minorities also depended on local deals, thereby directing our attention away from government policies and more toward their implementation or sabotage, from which we see just how different local realities could be from the image of a unified nation-state portrayed so convincingly by governments, cartographers, or statisticians.

While industrialists often undermined prevailing nationalist trends through their diverse business partnerships, their politics and legacy hardly constitute an easily "usable past" today, in an era of global economic crises, tax evasion scandals, and the rise of illiberal politics. Industrialists' views on economic policies are just as difficult to subsume under one label—such as economic liberalism—as their diverse and context-specific political ideas. Rather than being unconditional advocates of free trade and liberal economic policies more generally, the industrialists studied in this book professed malleable political ideologies and fostered allegiances that best served their interests across the changing and often chaotic political landscapes of Europe; we see them as supporters of protectionism, colonization, and total war, as well as of liberal, paternalistic, and even socialistic ideas on labor relations.

To further complicate things, those business elites who stood firmly behind a particular ideology or nation-building project also often gladly pursued economic activities that contradicted these professed ideas. The de Dietrichs of Alsace had a consistently pro-French politics throughout the nineteenth and twentieth centuries, yet this was hardly reflected in their business practices between 1871 and 1918, when their factories came under German sovereignty. This sort of divorce of economic interest from political ideology explains why the Hungarian Jewish Chorins thrived both under the liberal nationalist regimes of prewar Hungary and in Miklós Horthy's authoritarian state that embraced antisemitic agendas, and why they could make deals with Romanian nationalists to preserve their assets in Greater Romania after 1918. The businessmen featured in this book thus do not embody a better, more progressive, and tolerant social elite in an era of nationalist mobilization and ethnic discrimination. They feature as both the beneficiaries of imperialist policies between 1914 and 1918 (or, as in the case of Alsatian industrialists, through the 1920s) and ethnic minorities experiencing discrimination, at the center of attacks by ultranationalists and/or hostile governments. Most of them stood on the sidelines as their colleagues, such as Alsace-Lorraine's Germans or Transylvania's Romanians and subsequently Hungarians, were targeted by ethnic discrimination, or actively benefited from these and similar policies.

Official historiography in state socialist regimes in the 1950s made the bourgeoisie enemy number one of historical development and defunded academic research into the subject while social, labor, and cultural history turned away from the study of "elites" in Western Europe and the United States as well. Yet industrialists in late nineteenth- and early twentieth-century Europe wielded far less political power than was attributed to them in the Stalinist period, or what current discussions on the contemporary "top one percent's" role suggest.[10] While industrialists and businessmen often wielded far-reaching influence on economic policies, they did not trigger the First World War, the collapse of Germany and Austria-Hungary, or the emergence of successor states. Even the most powerful among them had no direct influence on the top government officials who decided on issues of war, peace, borders, the expulsion of and discrimination against ethnic minorities, or the administration of occupied territories. The unofficial mission of Hungarian industrialists to revise the country's borders in exchange for handing over key transportation companies to French industrialists failed, and Alsatian businessmen were similarly sidelined when it came to setting up the French administration of Alsace and Lorraine after 1918.

The rehabilitation of the historical role of the bourgeoisie in academia started after pro-market reforms in the Eastern Bloc in the late 1960s and gained further impetus after 1989. In the 1990s, the backlash against inefficient and collapsing socialist economies put the first era of capitalist development and the enterprising bourgeoisie of the Belle Epoque and even the entire presocialist era in East-Central Europe on a pedestal, while the enormous social inequalities and the embeddedness of business elites in the problematic politics of the first half of the twentieth century remained overlooked. They were seen as the predecessors of contemporary entrepreneurs shaking up and modernizing dusty socialist economies. As a result, business families emerged as the new creative heroes ushering in Western-style standards of living, while the negative consequences of capitalist transformation were viewed as a historical necessity. The argument that a muscular, preferably domestic bourgeoisie is a prerequisite for a strong liberal democracy was a salient ideological force behind privatization of state property on the cheap in postcommunist Eastern Europe and market fundamentalism more generally after 1989. As leading economists and policymakers argued at the time, "Processes of economic and political liberalisation are mutually reinforcing because the bourgeoisie would push for liberalisation and protect the rule of law."[11] Even so, the study of late nineteenth- and early twentieth-century business life during the first heyday of capitalism in East-Central Europe questions whether the existence of a wealthy business elite "reduces the scope for political patronage, and constitutes, together with economic liberalisation, an indispensable condition for maintaining democracy."[12] As the case studies in this book have explored, there seems to be no inherent connection between progressive politics and a powerful coterie of domestic industrialists, bankers, and businessmen. The trajectories of industrialists—who were neither villains nor heroes, neither pure victims nor oppressors—offer a perspective on how societies cope with or resist political change, how institutions like corporations are both dependent on and autonomous from governments, and the extent to which wealth can offer ways to opt out of or alleviate ethnic discrimination.

Postimperial Trajectories

While the industrialists of Austria-Hungary and Germany were remarkably successful in preserving their fortunes in the 1920s, the following two decades brought about genocide and massive social transformations. The 1930s pushed a number of industrialists into the Nazi orbit, a move that had fatal consequences for the Jews among them. Following the rise of Nazi Germany, both the de Dietrich and the Adler and Oppenheimer firms started to prepare their exodus from Central Europe. The de Dietrichs embarked on a plan to relocate to the interior of France; in the 1930s the company purchased shares in mechanical construction companies in Lyon and acquired two foundries in Vendôme. Finally, as an act of desperation, the firm founded an Algerian branch in 1938.[13] The choice of the less industrialized North African department was motivated not by profit seeking but solely by security concerns. The de Dietrichs had profited from the expropriation of Germans after 1918, which marked them as enemies to the Nazis, who reannexed the former Alsace-Lorraine to the Third Reich in 1940.

Less than two decades after the Adlers and Oppenheimers were expropriated by the French government for being German, the German government expropriated them for being Jewish. The Nazis used the firm's longtime patron, the Deutsche Bank, as the intermediary in these expropriations after 1937.[14] By then, the children of the founding families, Paul and Clemens Oppenheimer, who were the two managers of the firm, had relocated to England and Switzerland, respectively. Karl Adler remained in his villa in Berlin's Grünewald until 1938 before moving to Holland.[15] Mózes Farkas died in a Budapest sanatorium in 1941. By then, Nazi Germany had reannexed the former Alsace-Lorraine and granted northern Transylvania, including Farkas's native Cluj, to Hungary with the Second Vienna Arbitration of 1940, ushering in yet another convergence between Alsace-Lorraine and Transylvania between 1940 and 1944, this time around the Nazi orbit. In the meantime, the Hungarian government passed four anti-Jewish laws between 1938 and 1942 that banned people like Farkas from economic activity.[16]

The "long 1940s" brought about the mass murder of most Eastern European and many Alsatian Jewish industrialists during the Holocaust, and ended with the comprehensive expropriation of the remainder of the bourgeoisie in Eastern Europe after 1947 by communist regimes, the same region where Nazi extermination took the greatest toll.[17] Under these circumstances, physical survival and the perpetuation of family fortunes became extremely rare and at times involved controversial deals, yet chances of survival in Hungary, Romania, and Czechoslovakia were still better than in Poland and the rest of the territory that Timothy Snyder has aptly labeled "bloodlands."[18] Some of the industrialists discussed here were active during both world wars; Ferenc Chorin Jr. and tannery owner Karl Adler were among the Jewish industrialists who managed to emerge alive from the cataclysm of the 1940s. Karl Adler, like some other members of the Adler and Oppenheimer families, managed to leave Nazi Germany before the onset of the Second World War; Franz Ferdinand Oppenheimer, who was six when the French administration expelled the family from Strasbourg, died as a young man in Sachsenhausen in 1941.[19]

Hungarian Jews in Nazi-dominated Europe were the last to be targeted for extermination starting in the spring of 1944, years after French Jews had been deported. Ferenc Chorin Jr., who had converted to Catholicism, harbored a controversial friendship with Hungary's governor Miklós Horthy, even as Horthy condoned a series of anti-Jewish laws and failed to stop the deportation of provincial Jews to death camps in 1944 (figure E.1). But by then, even this friendship was not enough to save Chorin. In 1944, he found himself faced with a situation similar to the one in 1919 with regard to the potential loss of his fortune. Yet this time the field of play was profoundly different. In the last year

FIGURE E.1. Ferenc Chorin Jr. with Miklós Horthy at a Budapest industry fair in 1939. Source: Fortapan.

of the Second World War, unlike two and a half decades earlier, the stakes were not just foreign investments but also his family's deportation to death camps. Chorin made a controversial pact with the SS during the Nazi occupation of Hungary that allowed forty members of his family to escape to Switzerland and Portugal with their movable fortunes.[20] He had no idea at the time how little he had to lose economically given that the communist government of Hungary would expropriate his industrial conglomerate a mere five years after he had sold it to the Nazis.[21] His family's villa was converted into a school for the Hungarian Communist Party after 1945.[22]

Unlike any previous regimes, socialist people's republics managed to completely wipe out the bourgeoisie as a class that had emerged in nineteenth-century East-Central Europe in order to create a new class of cadres that took over the social privileges, high-ceilinged apartments, and summer homes of the bourgeoisie.[23] During the Stalinist period, those who remained were often deported to rural areas (as was the case of Budapest's aristocrats and industrialists), interned in labor camps in Hungary, Romania, and the USSR, or allowed to remain in their factories as unskilled laborers or foremen—like Ervin Renner, the grandson of Johann Renner, who founded the family's tannery in Kolozsvár in the 1910s. The young Ervin, who stood a lanky 6'5" with broad shoulders and curly blonde hair, met Zsuzsanna in a hair salon in Cluj where she worked in the 1950s. He immediately asked for her hand in marriage, but she was advised by her boss at the time not to ruin her life by marrying a former industrialist.[24] The pair eventually reunited after 1989, and Zsuzsanna is among the most dedicated guardians of the Renner heritage in Cluj.[25]

In the 1940s, amid genocide and Sovietization, East-Central Europe's bourgeoisie did brutally "catch up" to and surpass the plight of the Alsatian German industrialists who had been expelled by the French after 1918. Like a volcanic eruption, the era of the Second World War also destroyed business archives, family papers, and government documents that revealed convergences among Central European industrialists and their companies in the first three decades of the twentieth century. As Tony Judt observed, "German-speaking central Europe—the engine room of European culture for the first third of the twentieth century—had ceased to exist."[26]

There were numerous similarities between societies in communist "Eastern Europe" and the "free" states of the continent by the 1960s and 1970s. These ranged from the spread of public housing blocks that were built following similar models in both the East and the West to the popularity of the same music across the continent.[27] Despite these convergences, however, the image of a developed Western Europe and its "Other," an Eastern Europe trying and failing to "catch up" economically and culturally, remained remarkably persistent during the Cold War—and is still persistent to this day.[28] At the time, it was easier to believe in and observe long-standing divisions of Eastern and Western Europe, going back to the Middle Ages, than to notice alternative divisions and projects of integration in European history.[29] Understandably, in the shadow of the Second World War there was little interest in excavating a past that bore so little resemblance to the apparent East-West split of the continent reinforced and made visible by the Iron Curtain.[30] More surprisingly, however, very few historians have explored the connected histories of Central Europe in the era of the Great War even after the fall of the Iron Curtain and the expansion of the European Union to many states of the former Eastern Bloc.

While the lifestyles of Central Europe's middle classes, both East and West, not to mention the consumption habits of the super wealthy, may have started to converge after 1989, there is also convergence in the decay of the two regions' industrial heritage despite the continued economic importance of such cities as Strasbourg and Cluj-Napoca (Cluj).[31] The once-coveted factories and mines from which the Chorins, Adlers, Oppenheimers, and other families drew their fortunes have fallen into disrepair and hardly constitute sites of hope and potential for prosperity. A small Italian tannery bought parts of the former Adler and Oppenheimer site in the 2000s but folded after just five years. Since then, the factory's premises have been transformed into a housing project dubbed the Éco-quartier Les Tanneries, a self-proclaimed environmentally conscious neighborhood that nonetheless had no public transportation access for years.[32] In the 1970s, the Strasbourg municipality demolished the Maison Rouge hotel and built a shopping mall on its location, despite citizen protests.[33] Other buildings key to actors in this book continue to flourish in their onetime beauty. The Strasbourg villa from which the French army expelled the Oppenheimers now serves as the headquarters of France's permanent representation at the Council of Europe. France emerged as a victim of Nazi aggression in the 1940s, and it later became a main driver of European unification and reconciliation in the 1950s. As a result, the ethnic cleansing of Germans by the French army after the First World War receded into the background in politics, education, and collective memory, and even in French historiography and public memory. France has so far paid no restitution to expelled Germans.[34] While Annelies Oppenheimer, who was a child during the family's expulsion, donated her collection of early modern paintings to the Strasbourg Fine Arts Museum in 2004, the exhibition makes no mention of the family's troubled past with the French administration.[35]

The steel towns of Lorraine have rarely enjoyed positive press over the past half century. Hagondange appeared in Jean-Paul Wenzel's 1975 existentialist play *Far from Hagondange* as a byword for the emptiness of the working-class lifestyle and consumerism in a welfare state.[36] At present, only the few lively restaurants of North African immigrants constitute islands of hope in these steel towns, at least according to a journalist from *Le Monde*.[37] In the first round of France's 2017 presidential elections, protest parties thrived as the National Front's Marine Le Pen finished first with 28 percent followed by the Far Left Euroskeptic Jean-Luc Mélenchon with 22 percent.[38]

Since 2014, miners at the Hunedoara Energy Complex (Complexul Energetic Hunedoara) have been engaging in periodic strikes protesting against the massive and ongoing layoffs of the corporation's remaining 6,600 employees.[39] Given that the demand for coal has plummeted since the 1990s, the currently state-owned company has been put up for sale, but to date no acceptable proposal has reached the desk of the Romanian minister of the economy.[40] The local press has occasionally published news about potential saviors of the Jiu valley's economically depressed population: "The Americans are coming," read one article title from 2014.[41] That plan, too, has since failed, while striking miners showed their anger in the 2010s by breaking into the management office and pressuring the government-appointed board of directors to resign.[42] Nor is the situation any better at the former Renner tannery. The firm advertised itself in 1992 during Romania's capitalist transformation with recollections of its former prosperity, yet it went bankrupt in 1999 (figure 9.8). The Clujana tannery gained a new lease on life when Cluj-Napoca's municipality salvaged it in 2004; the indebted firm is now nearing bankruptcy again while its formerly bustling factory has become dilapidated (figure E.2).[43] One of the proposed solutions, as in Strasbourg, is to transform the tannery's grounds into apartments in Romania's "IT capital," where information technology and engineering firms like the German Bosch corporation employ a sizable portion of the city's population.[44]

Yet decay alone fails to capture the current economic situation of Alsace, Lorraine, Transylvania, and Central Europe. The pre-pandemic Strasbourg and Cluj of the 2010s were teeming with thousands of exchange students from all over Europe thanks to the EU's Erasmus student mobility program, seeking out similar bars, coffee shops, and fast fashion stores and sporting the same haircuts. The upsurge of the IT sector managed to solve at least some problems of postindustrial and postsocialist transition in Cluj, if not for the workers, then at least for the middle class, including first-generation Romanian college students who find well-paid employment in the sector, alongside French, Italian, and other colleagues who have recently moved to the city. While Romania has lost around one-fifth of its population to emigration since 2000, the population of Cluj has increased slightly over the past decade owing mainly to the influx of people from other Romanian cities, including Bucharest.

Newcomers to the city have ratcheted up property prices and rents, which now surpass those in Budapest and Bucharest and comparable to prices in Spanish, Italian, and French cities of a similar population size. Support from the European Union as well as politically motivated subventions from Hungary's Viktor Orbán to businesses and organizations acting as representatives of the "Hungarian community" of Transylvania, contributed to the renova-

FIGURE E.2. The former Renner tannery in 2018 with the old shoe ad on top of a factory tower. Photo: Author (2017).

tion of historical buildings, churches, and public spaces, while incentives to install insulation on Ceaușescu-era housing projects in the outskirts gave socialist-era concrete blocks a face-lift.

As a result of European unification since the 1950s, the border city of Strasbourg has managed to both retain its traditional heavy industries and emerge as a hub of pharmaceutical, plastics, and other industries. Some of the firms discussed in this book, like the Alsatian Mechanical Construction Company, have fused with larger firms, yet the "Al" prefix in their names—for example, Alcatel or Alstom—still speaks to their Alsatian roots. Strasbourg also emerged as the symbol of Franco-German reconciliation that brought the European Parliament and a series of European Union offices to the city, along with well-paid Eurocrats who work in offices overlooking the Cité Ungemach, a garden city made up of small houses built by Léon Ungemach as compensation for his spectacular profits during the First World War. Some of the family businesses of Alsace are still active today, and descendants of Eugene de Dietrich still live in the family mansion, while their castle now serves as the company's headquarters and archives. Yet the histories of the De Dietrichs, Renners, and other businesses and families of Central and East-Central Europe since the 1930s has to be the subject of a different book.

Notes

Note on Place-Names

1. Tara Zahra, "The 'Minority Problem' and National Classification in the French and Czechoslovak Borderlands," *Contemporary European History* 17, no. 2 (2008): 137–65.

Introduction

1. Jochen Böhler, "Enduring Violence: The Postwar Struggles in East-Central Europe, 1917–21," *Journal of Contemporary History* 50, no. 1 (2015): 58–77.

2. Simone Derix, *Die Thyssens: Familie und Vermögen, Familie - Unternehmen - Öffentlichkeit: Thyssen im 20. Jahrhundert* (Paderborn, Germany: Ferdinand Schöningh, 2016), 379.

3. Horst A. Wessel, *Thyssen & Co., Mülheim a.d. Ruhr: Die Geschichte einer Familie und ihrer Unternehmung* (Stuttgart: Franz Steiner Verlag, 1991), 44–45.

4. John Maynard Keynes, *The Economic Consequences of the Peace* (Cham: Palgrave Macmillan, 2019), 181.

5. Éva Kovács, "Overcoming History through Trauma: The Hungarian Historikerstreit," *European Review* 24, no. 4 (October 2016): 523–534.

6. Fernand Braudel quoted in Immanuel Maurice Wallerstein, *Unthinking Social Science: The Limits of Nineteenth-Century Paradigms* (Philadelphia: Temple University Press, 2001), 136.

7. Quoted in Tony Judt, *Postwar: A History of Europe since 1945* (New York: Penguin Press, 2005), 202.

8. Some notable exceptions include Tara Zahra, "The 'Minority Problem' and National Classification in the French and Czechoslovak Borderlands," *Contemporary European History* 17, no. 2 (2008): 137–165; Jürgen Kocka and Heinz-Gerhard Haupt, "Comparison and Beyond: Traditions, Scope, and Perspectives of Comparative History," in *Comparative and Transnational History: Central European Approaches and New Perspectives*, ed. Heinz-Gerhard Haupt and Jürgen Kocka (New York: Berghahn Books, 2012), 12.

9. James Mahoney and Dietrich Rueschemeyer, "Comparative Historical Analysis, Achievements and Agendas," in *Comparative Historical Analysis in the Social Sciences*, ed. James Mahoney and Dietrich Rueschemeyer (Cambridge: Cambridge University Press, 2003), 8–9.

10. Philipp Ther, "Comparisons, Cultural Transfers, and the Study of Networks: Toward a Transnational History of Europe," in *Comparative and Transnational History: Central European Approaches and New Perspectives*, ed. Heinz-Gerhard Haupt and Jürgen

Kocka (New York: Berghahn Books, 2012), 204; Jürgen Kocka, "Comparison and Beyond," *History and Theory* 42, no. 1 (2003): 40–41.

11. Georges-Henri Soutou, "L'Impérialisme du pauvre," *Relations Internationales*, no. 7 (1976): 219–239; Adam Tooze, *The Deluge: The Great War, America, and the Remaking of the Global Order, 1916–1931* (New York: Viking, 2014), 3–31.

12. Henri Mathias Berthelot to "Georges," January 7, 1919, in *General Henri Berthelot and Romania, Mémoires et correspondance, 1916–1919*, ed. Glenn Torrey (Boulder, CO: EEM, 1987), 203.

13. Ther, "Comparisons," 214.

14. Holly Case, "Reconstruction in East-Central Europe: Clearing the Rubble of Cold War Politics," *Past & Present* 210, Supplement 6 (January 1, 2011): 71–86; György Péteri, "Nylon Curtain—Transnational and Transsystemic Tendencies in the Cultural Life of State-Socialist Russia and East-Central Europe," *Slavonica* 10, no. 2 (November 1, 2004): 113–123.

15. Tara Zahra's pioneering study on Alsatian and Bohemian practices of ethnic discrimination reached similar conclusions. Zahra, "'Minority Problem.'"

16. Zahra, "'Minority Problem.'"

1. Industrialists and Consolidation in Central Europe (1867–1914)

1. Isaac Adler was born in Heilbronn, while Renner's family originated from Degingen.

2. *Bericht des Vorstandes über das 13. Geschäftsjahr vom 1. Juli 1911 bis 30 Juni 1912* (Strasbourg: A.O., 1912), 1–4; "Gyártörténet," in Clujana, DJAN Cluj.

3. Mack Walker, *German Home Towns: Community, State, and General Estate, 1648–1871* (Ithaca, NY: Cornell University Press, 1971), 73–107.

4. Andrew C. Janos, *The Politics of Backwardness in Hungary, 1825–1945* (Princeton, NJ: Princeton University Press, 1982), 155–156; Ignác Romsics, *Magyarország története a XX. században* (Budapest: Osiris, 2005), 61.

5. Vicki Caron, *Between France and Germany: The Jews of Alsace-Lorraine, 1871–1918* (Stanford, CA: Stanford University Press, 1988), 1–37.

6. Tara Zahra, *The Great Departure: Mass Migration from Eastern Europe and the Making of the Free World* (New York: W. W. Norton, 2016); Michel Hubert, *Deutschland im Wandel: Geschichte der deutschen Bevölkerung seit 1815* (Stuttgart: Franz Steiner Verlag, 1998), 9–19, 68–81.

7. Steven Beller, *The Habsburg Monarchy, 1815–1918* (Cambridge: Cambridge University Press, 2018), 179–240; Pieter M. Judson, *The Habsburg Empire: A New History* (Cambridge, MA: Harvard University Press, 2016), 269–328.

8. Péter Hanák and Éva Somogyi, *1867 - európai térben és időben* (Budapest: MTA TTI, 2001); Éva Somogyi, *Abszolutizmus és kiegyezés, 1849–1867* (Budapest: Gondolat, 1981); István Deák, *Beyond Nationalism: A Social and Political History of the Habsburg Officer Corps, 1848–1918* (New York: Oxford University Press, 1990); Judson, *Habsburg Empire*, 249–309.

9. Hanák and Somogyi, *1867 - európai térben és időben*.

10. Rachel Chrastil, *The Siege of Strasbourg* (Cambridge, MA: Harvard University Press, 2014), 1–15, 203–233.

11. Dan P. Silverman, "The Economic Consequences of Annexation: Alsace-Lorraine and Imperial Germany, 1871–1918," *Central European History* 4, no. 1 (March 1, 1971): 34–53.

12. Isabel V. Hull, *Absolute Destruction: Military Culture and the Practices of War in Imperial Germany* (Ithaca, NY: Cornell University Press, 2005).

13. Móric Szentkirályi, "Elzász, Magyarország, Bosznia," *Budapesti Szemle* 18, no. 36 (1878): 318–358.

14. Szentkirályi, "Elzász, Magyarország, Bosznia," 321. (Translations from non-English language sources are all mine. M. R)

15. Szentkirályi, "Elzász, Magyarország, Bosznia"; Charles Grad, *Wiener Weltausstellung, Bericht über die Industrie des Elsasses* (Colmar, Buchdruckerei und Lithographie von Camille Decker>, 1873).

16. N. B., "Egy annektált tartományról," *Vasárnapi Újság*, XXIII, vol. 50, 1876, p. 792.

17. Szentkirályi, "Elzász, Magyarország, Bosznia," 327.

18. István Nagy, "Egy kolozsvári nagyüzem múltjából," *Korunk*, 16, vol. 2–3 (1957): 248–249.

19. Iván T. Berend, "A közép- és kelet-európai gazdasági integráció kérdéséhez (Történelmi előzmények)," *Közgazdasági Szemle*, 3, no. 15 (1968): 311.

20. Niall Ferguson, *The World's Banker: The History of the House of Rothschild* (London: Weidenfeld & Nicolson, 1998).

21. Harold James, *Monetary and Fiscal Unification in Nineteenth-Century Germany: What Can Kohl Learn from Bismarck?* Essays in International Finance, no. 202 (Princeton, NJ: International Finance Section, Department of Economics, Princeton University, 1997), 11–13; Andres Solimano, *Economic Elites, Crises, and Democracy: Alternatives beyond Neoliberal Capitalism* (Oxford: Oxford University Press, 2014), 89–91.

22. Ronmyana Preshlenova, "Austro-Hungarian Trade and the Economic Development of Southeastern Europe before 1914," in *Economic Transformations in East and Central Europe: Legacies from the Past and Policies for the Future*, ed. David F. Good (London: Routledge, 1994), 235–236; Petra Balaton, "Szterényi József erdélyi pályafutása," *Levéltári Közlemények* 82, no. 2 (2011): 150–151.

23. Preshlenova, "Austro-Hungarian Trade," 235–236.

24. Scott, Eddie. "Economic Policy and Economic Development in Austria-Hungary, 1867–1913." In *The Cambridge Economic History of Europe from the Decline of the Roman Empire*, edited by Peter Mathias and Sidney Pollard, 827. Cambridge: Cambridge University Press, 1989.; Sándor Ullmann, "Segélyt Erdély iparának!," *Pesti Hírlap*, June 17, 1886, 9.

25. *Magyar statisztikai évkönyv, 1915* (Budapest: M.K.K.S.H., 1918), 23:149.

26. *Magyar statisztikai évkönyv*, 23:149.

27. *A Kolozsvári Kereskedelmi és Iparkamara jelentése kerülete közgazdasági viszonyairól az, 1886-, 1887-, 1888-, 1889. években* (Cluj: Kolozsvári Kereskedelmi és Iparkamara, 1890), 45–47.

28. Botond Nagy, "Székelyföld gazdasági fejlődése a 19. század második felében: Határszéli gazdasági környezet és üzleti modellek Háromszéken" (PhD diss., Eötvös Loránd University, 2016), 3–11.

29. Nagy, "Székelyföld gazdasági fejlődése," 3–11.

30. *A Kolozsvári Kereskedelmi és Iparkamara jelentése*, 45–47.

31. Miklós Koren and Bálint Menyhért, "Ideas off the Rails: Railroads and Institutional Development in the Austro-Hungarian Monarchy," in Bálint Menyhért, "History as an Agent of Growth: Natural Experiments from Central Europe," PhD diss., Central European University, 2017; Frigyes Fellner, *A magyar szent korona országai nemzeti vagyonának és nemzeti jövedelmének megoszlása a mai Magyarország és az utódállamok között* (Budapest: Franklin, 1923), 13.

32. The trip from Budapest to Brassó/Brașov took twenty hours. Zoltán Szász, ed., *Erdély története* (Budapest: Akadémiai Kiadó, 1986), 3:1509–1517.

33. Fellner, *A magyar szent korona*, 13.

34. Eddie, "Economic Policy and Economic Development in Austria-Hungary," 864–880.

35. Nagy, "Egy kolozsvári nagyüzem múltjából."

36. Ákos Szentkirályi, *Néhány mozzanat Kolozsvár szab. Kir. Város közgazdasági életének 1909. évi történetéből* (Kolozsvár: Ajtai, 1910), 1–18; Lajos Kántor and György Kovács Kis, *Kulcsok Kolozsvárhoz: A föl nem adható város* (Kolozsvár: Korunk Baráti Társaság, 2000), 347–348.

37. Sándor Ilyés, "Történeti szubkultúrák, csoportkultúrák Kolozsváron a 20. Században," *Korunk* 10 (2006): 61–69.

38. Vlad Popovici, "Elita românească din Transilvania și Ungaria perioadei dualiste în perspectivă istoriografică, între 'național' și 'social,'" in *Elitele Puterii: Puterea Elitelor În Spațiul Românesc (Secolele XV-XX)*, ed. Cristian Ploscaru (Iași, Romania: Editura Universității "Alexandru Ioan Cuza," 2018), 49–59.

39. Gábor Egry, *Nemzeti védgát vagy szolid haszonszerzés? Az erdélyi szászok pénzintézeti rendszere és szerepe a nemzeti mozgalomban (1835–1914)* (Csíkszereda, Romania: Pro-Print, 2009), 316–344; Mihai D. Drecin, *Banca "Albina" din Sibiu: Instituție natională a Românilor Transilvăni: 1871–1918* (Cluj-Napoca: Ed. Dacia, 1982), 83–116.

40. Petru Suciu, *Probleme Ardelene, reforma agrară în Ardeal, problema orașelor Ardelene, Clasele sociale în Ardeal* (Cluj: Editura Revistei Societatea de mâine, 1924); Barna Ábrahám, "The Idea of Independent Romanian National Economy in Transylvania at the Turn of the 20th Century," in *Nation-Building and Contested Identities: Romanian and Hungarian Case Studies*, edited by Balázs Trencsényi and Dragos Petrescu. (Budapest: Regio Books, 2001), 209–216; Szász Zoltán, "Az erdélyi román polgárság szerepéről 1918 őszén," *Századok* 2 (1972): 304–335.

41. *Renner Testvérek és Társai Bőrgyár R.t III-ik rendes közgyűlése*, ANR Cluj, Fond Clujana, 1/1948 [1916].

42. John Komlos, *The Habsburg Monarchy as a Customs Union: Economic Development in Austria-Hungary in the Nineteenth Century* (Princeton, NJ: Princeton University Press, 1983), 158–162; Eddie, "Economic Policy and Economic Development in Austria-Hungary," 816–817; Janos, *Politics of Backwardness*, 127–132.

43. Eddie, "Economic Policy and Economic Development in Austria-Hungary," 864–880; Janos, *Politics of Backwardness*, 131–132.

44. Gábor Egry, "Regionalizmus, erdélyiség, szupremácia: Az Erdélyi Szövetség és Erdély jövője, 1913–1918," *Századok* 1 (2013): 3–6.

45. Egry, "Regionalizmus, erdélyiség, szupremácia," 3–6.

46. Transylvania was understood as the entirety of territories annexed from Hungary by Romania after the First World War.

47. Stephen G. Gross, *Export Empire: German Soft Power in Southeastern Europe, 1890–1945* (Cambridge: Cambridge University Press, 2015), 62–102.

48. François Roth, *La Lorraine annexée: étude sur la présidence de Lorraine dans l'Empire allemand, 1870–1918* (Nancy, France: Université de Nancy II), 308–364.

49. Jennifer Siegel, *For Peace and Money: French and British Finance in the Service of Tsars and Commissars* (Oxford: Oxford University Press, 2014), 12–49.

50. Róbert Nagy, *Capitalul-forță a transformării: Rolul capitalului german în industrializarea Transilvaniei (1880–1918)* (Cluj-Napoca: Presa Universitară Clujeană, 2011).

51. "Czukorgyár-részvénytársaságok," in *Pénzügyi Compass, 1908–1909*, ed. Alfréd Kormos (Budapest: Apollo, 1909), 173

52. "Czukorgyár-részvénytársaságok."

53. *Pallas Nagy Lexikona* (Budapest: Pallas I. Ny. Rt., 1895), 10:939.

54. Michael Stephen Smith, *The Emergence of Modern Business Enterprise in France, 1800–1930* (Cambridge, MA: Harvard University Press, 2006), 170–172.

55. Jeremi Suri, *Power and Protest: Global Revolution and the Rise of Detente* (Cambridge, MA: Harvard University Press, 2009), 29–32; "Les Charbonnages D'Urikany," *Paris-capital: journal financier*, July 8, 1896, 2; J. Hajek, "Les Charbonnages D'Urikany," *L'Écho des mines et de la métallurgie*, March 22, 1891; "Causerie Financière," *Journal du Dimanche*, April 3, 1892, 2–3; "Chronique Financière," *La Caricature, publication de la Librairie illustrée*, March 14, 1891, 87; Smith, *Emergence of Modern Business Enterprise in France*, 170–172.

56. *The Encyclopaedia Britannica* (New York: Encyclopaedia Britannica, 1910), 6:579.

57. *Encyclopaedia Britannica*, 6:579.

58. Gábor Téglás, "Hunyad megye közgazdasági leírása," *Közgazdasági Szemle* 27, no. 30 (1903): 766.

59. "Oraviczai bányakapitányság," *Magyar Bánya-Kalauz*, no. 4 (1896): 68.

60. "Oraviczai bányakapitányság," 68; "Salgótarjáni kőszénbánya rt.," in *Mihók-féle Magyar Compass* 27, no. 2 (1899). 465.

61. György Kövér, *Iparosodás agrárországban* (Budapest: Gondolat, 1982).

62. Sándor Galánthai Nagy, ed., *Mihók-féle Magyar Compass 1899–1900* (Budapest: Légrády, 1900), 465.

63. Rudolf Gräf, *Domeniul bănățean al StEG 1855–1920: Din istoria industrială a Banatului montan* (Reșița, Romania: Editura Banatica, 1997), 56–58.

64. Jean-Luc Pinol, "Elites et cercles à Lyon avant et après la première guerre mondiale," in *Eliten in Deutschland und Frankreich im 19. und 20. Jahrhundert: Strukturen und Beziehungen*, ed. Rainer Hudemann and Georges-Henri Soutou (Munich: R. Oldenbourg, 1994), 1:47–48.

65. "Compagnie Algérienne de Glace Hygiénique," *Les entreprises coloniales françaises* database, accessed June 25, 2015, http://www.entreprises-coloniales.fr/afrique-du-nord/Alger._glace_hygienique.pdf.

66. "Société Anonyme des Mines de la Loire," *Le Constitutionnel, journal politique littéraire, universel*, January 24, 1855, 4.

67. Béla Kempelen, *Magyar nemes családok* (Budapest: Grill K., 1931), 10:450.

68. "Compagnie Algérienne de Glace Hygiénique."

69. Rondo Cameron defines Central and East-Central Europe as Switzerland, Germany, and Austria-Hungary. Rondo E. Cameron, *France and the Economic Development*

of Europe, 1800–1914 (Chicago: Rand McNally, 1965), 88; Rondo Cameron and V. I. Bovykin, *International Banking, 1870–1914* (Oxford: Oxford University Press, 1992), 1–15.

70. Raymond Poidevin, *Les relations économiques et financières entre la France et l'Allemagne de 1898 à 1914* (Paris: A. Colin, 1969), xi; Volker R. Berghahn, ed., *Quest for Economic Empire: European Strategies of German Big Business in the Twentieth Century* (Providence, RI: Berghahn Books, 1996); Volker Berghahn, "German Big Business and the Quest for a European Economic Empire in the Twentieth Century," in *German Big Business and Europe in the Twentieth Century*, ed. Volker Berghahn, Reinhard Neebe, and Jeffrey J. Anderson (Providence, RI: Thomas J. Watson Jr. Institute for International Studies, Brown University, 1993).

71. The full name of the German company was Oberschlesische Kokswerke und Chemische Fabriken AG, or Upper Silesian Coke Works and Chemical Products Company. Poidevin, *Les relations économiques*, xi; Berghahn, *Quest for Economic Empire*; Berghahn, "German Big Business."

72. "La Laenderbank," *Le Capitaliste: Journal de la banque Parisienne*, March 8, 1882, 213; László Szűcs, "A Petrozsényi Kőszénbánya Rt. átadása a Szovjetuniónak, a magyar jóvátétel különleges fejezete," *Történelmi Szemle* 1 (2010): 70.

73. "Les Charbonnages D'Urikany," *Paris-capital: journal financier*, July 8, 1896, 2; J. Hajek, "Les Charbonnages D'Urikany," *L'Écho des mines et de la métallurgie*, March 22, 1891; "Causerie Financière," *Journal du Dimanche*, April 3, 1892, 2–3; "Chronique Financière," *La Caricature, publication de la Librairie illustrée*, March 14, 1891, 87.

74. "Közgazdasági havi értesítő," *Közgazdasági és Közigazgatási Szemle* 2 (1894): 292–295; "Krónika," *A Bánya*, February 28, 1909, 2–3.

75. "Les Charbonnages d'Urikany," *Voleur Illustré, Revue pour Tous*, March 19, 1891, 190–191.

76. Janos, *Politics of Backwardness*, 149–150.

77. "Les Charbonnages D'Urikany," 149–150.

78. Lajos Varga, "Munkásság, munkásmozgalom Erdélyben 1914-ig," *História* 3 (1987): 31–32.

79. Varga, "Munkásság, munkásmozgalom Erdélyben 1914-ig," 31–32

80. György Kövér, "Bécsi és pesti bankok a Balkánon a századfordulón," in. *A pesti City öröksége: Banktörténeti tanulmányok* (Budapest: BFL, 2012), 360–362; Kövér, *Iparosodás agrárországban*; S. N. Broadberry and Kevin H. O'Rourke, eds., *The Cambridge Economic History of Modern Europe* (Cambridge: Cambridge University Press, 2010); Rondo E. Cameron, *France and the Economic Development of Europe, 1800–1914* (Princeton, NJ: Princeton University Press, 1961), 88.

81. Robert Nemes, *Another Hungary: The Nineteenth-Century Provinces in Eight Lives* (Stanford, CA: Stanford University Press, 2016).

82. Kálmán Mikszáth, "Chorin császári biztos;" in *Ezredvég* 5 (2010): 77–80; Daisy Strasser Chorin, "*Az Andrássy úttól a Park Avenue-ig: fejezetek Chorin Ferenc életéből (1879–1964)* (Budapest: Osiris, 1999), 13–17.

83. "Chorin Ferencz," in Albert Sturm, ed., *Országgyülési Almanach, 1897–1901* (Budapest: Pesti Lloyd, 1897), 214–215.

84. "Dr. Chorin Ferenc," *A Bánya*, February 20, 1920, 5.

85. "A Salgótarjáni Kőszénbánya Rt. története és a magyar közgazdasági életben elfoglalt szerepe [1917–1918]," MNL-OL, Z 223, 24. cs. 71/1. tétel.

86. "Egyesületünk és a gyáriparosok szövetsége," *Magyar Ipar* 26 (1902): 776.

87. Géza Somogyi, "Az állami szénbányászatról," *A Bánya*, December 25, 1910, 34.

88. Antal Vörös, "A magyar bányaigazgatás szervezete," *Levéltári Szemle* 55, no. 2 (1984): 205–207; "Szemelvény az aradi kereskedelmi és iparkamara 1909. évi jelentéséből," *A Bánya*, August 21, 1910, 2–4.

89. "Salgótarjáni kőszénbánya rt.," *Mihók-féle Magyar Compass* 27, no. 2 (1899). 465; *Mihók-féle Magyar Compass* 36, no 2. (1908): 378; Julianna Puskás, *Kivándorló magyarok az Egyesült Államokban, 1880–1940* (Budapest: Akadémiai Kiadó, 1982), 62.

90. Béla Tomka, "Interlocking Directorates between Banks and Industrial Companies in Hungary at the Beginning of the Twentieth Century," *Business History* 43, no. 1 (January 2001): 32–35.

91. Tomka, "Interlocking Directorates," 32–35; Béla Tomka, "Bankuralom, bankérdekeltség, bankellenőrzés: A magyarországi pénzintézetek ipari kapcsolatai a századfordulón, 1895–1913," *Történelmi Szemle* 2 (1995): 183–185.

92. Andrea Colli, *The History of Family Business, 1850–2000* (New York: Cambridge University Press, 2002); David S. Landes, *Dynasties: Fortunes and Misfortunes of the World's Great Family Businesses* (New York: Viking, 2006), 261–273.

93. "Milliomos adózók a Lipótvárosban," *Az Est*, September 9, 1917.

94. Alison F. Frank, *Oil Empire: Visions of Prosperity in Austrian Galicia* (Cambridge, MA: Harvard University Press, 2005), 77.

95. *A magyar korona országaiban az 1870. év elején végrehajtott népszámlálás eredményei a hasznos házi állatok kimutatásával együtt* (Pest, Hungary: Atheneaum, 1871); *Magyar Korona országainak 1900. évi népszámlálása, A népesség általános leírása községenkint* (Budapest: Magyar Királyi Központi Statisztikai Hivatal, 1902), 1:404–405; *A Magyar Szent Korona országainak 1910. évi népszámlálása, A népesség főbb adatai községek és népesebb puszták, telepek szerint, Magyar statisztikai közlemények* (Budapest: M. K. S. H., 1912), 42: 404–405.

96. Alajos Kovács, "Az 1910.-i népszámlálás eredménye," *Közgazdasági Szemle* 35, part 1 (1911): 231.

97. *A Magyar Szent Korona országainak 1910. évi népszámlálása, 2. rész, A népesség foglalkozása és a nagyipari vállalatok községenkint, Magyar statisztikai közlemények*, vol. 48 (Budapest: Magyar Királyi Központi Statisztikai Hivatal), 1068–1069.

98. MSK, vol. 48, 806.

99. Joseph Rossé, Marcel Stürmel, Albert Bleicher, Fernand Deiber, and Jean Keppi, *Das Elsass von 1870–1932* (Colmar, France: Verlag Alsatia, 1936), 4:48–52; Illés Edvi, ed., *A magyar béketárgyalások: Jelentés a Magyar békeküldöttség működéséről Neuilly s/S.-ben 1920 januárius - marcius havában* (Budapest: M. kir. tudományegyetemi nyomda, 1920), 3/a:117–118.

100. Walker, *German Home Towns*, 73–107.

101. François Igersheim, *L'Alsace des notables (1870–1914): La bourgeoisie et le peuple alsacien* (Strasbourg: Bf, 1981); Laufenburger, *Cours d'economie*, 97–111.

102. Michel Hau, *L'Industrialisation de l'Alsace: 1803–1939* (Strasbourg: Association des publications près les universités de Strasbourg, 1987), 238–239.

103. David Allen Harvey, *Constructing Class and Nationality in Alsace, 1830–1945* (DeKalb: Northern Illinois University Press, 2001), 77; Alfred Wahl and Jean-Claude

Richez, *La vie quotidienne en Alsace entre France et Allemagne: 1850–1950* (Paris: Hachette, 1993), 241–243.

104. Alfred Wahl, *L'option et l'émigration des Alsaciens-Lorrains, 1871–1872* (Paris: Ophrys, 1977), 174.

105. Christopher J. Fischer, *Alsace to the Alsatians? Visions and Divisions of Alsatian Regionalism, 1870–1939* (New York: Berghahn Books, 2010), 8.

106. Caron, *Between France and Germany*, 45–73.

107. Alexander C. T. Geppert, *Fleeting Cities: Imperial Expositions in Fin-de-Siècle Europe* (Houndmills, Basingstoke, Hampshire, UK: Palgrave Macmillan, 2010), 29–33; Nikolaus Wolf, "Was Germany Ever United? Evidence from Intra- and International Trade, 1885–1933," *Journal of Economic History* 69, no. 3 (2009): 877; Béatrice Dedinger, "The Franco-German Trade Puzzle: An Analysis of the Economic Consequences of the Franco-Prussian War." *The Economic History Review* 65, no. 3 (2012): 1038–1042.

108. Achille Mercier, "M. Pouyer Quartier et l'article XI de la traité du Francfort," *L'Économiste français: Journal hebdomadaire*, September 26, 1885, 385; Hau, *L'Industrialisation de l'Alsace*, 233–234; Dan P. Silverman, *Reluctant Union, Alsace-Lorraine and Imperial Germany, 1871–1918* (University Park: Pennsylvania State University Press, 1972), 166–167.

109. Silverman, *Reluctant Union*, 177.

110. Michel Hau, *La Maison De Dietrich, de 1864 à nos jours* (Strasbourg: Oberlin, 1998), 140–141.

111. Otto Hellmann, *Die staatsrechtliche Stellung des Reichslandes Elsass-Lothringen nach seiner geschichtlichen Entwicklung und dem geltenden Recht* (Freising, Germany: Buchdr. von A. Warmuth, 1907), 52.

112. Rossé et al., *Das Elsass*, 1:391–403.

113. Continuities are remarkable even in relatively high-ranking positions. The German administration, for instance, retained Strasbourg's municipal architects Geoffroy Conrath and Joseph Klotz as well. Klaus Nohlen, *Construire une capitale: Strasbourg impérial de 1870 à 1918: les bâtiments officiels de la Place impériale* (Strasbourg: Publications de la Société Savante d'Alsace, 1997), 28–36.

114. Gerald D. Feldman, *Army, Industry, and Labor in Germany, 1914–18* (Princeton, NJ: Princeton University Press, 1966), 9.

115. Feldman, *Army, Industry, and Labor in Germany*, 9.

116. Hellmann, *Die staatsrechtliche Stellung des Reichslandes*, 43–45; Silverman, *Reluctant Union*; Volker Rolf Berghahn, *Imperial Germany, 1871–1918: Economy, Society, Culture, and Politics* (New York: Berghahn Books, 2005), 109.

117. Börries Kuzmany, "Habsburg Austria: Experiments in Non-territorial Autonomy," *Ethnopolitics* 15, no. 1 (January 1, 2016): 43–65; Jeremy King, "The Municipal and the National in the Bohemian Lands, 1848–1914," *Austrian History Yearbook* 42 (April 2011): 89–109; Tara Zahra, *Kidnapped Souls: National Indifference and the Battle for Children in the Bohemian Lands, 1900–1948* (Ithaca, NY: Cornell University Press, 2008), 33–36.

118. Judson, *Habsburg Empire*, 329–331.

119. Berghahn, *Imperial Germany*, 105–113.

120. Berghahn, *Imperial Germany*, 105–113.

121. Berghahn, *Imperial Germany*, 105–113; Stefan Berger, "Building the Nation among Visions of German Empire," in *Nationalizing Empires*, ed. Stefan Berger and Alexei Miller (Budapest: Central European University Press, 2015), 253–255.

122. Versailles Treaty, Art. 297.

123. Rossé et al., *Das Elsass*, 4:47.

124. Daniela L. Caglioti, "Property Rights in Time of War: Sequestration and Liquidation of Enemy Aliens' Assets in Western Europe during the First World War," *Journal of Modern European History* 12, no. 4 (2014): 526.

125. Hermann Hiery, *Reichstagswahlen im Reichsland: Ein Beitrag zur Landesgeschichte von Elsass-Lothringen und zur Wahlgeschichte des Deutschen Reiches, 1871–1918* (Düsseldorf: Droste, 1986), 150–170, 313–330.

126. Mark Hewitson, *Germany and the Causes of the First World War* (London: Bloomsbury, 2004), 148–150.

127. Igersheim, *L'Alsace des notables*, 1–11.

128. François Uberfill, *La société strasbourgeoise entre France et Allemagne (1871–1924): la société strasbourgeoise à travers les mariages entre Allemands et Alsaciens à l'époque du Reichsland: le sort des couples mixtes après 1918* (Strasbourg: Société Savante d'Alsace, 2001), 175.

129. Hau, *La Maison De Dietrich*, 15–16.

130. Hau, *La Maison De Dietrich*, 16–17.

131. Simon Schama, *Citizens: A Chronicle of the French Revolution* (New York: Knopf, 1989), 596–598; Thomas Amédée Rouget de Lisle, *La vérité sur la paternité de la Marseillaise* (Paris, 1865), 7.

132. "Dietrich," in Jean Chrétien Ferdinand Hoefer, *Nouvelle biographie générale depuis les temps les plus reculés jusqu'à nos jours, avec les renseignements bibliographiques et l'indication des sources à consulter* (Paris: Firmin Didot frères, fils et cie, 1855), 154–156.

133. Hau, *La Maison de Dietrich*, 81–98.

134. Hau, *La Maison De Dietrich*, 100.

135. Hau, *La Maison De Dietrich*, 128; "La guerre du 1870: La déchirure, exploitation pédagogique," Fiche 8, pp. 5–6, ADBR, http://archives.bas-rhin.fr; Antoinette Spindler-Theis, "Susan de Diétrich," in *Bulletin de la Societe de l'Histoire du Protestantisme Francais* (Paris: Librairie Droz), 501–509.

136. Hau, *La Maison De Dietrich*, 144.

137. Hau, *L'Industrialisation de l'Alsace*, 249–251; Silverman, *Reluctant Union*, 177.

138. Roth, *La Lorraine annexée*, 308, 352.

139. Uberfill, *La société strasbourgeoise*, 40–44.

140. Dedinger, "Franco-German Trade Puzzle," 1040; Rossé et al., *Das Elsass*, 4:16, 46.

141. Uberfill, *La société strasbourgeoise*, 35.

142. Jean Daltroff, "Les Adler et Oppenheimer," *Revue d'Alsace*, no. 136 (October 1, 2010): 183.

143. Uberfill, *La société strasbourgeoise*, 83–86.

144. Heinrich von. Treitschke, *What We Demand from France* (London: Macmillan, 1870), 28–29.

145. George Delahache, *Petite histoire de l'Alsace-Lorraine* (Paris: Libraire Bernard Grasset, 1918), 72.

146. Roth, *La Lorraine annexée*, 216.

147. Roth, *La Lorraine annexée*, 315.

148. Hau, *L'Industrialisation de l'Alsace*, 240–247.

149. Roth, *La Lorraine annexée*, 267.

150. Roth, *La Lorraine annexée*, 305.

151. The construction of the Moselle canal would have helped transport Lorraine steel to German markets, but the Prussian government rejected the canal and it was never built. Roth, *La Lorraine annexée*, 259–352; Silverman, *Reluctant Union*, 186.

152. Roth, *La Lorraine annexée*, 331–335.

153. Roth, *La Lorraine annexée*, 216, 370–371.

154. Roth, *La Lorraine annexée*, 370.

155. Werner Wittich, *Deutsche und französische Kultur im Elsass* (Strassburg: Schlesier & Schweikhardt, 1900), 55.

156. *Handbuch für nichtsozialdemokratische Wähler* (Berlin: Reichsverbandsverl., 1911); *Verzeichnis der in der Bücherei der Firma Adler und Oppenheimer Lederfabrik A. G. Lingolsheim enthaltenen Bücher* (Strassburg: DuMont Schauberg, 1917).

157. Uberfill, *La société strasbourgeoise*, 163–164.

158. Uberfill, *La société strasbourgeoise*, 163–164; Rossé et al., *Das Elsass*, 4:55.

159. Rossé et al., *Das Elsass*, 4:55.

160. Landes, *Dynasties: Fortunes and Misfortunes.*

161. Hau, *La Maison De Dietrich*; Igersheim, *L'Alsace des notables*, 1–11.

162. Daltroff, "Les Adler et Oppenheimer," 179.

163. Daltroff, "Les Adler et Oppenheimer," 189.

164. Caron, *Between France and Germany*, 24–25, 73.

165. Eugen Jacobi, *Fragen der Übergangswirtschaft: Vortrag Gehalten in der Strassburger Gesellschaft für Deutsche Kultur, Januar 1917* (Strassburg: Dumont Schauberg, 1917); Eugen Jacobi, *Wirtschaftliche Tages- und Zukunfts-Fragen: Vortrag gehalten in der Strassburger Gesellschaft für deutsche Kultur, am 14 März 1918* (Strassburg: Dumont Schauberg, 1918).

166. Daltroff, "Les Adler et Oppenheimer."

167. Alain Kahn, "Eléments concernant l'Ecole Israélite du Travail de Strasbourg," Judaisme database, accessed November 7, 2017, http://judaisme.sdv.fr/histoire/villes/strasbrg/travail.htm.

168. Daltroff, "Les Adler et Oppenheimer," 191–193.

169. "Auszug aus dem Register der Beratungen des Gemeinderats der Strassburg i. E," AVES 77 MW 250, Fondation Adler; Harvey, *Constructing Class*, 48, 79; Daltroff, "Les Adler et Oppenheimer," 187–188.

170. Hau, *La Maison De Dietrich*, 93–101.

171. *Statuten der Aktiengesellschaft Adler-Oppenheimer, Lederfabrik Strassburg i. E.* (Strasbourg: Strassburger Druckerei, 1914).

172. *Adler-Oppenheimer, Lederfabrik.*

173. *Adler-Oppenheimer, Lederfabrik.*

174. *Adler-Oppenheimer, Lederfabrik.*

175. Jean Keppi, "Rapport au Conseil municipal sur la Crise des Habitations à Strasbourg," May 1920, ADBR 94 J 71.

176. *Adler-Oppenheimer, Lederfabrik*, 14–16.

177. Szentkirályi, "Elzász, Magyarország, Bosznia," 342.

178. Szentkirályi, "Elzász, Magyarország, Bosznia," 342.

179. Colli, *History of Family Business*, 76.

180. Karl Polanyi, *The Great Transformation* (New York: Beacon Press, 1957), 76.

181. Stefan Zweig, *The World of Yesterday*, trans. Anthea Bell (Lincoln: University of Nebraska Press, 2013); Hannah Arendt, *The Origins of Totalitarianism* (New York: Harcourt Brace Jovanovich, 1973), 50–53; Keynes, *Economic Consequences of the Peace*, 49–58.

182. Alison Frank, "The Petroleum War of 1910: Standard Oil, Austria, and the Limits of the Multinational Corporation," *American Historical Review* 114 (2009): 17.

2. Costly Nationalism

1. On the critique of the "borderland" concept, see Pieter M. Judson, *Guardians of the Nation: Activists on the Language Frontiers of Imperial Austria* (Cambridge, MA: Harvard University Press, 2006), 1–11.

2. Gusztáv Beksics, *La question roumaine et la lutte des races en Orient* (Paris: Chailley, 1895), 59–117; Gusztáv Beksics, *A magyar politika uj alapjai kapcsolatban a magyar faj terjeszkedő képességével és a földbirtokviszonyokkal* (Budapest: Athenaeum, 1899), 84–119.

3. Robert Gerwarth and Erez Manela, eds., *Empires at War: 1911–1923* (Oxford: Oxford University Press, 2014), 1–16; Heather Jones, James O'Brien, and C. Schmidt-Supprian, *Untold War: New Perspectives in First World War Studies* (Leiden: Brill, 2008), 1–20; Phillip Ther, "Pre-negotiated Violence: Ethnic Cleansing in the 'Long First World War,'" in *Legacies of Violence: Eastern Europe's First World War*, ed. J. Böhler, W. Borodziej, and J. von Puttkamer (Munich: Oldenbourg, 2014), 259.

4. József Galántai, *Magyarország az első világháborúban, 1914–1918* (Budapest: Akadémiai Kiadó, 1974), 90–112; Tibor Hajdu and Ferenc Pollmann, *A régi Magyarország utolsó háborúja, 1914–1918* (Budapest: Osiris, 2014), 45–53.

5. Irina Marin, *Peasant Violence and Antisemitism in Early Twentieth-Century Eastern Europe* (New York: Palgrave Macmillan, 2018), 77–154.

6. Ferenc Pölöskei, "István Tisza's Policy toward the Romanian Nationalities on the Eve of World War I," *Acta Historica Academiae Scientiarum Hungaricae* 18, nos. 3/4 (1972): 267–291.

7. Janos, *Politics of Backwardness*, 113.

8. András Cieger, *Politikai korrupció a Monarchia Magyarországán, 1867–1918* (Budapest: Napvilág, 2011), 35–47.

9. Judson, *Habsburg Empire*, 370–384.

10. Ágoston Berecz, *The Politics of Early Language Teaching: Hungarian in the Primary Schools of the Late Dual Monarchy* (Budapest: CEU Press, 2013), 183–234.

11. "Egyről-másról," *Köztelek*, May 2, 1914, 1; Károly Irinyi, *Mitteleuropa-tervek és az osztrák-magyar politikai közgondolkodás* (Budapest: Akadémiai Kiadó, 1973), 225–264.

12. Irinyi, *Mitteleuropa-tervek*, 225–264.

13. Maureen Healy, *Vienna and the Fall of the Habsburg Empire: Total War and Everyday Life in World War I* (Cambridge: Cambridge University Press, 2004), 31–86.

14. [Lajos Litschauer], "A nagy és hatalmas, Európa bányászati iparának terén vezérlő szerepet vívő Németország . . ." *Jó Szerencsét*, February 2, 1908, 283–284; Géza Somogyi, "Az állami szénbányászatról," *A Bánya*, December 25, 1910, 34.

15. Antal Vörös, "A magyar bányaigazgatás szervezete," *Levéltári Szemle* 55, no. 2 (1984): 205–207; "Szemelvény az aradi kereskedelmi és iparkamara 1909. évi jelentéséből," *A Bánya*, August 21, 1910, 2–4.

16. "Petrozsény, a bérletben volt zsilvölgyi kőszénbányák házi kezelésbe vétele," *A Bánya*, December 25, 1909, 37.

17. Janos, *Politics of Backwardness*, 141.

18. "Az ipartanács beosztása és szabályzata," *Magyar Ipar* 30, no. 10 (1909): 31.

19. Janos, *Politics of Backwardness*, 127–142.

20. Law III of 1907, Net Jogtár database, accessed January 8, 2017, https://net.jogtar.hu/ezer-ev-torvenyei.

21. Law III of 1907.

22. László Katus, "Az iparosodás fellendülése," in Péter Hanák and Ferenc Mucsi, eds. *Magyarország története tíz kötetben, 7. Magyarország története. 1890–1918*, vol. 1, (Budapest: MTA TTI, 1978), 351–358.

23. Law III of 1907.

24. Bálint Varga, *The Monumental Nation: Magyar Nationalism and Symbolic Politics in Fin-de-Siècle Hungary* (New York: Berghahn Books, 2016), 1–20.

25. Komlos, *Habsburg Monarchy as a Customs Union*, 159.

26. Komlos, *Habsburg Monarchy as a Customs Union*, 159.

27. "Egy magyar főpap az iparpártolásról," *Honi Ipar*, October 15, 1906, 5.

28. "Tulipános tollak- Angliából," *Honi Ipar*, December 1, 1906, 9.

29. "Magyar lópatkó szeg a hadseregnél," *Honi Ipar*, October 15, 1906, 5.

30. Komlos, *Habsburg Monarchy as a Customs Union*, 159.

31. In 1910, the city of Kolozsvár employed seventy-eight tanners, while Kolozs County around it employed thirty-four. *Magyar statisztikai közlemények*, 48:52.

32. János Fodor, *Bernády György: Politikai életrajz* (Marosvásárhely, Romania: Lector Kiadó, 2017), 56–108.

33. Nemes, *Another Hungary*, 8.

34. Nemes, *Another Hungary*, 7.

35. R. Frank, "Renner Testvérek és Társai Bőrgyárt R.t. Cluj Monographiája" [c. 1926] 6/1924 Date monografice, Clujana, DJAN Cluj

36. "Üdvözlet a harczosoknak!," *Független Magyarország*, October 2, 1903, 5.

37. Nathaniel Katzburg, *Fejezetek az újkori zsidó történelemből Magyarországon* (Budapest: Osiris-MTA Judaisztikai Kutatócsoport, 1999), 103–115; Anikó Prepuk, "Religious Equality and Jewish Emancipation: The Acceptance of the Jewish Denomination in Hungary in the 1890s," in *Tolerance and Intolerance in Historical Perspective*, ed. Csaba Lévai and Vasile Vese (Pisa: PLUS, 2003), 12–23.

38. Deák, *Beyond Nationalism*.

39. "Üdvözlet a harczosoknak!"

40. Michael Laurence Miller, "A Monumental Debate in Budapest: The Hentzi Statue and the Limits of Austro-Hungarian Reconciliation, 1852–1918," *Austrian History Yearbook* 40 (2009): 231–233.

41. "Üdvözlet a harczosoknak!," 5.

42. Lawyer Kálmán Frankl, Memorandum, September 10, 1941, ANR Cluj, Fond Clujana, Testamentului Dr. Farkas, 8/1932, pp. 10–14.

43. István Nagy, "Egy kolozsvári nagyüzem múltjából," *Korunk*, 16, no. 2–3 (1957): 249.

44. Nagy, "Egy kolozsvári nagyüzem múltjából," 249.

45. Pálffy József, "Kolozsvár, mint iparváros," *Kolozsvári Városi Közlöny*, May 1910, 1–3.

46. "Renner Testvérek és Társai Bőrgyár Alapszabályai," September 2, 1911, Clujana 1/1915, DJAN Cluj.

47. "Jegyzőkönyv," 1913, 1914, "Rapoarte și Procese Verbale," Clujana 1/1915, DJAN Cluj.

48. Béla Katona, *Magyarország közgazdasága, Pénzügyi és közgazdasági évkönyv 1913. évről.* (Budapest: Légrády, 1914, 11–14; "Szemle," *Magyar Gyáripar* 4, no. 24 (July 1914): 2.

49. "Jegyzőkönyv," April 11, 1915, Clujana 1/1915, "Rapoarte și Procese Verbale," DJAN Cluj;, , 1915/1.

50. Minutes of the assembly of the Renner Brothers' and Partners' Tannery, April 11, 1915, DJAN, Clujana, 1915/1.

51. "A kolozsvári csizmadia-munkások szervezkedéséhez," *Kolozsvári Munkás*, September 15, 1905.

52. Irina Livezeanu, *Cultural Politics in Greater Romania: Regionalism, Nation Building & Ethnic Struggle, 1918–1930* (Ithaca, NY: Cornell University Press), 6–9, 129–135.

53. Constantin Iordachi, *Liberalism, Constitutional Nationalism, and Minorities: The Making of Romanian Citizenship, c. 1750–1918* (Leiden: Brill, 2019), 195–264; Ezra Mendelsohn, *The Jews of East Central Europe between the World Wars* (Bloomington: Indiana University Press, 1983), 171–178; Marin, *Peasant Violence and Antisemitism*, 5.

54. R[óbert] B[raun], "Társadalmi, politikai és egyéb aktuális kérdések," *Huszadik Század* 1 (1913): 133; László Bizony, *A keleti határról* (Budapest: Szerző, 1912), 48.

55. Illés Edvi, ed., *A magyar béketárgyalások: Jelentés a Magyar békeküldöttség működéséről Neuilly s/S.-ben 1920 január'us - marcius havában* (Budapest: M. kir. tudományegyetemi nyomda, 1920), 3/a:67–80.

56. Gusztáv Beksics, *A román kérdés és a fajok harcza Európában és Magyarországon* (Budapest: Athenaeum, 1895), 168; Éva Kovács, "Az agrárius beszédmód rekonstrukciója az 1920-as földbirtokreform parlamenti vitája alapján," in *A tudomány és az oktatás vonzásában: Tanulmánykötet Tóth Tibor professzor emlékére*, ed. Zoltán Kaposi, Tamás Lendvai, and Oroszi Sándor (Pécs: PTE-FEEK KTK, 2012), 311–333.

57. B[raun], "Társadalmi, politikai és egyéb aktuális kérdések," 133; Bizony, *A keleti határról*, 48.

58. Miklós Bánffy, *The Transylvanian Trilogy: They Were Counted* (Toronto: Knopf Doubleday Publishing Group, 2013), 507–508.

59. Egry, "Regionalizmus, erdélyiség, szupremácia," 27–29.

60. Egry, "Regionalizmus, erdélyiség, szupremácia," 27–29.

61. Egry, "Regionalizmus, erdélyiség, szupremácia," 27–29.

62. "Hantos Elemér," in Bizony, *A keleti határról*, 122.

63. "Hantos Elemér," 122.

64. Egry, *Nemzeti védgát vagy szolid haszonszerzés?*, 192–200.

65. "Sonderausdruck aus den stenographischen Bericht der 9. Sitzung der ersten Kammer von 29. April 1912," in AVES, 81 Z 39/1.

66. Schama, *Citizens*, 596–598.

67. "Protokoll der ausserordentlichen Sitzung vom 17. Mai 1912, Handelskammer zu Strassburg i. E.," AVES 81 Z 39/1.

68. "Programme de la Fête Ste Cécile de la Chorale de l'usine de Grafenstaden, 14 janvier, 1882," retieved from BNU Strasbourg at https://www.numistral.fr/ark:/12148/btv1b102031247, October 17, 2018.

69. Joseph Rossé, Marcel Stürmel, Albert Bleicher, Fernand Deiber, and Jean Keppi, *Das Elsass von 1870–1932* (Colmar: Verlag Alsatia, 1936), 1:160; Bernhard Menne, *Blood and Steel: The Rise of the House of Krupp* (New York: L. Furman, 1938), 257–300.

70. Frank Bösch, *Öffentliche Geheimnisse: Skandale, Politik und Medien in Deutschland und Grossbritannien 1880–1914* (Oldenbourg, Germany: Oldenbourg Verlag, 2009), 449–454.

71. "Sonderausdruck."

72. Schama, *Citizens*, 596–598.

73. Schama, *Citizens*, 596–598.

74. "Annoncen," *Illkirch-Grafenstadener Anzeiger*, February 17, 1912, 1.

75. "Annoncen," 1.

76. Nicolas Stoskopf, "André Koechlin & Cie," *SACM, Wärtsilä, Histoire de La Fonderie (D'Giesserei) à Mulhouse (1826–2007)*, 2007, 1–52, https://hal.archives-ouvertes.fr/hal-00544984.

77. Stoskopf, "André Koechlin," 38–40.

78. Hau, *L'Industrialisation de l'Alsace*, 242; Luc Jeanvoine, "Conflit intra-allemand sous-jacent au conflit franco-allemand: L'exemple de la S.A.C.M. (1914–1918)?," *Guerres mondiales et conflits contemporains* 265, no. 1 (2017): 34.

79. Stoskopf, "André Koechlin," 36–39.

80. Stoskopf, "André Koechlin," 39.

81. Stoskopf, "André Koechlin," 39.

82. Stoskopf, "André Koechlin," 40.

83. Stoskopf, "André Koechlin," 40.

84. Hartmut Kaelble, *Industrielle Interessenpolitik in der Wilhelminischen Gesellschaft: Centralverband Deutscher Industrieller 1895 bis 1914* (Berlin: Walter de Gruyter GmbH, 2016), 220–224.

85. Chlodwig Karl Viktor Hohenlohe-Schillingsfürst and Alexander Hohenlohe-Schillingsfürst, *Memoirs of Prince Chlodwig of Hohenlohe-Schillingsfuerst* (New York: Macmillan, 1906), 2:404–406.

86. Kaelble, *Industrielle Interessenpolitik*, 220–224.

87. Kaelble, *Industrielle Interessenpolitik*, 220–224.

88. Sean Andrew Wempe, *Revenants of the German Empire: Colonial Germans, Imperialism, and the League of Nations* (New York: Oxford University Press, 2019), 120–124; Matthew P. Fitzpatrick, *Liberal Imperialism in Germany: Expansionism and Nationalism, 1848–1884* (Oxford, UK: Berghahn Books, 2008), 116–134.

89. Roger Chickering, *We Men Who Feel Most German: A Cultural Study of the Pan-German League, 1886–1914* (New York: Routledge, 2019); Barry A. Jackisch, *The Pan-German League and Radical Nationalist Politics in Interwar Germany, 1918–39* (Farnham, UK: Ashgate, 2012), 1–14.

90. Kaelble, *Industrielle Interessenpolitik*, 120, 210.

91. Gary D. Stark, *Banned in Berlin: Literary Censorship in Imperial Germany, 1871–1918* (New York: Berghahn Books, 2009), 86–149.

92. "Sonderausdruck."

93. A. Plate, *Handbuch für das Preussische Abgeordnetenhaus: Ausgabe für die 20. Legislaturperiode* (Berlin: Moeser, 1904), 362.

94. "Sonderausdruck," 1.

95. "Sonderausdruck," 1.

96. Hau, *La Maison De Dietrich*, 101–102.

97. Hau, *La Maison De Dietrich*, 101–102.

98. Hau, *La Maison De Dietrich*, 101–102; *Verhandlungen: Stenographische. Berichte über die Verhandlungen* (Berlin: Preussische Verlagsanstalt, 1912), 4206–4207.

99. Fischer, *Alsace to the Alsatians?*, 89.

100. Fischer, *Alsace to the Alsatians?*, 89.

101. Fischer, *Alsace to the Alsatians?*, 89.

102. "Alsace-Lorraine," *Journal des Débats*, May 9, 1912, 2.

103. "Alsace-Lorraine," 2.

104. Igersheim, *L'Alsace des notables*, 1–11.

105. Hau, *La Maison De Dietrich*, 147–148.

106. "En attendant les interpellations sur l'affaire Grafenstaden," *Journal D'Alsace-Lorraine, Ancien Journal D'Alsace et Courrier du Bas-Rhin* 125, no. 123 (May 4, 1912): 1–3.

107. "Après la bataille," *Nouvelliste*, June 5, 1912, 1.

108. "En attendant les interpellations."

109. "En attendant les interpellations," 1.

110. "En attendant les interpellations," 1.

111. Hau, *La Maison De Dietrich*, 147–148.

112. Hau, *La Maison De Dietrich*, 147–148.

113. "Protokoll der ausserordentlichen Sitzung."

114. *Bericht des Vorstandes über das 15. Geschäftsjahr vom 1. Juli 1911 bis 30 Juni 1912* (Strasbourg: A.O., 1912), 1–3.

115. Stoskopf, "André Koechlin," 40–41.

116. Fischer, *Alsace to the Alsatians?*, 94.

117. Hull, *Absolute Destruction*, 230.

118. Rossé et al., *Das Elsass*, 1:167–173; Erwin Schenk, Der Fall Zabern, (Stuttgart, Germany: W. Kohlhammer 1927), 120–121; Frédéric Eccard, *L'Alsace sous la domination allemande* (Paris: A. Colin, 1919), 238–269.

119. Hans Ulrich Wehler, *Krisenherde des Kaiserreichs: 1871–1918. Studien z. dt. Sozial- u. Verfassungsgeschichte* (Göttingen: Vandenhoeck u. Ruprecht, 1970), 66.

120. Wehler, *Krisenherde des Kaiserreichs*, 83.

121. Ignác Romsics, *Erdély elvesztése, 1918–1947* (Budapest: Helikon Kiadó, 2018), 88–124.

3. Millionaires of Mitteleuropa

1. Heather Jones and Laurence van Ypersele, "Introduction to Part III," in *The Cambridge History of the First World War*, ed. Jay Murray Winter (Cambridge: Cambridge University Press, 2014), 3:181–185.

2. David D. Hamlin, *Germany's Empire in the East: Germans and Romania in an Era of Globalization and Total War* (Cambridge: Cambridge University Press, 2017), 251–322;

Alexander Watson, *Ring of Steel: Germany and Austria-Hungary at War,1914–1918* (London: Allen Lane, 2014), 259–265.

3. Niall Ferguson, *The House of Rothschild: The World's Banker, 1849–1999* (New York: Penguin, 1999), 284–317.

4. Charles S. Maier, *Recasting Bourgeois Europe: Stabilization in France, Germany, and Italy in the Decade after World War I* (Princeton, NJ: Princeton University Press, 1975), 3–15, 70–87.

5. Hew Strachan, *Financing the First World War* (Oxford: Oxford University Press, 2004), 63–105.

6. Tobias Grill, "'Pioneers of Germanness in the East'? Jewish-German, German, and Slavic Perceptions of East European Jewry during the First World War," in *Jews and Germans in Eastern Europe: Shared and Comparative Histories*, ed. Tobias Grill (Berlin: Walter de Gruyter, 2018), 125–159; Marsha L. Rozenblit, *Reconstructing a National Identity: The Jews of Habsburg Austria during World War I* (Oxford: Oxford University Press, 2001), 106–119.

7. Strachan, *Financing the First World War*, 63–105.

8. Tooze, *Deluge*, 204–205.

9. Niall Ferguson, *The Pity of War* (New York: Basic Books, 1999), 248–281; Feldman, *Army, Industry, and Labor*, xix–xxi.

10. Adam Tooze and Ted Fertik, "The World Economy and the Great War," *Geschichte und Gesellschaft* 40, no. 2 (2014): 214–238.

11. Jürgen Kocka, *Facing Total War: German Society, 1914–1918* (Cambridge, MA: Harvard University Press, 1985), 28–31; Max-Stephan Schulze, "Austria-Hungary's Economy in World War I," in *The Economics of World War I*, ed. Stephen N. Broadberry and Mark Harrison (Cambridge: Cambridge University Press, 2005), 28–31.

12. Reinhart Koselleck, "Crisis," trans. Michaela W. Richter, *Journal of the History of Ideas* 67, no. 2 (2006): 358.

13. Tooze and Fertik, "World Economy."

14. Tooze and Fertik, "World Economy."

15. Feldman, *Army, Industry, and Labor*, 3–36.

16. "A Magyar Bőriparosok Országos Szövetségének alakuló közgyűlése," *Bőripari Szemle*, September 1, 1917, 1.

17. "Magyar Bőriparosok," 1.

18. Strachan, *Financing the First World War*, 106; Hans Ulrich Wehler, *The German Empire, 1871–1918* (Leamington Spa, Warwickshire, UK: Berg Publishers, 1985), 202.

19. Economic historian Albrecht Ritschl admits that scarce statistical evidence on imperial "trade balance . . . provides only an incomplete account of Germany's access to and use of foreign resources." Albrecht Ritschl, "The Pity of Peace: Germany's Economy at War, 1914–1918 and Beyond," in *The Economics of World War I*, ed. Stephen N. Broadberry and Mark Harrison (Cambridge: Cambridge University Press, 2005), 52.

20. Ritschl, "Pity of Peace," 41.

21. Schulze, "Austria-Hungary's Economy," 78–79.

22. Norman Stone, *The Eastern Front, 1914–1917* (New York: Scribner, 1975), 265.

23. Hull, *Absolute Destruction*, 226–262; Hamlin, *Germany's Empire in the East*, 172–250; Jesse Kauffman, *Elusive Alliance: The German Occupation of Poland in World War I* (Cambridge, MA: Harvard University Press, 2015), 23–63.

24. Paul C. Vincent, *The Politics of Hunger: The Allied Blockade of Germany, 1915–1919* (Athens: Ohio University Press, 1985), 1–59.

25. "A drezdai tanácskozás," *Magyar Gyáripar* 5, no. 24 (December 16, 1915): 9–10; Galántai, *Magyarország az első világháborúban*, 241.

26. Friedrich Naumann, *Central Europe* (London: King, 1916), 3.

27. Károly Irinyi, *A Naumann-féle "Mitteleuropa"-tervezet és a magyar politikai közvélemény* (Budapest: Akadémiai Kiadó, 1963).

28. "Folytatólagos ülés," *Magyar Gyáripar* 8, no. 10–12 (May 16, 1918): 27.

29. "Középeurópa," *Huszadik Század* 33, no. 17 (January–July 1916): 456–460.

30. "Középeurópa," 456.

31. "Középeurópa," 456.

32. Charles S. Maier, *Once within Borders: Territories of Power, Wealth, and Belonging since 1500* (Cambridge, MA: Belknap Press of Harvard University Press, 2016), 13–14; Mark Hewitson, *Germany and the Modern World, 1880–1914* (Cambridge: Cambridge University Press, 2018), 1–18.

33. Galántai, *Magyarország az első világháborúban*, 242–243.

34. Galántai, *Magyarország az első világháborúban*, 242–243.

35. "Recommendations of the Economic Conference of the Allied Governments," *American Journal of International Law* 10, no. 4 (October 1916): 227–233.

36. Henry Cord Meyer, *Mitteleuropa in German Thought and Action, 1815–1945* (The Hague: Nijhoff, 1955), 240.

37. Meyer, *Mitteleuropa in German Thought and Action*, 231.

38. Meyer, *Mitteleuropa in German Thought and Action*, 231.

39. Caglioti, "Property Rights in Time of War," 529.

40. Friedrich Kahl, "Die Pariser Wirtschaftskonferenz," *Weltwirtschaftliches Archiv* 9 (1917): 217–229; Eugen Jacobi, *Fragen der Übergangswirtschaft, Vortrag gehalten in der Strassburger Gesellschaft für Deutsche Kultur, Januar 1917* (Strasbourg: Dumont Schauberg, 1917), 16–19.

41. Jacobi, *Fragen der Übergangswirtschaft*, 15–17; Hull, *Absolute Destruction*, 1–16, 141–166.

42. Ferenc Chorin Jr., "A magyar ipar a háborúban," *Magyar Figyelő* 4 (1914): 381–385.

43. Chorin, "A magyar ipar a háborúban," 385.

44. Jacobi, *Fragen der Übergangswirtschaft*, 16–17.

45. Nagy Magyar Compass, 44, vol. 2 (Budapest: Galánthai Nagy Sándor, 1915), 461–462.

46. Nesting imperialism was also related to what Milica Bakić-Hayden defined as "nesting orientalism" in her "Nesting Orientalisms: The Case of Former Yugoslavia," *Slavic Review* 54, no. 4 (1995): 917–931.

47. Galántai, *Magyarország az első világháborúban*, 280–284.

48. Galántai, *Magyarország az első világháborúban*, 280–284.

49. Vilmos Laurentzi, "A vilagháború nagy problémája," *Magyar Figyelő* 5, no. 2 (1915): 425; Sean McMeekin, *The Berlin-Baghdad Express: The Ottoman Empire and Germany's Bid for World Power* (Cambridge, MA: Belknap Press of Harvard University Press, 2010), 123–179.

50. B., "Jogászi közeledés a Balkán államok felé," *Jogtudományi Közlöny* 29 (1916): 255.

51. Balázs Ablonczy, *Keletre, magyar! A magyar turanizmus története* (Budapest: Jaffa, 2016), 64–65.

52. Ferenc Szécsén, "Iparművészeti kiállításunk Szofiában," *Magyar Iparművészet* 21, no. 7–8.(1918): 105–108.

53. Jenő Cholnoky, "A magyar medence kapcsolata a Balkánnal," *Turán*, no. 2 (1917): 80.

54. Quoted in Irinyi, *Mitteleuropa-tervek*, 231.

55. "A keleti kereskedelmi akadémia jubileuma," *Magyar Ipar* 27, no. 37 (1916): 514–515.

56. "A keleti kereskedelmi akadémia jubileuma," 514–515.

57. *Jelentés a Magyar Keleti Kulturközpont (Turáni Társaság) két évi müködéséröl* (Budapest: M.K.K.K. (T.T.), 1918), 20–22; Tamara Scheer, "Etappenliebe: Belgrad, Cetinje und Lublin unter österreichisch-ungarischer Besatzungsmacht im Ersten Weltkrieg," *Medizin, Gesellschaft und Geschichte* 34 (2015): 35–63.

58. *Jelentés*, 7.

59. "Bárczy István elnöki megnyitóbeszéde, mondotta az O. M. Iparművészeti Társulat 1918. évi május hó 5-én tartott közgyűlésén," in Kálmán Györgyi ed., *Magyar Iparművészet* 21, nos. 4–6 (1918): 54.

60. Stephan Haggard, "Import Substitution Industrialization," in *The Oxford Companion to Politics of the World*, ed. Joel Krieger and Margaret E. Crahan (Oxford: Oxford University Press, 2001), 385.

61. István Deák, *The Lawful Revolution: Louis Kossuth and the Hungarians, 1848–1849* (New York: Columbia University Press, 1979).

62. Sophie Charlotte Preibusch, *Verfassungsentwicklungen im Reichsland Elsass-Lothringen 1871–1918: Integration durch Verfassungsrecht?* (Berlin: Humboldt-Universität, 2004), 521–548.

63. The request of the management of the Jádvölgy Aluminum Mines Company (Jádvölgyi Alumínium Bányatársaság) and Károly Kornis to Hungarian minister of commerce and industry János Harkányi, c. 1917, Hungarian National Archives, MNL-OL Z 323/2, item 52, 12; "A Német Birodalomhoz való gazdasági közeledés iránti tárgyalások ismertetése," MNL-OL K 69, 16. cs.

64. Béla Katona, *Magyarország közgazdasága. Pénzügyi és közgazdasági évkönyv az 1917. évről.* (Budapest: Benkő Gyula cs. és kir. udvari könyvkereskedése, 1917), 377; Frigyes Fellner, "Az átmeneti gazdaság kérdéséről," *Budapesti Szemle* 172, nos. 490–492 (1917): 250–263.

65. Katona, *Magyarország közgazdasága.*

66. "Tervezet," 778/1944 (1917), Fond Clujana, DJAN Cluj, 37–40.

67. Máté Rigó, "The Long First World War and the Survival of Business Elites in East-Central Europe: Transylvania's Industrial Boom and the Enrichment of Economic Elites," *European Review of History* 24, no. 2 (2017): 250–272.

68. "Rapoarte și procese verbale," 1/1914–1918, Fond Clujana, DJAN Cluj.

69. Schulze, "Austria-Hungary's Economy," 97–103.

70. "Tervezet," 778/1944 (1917), Fond Clujana, DJAN Cluj.

71. "Tervezet," 778/1944 (1917), Fond Clujana, DJAN Cluj.

72. "Rapoarte și procese verbale," 1/1917.

73. "Erdélyi Magyar Nemzeti Bank" [Transylvanian Hungarian National Bank], *Erdélyi Közgazdaság*, August 2, 1917.

74. Thomas Nipperdey, *Deutsche Geschichte, 1866–1918: Machtstaat vor der Demokratie* (Munich: C. H. Beck, 1990), 308–311.

75. "Szemle," *Magyar Gyáripar* 6, no. 13 (July 1, 1916): 1–2.

76. Jonathan Levy, "Accounting for Profit and the History of Capital," *Critical Historical Studies* 1, no. 2 (September 2014): 171.

77. Hantos, "Pénzügyi mozgósításunk," 168–174.

78. "Szemle," *Magyar Gyáripar.*

79. Strachan, *Financing the First World War*, 100–104; Wehler, *German Empire*, 202.

80. Strachan, *Financing the First World War*, 102–103; Wehler, *German Empire*, 202.

81. Strachan, *Financing the First World War*, 100.

82. Strachan, *Financing the First World War*, 101.

83. Strachan, *Financing the First World War*, 85–86.

84. Emil Klug, "Az új adók képviselőházi módosításai," *Magyar Ipar* 37, no. 39 (September 24, 1916): 1–2.

85. Klug, "Az új adók képviselőházi módosításai," 1–2.

86. Klug, "Az új adók képviselőházi módosításai," 1–2.

87. Kocka, *Facing Total War*, 31.

88. "Law department" [of the Hungarian Bank] to the Renner tannery, August 24, 1918, Clujana, 778/1944 [1917], p. 183.

89. "Hírek," *Az Est*, July 27, 1916, 7.

90. Tomka, "Interlocking Directorates," 1–35.

91. Tomka, "Interlocking Directorates," 25–42.

92. Katona, *Magyarország közgazdasága*, 1–8; "A lakéskérdés," *Pesti Hirlap*, September 9, 1917, 8.

93. Schulze, "Austria-Hungary's Economy," 107.

94. *Nagy Magyar Compass* 43, no. 2 (1915), 461–462.

95. "Tervezet," Clujana 778/1944.

96. "A Magyar Bőriparosok Országos Szövetségének alakuló közgyűlése," *Bőripari Szemle*, September 1, 1917, 1.

97. "Magyar Szent Korona Országának Bőripari Központja rt," *Bőripari Szemle*, June 15, 1917, 5; *Nagy Magyar Compass* 43, no. 2 (1915), 461–462.

98. *Nagy Magyar Compass* 43, no. 2 (1915), 461–462.

99. "A Magyar Bőriparosok Országos Szövetségének alakuló közgyűlése," 1.

100. "Magyar Szent Korona Országának Bőripari Központja rt," *Nagy Magyar Compass* 43, no. 2 (1915), 461–462.

101. "A Magyar Bőriparosok Országos Szövetségének alakuló közgyűlése," *Bőripari Szemle*, June 15, 1917, 5.

102. War Ministry, Vienna, to the Renner tannery, February 17, 1917, Clujana 778/1944, 45–46; Anglo-Austrian Bank to M.F., June 2, 1917, October 2, 1917, Clujana 778/1944, 69, 87–89.

103. "A Magyar Bőriparosok Országos Szövetségének alakuló közgyűlése," 1.

104. "A Magyar Bőriparosok Országos Szövetségének alakuló közgyűlése," 1.

105. Pál Ranschburg, "Orvosi bizonyítvány," February 4, 1933, Clujana 37/1943.

106. "Végrendelet," April 19, 1932, DJAN Cluj, Fond Clujana, Secretariat 8/1932.

107. "A nagyváradi művésznő és a kolozsvári urak," *Ellenőr*, July 18, 1927, 30.

108. War Ministry, Vienna, to the Renner tannery, February 17, 1917.

109. KLAG to Royal Prussian War Ministry, Kriegsamt., October 11, 1918, BArch, Kriegsleder AG 8736/191, p. 21.

110. Géza Lengyel, "A külkereskedelmi forgalom mai szabályozása Mo-on és a szomszéd államokban", *Közgazdasági Szemle* 44, no. 62 (1920): 587–588.

111. Glenda Sluga, *Internationalism in the Age of Nationalism* (Pennsylvania Studies in Human Rights) (Philadelphia: University of Pennsylvania Press, 2013), 5.

112. Hewitson, *Germany and the Modern World*, 1–18; Charles S. Maier, "Consigning the Twentieth Century to History: Alternative Narratives for the Modern Era," *American Historical Review* 105, no. 3 (2000): 807–812; Maier, *Once within Borders*, 1–13, 269–296; Roland Robertson, *Globalization: Social Theory and Global Culture* (London: Sage, 1992), 10; Sebastian Conrad, *Globalisierung und Nation im deutschen Kaiserreich* (Munich: Beck, 2006), 325; on the post-1918 legacy of deglobalization, see Tara Zahra, "Colonizing the Homeland: Deglobalization in Interwar Austria" (presentation at the American Historical Association convention, January 5, 2020); Quinn Slobodian, *Globalists: The End of Empire and the Birth of Neoliberalism* (Cambridge, MA: Harvard University Press, 2018), 27–54.

113. Hewitson, *Germany and the Modern World*, 12–13; Maier, "Consigning the Twentieth Century to History," 807–831; Maier, *Once within Borders*, 227–229; Slobodian, *Globalists*, 27–54.

114. Ernst Zander, *Der Wirtschaftliche Wiederaufbau von Elass-Lothringen nach dem Kriege* (Strassburg: Karl Trübner, 1917), 8, 9–10.

115. Zander, *Der Wirtschaftliche Wiederaufbau von Elass-Lothringen nach dem Kriege*, 9–11.

116. Jacobi, *Fragen der Übergangswirtschaft*, 28–29.

117. Bertrand Risacher and Nicolas Stoskopf, "L'industrie alsacienne dans la Grande Guerre: Un désastre économique?," *Revue d'Alsace* 139 (2013): 77–104.

118. Fischer, *Alsace to the Alsatians?*, 100–127.

119. Risacher and Stoskopf, "L'industrie alsacienne," 77–104.

120. Risacher and Stoskopf, "L'industrie alsacienne," 77–104.

121. Risacher and Stoskopf, "L'industrie alsacienne," 77–104.

122. Hau, *La Maison De Dietrich*, 148–149; Joseph Rossé, Marcel Stürmel, Albert Bleicher, Fernand Deiber, and Jean Keppi, *Das Elsass von 1870–1932* (Colmar: Verlag Alsatia, 1936), 1:306–317.

123. Hau, *La Maison De Dietrich*, 148–151.

124. Jacqueline to Dominique de Dietrich, August 27, 1914, ADD, unsorted.

125. Jacqueline to Dominique de Dietrich, August 27, 1914.

126. "Survey form of the Kriegsamt, Berlin," ADBR 47AL101/1; Hau, *La Maison De Dietrich*, 148–149.

127. "Zusammenstellung der Monats Grund-Quoten an Grossviehauten," October 8, 1917, BArch, R 8736/221, pp. 13–14.

128. "Zusammenstellung der Monats Grund-Quoten an Grossviehauten," October 8, 1917, pp. 13–14.

129. Becker, *Die Wirtschaftliche Entwickelung der Deutschen Lederindustrie*, 71–75; Adolf Link, *Die Deutsche Lederindustrie, Eine Standortsstudie* (Tübingen: H. Laupp, 1913), 15–16.

130. *Magyar statisztikai közlemények*, vol. 37 (1911), 38–39.

131. Leather imports made up more than 3 percent of the value of total Hungarian imports. *Magyar statisztikai közlemények*, 37:38–39; Link, *Die Deutsche Lederindustrie, Eine Standortsstudie*, 15–16.

132. Eric W. Osborne, *Britain's Economic Blockade of Germany, 1914–1919* (London: Frank Cass, 2004), 58–82, 145.

133. KLAG to Royal Prussian War Ministry, Kriegsamt., October 11, 1918, BArch, Kriegsleder AG 8736/191, p. 21; Osborne, *Britain's Economic Blockade of Germany*, 145.

134. *Bericht des Vorstandes über das 13. Geschäftsjahr vom 1. Juli 1911 bis 30 Juni 1912* (Strasbourg: A.O., 1912), 1–4; for years 1913–1928, see Norddeutsche Lederwerke A.G. in ZBW - Leibniz-Informationszentrum Wirtschaft (Leibnitz Information Centre for Economics) database, accessed May 15, 2019, http://zbw.eu/beta/p20/company/41419/about.de.html.

135. *Bericht über das 19. Geschäftsjahr*, 4, Retrieved from ZBW database at https://zbw.eu/beta/p20/company/41419/about.de.html on November 5, 2021.

136. Kocka, *Facing Total War*, 31–32.

137. Strachan, *Financing the First World War*, 105.

138. Strachan, *Financing the First World War*, 63–87.

139. "Adler & Oppenheimer Lederfabrik A.-G.," *Frankfurter Zeitung*, December 8, 1915.

140. KLAG to Royal Prussian War Ministry, Kriegsamt., October 11, 1918, BArch, Kriegsleder AG 8736/191, p. 21.

141. "Sitzung der Verteilungskommission für Grossviehhaute," March 23, 1917, BArch, R 8736/218, 7–8.

142. "Sitzung der Verteilungskommission für Grossviehhaute," March 23, 1917, 7–8.

143. "Sitzung der Verteilungskommission für Grossviehhaute," March 23, 1917, 7–8.

144. "Sitzung der Verteilungskommission für Grossviehhaute," March 23, 1917, 7–8.

145. Detlef Krause, *Die Commerz- und Disconto-Bank, 1870–1920/23: Bankgeschichte als Systemgeschichte* (Stuttgart: F. Steiner, 2004), 264.

146. "Sitzung der Verteilungskommission für Grossviehhaute," March 23, 1917, 7–8.

147. "Sitzung der Verteilungskommission für Grossviehhaute," March 23, 1917, 7–8.

148. "Sitzung der Verteilungskommission für Grossviehhaute," July 7, 1919, BArch, R 8736/218.

149. John Deak and Jonathan E. Gumz, "How to Break a State: The Habsburg Monarchy's Internal War, 1914–1918," *American Historical Review* 122 (2017): 1106.

4. The Enemy's Money

1. Rudolf Kučera, *Rationed Life: Science, Everyday Life, and Working-Class Politics in the Bohemian Lands, 1914–1918* (New York: Berghahn Books, 2016), 12–54.

2. Caglioti, "Property Rights"; Daniela L. Caglioti, *War and Citizenship, Enemy Aliens and National Belonging from the French Revolution to the First World War* (Cambridge: Cambridge University Press, 2020). I am grateful to Daniela L. Caglioti for sharing her manuscript with me.

3. Caglioti, "Property Rights," 531; Georges-Henri Soutou, *L'Or et le sang: Les buts de guerre écnomiques de la première guerre mondiale* (Paris: Fayard, 1989), 233–303; ADBR 116 AL 199–203; ADBR 116 AL; ADBR 67 AL 1–4.

4. Roger Chickering, *Imperial Germany and the Great War, 1914–1918*, 3rd ed. (Cambridge: Cambridge University Press, 2014), 71–80.

5. Holly Case offers an argument on why "small states mattered" in the Second World War. See Holly Case, *Between States: The Transylvanian Question and the European Idea during World War II* (Stanford, CA: Stanford University Press, 2009), 1–8.

6. Eugen Jacobi, *Fragen der Übergangswirtschaft, Vortrag gehalten in der Strassburger Gesellschaft für Deutsche Kultur, Januar 1917* (Strasbourg: Dumont Schauberg, 1917), 1–19; Pölöskei, "István Tisza's Policy toward the Romanian Nationalities on the Eve of World War I."

7. "Dr. Schwander német birodalmi államtitkár az elzászi kérdésről," *Pesti Napló*, November 1, 1917, 5.

8. Borut Klabjan, "The Outbreak of War in Habsburg Trieste," in *Sarajevo 1914: Sparking the First World War*, ed. Mark Cornwall (Bloomsbury, UK: Bloomsbury Academic, 2020), 233–252; Brendan Jeffrey Karch, *Nation and Loyalty in a German-Polish Borderland: Upper Silesia, 1848–1960* (Cambridge: Cambridge University Press, 2018), 96–104; Deak and Gumz, "How to Break a State," 1110.

9. Deak and Gumz, "How to Break a State," 1110.

10. Caglioti, "Property Rights," 530–531; André Pinoche, *Le Séquestre et la liquidation des biens de sujets ennemis en France et en Allemagne, thèse pour le doctorat sciences politiques et économiques* (Bar-le-Duc,France: impr. de Constant-Laguerre, 1920), 1–9; Richard Mercier, *Le Sequestre des biens alsaciens-lorrains en France pendant la guerre de 1914–1918*, 1970, BDIC, 1–8; Frédéric Manfrin, Laurent Veyssière, and Thomas Cazentre, *Été 14: Les derniers jours de l'ancien monde* (Paris: Bibliothèque nationale de France, 2014).

11. "Bekanntmachung," *Reichs-Gesetzblatt*, no. 71 (1914): 397.

12. "Bekanntmachung," 397.

13. John Scobell Armstrong, *War and Treaty Legislation: Affecting British Property in Germany and Austria, and Enemy Property in the United Kingdom* (London: Hutchinson, 1921), 77; Caglioti, *War and Citizenship*, 294–296.

14. October 14, 1914, Circular of the Garde des Sceaux on the exemption of Alsatians-Lorrainers, Czechs and Poles from sequesters. Pinoche, *Le séquestre et la liquidation*, 30–35.

15. October 14, 1914, Circular; Caglioti, "Property Rights," 534.

16. Mercier, *Le Séquestre*, 68–81; Farmer Albert Hotz to French minister of justice, June 29, 1923, ADBR 121AL 676; "Séquestre des biens ennemis situés en France 1915–1919," ANF, F 12, 7845.

17. A. J. P. Taylor, *The First World War: An Illustrated History* (New York: Putnam, 1980), 106.

18. "Nouvelles mesures concernant les entreprises ennemies places sous séquestre," BDIC, F D 801/53.

19. Kaiserlicher Bezirkspräsident of Lothringen to the minister for Alsace-Lorraine, Department of the Interior (Abteilung des Innern), April 20, 1917, ADBR 22 AL 107.

20. Max Weber, *Economy and Society: An Outline of Interpretive Sociology* (Berkeley: University of California Press, 1978), 1400.

21. Hull, *Absolute Destruction*, 5–30.

22. Caglioti, "Property Rights," 529; Paul Frederick Simonson, *Private Property and Rights in Enemy Countries: and Private Rights against Enemy Nationals and Governments under the Peace Treaties with Germany, Austria, Hungary, Bulgaria, and Turkey* (London: E. Wilson, 1921), i–viii.

23. Mark Hewitson, *Germany and the Modern World, 1880–1914* (Cambridge: Cambridge University Press, 2018), 8.

24. Caglioti, "Property Rights," 528–529.

25. Vincent, *Politics of Hunger*, 1–34; Caglioti, *War and Citizenship*, 280–282.

26. Frank, "Petroleum War of 1910."

27. Emil Petri, *Zwangsverwaltung und Liquidation des feindlichen Vermögens im Inlande* (Strassburg: Strassburger Druckerei und Verlagsanstalt, 1917), 1–4.

28. Risacher and Stoskopf, "L'industrie alsacienne," 81–97.

29. Hans Schultz Hansen, "Minorities in Germany (Denmark)," in *1914–1918 Online: International Encyclopedia of the First World War*, ed. Ute Daniel, Peter Gatrell, Oliver Janz, Heather Jones, Jennifer Keene, Alan Kramer, and Bill Nasson, https://encyclopedia.1914-1918-online.net/article/minorities_in_germany_denmark.

30. Risacher and Stoskopf, "L'industrie alsacienne," 77–104.

31. Preibusch, *Verfassungsentwicklungen im Reichsland Elsass-Lothringen*, 578–595; Paul Matter, "Les tentatives de colonisation allemande en Alsace-Lorraine," *Revue des Sciences Politiques* 43, no. 2 (April 15, 1920): 184–196; Frédéric Eccard and Louis Renault, *Biens et intérêts français en Allemagne et en Alsace-Lorraine pendant la guerre ouvrage accompagné de la traduction des textes allemands relatifs aux mesures législatives et administratives prises à l'égard des biens français, anglais et alliés et d'une liste des principales enterprises françaises séquestrées et liquidées en Alsace-Lorraine et en Allemagne* (Paris: Libr. Payot et cie, 1917).

32. Risacher and Stoskopf, "L'industrie alsacienne," 77–104.

33. Risacher and Stoskopf, "L'industrie alsacienne," 84.

34. Strassburger Post quoted in Eccard and Renault, *Biens et intérêts français*, 20.

35. Eccard and Renault, *Biens et intérêts français*, 84–85.

36. Eccard and Renault, *Biens et intérêts français*, 84; Charles Schmidt, *Les Plans secrets de la politique allemande en Alsace-Lorraine (1915–1918)* (Paris: Payot, 1922), 53–54.

37. "Dr. Schwander."

38. P. de Retz, "Rapport sur le bassin de potasse d'Alsace," *Bulletin de la Société industrielle de l'Est* 160 (January–March 1920): 34–35.

39. Risacher and Stoskopf, "L'industrie alsacienne," 78–79.

40. Risacher and Stoskopf, "L'industrie alsacienne," 78–79.

41. *Procès-Verbaux de La Conférence d'Alsace-Lorraine, 1e–24e séances, 18 février 1915–22 mai 1916* (Paris: Imprimerie Nationale, 1917), 1:334.

42. Bertrand Risacher, "Une dynastie de petits capitaines d'industrie face aux vicissitudes de l'histoire: Les Latscha de Jungholtz (1834–1920)," *Revue d'Alsace*, no. 140 (2014): 302.

43. Risacher and Stoskopf, "L'industrie alsacienne," 82.

44. Risacher and Stoskopf, "L'industrie alsacienne," 82.

45. Risacher and Stoskopf, "L'industrie alsacienne," 82.

46. Secretary von Roedern to the Bezirkspräsidenten, September 14, 1914, ADBR 67 AL 1.

47. Secretary von Roedern to the Bezirkspräsidenten, September 14, 1914.

48. Zilch Reinhold, "Roedern, Siegfried Graf von," *Neue Deutsche Biographie* 21 (2003): 710–711.

49. Bezirkspräsident of Lothringen to the minister for Alsace-Lorraine, September 14, 1914, ADBR, 67 AL 1.

50. Joseph Rossé, Marcel Stürmel, Albert Bleicher, Fernand Deiber, and Jean Keppi, *Das Elsass von 1870–1932* (Colmar: Verlag Alsatia, 1936), 1:244. Numbers are postwar estimates by the association of interned; Alsace-Lorrainers, the Proscrits d'Alsace-Lorraine.

51. AEB to Ministry of Alsace-Lorraine, September 24, 1914, ADBR 67 AL 1.

52. Memorandum by supervisory commissioner [of banks] Ad. Strauss to Ministry of Alsace-Lorraine, December 23, 1914, ADBR 67 AL 1.

53. AEB to Ministry of Alsace-Lorraine, September 24, 1914.

54. Memorandum, no. IV A 10799, Reich Chancellor (Reich Office of the Interior) to the Statthalter, September 20, 1914, ADBR 67 AL 1.

55. AEB to Ministry for Alsace-Lorraine, September 24, 1914; Manfred Pohl, *Handbook on the History of European Banks* (Frankfurt: Edward Elgar Publishing, 1994), 290.

56. AEB to Ministry for Alsace-Lorraine, September 24, 1914.

57. AEB to Ministry for Alsace-Lorraine, January 8, 1915, ADBR 67 AL 1.

58. *Allgemeine Elsässische Bankgesellschaft/Société générale alsacienne de banque, Geschäftsbericht für das Geschäftsjahr 1919* (Strassburg: S. G. A. B., 1919).

59. Memorandum of anonymous supervisory commissionary, December 23, 1914, ADBR 67 AL 1.

60. Memorandum of anonymous supervisory commissionary, December 23, 1914.

61. Memorandum of anonymous supervisory commissionary, December 23, 1914.

62. Memorandum of Ministry of Alsace-Lorraine, Dept. of Finance, Commerce and Domains, December 24, 1914, ADBR 67 AL 1.

63. "Survey form of the Kriegsamt, Berlin," ADBR 47AL 101/1; Hau, *La Maison De Dietrich*, 148–149.

64. Hau, *La Maison De Dietrich*, 148–149.

65. Hau, *La Maison De Dietrich*, 148–149.

66. Hau, *La Maison De Dietrich*, 151.

67. Chickering, *Imperial Germany and the Great War*, 76–82.

68. Rossé et al., *Das Elsass*, 4:149; Ritschl, "Pity of Peace," 46–49; Risacher and Stoskopf, "L'industrie alsacienne," 77–82.

69. Risacher and Stoskopf, "L'industrie alsacienne," 93.

70. Fischer, *Alsace to the Alsatians?*, 77–97.

71. Risacher and Stoskopf, "L'industrie alsacienne."

72. Auguste Zundel, *1914–1918, Journal de la Grande Guerre vécue à Mulhouse* (Colmar, France, 2004); Risacher and Stoskopf, "L'industrie alsacienne," 81.

73. Risacher and Stoskopf, "L'industrie alsacienne," 100.

74. Risacher and Stoskopf, "L'industrie alsacienne," 100.

75. Risacher and Stoskopf, "L'industrie alsacienne," 100.

76. Risacher and Stoskopf, "L'industrie alsacienne," 97.

77. Risacher, "Une dynastie de petits capitaines d'industrie," 306–308.

78. Risacher, "Une dynastie de petits capitaines d'industrie, 307.

79. Maureen Healy, "Introductory Remarks: Space, Chronology and the Habsburg Home Fronts," *European Review of History: Revue Européenne d'histoire* 24, no. 2 (March 4, 2017): 176–184.

80. "Abschrift," Pagaschuh G. m. b. H. Arbeitsstelle für Papiergarnschuhe, Städtische Kriegfürsorge, Mulhouse, July 11, 1918, ADBR 47 AL 63/7; Risacher and Stoskopf, "L'industrie alsacienne," 101.

81. "Abschrift," Pagaschuh, July 11, 1918.

82. "Abschrift," Pagaschuh G. m. b. H., July 11, 1918.

83. Pagaschuh Company, War Relief Office, Mulhouse, to secretary of state at the Reich Economic Office, July 11, 1918, ADBR 47 AL 63/7.

84. Pagaschuh Company, War Relief Office, Mulhouse, to secretary of state at the Reich Economic Office, July 11, 1918.

85. Pagaschuh Company, War Relief Office, Mulhouse, to secretary of state at the Reich Economic Office, July 11, 1918.

86. Pagaschuh Company, War Relief Office, Mulhouse, to secretary of state at the Reich Economic Office, July 11, 1918.

87. Robert Lévy, *Histoire économique de l'industrie cotonnière en Alsace: Étude de sociologie descriptive* (Paris: F. Alcan, 1912), 238.

88. The industrialist Weyl argued that teachers hung posters in classrooms and advised students to wear shoes made by Paga. R. und L. Weyl Co., Benfeld (Alsace) to Strassburg auditor Fritz Fahr, July 17, 1917, ADBR 47 AL 63/4; John M. Turner, *Trade Development in Latin America* (Washington, DC: US Government Printing Office, 1912), 44.

89. R. und L. Weyl Co., to Fritz Fahr, July 17, 1917

90. "Bundesratsausschusse IV und VI," July 18, 1917, ADBR 47AL 63/4.

91. "Bundesratsausschusse IV und VI," July 18, 1917.

92. "Bundesratsausschusse IV und VI," July 18, 1917.

93. "Abschrift," Pagaschuh G. m. b. H., July 11, 1918, ADBR 47AL 63/7.

94. "Abschrift," Pagaschuh G. m. b. H., July 11, 1918.

95. "Abschrift," Pagaschuh G. m. b. H., July 11, 1918.

96. "Abschrift," Pagaschuh G. m. b. H., July 11, 1918.

97. "Abschrift," Pagaschuh G. m. b. H., July 11, 1918.

98. "Abschrift," Pagaschuh G. m. b. H., July 11, 1918.

99. "A Keleti vásár," *8 Órai Újság*, August 20, 1917.

100. Preibusch, *Verfassungsentwicklungen*, 521–548.

101. Holly Case, *The Age of Questions: Or, A First Attempt at an Aggregate History of the Eastern, Social, Woman, American, Jewish, Polish, Bullion, Tuberculosis and Many Other Questions over the Nineteenth Century, and Beyond* (Princeton, NJ: Princeton University Press, 2018), 92.

102. Case, *Age of Questions*, 92.

103. Matter, "Les tentatives," 194.

104. Matter, "Les tentatives" 184–196.

105. Memorandum of almoner Didio of the Service Penitentiaire et Aumonier de la Maison de Correction de Strassburg, after 1918, ADBR 121 AL 94; Rossé et al., *Das Elsass*, 1:370.

106. Matter, "Les tentatives," 194–196.

107. Roth, *La Lorraine annexée*, 259–352.

108. "Verzeichnes der Mitglieder des Aufsichtsrates und der Vertreter" [List of supervisory board members and representatives], AVES, 273 MW 200.

109. Ernst Zander to the Kaiserliches Ministerium für Elsass-Lotharingen, Department of the Interior, June 7, 1917, AVES, 273 MW 200; on Zander, see *Schweizerische Bauzeitung* 63, no. 13 (March 28, 1914): 186n2.

110. Zander to Ministerium, June 7, 1917, 3.

111. Zander to the Ministerium, June 7, 1917, 3.

112. Zander to the Ministerium, June 7, 1917, 3.

113. Zander to the Ministerium, June 7, 1917, 4–5.

114. Fischer, *Alsace to the Alsatians?*, 47–48.

115. Fischer, *Alsace to the Alsatians?*, 47–48.

116. Galántai, *Magyarország az első világháborúban*, 175–179; Watson, *Ring of Steel*, 53–103.

117. Galántai, *Magyarország az első világháborúban*, 178.

118. Zsombor Bódy, "Gyár és földbirtok a nagy háborúban és az összeomlásban," *Századok* 6 (2018): 1263–1264; Harvey, *Constructing Class*, 48–79.

119. Marin, *Peasant Violence and Antisemitism*, 77–154.

120. Ákos Bartha, *Populizmus, népiség, modernizáció: Fejezetek a kelet-közép-európai politikai gondolkodás 20. századi történetéből* (Budapest: MTA Bölcsészettudományi Kutatóközpont, 2017), 69–119; Lajos Beck, *A magyar földbirtok megoszlása: Agrár-statisztikai tanulmány* (Budapest: Pallas, 1918).

121. Beck, *A magyar földbirtok*, 22–23.

122. László Bizony, *A keleti határról* (Budapest: Szerző, 1912), 9–39; Egry, "Regionalizmus, erdélyiség, szupremácia," 27–29.

123. Tibor Vadnay, *A magyar jövő: Közgazdaság- és szociálpolitikai tanulmány* (Budapest: Athenaeum, 1918), 96.

124. Vadnay, *A magyar jövő*, 96–97.

125. Vadnay, *A magyar jövő*, 96.

126. Vadnay, *A magyar jövő*, 96.

127. Péter Bihari, *Lövészárkok a hátországban: Középosztály, zsidókérdés, antiszemitizmus az első világháború Magyarországán* (Budapest: Napvilág, 2008), 204–205.

128. Bihari, *Lövészárkok a hátországban*, 204–205.

129. Pál Hatos, *Az elátkozott köztársaság: Az 1918-as összeomlás és az őszirózsás forradalom története* (Budapest: Jaffa Kiadó, 2018), 23.

130. Paul Hanebrink, "Transnational Culture War: Christianity, Nation, and the Judeo-Bolshevik Myth in Hungary, 1890–1920," *Journal of Modern History* 80, no. 1 (2008): 64–72; Paul Hanebrink, *A Specter Haunting Europe: The Myth of Judeo-Bolshevism* (Cambridge, MA: Harvard University Press, 2018), 1–44; Deák, *Beyond Nationalism*, 196.

131. Bihari, *Lövészárkok a hátországban*, 201–203.

132. Bihari, *Lövészárkok a hátországban*, 201–203.

133. Galántai, *Magyarország az első világháborúban*, 268–272.

134. Healy, *Vienna and the Fall of the Habsburg Empire*, 31–86; Belinda Davis, *Home Fires Burning: Food, Politics, and Everyday Life in World War I Berlin* (Chapel Hill: University of North Carolina Press, 2000), 127–133.

135. "Testimony of Dénes Berinkey," in Hatos, *Az elátkozott*, 69, 435.

136. Reinhold Zilch and Jürgen Koppatz, *Okkupation und Währung im Ersten Weltkrieg: Die deutsche Besatzungspolitik in Belgien und Russisch-Polen 1914–1918* (Goldbach, Germany: Keip, 1994).

137. Healy, "Introductory Remarks," 176–184.

138. Tim Grady, *The German-Jewish Soldiers of the First World War in History and Memory* (Liverpool, UK: Liverpool University Press, 2011), 31–36; Davis, *Home Fires Burning*, 127–133; George O. Liber, *Total Wars and the Making of Modern Ukraine, 1914–1954* (Toronto: University of Toronto Press, 2016), 44–46; William W. Hagen, *Anti-Jewish Violence in Poland, 1914–1920* (Cambridge: Cambridge University Press, 2018), 61–122; Robert Nemes, "Refugees and Antisemitism in Hungary during the First World War," in *Sites of European Antisemitism in the Age of Mass Politics, 1880–1918*, ed. Robert Nemes and Daniel Unowsky (Waltham, MA: Brandeis University Press, 2014), 249–253.

139. Bihari, *Lövészárkok a hátországban*, 196–201.

140. "Cholnoky Jenő," in *A zsidókérdés Magyarországon* (Budapest: Társtud. Társ., 1917), 75.

141. Davis, *Home Fires Burning*, 133.

142. "Agrárius 'élelmesség,'" *Népszava*, June 20, 1916, 1–2.

143. "Uj milliomosok," *Népszava*, August 27, 1916, 13–14.

144. "Uj milliomosok," 13.

145. "Uj milliomosok;" József Balassa, "Komisz és hadi," in *Magyar Nyelvőr*, ed. Zsigmond Simonyi (Budapest: Magyar Nyelvőr Kiadóhivatala, 1918), 48:44.

146. József Balassa, "Komisz és hadi," in *Magyar Nyelvőr*, ed. Zsigmond Simonyi (Budapest: Magyar Nyelvőr Kiadóhivatala, 1918), 48:44.

147. Lajos Pilisi, *A megrohant és felszabadított Erdély* (Budapest: Auktor, 2005), 41–155.

148. Lajos Stern, *Emlék könyvecske*, MNL-OL, X 10815. I am grateful to Béla Mihalik for sharing his family archives with me.

149. Paul Freedman, "A dossier of peasant and seigneurial violence" in Justine Firnhaber-Baker, Dirk Schoenaers eds., *The Routledge History Handbook of Medieval Revolt* (London: Routledge, 2017), 267–278.

150. Tibolt Schmidt Papers, MNL-OL, P 2287, d. 1.

151. Tibolt Schmidt Papers, MNL-OL, P 2287, d. 1.

152. Hague, IV, 1907, art. 42–56.

153. Major Constantin G. Pietraru's "Appeal to inhabitants," September 1916, Tibolt Schmidt Papers, MNL-OL, d. 1, p. 323.

154. "Appeal to inhabitants," September 1916, p. 323.

155. Dietmar Müller, "The Concept of Property in Romania's Economic-Legal History," in *Key Concepts of Romanian History Alternative Approaches to Socio-Political Languages*, ed. Victor Neumann and Armin Heinen (Budapest: Central European University Press, 2013), 187; Major Constantin G. Pietraru, "Ordonanța Nr. 1," September 10, 1916, Tibolt Schmidt Papers, MNL-OL, d. 1, p. 319.

156. Egry, "Regionalizmus, erdélyiség, szupremácia," 1–5.

157. Egry, "Regionalizmus, erdélyiség, szupremácia," 1–5; Nándor Bárdi, "Az erdélyi magyar (és regionális) érdekek megjelenítése az 1910-es években. Az Erdélyi Szövetség programváltozatai," *Magyar Kisebbség*, 8, no. 2–3 (2003): 93–105.

158. Bárdi, "Az Erdélyi Szövetség programváltozatai."

159. Stern, *Emlék könyvecske.*

160. *Nagy Magyar Compass* 46–47, no. 2, (1918): 305–307.

161. Decree 4000/1917.

162. "Rendelettervezet az ingatlanokra vonatkozó magánjogi szabályok kiegészítése tárgyában," October 8, 1918, in Emma Iványi, ed. *Magyar minisztertanácsi jegyzőkönyvek az első világháború korából, 1914–1918* (Budapest: Akadémiai Kiadó), 1960.

163. The Transylvanian Land Relief Action had been in the making since 1911, when István Bethlen lobbied for the creation of a state-funded bank (the so-called Altruistic or Non-Profit Bank) that would defend Magyar gentries from Romanian land buyers. Council of Min., November 28, 1913, in Iványi, *Magyar minisztertanácsi jegyzőkönyvek*, 119.

164. Law XV of 1911 established the National Alliance of Land Credit Institutes (Földhitelintézetek Országos Szövetsége). Egry, "Regionalizmus, erdélyiség, szupremácia," 26; *Stenographische Berichte über die Verhandlungen, Preussischen Hause der Abgeordneten* (Berlin: W. Buchdruckerei, 1908), 1591; István Bethlen, *Bethlen István gróf beszédei és írásai* (Budapest: Géniusz R.t., 1933), 68; Gábor Egry, "National Economy vs. Economic Efficiency? Economic Nationalism, Nationalizing State(s) and Transitory Effects in Interwar Transylvania" (paper presented at the Society for Romanian Studies International Conference, Bucharest, June 2015).

165. Council of Min., October 12, 1917, 303–304.

166. Council of Min., August 17, 1914; October 13, 1916, 79–80, 236–237.

167. Council of Min., October 12, 1917, 303–304.

168. "Közgazdaság," *Pesti Hirlap*, December 9, 1917, 12.

169. Egry, *Nemzeti védgát vagy szolid haszonszerzés?*, 274–275, 338–342.

170. "Napi hirek," *Pesti Hirlap*, September 8, 1916, 13.

171. Iványi, *Magyar minisztertanácsi jegyzőkönyvek*, 252.

172. Memorandum of Counselor of Border Police Pietsch to minister of interior, June 9, 1917, DJAN Cluj, 1426/1172, Primul Război Mondial, III/23 "Rapoarte ale poliției politice."

173. Memorandum of Counselor of Border Police Pietsch to minister of interior, June 9, 1917.

174. "Törvénykezés," *Pesti Hirlap*, March 9, 1917, 9.

175. "Törvénykezés," 9.

"Törvénykezés," 7.

176. Hamlin, *Germany's Empire in the East*, 251–322.

177. "*A Romániában Érdekeltek Központja a Budapesti Kereskedelmi és Iparkamarában* 1917 február 24-i ülése;" Monatsbericht des Wirtschaftsstaabes." ÖeStA, 136 F 36 Krieg 1914–1918 Dep. 16. Abt. 57- Rumänien, folder 7.

178. "*A Romániában Érdekeltek Központja a Budapesti Kereskedelmi és Iparkamarában* 1917 február 24-i ülése."

179. Gyula Walter, "A balkanológiai katedra körül," *Egyetem, a Kolozsvári Magyar Királyi Ferencz József-Tudományegyetem Társadalmi és Tudományos Közlönye* 1, nos. 3–4 (October 1917): 6–8.

180. Gábor Egry, "'Der Kampf um Bodenbesitz' Az erdélyi szászok földbirtokviszonyai és a szász nemzetpolitika 1890-1918-ig," *Korunk* 15 no. 9 (September 2005): 94–107.

181. József Geml, *Emlékiratok polgármesteri müködésem idejéből* (Timișoara, Romania: Helikon könyvnyomdai műintézet, 1924), 75–87.

182. Geml, *Emlékiratok polgármesteri müködésem idejéből*, 75–87.

183. Egry, "'Der Kampf.'"

184. Irinyi, *Mitteleuropa-tervek*; Károly Koffler, "A földgázszerződés," *Magyar Ipar*, December 16, 1915, 8–9; "Balkán-akadémia Szegeden," *Honi Ipar*, July 15, 1916, 8; *A Bánya-Das Bergwerk* 10, no. 48 (1915): 1; *Képviselőházi Napló* [Minutes of the House of Representatives], January 21, 1916, 350–377, http://mpgy.ogyk.hu/.

185. Gyula Rácz, "A földgázszerződés," *Huszadik Század* 33, no. 17, no 1 (January–July 1916): 123–125.

186. "Középeurópa," 416.

5. Profiting from Victory

1. Larry Wolff, *Woodrow Wilson and the Reimagining of Eastern Europe* (Stanford, CA: Stanford University Press, 2020), 56–114.

2. Jochen Böhler, *Civil War in Central Europe, 1918–1921: The Reconstruction of Poland* (Oxford: Oxford University Press, 2018), 3–88, 66–94.

3. Romanian National Council (RNC) Budapest to RNC Alba Iulia [n/a] in Fond Hațieganu, pachetul 16., ANR Bucharest; Memorandum on Tornyai Schosberger Rezső, c. November 1918, BFL, Fond IV.1411.b., 1886/1139.

4. Maier, *Recasting Bourgeois Europe*.

5. Siegel, *For Peace and Money*, 12–49, 168–209.

6. Arendt, *Origins of Totalitarianism*, 271; Tooze, *Deluge*, 3–31.

7. Georges Dazet, *La liquidation des séquestres* (Paris: Éditions et librairie, 1916).

8. Denis Nohlen, *Strasbourg Architecture: 1871–1918* (Strasbourg, France: Le Verger, 1991), 98; R. Heusch, "La Brique," *Bulletin, Société des Sciences, Agriculture et Arts de la Basse-Alsace* 61 (1907): 50.

9. *The Traveller's Handbook for Belgium and the Ardennes* (London: Thomas Cook & Son, 1911), 90.

10. Uberfill, *La société strasbourgeoise*, 215–223.

11. Jules Jaeger, testimony at the chamber of deputies on December 23, 1921, in *Journal Officiel* no. 152, December 24, 1921, p. 5208.

12. Jaeger, testimony, December 23, 1921, JO, no. 152, December 24, 1921.

13. Comptroller general to the prefect of Bas-Rhin, February 7, 1933, ADBR 157 AL 105.

14. Commissaire Général to the Garde des Sceaux, November 26, 1923, ANF, AJ 30, 180.

15. Shannon Monaghan, *Protecting Democracy from Dissent: Population Engineering in Western Europe, 1918–1926* (Milton Park, Abingdon, Oxon: Routledge, 2018), 99–104.

16. Uberfill, *La société strasbourgeoise*, 215–223; Zahra, "'Minority Problem,'" 139–140.

17. Carolyn Grohmann, "From Lotharingen to Lorraine: Expulsion and Voluntary Repatriation," in Conan Fischer and Alan Sharp, eds. *After the Versailles Treaty, Enforcement, Compliance, Contested Identities* (London and New York: Routledge, 2008), 153–166.

18. Grohmann, "From Lotharingen," 156–157.

19. Comptroller General to Prefect of Bas-Rhin, February 7, 1933, ADBR 157 AL 105.

20. Jaeger, testimony, December 23, 1921, JO, p. 5209.

21. Minister of justice Laurent Bonnevay at chamber of deputies, December 29, 1921, JO, no. 157, p. 5391.

22. "Sénat, Année 1917," *Journal Officiel de la République Française*, September 26–27, 1917, 7648–7649.

23. Dazet, *La liquidation*.

24. Wilhelm Wiesmayer to Dr. Schwalb at the Reich Interior Ministry, Department of Alsace-Lorraine, April 4, 1925, BArch, R 1501/125452.

25. Jaeger, testimony, December 23, 1921.

26. Jaeger, testimony, December 23, 1921.

27. Cyrus Adler and Henrietta Szold, *American Jewish Year Book* (Philadelphia: Jewish Publication Society of America, 1920), 67–68.

28. Adler and Szold, *American Jewish Year Book*.

29. Jaeger, testimony, December 23, 1921, p. 5410.

30. Report of deputy Jaeger, January 29, 1922, 30 AJ 187; "Chamber of Deputies Session 2 of December 29, 1921," in *Journal Officiel*, no. 157 (December 30, 1921).

31. Report of deputy Jaeger, January 29, 1922; Wiesmayer to Dr. Schwalb, April 4, 1925.

32. Jaeger, testimony, December 23, 1921, JO, p. 5408.

33. "Jaeger, Jules Othon," in *Encyclopédie de l'Alsace* (Strasbourg: Ed. Publitotal, 1984), 7:4305.

34. "Chamber of Deputies Session 2 of December 29, 1921," 5402.

35. "Jaeger, Jules Othon," 4305.

36. Zahra, "'Minority Problem,'" 137.

37. "Chamber of Deputies Session 2 of December 29, 1921," 5402.

38. "Chamber of Deputies Session 2 of December 29, 1921," 5402.

39. Joseph Schmauch, "Novembre 1918. L'administration française s'établit en Alsace-Lorraine," *Revue d'Alsace*, no. 139 (October 1, 2013): 261.

40. Schmauch, "Novembre 1918," 265.

41. Schmauch, "Novembre 1918," 263.

42. Schmauch, "Novembre 1918," 263.

43. Schmauch, "Novembre 1918," 263.

44. Bonnevay at chamber of deputies, December 29, 1921.

45. Jaeger, testimony, December 23, 1921, JO, p. 5408.

46. Jaeger, testimony, December 23, 1921, JO, p. 5403.

47. Comptroller general to the prefect of Bas-Rhin, February 7, 1933, ADBR 157 AL 105.

48. Comptroller general to the prefect of Bas-Rhin, February 7, 1933, ADBR 157 AL 105.

49. Bonnevay at chamber of deputies, December 29, 1921; Memorandum, June 23, 1923, SAEF, box 31958.

50. Jaeger, testimony, December 23, 1921, JO, p. 5408.

51. Bonnevay at chamber of deputies, December 29, 1921, pp. 5386–5403.

52. DNS to Commissaire Général, June 3, 1925, ADBR 121 AL 595.

53. Soon after, the new Alsatian owners started to print a German-language paper that was still in a Gothic script but with a French heading (*Dernières Nouvelles de Strasbourg*) and a pro-French slant.

54. General commissioner Cura at the regional tribunal of Strasbourg to the high commissioner, February 25, 1919, ADBR 121 AL 877.

55. Alison Carrol, *The Return of Alsace to France, 1918–1939* (Oxford: Oxford University Press, 2018), 118–128.

56. Carrol, *Return of Alsace to France*, 118–128; Harvey, *Constructing Class and Nationality in Alsace*, 130–152.

57. Police report on socialist party meeting on August 17, 1919, ADBR 121 AL 864.

58. Marcel Dumuis, "Note sur le projet d'achat," April 2, 1919, ADBR 121 AL 1448.

59. Dumuis, "Note sur le projet d'achat," April 2, 1919.

60. Dumuis, "Note sur le projet d'achat," April 2, 1919; Loucheur to Jeanneney, February 5, 1919, ADBR 121AL 1448.

61. Dumuis, "Note sur le projet d'achat," April 2, 1919.

62. Dumuis, "Note sur le projet d'achat," April 2, 1919.

63. Loucheur to Dumuis, February 18, 1919, ADBR 121 AL 1448.

64. Dumuis, "Note sur le projet d'achat," April 2, 1919.

65. Firminy's paid-up capital amounted to four million francs, less than the net worth of the WNJ firm. "Société des acieries et forges de Firminy," *France: Economic and Commercial Conditions in France* (H.M. Stationery Office and Department of Commercial Relations and Exports, Great Britain: London, 1923), 94, 279; Confédération générale du travail, *Rapport de la Commission d'enquête du Conseil économique du Travail dans les régions dévastées: une politique de reconstruction* (Villeneuve, France: St. Georges, 1921), 1–12; Robert Pinot, *Le Comité Des Forges de France Au Service de La Nation (Août 1914 - Novembre 1918)* (Paris: A. Colin, 1919), 253–254.

66. Loucheur to Jeanneney, February 13, 1919.

67. Loucheur to Dumuis, February 18, 1919.

68. Bernard Vogler and Michel Hau, *Histoire économique de l'Alsace: croissance, crises, innovations: vingt siècles de développement régional* (Strasbourg: Editions la nuée bleue, 1997), 261.

69. *Geschäftsbericht für das 20., 21. und 22. Geschäftsjahr*, ZBW database.

70. Albert Bleicher and Joseph Rossé, *Die einträglichste Plünderung, die je begangen wurde: die Verschleuderung der elsaß-lothr. Industrien u. Bodenschätze; nach offiz. Berichten* (Kolmar [Colmar]: Alsatia, 1940).

71. "Oppenheimer villa," in "Dossier de la Police du bâtiment," Archive de la Ville et de la Communauté Urbaine, Strasbourg, 709 W 105.

72. "Notice sur les biens séquestrés," Industrial Services of Alsace-Lorraine, May 12, 1919, ADBR 121 AL 1448.

73. "Notice sur les biens séquestrés," May 12, 1919.

74. "Notice sur les biens séquestrés," May 12, 1919; Jaeger, testimony, December 29, 1921, JO, no. 157, p. 5392.

75. Memorandum "Maison allemandes sous séquestre," ADBR 121 AL 1448.

76. Alain Kahn, "Eléments concernant l'Ecole Israélite du Travail de Strasbourg," *Judaisme* database, accessed November 7, 2017, http://judaisme.sdv.fr/histoire/villes/strasbrg/travail.htm.

77. Georges Schmoll, "L'Alsace et la Lorraine françaises," *L'Univers israélite* 74, no. 15 (December 20, 1918): 345; Philippe-Efraïm Landau, "La communauté juive de France et la Grande Guerre," *Annales de demographie historique* 103, no. 1 (2002): 101.

78. Caron, *Between France and Germany*, 184; Landau, "La communauté juive," 102.

79. Landau, "La communauté juive."

80. "Questionnaire to Mr. Adler & Oppenheimer," January 9, 1919, ADBR 121 AL 1449.

81. David Allen Harvey, "Lost Children or Enemy Aliens? Classifying the Population of Alsace after the First World War," *Journal of Contemporary History* 34, no. 4 (October 1, 1999): 552–553.

82. Dr. Sándor Bottka, "Hirdetés finom bőrgyártelep létesítéséhez," August 6, 1918, Clujana 1/1920, ANR Cluj.

83. Memorandum of Pál Engel, director of the Austro-Hungarian Bank, August 23, 1919, DJAN Cluj, Fond Clujana 1/1919.

84. Gyula Kormos, ed., *Magyar pénzügyi compass* (Budapest: Apollo, 1924), 681–766.

85. Illés Edvi, ed., *A magyar béketárgyalások: Jelentés a Magyar békeküldöttség működéséről Neuilly s/S.-ben 1920 január ius - marcius havában* (Budapest: M. kir. tudományegyetemi nyomda, 1920), 3/a:124.

86. "Külföldi részvénytársaságok," in Kormos, *Magyar pénzügyi compass*, 722–743.

87. Traian Sandu, *La Grande Roumanie alliée de la France: Une péripétie diplomatique des Années Folles? (1919–1933)* (Paris: Harmattan, 1999), 1–10.

88. Bruno Cabanes, *La victoire endeuillée: La sortie de guerre des soldats français, 1918–1920* (Paris: Seuil, 2004), 277–333; Ignác Romsics, *Erdély elvesztése, 1918–1947* (Budapest: Helikon, 2018), 51–53.

89. Romanian general Henri Chiski's memorandum from November 23, 1919, quoted in Lucian Leuștean, *România, Ungaria și Tratatul de la Trianon 1918–1920* (Iași, Romania: Polirom, 2002), 197; Balázs Ablonczy, *Ismeretlen Trianon: Az összeomlás és a békeszerződés történetei, 1918–1921* (Budapest: Jaffa Kiadó, 2020), 141.

90. Edvi, *A magyar béketárgyalások*, 1:390–395; Zsombor Bódy, "A semleges, független Bánát mint ütközőállam," Trianon 100 database, accessed May 17, 2021, http://trianon100.hu/blog-cikk/a-semleges-fuggetlen-banat-mint-utkozoallam.

91. "Berthelot Nagyváradon," *Világ*, December 31, 1918, 4; *Nagyvárad*, December 31, 1918; Nemes, "Refugees and Antisemitism in Hungary during the First World War," 249–253.

92. "Minutes of the Timișoara chamber of commerce," January 10, 1920, Fond Camera de Comerț, ANR, DJAN Timiș.

93. Romsics, *Erdély elvesztése*, 77–165; Leuștean, *România, Ungaria*, 16–39.

94. Ablonczy, *Ismeretlen Trianon*, 136.

95. Leuștean, *România, Ungaria*, 18–24.

96. Romsics, *Erdély elvesztése*, 51–77.

97. Ablonczy, *Ismeretlen Trianon*, 91–92; Tamás Révész, *Nem akartak katonát látni? A magyar állam és hadserege 1918-1919-ben* (Budapest: Bölcsészettudományi Kutatóközpont, Történettudományi Intézet, 2019), 107–108.

98. Peter Pastor, *Hungary between Wilson and Lenin: The Hungarian Revolution of 1918–1919 and the Big Three* (Boulder, CO: East European Quarterly, 1976), 70–135; Révész, *Nem akartak katonát látni?*, 50–78.

99. Pastor, *Hungary between Wilson and Lenin*, 88.

100. Glenn E. Torrey, *The Romanian Battlefront in World War I* (Lawrence: University Press of Kansas, 2011), 15–21; Jean-Noël Grandhomme, Michel Roucaud, and Thierry Sarmant, eds., *La Roumanie dans la Grande Guerre et l'effondrement de l'armée Russe: Edition critique des rapports du général Berthelot, chef de la mission militaire française en Roumanie, 1916–1918* (Paris: Harmattan, 2000).

101. Henri Mathias Berthelot to "Georges," January 7, 1919, in *General Henri Berthelot and Romania, Mémoires et correspondance*, ed. Glenn Torrey (Boulder, CO: EEM, 1987), 203.

102. Dénes Sebess, *Az új agrárdemokráciák* (Budapest: Légrády, 1925), 110.

103. Romsics, *Erdély elvesztése*, 142–146.

104. Gábor Egry, "Negotiating Post-Imperial Transitions: Local Societies and Nationalizing States in East Central Europe," in *Embers of Empire, Continuity and Rupture in the Habsburg Successor States after 1918*, Austrian and Habsburg Studies, ed. Paul Miller and Claire Morelon (New York: Berghahn, 2019), 15–42.

105. Romsics, *Erdély elvesztése*, 161–171, 216–237.

106. Leuștean, *România, Ungaria*, 31.

107. Leuștean, *România, Ungaria*, 29–31.

108. Leuștean, *România, Ungaria*, 36–37; Pastor, *Hungary between Wilson and Lenin*, 63–65.

109. Sherman David Spector, *Rumania at the Paris Peace Conference: A Study of the Diplomacy of Ioan I.C. Brătianu* (New York: Bookman Associates, 1962), 78–87.

110. Romsics, *Erdély elvesztése*, 171–178.

111. "Általános sztrájk Erdélyben," *Népszava*, January 25, 1919, 3.

112. Balázs Schuller, "Impériumváltás a Zsil-Völgyében, 1918," *Bányászati és Kohászati Lapok* 3 (2005): 35–38.

113. Romsics, *Erdély elvesztése*, 171–178.

114. Romsics, *Erdély elvesztése*, 171–178.

115. "Visa petition of Adolf Renner," ANIC, Fond Consiliul Dirigent, 1920/9; "Jegyzőkönyv," June 7, 1919, in "Procesele Verbale, 1918–1926," Fond Camera de Comerț și de Industrie, DJAN Cluj.

116. Nándor Bárdi, *Otthon és haza, Tanulmányok a romániai magyar kisebbség történetéről* (Csíkszereda, Romania: Pro-Print, 2013), 106.

117. Sandu, *La Grande Roumanie*, 7–9.

118. Romsics, *Erdély elvesztése*, 248–250.

119. David Mitrany, *The Land and the Peasant in Rumania: The War and Agrarian Reform (1917–21)* (New Haven, CT: Yale University Press, 1930).

120. Mitrany, *Land and the Peasant in Rumania*.

121. Antal Berkes, "The League of Nations and the Optants Disputes of the Hungarian Borderlands: Romania, Yugoslavia and Czechoslovakia," in *Remaking Central Europe: The League of Nations and the Former Habsburg Lands*, ed. Natasha Wheatley and Peter Becker (Oxford: Oxford University Press, 2020).

122. Müller, "Concept of Property in Romania's Economic-Legal History," 183–222.

123. Müller, "Concept of Property in Romania's Economic-Legal History," 197.

124. Müller, "Concept of Property in Romania's Economic-Legal History," 197.

125. Royal decree No. 3603 passed on December 8, 1918; Ludovic Báthory, *Societățile carbonifere și sistemul economic și politic al României: 1919–1929* (Cluj-Napoca: Presa Universitară Clujeană, 1999), 72.

126. *Monitorul Oficial*, No. 16, du 6 Mai 1919, p. 902; Memorandum of Robert de Flers to French minister of foreign affairs, March 20, 1919, AAE 110CPCOM/98 P/17444—Roumanie, Commerce, p. 42.

127. Ștefan Cristian Ionescu, *Jewish Resistance to "Romanianization," 1940–44* (Basingstoke: Palgrave Macmillan, 2015).

128. Nicolae Iorga, "Egy ember élete - úgy, amint volt," in Andor Horváth, ed., *Tanúskodni jöttem: Válogatás a két világháború közötti roman emlékirat- és naplóirodalomból* (Kolozsvár, Romania, Kriterion 2003), 243–244.

129. Board meeting of the Economic Bank (Közgazdasági Bank), March 29, 1920, ANR, DJAN Timiș, Prefectura Jud. Timiș-Torontal 80/1920, pp. 67–70.

130. *Drapelul*, 104/19, October 8, 1919.

131. Lawyer Móric Rosenthal to prefect Aurel Cosma, April 16, 2016, ANR, Timiș, Prefectura Jud. Timiș-Torontal 80/1920, p. 65; Dumitru Ogășanu, *Consiliul Dirigent al Transilvaniei, Activitatea legislativă, 1918–1920* (Oradea, Romania: Editura Universității din Oradea, 2002), 13–29, 59–68; Board meeting of the Economic Bank (Közgazdasági Bank), March 29, 1920, ANR, DJAN Timiș, Prefectura Jud. Timiș-Torontal 80/1920, pp. 67–70.

132. Rosenthal to Cosma, April 16, 2016.

133. "Jegyzőkönyv," April 2, 1921, in "Procesele Verbale, 1918–1926."

134. Based on the February 13, 1919, decree on the support of national industries (711/1919), *Gazeta Oficiala*, January 27, 1921, 1.

135. Kormos, *Magyar pénzügyi compass*, 681–766.

136. Kormos, *Magyar pénzügyi compass*, 681–766.

137. István Gaucsík, *A jog erejével: a szlovákiai magyarság gazdasági önszerveződése, 1918–1938: dokumentumok* (Pozsony/Bratislava, Slovakia: Kalligram, 2008), 14–18.

138. Borzu Sabahi, *Compensation and Restitution in Investor-State Arbitration: Principles and Practice* (Oxford: Oxford University Press, 2011), 48–49.

139. Berkes, "League of Nations and the Optants Dispute."

140. Detlev F. Vagts, "Coercion and Foreign Investment Rearrangements," *American Journal of International Law* 72, no. 1 (January 1978): 18.

141. David C. Kang, "Transaction Costs and Crony Capitalism in East Asia," *Comparative Politics* 35, no. 4 (2003): 439.

142. Cieger, *Politikai korrupció a Monarchia Magyarországán*, 151–188.

143. Laura Lee Downs, *Manufacturing Inequality: Gender Division in the French and British Metalworking Industries, 1914–1939* (Ithaca, NY: Cornell University Press, 1995), 1–14, 186–226.

144. Spector, *Rumania at the Paris Peace Conference*, 64–97; Zahra, "'Minority Problem'"; Wolff, *Woodrow Wilson*, 189–204.

145. Berkes, "League of Nations and the Optants Dispute," 283–314.

146. Edvi, *A magyar béketárgyalások*, 3a:60–124.

147. Roman Holec, *Dejiny plné dynamitu: Bratislavský podnik Dynamit Nobel na križovatkách novodobých dejín* (Bratislava, Slovakia: Kalligram, 2011), 1–37; Roman Holec, "Economic Aspects of Slovak National Development," in *Economic Change and*

the National Question in Twentieth-Century Europe, ed. Alice Teichova (Cambridge: Cambridge University Press, 2000), 280–285; Alice Teichova, *Wirtschaftsgeschichte der Tschechoslowakei: 1918–1980* (Vienna: Böhlau, 1988), 59–66.

6. France's East-Central European "Empire" after Versailles

1. George Bradshaw, *Bradshaw's Illustrated Hand-Book to Switzerland and the Tyrol* (London: W. J. Adams & Sons, 1857), 14.

2. Henrik Fellner to Ferenc Chorin Jr., September 20, 1919, MNL-OL, 71/1 t. 24. Cs. Z 223.

3. Wessel, *Thyssen & Co.*, 44–45.

4. Samuel Goodfellow, "Fascism and Regionalism in Interwar Alsace," *National Identities* 12, no. 2 (2010): 133–145; Fischer, *Alsace to the Alsatians?*, 128–151.

5. Philip Shukry Khoury, *Syria and the French Mandate: The Politics of Arab Nationalism, 1920–1945* (Princeton, NJ: Princeton University Press, 1989), 44–46.

6. Idir Ouahes, *Syria and Lebanon under the French Mandate: Cultural Imperialism and the Workings of Empire* (London: I.B. Tauris, 2018), 224–228; Philippe Marguerat, "Les investissements français dans le Bassin danubien durant l'entre-deux-guerres: Pour une nouvelle interprétation," *Revue Historique* 306: 629, no. 1 (2004): 126.

7. Keynes, *Economic Consequences of the Peace*, 181.

8. Alice Teichova, *Economic Change and the National Question in Twentieth-Century Europe* (Cambridge: Cambridge University Press, 2000); Peter Mathias and Sidney Pollard, *The Industrial Economies: The Development of Economic and Social Policies* (Cambridge: Cambridge University Press, 1989), 893–905; Sean McMeekin, *History's Greatest Heist: The Looting of Russia by the Bolsheviks* (New Haven, CT: Yale University Press, 2009), 93–222.

9. Berkes, "League of Nations and the Optants Dispute," 283–314.

10. Teichova, *Economic Change and the National Question*; Mathias and Pollard, *Industrial Economies*, 893–905.

11. Georges-Henri Soutou, "La France et les Marches de l'Est 1914–1919," *Revue Historique* 260: 528, no. 2 (1978): 341–388; Sandu, *La Grande Roumanie*, 1–14.

12. Victoria De Grazia, *Irresistible Empire: America's Advance through Twentieth-Century Europe* (Cambridge, MA: Belknap Press of Harvard University Press, 2005), 1–10; Wolff, *Woodrow Wilson*, 56–114.

13. Peter Jackson, *Beyond the Balance of Power: France and the Politics of National Security in the Era of the First World War* (Cambridge: Cambridge University Press, 2013), 235.

14. Marguerat, "Les investissements français," 157–162.

15. Elisabeth Gläser, "The Making of the Economic Peace," in *The Treaty of Versailles: A Reassessment after 75 Years*, ed. Manfred F. Boemeke, Gerald D. Feldman, and Elisabeth Gläser (Cambridge: Cambridge University Press, 1998), 392–393.

16. Sergio Romano, "Italy in Post-World War 1 Diplomacy," in *Italy and East Central Europe: Dimensions of the Regional Relationship*, ed. Vojtech Mastny (New York: Routledge, 2019), 17–34.

17. Georges-Henri Soutou, *La grande illusion: Quand la France perdait la paix, 1914–1920* (Paris: Texto, 2015), 305–362.

18. Georges-Henri Soutou, "The French Peacemakers and Their Home Front," in Boemeke et al., *Treaty of Versailles*, 180–186; Tooze and Fertik, "World Economy and the Great War," 231–232.

19. Ronald Findlay, *Power and Plenty: Trade, War, and the World Economy in the Second Millennium* (Princeton, NJ: Princeton University Press, 2007), 461.

20. Piotr Stefan Wandycz, *France and Her Eastern Allies, 1919–1925* (Minneapolis: University of Minnesota Press, 1962), 3–23.

21. Jackson, *Beyond the Balance of Power*, 197–235.

22. Martin Thomas, "French Empire Elites and the Politics of Economic Obligation in the Interwar Years," *Historical Journal* 52, no. 4 (2009): 989–1016; Heather Streets-Salter, *World War One in Southeast Asia: Colonialism and Anticolonialism in an Era of Global Conflict* (Cambridge: Cambridge University Press, 2017), 169–213.

23. "Institut Français, Bucarest," AAE, Nantes, 126PO/1/35-36.

24. "Institut Français, Bucarest."

25. Siegel, *For Peace and Money*, 168–209.

26. David Harvey, *The Limits to Capital* (New York: Verso Books, 2018), xviii–xxxi; Michael Jabara Carley, "From Revolution to Dissolution: The Quai d'Orsay, the Banque Russo-Asiatique, and the Chinese Eastern Railway, 1917–1926," *International History Review* 12, no. 4 (1990): 721–761.

27. Benjamin F. Martin, *France and the Après Guerre, 1918–1924: Illusions and Disillusionment* (Baton Rouge: Louisiana State University Press, 1999). 34; Francis Delaisi, René Cassin, and Stéphane Lauzanne, *Les Soviets et la Dette Russe en France* (Paris: Publications de la Conciliation Internationale, 1930; Soutou, "L'Impérialisme du pauvre," 219–239.

28. Siegel, *For Peace and Money*, 12–49, 168–209; Haim Shamir, *Economic Crisis and French Foreign Policy: 1930–1936* (Leiden: Brill Archive, 1989), 35–37.

29. Minister Isaac to the President, December 10, 1920, ANF F 12 9174.

30. McMeekin, *History's Greatest Heist*, 1–8.

31. Balázs Ablonczy, *Pál Teleki (1874–1941): The Life of a Controversial Hungarian Politician* (Boulder, CO: Social Science Monographs, 2006), 65.

32. Ablonczy, *Pál Teleki*, 121–162.

33. Abraham Berglund, "The Iron-Ore Problem of Lorraine," *Quarterly Journal of Economics* 33, no. 3 (1919): 532.

34. Berglund, "Iron-Ore Problem of Lorraine," 537.

35. Robert Gerwarth, *The Vanquished: Why the First World War Failed to End, 1917–1923* (London: Allen Lane, 2016), 1–14.

36. "Légitimation," June 20, 1919, ANF F7, 13377.

37. Marguerat, "Les investissements français," 129.

38. Richard F. Kuisel, *Capitalism and the State in Modern France: Renovation and Economic Management in the Twentieth Century* (Cambridge: Cambridge University Press, 1983), 37–50; Maier, *Recasting Bourgeois Europe*, 71–73.

39. John F. Godfrey, *Capitalism at War: Industrial Policy and Bureaucracy in France, 1914–1918* (Leamington Spa, UK: Berg, 1987), 1–6.

40. Louis Loucheur to Marcel Dumuis, February 18, 1919, ADBR 121 AL 1448.

41. Artillery Squadron Chief Hausser, General Inspector of the Bureau of Industries for Alsace-Lorraine (Service Industriel d'Alsace et de Lorraine), to the General Commissioner, March 28, 1919, ADBR 121 AL 1448.

42. Marc Trachtenberg, *Reparation in World Politics: France and European Economic Diplomacy, 1916–1923* (New York: Columbia University Press, 1980), i–v, 1–10.

43. "Chamber of Deputies Session 2 of December 29, 1921," *Journal Officiel*, no. 157 (December 30, 1921): 5399–5402.

44. Maier, *Recasting Bourgeois Europe*, 71–73.

45. Robert Pinot, *Le Comité des forges de France au service de la nation (août 1914 - novembre 1918)* (Paris: A. Colin, 1919), 232; Jacques Bariéty, "Les conséquences pour l'économie française du retour de l'Alsace-Lorraine à la France en 1919," *Francia: Forschungen zur Westeuropäischen Geschichte* 3 (1975): 535–536.

46. Pinot, *Le Comité des forges*; Bariéty, "Les conséquences pour l'économie française," 535–536.

47. Pinot, *Le Comité des forges*, 232.

48. Pinot, *Le Comité des Forges*, 230–232; Bulletin No. 3707; "Les Mines de Fer de l'Alsace et de Lorraine en 1923," Bulletin No. 3806, *Le Comité des Forges*, 8. AAE C 24/4.

49. The net worth of these plants was around $10 billion as of 2015. All dollar estimates in the book are based on currency conversion rates in force at the time. I rely on economic historian Rodney Edvinsson's exchange rate estimates. Historical Currency Converter database, accessed June 3, 2016, http://www.historicalstatistics.org/Currencyconverter.html.

50. The French minister of commerce and industry, Auguste Isaac, to President Alexandre Millerand, December 10, 1920, ANF F 12 9174; Kenneth Mouré, *Managing the Franc Poincaré: Economic Understanding and Political Constraint in French Monetary Policy, 1928–1936* (Cambridge: Cambridge University Press, 1991), 11.

51. Jeffrey R. Fear, *Organizing Control* (Cambridge, MA: Harvard University Press, 2005), 291; Manfred Rasch, "August Thyssen die Katholische Grossindustrielle der Wilhelminischen Epoche," in *August Thyssen und Hugo Stinnes: Ein Briefwechsel 1898–1922*, ed. M. Rasch and Gerald D. Feldman (Munich: C. H. Beck, 2003), 50–54.

52. Roth, *La Lorraine annexé*, 610; Maurer Mauere, ed., *The U.S. Air Service in World War I* (Washington, DC: Government Printing Office, 1979), 4:382–392; *Journal of the Iron and Steel Institute* 104, no. 2 (London: The Institute, 1921), 311–312.

53. Wessel, *Thyssen & Co.*, 44–45.

54. Wessel, *Thyssen & Co.*, 44–45.

55. "Verhaftung deutscher Großindustriellen wegen Landesverrates," *Pester Lloyd*, December 9, 1918, 4.

56. "Verhaftung deutscher Großindustriellen wegen Landesverrates"; Wessel, *Thyssen & Co.*, 44–45.

57. "Report on Hagondange firm," AAE, 45RC20 Relations Commerciales (1919–1940) C 24, Alsace Lorraine; "Tableau synoptique des opérations" annex to Louis Cluzel, *Annexe au procès-verbal de la 2e séance du 19 janvier 1928. Rapport fait au nom de la Commission des Marchés et les Spéculations sur les séquestres des biens des ressortissants anciens ennemis en France et dans les départements recouvrés et sur la liquidation des usines métallurgiques de Lorraine*, PAAA, box 762.

58. Youssef Cassis, *Big Business: The European Experience in the Twentieth Century* (New York: Oxford University Press, 1997), 54–57.

59. Michel Prosic, *L'usine créatrice: L'usine de Hagondange, naissance de la vie ouvrière, 1910–1938* (Hagondange, FranceVille de Hagondange, 1996), 34.

60. H. Mornard, *Mémoire sur la situation des sociétés acquéreurs des usines métallurgiques allemandes en Lorraine* (Paris: n.p., 1922), 8; AAE C 24 Dossier 3, 1920.

61. Senator Henri Marguerie, Memorandum "Au sujet des usines d'Hagondange," AAE, 45RC20 Relations Commerciales (1919–1940) C 22–24, Alsace Lorraine.

62. "L'attentat d'Hagondange," *L'Est Républicain*, March 30, 1920, 2.

63. Louis Renault to the Union of Consumers, November 5, 1919, cited by Gilbert Hatry, *Louis Renault, patron absolu* (Paris: Éditions JCM, 1990), 206.

64. Renault to the Union of Consumers, 206.

65. As of the early twentieth century, the Dingler-Karcher plant, which employed one thousand workers and produced two hundred tons of steel a day, was even superior to the capacity of the de Dietrich company when measured in the capacity of its open hearth furnaces. *Gemeinfassliche Darstellung des Eisenhüttenwesens* (Düsseldorf: Bagel, 1903), 146; "Germany's Mineral Losses under the Treaty," *Iron Age* 104 (July 24, 1919): 253; Hau, *La Maison De Dietrich*, 155.

66. Hau, *La Maison De Dietrich*, 155.

67. "Report on Hagondange firm," AAE; Prosic, *L'usine créatrice*, 99.

68. The comparison of the value of 1914 and 1919 currencies is based on the value of the gold mark and the French franc as compared with the value of gold and silver. Historical Currency Converter database, accessed June 3, 2016, http://www.historicalstatistics.org/Currencyconverter.html.

69. "Report on Hagondange firm," AAE.

70. "Report on Hagondange firm," AAE.

71. "Report on Hagondange firm," AAE.

72. "Report on Hagondange firm," AAE, 1–2.

73. "Tableau synoptique des opérations," in Cluzel, *Annexe au procès-verbal de la 2e séance du 19 janvier 1928*.

74. In 1932, the company was still waiting on its shareholders to pay as much as 65,490,000 francs in exchange for their shares. *Denkschrift*, 39.

75. "Tableau synoptique des opérations" in No. 5357, Chambre des Députés. Treizième Législature, Session du 1928 in Cluzel, *Annexe au procès-verbal de la 2e séance du 19 janvier 1928*.

76. "Tableau synoptique des opérations" in Cluzel, *Annexe*.

77. Denis Woronoff, *François de Wendel* (Paris: Presses de Sciences Po, 2001), 76.

78. Ablonczy, *Pál Teleki*, 65–66; Gyula Juhász, *Hungarian Foreign Policy, 1919–1945* (Budapest: Akadémiai Kiadó, 1979), 46.

79. Marguerat, "Les investissements français," 121–129.

80. Marguerat, "Les investissements français," 135–141.

81. Francis Deák, *Hungary at the Paris Peace Conference: The Diplomatic History of the Treaty of Trianon* (New York: Columbia University Press, 1942), 256.

82. Marguerat, "Les investissements français," 131–141.

83. Marguerat, "Les investissements français," 130–133.

84. André Tardieu, *The Truth about the Treaty* (Indianapolis, IN: Bobbs-Merrill, 1921), 249.

85. Roman Holec, *Dinamitos történelem: A pozsonyi Dynamit Nobel Vegyipari Konszern a közép-európai történelem keresztútján: 1873–1945* (Bratislava: Kalligram, 2009), 29–42; "The Factory at Chorzow, Germany v. Poland," *Permanent Court of Interna-*

tional Justice, File E. c. XIII., Docket XIV: I. Judgment No. 13, September 13, 1928, http://www.worldcourts.com/pcij/eng/decisions/1928.09.13_chorzow1.htm; Karch, *Nation and Loyalty*, 135–185.

86. Báthory, *Societățile carbonifere*, 19.

87. Báthory, *Societățile carbonifere*, 67–74.

88. Báthory, *Societățile carbonifere*, 67–70.

89. Romsics, *Erdély elvesztése*, 173–178.

90. *Monitorul Oficial*, No. 16, du 6 Mai 1919, p. 902; AAE 110CPCOM/98 P/17444—Roumanie, Commerce, 42.

91. Murgescu Bogdan, *România și Europa: Acumularea decalajelor economice: 1500–2010* (Iași, Romania: Polirom, 2010), 252.

92. Báthory, *Societățile carbonifere*, 89.

93. Báthory, *Societățile carbonifere*, 89–90.

94. Báthory, *Societățile carbonifere*, 67–78.

95. "Salgótarjáni kőszénbánya rt.," in *Magyar Pénzügyi Compass 1917–1918*, vol. 3, ed. Gyula Kormos (Budapest: Apollo, 1918), 1:171; "Salgótarjáni kőszénbánya rt.," *Nagy Magyar Compass* 45–46, no. 2: 304.

96. "F. F. Wiesenberger—Lopás büntette," Kr.1534/1919, HU BFL XVI.2, 7. nagydoboz, Budapesti Forradalmi Törvényszék, Kísérleti Kriminológiai Osztály iratai.

97. "A svábhegyi új erdei iskola (volt Chorin villa)," *Új Idők* 25, no. 19 (June 5, 1919): 358; Szomaházy István, "Az angora cica," *Szinházi Élet*, June 22–28, 1919, 27–28.

98. Rozenblit, *Reconstructing a National Identity*, 128–161.

99. Miklós Konrád, *Zsidóságon innen és túl: Zsidók vallásváltása Magyarországon a reformkortól az első világháborúig* (Budapest: MTABTK TTI, 2014), 17, 267.

100. "Báró Ullmann Adolf a Hitelbank vállalatainak helyzetéről," *Magyar Tőzsde*, February 4, 1920, 4.

101. "Báró Ullmann," 4.

102. "Darier et Cie," Diplomatische Dokumente der Schweiz Database, accessed June 3, 2016, https://dodis.ch/R1645.

103. "Les Charbonnages D'Urikany," *Paris-capital: Journal financier*, July 8, 1896, 2.

104. "Le Marché Roumain," *France-Europe Orientale: Bulletin Officiel du Comité National d'Expansion Économique dans l'Europe Orientale*, April 1, 1919, 33.

105. "Fónagy Aladár a Foresta uj tranzakcióiról," *Magyar Tőzsde*, February 7, 1920, 3.

106. The Romanian leu had lost over two-thirds of its value by early 1919. The French franc, the Romanian leu, and the Hungarian crown were heavily inflated compared with the Swiss franc. Costin C. Kirițescu, *Sistemul bănesc al leului și precursorii lui*, vol. 2 (Bucharest: Editura Academiei Republicii Populare Romîne, 1964), 255–271.

107. "Memorandum über die Steinkohlengruben," MNL-OL, Z 223, 24 cs.

108. Dominique Kirchner Reill, *The Fiume Crisis: Life in the Wake of the Habsburg Empire* (Cambridge, MA: Belknap Press of Harvard University Press, 2020); Ablonczy, *Ismeretlen Trianon*, 105.

109. "Báró Ullmann"; "Fónagy Aladár."

110. Engineer Balasinovici to SCMC, January 11, 1920, MNL-OL, Z 223, 24. cs. 71/1.

111. Engineer Balasinovici to SCMC, January 11, 1920.

112. "Báró Madarassy-Beck Gyula Párizsban," *Magyar Tőzsde*, February 21, 1920, 2.

113. Memorandum, MNL-OL, Z 223, 24 cs, 71/1.

114. Báthory, *Societățile carbonifere.*

115. "Jegyzőkönyv," [1920], MNL-OL, Z 223, 24 cs., 71/3.

116. "Jegyzőkönyv," February 8, 1921, MNL-OL, Z 223, 24 cs, 71/3.

117. "A Petrozsényi szénbánya helyzete," Z 223, 24 cs, 71/2 t.

118. Jackson, *Beyond the Balance of Power*, 368.

119. Note 353 of Hungarian minister to France Iván Praznovszky to prime minister István Bethlen, August 24, 1920, MNL-OL, K64 1. cs. 27. t. 294/res.pol. 1920.

120. Albert Apponyi, "On the Transylvanian Question," in *The Hungarian Peace Negotiations*, ed. Jenő Cholnoky (Budapest: M. kir. tudományegyetemi nyomda, 1921), 1:130–150.

121. "Magyar Jelzálog-Hitelbank," *Nagy Magyar Compass*, 42/1 (1914), 154–156; *Mihók-féle Magyar Compass* 33, no. 1 (1905): 112–115.

122. Ablonczy, *Pál Teleki*, 65.

123. Francis Deák, *Hungary at the Paris Peace Conference: The Diplomatic History of the Treaty of Trianon* (New York: Columbia University Press, 1942), 256.

124. Loucheur to the French minister of foreign affairs, December 21, 1918, AAE, mf. 90CPCOM28.

125. Deák, *Hungary at the Paris Peace Conference*, 264–265.

126. Deák, *Hungary at the Paris Peace Conference*, 267–268.

127. Deák, *Hungary at the Paris Peace Conference*, 267–268; Ablonczy, *Pál Teleki*, 66.

128. Romsics, *Erdély elvesztése*, 290.

129. Treaty of Trianon, Article 47.

130. Document no. 13733, Dossier no. 12885, 1920/1921, R 1661–1663, LoNa; Francis Deák, "The Rumanian-Hungarian Dispute before the Council of the League of Nations," *California Law Review* 120, no. 16 (1928): 120–133; Deák, *Hungary at the Paris Peace Conference*, 281.

131. Deák, *Hungary at the Paris Peace Conference*, 281.

132. "Note Appel," *France Europe-Orientale* 1, no. 1 (1919): 4.

133. "Souscripteurs fondateurs," *France Europe-Orientale* 1, no. 2 (1919): 3.

134. "Souscripteurs fondateurs," 3; Henri Hauser, *Les méthodes allemandes d'expansion économique*, 3rd ed. (Paris: A. Colin, 1916), 277–278.

135. Hauser, *Les méthodes allemandes*, 277–278.

136. E. V. Letzgus, "Le Marché Roumain," *France Europe-Orientale* 1, no. 1 (1919): 6–10.

137. I. Boamba, *Banque Marmorosch Blank & Co. Société Anonyme, 1828–1923* (Bucharest: Cultură Natională, 1924), 107.

138. Christie, *Murder on the Orient Express* (New York: HarperPaperbacks, 1991), 98.

139. Auguste Jardé, "Les Chemins de Fers en Europe en 1921," *Annales de Géographie* 31, no. 174 (November 15, 1922): 503–506.

140. "A 'felszabadítók' a Bácskában," *Pesti Napló*, January 22, 1920, 4.

141. Jardé, "Les Chemins de Fers en Europe en 1921," 505.

142. "Conseil d'Administration de la Compagnie," *Bulletin de Renseignements*, CFRNA, December 1, 1923, 2, ANF Nantes, Legation Bucharest, 124 PO/1.

143. "Légiposta közlekedés létesítése Párizs és Konstantinápoly között Budapesten át," memorandum by Hungarian Foreign Ministry, September 17, 1920, MNL-OL, K 69, 735 cs. 3. t., p. 16.

144. "Le survol de l'Allemagne," *Bulletin de Renseignements*, CFRNA, December 1, 1923, 2.

145. Versailles Treaty, Article 297 b.

146. Judson, *Habsburg Empire*, 442–446.

147. Versailles Treaty, Article 256, TT Article 191, T St. G. Article 78, 208, 249, 250.

148. Keynes, *Economic Consequences of the Peace*, 233.

7. Imperial Currencies after the Fall of Empires

1. "Traffic de monnaie," December 31, 1919, ADBR 157 AL 50; "Starea de spirit in Transilvania," Direcția Generală a Poliției, 3/1919-1920, ANR Bucharest, Fond Consiliul Dirigent; "Jenő Veszprémi," Vama Curtici 1/1921, DJAN Arad.

2. Reill, *Fiume Crisis*, 81.

3. Livezeanu, *Cultural Politics in Greater Romania*; Roland Clark, *Holy Legionary Youth: Fascist Activism in Interwar Romania* (Ithaca, NY: Cornell University Press, 2015), 1–28; Gábor Egry, "Unholy Alliances? Language Exams, Loyalty, and Identification in Interwar Romania," *Slavic Review* 76, no. 4 (2017): 959–982; Zahra, "'Minority Problem,'" 137.

4. Gregor von Rezzori, *The Snows of Yesteryear: Portraits for an Autobiography* (New York: New York Review of Books, 2009), 72.

5. Marguerat, "Les investissements français," 121–162.

6. Ion I. Lapedatu, *Chestiunea valutei* (Bucharest: Imprimeria Statului, 1920), 1–18.

7. Horia Maniu, *Unificarea monetară* (Bucharest: Cartea Românească, 1924), 9.

8. Zahra, "'Minority Problem.'"

9. Joseph Rossé, Marcel Stürmel, Albert Bleicher, Fernand Deiber, and Jean Keppi, *Das Elsass von 1870–1932* (Strasbourg: Verlag Alsatia, 1938), 1:185–250.

10. "Question monétaire" memorandum [1916], ADBR 1 AL 1020; Memorandum by the État-majeur de l'Armée, 2e Bureau I, Section Économique, "Mesures Financières de guerre et d'après-guerre en Allemagne," February 9, 1918, SHD, 16 N 1375.

11. "Question monétaire" [1916]; *Procès-Verbaux de La Conférence d'Alsace-Lorraine, 1e–24e séances, 18 février 1915–22 mai 1916* (Paris: Imprimerie Nationale, 1917), 1:334.

12. *Procès-Verbaux*, 1:330–334.

13. Harold William Vazeille Temperley, *A History of the Peace Conference of Paris* (London: H. Frowde, and Hodder & Stoughton, 1920), 2:459–461.

14. Raphaël Milliès-Lacroix, *Annex*, ANF, F 12 8044, p. 4; "French propaganda on Alsace-Lorraine," ANF, AJ/30/103.

15. Sally Marks, *The Illusion of Peace: International Relations in Europe, 1918–1933* (New York: Palgrave Macmillan, 2003), 5.

16. Decree of President Clemenceau, November 26, 1918, *Journal Officiel de la République Français*, December 7, 1918, 10544.

17. Laird Boswell, "From Liberation to Purge Trials in the 'Mythic Provinces': Recasting French Identities in Alsace and Lorraine, 1918–1920," *French Historical Studies* 23, no. 1 (2000): 130; Monaghan, *Protecting Democracy from Dissent*, 133–135.

18. Raymond Poincaré, *Au service de la France, neuf années de souvenirs* (Paris: Plon, 1974), 11:10–12.

19. David Chuter, *Humanity's Soldier: France and International Security, 1919–2001* (Providence, RI: Berghahn Books, 1996), 58.

20. Ministry of Finance to the Senate and chamber financial committee, January 30, 1919, Milliès-Lacroix, *Annex*, ANF F 12 8044, p. 12.

21. Dan P. Silverman, *Reconstructing Europe after the Great War* (Cambridge, MA: Harvard University Press, 1982), 1–5, 70–94.; Kenneth Mouré, *The Gold Standard Illusion: France, the Bank of France, and the International Gold Standard, 1914–1939* (Oxford: Oxford University Press, 2002), 43–44.

22. Charles Kindleberger, *A Financial History of Western Europe* (London: Allen & Unwin, 1984), 239–249.

23. Mitchell Allen and Michael Hughes, *German Parliamentary Debates, 1848–1933* (New York: P. Lang, 2003), 220.

24. Jean-Baptiste Duroselle, *Clemenceau* (Paris: Fayard, 1988), 830.

25. "Note au Ministre," November 23, 1918, AAE 90 CPCOM 24, p. 29.

26. Michael Angelo Heilperin, *Aspects of the Pathology of Money: Monetary Essays from Four Decades* (London: Graduate Institute of International Studies, 1968), 125–127.

27. Milliès-Lacroix, *Annex*, ANF F 12 8044, p. 4.

28. Georges Delahache, *Strasbourg 1918–1920* (Paris: Pochy, 1920), 5.

29. Milliès-Lacroix, *Annex*, ANF F 12 8044, p. 12; Duroselle, *Clemenceau*, 829–831; Alan Sharp, *The Versailles Settlement: Peacemaking after the First World War, 1919–1923* (Basingstoke: Palgrave Macmillan, 2008), 82–84.

30. *Allgemeine Elsässische Bankgesellschaft, Société générale alsacienne de banque, Geschäftsbericht für das Geschäftsjahr für das Bilanzjahr 1918* (Strasbourg: Imprimerie Française, 1919), 6.

31. *Geschäftsbericht für das Geschäftsjahr 1918*, 6.

32. *Allgemeine Elsässische Bankgesellschaft / Société générale alsacienne de banque, Geschäftsbericht für das Geschäftsjahr für das Bilanzjahr 1919 an die Generalversammlung der Aktionäre vom 9. März 1920* (Strasbourg: Imprimerie Française, 1920), 1–19.

33. Gérard Noiriel, *Longwy: Immigrés et prolétaires, 1880–1980* (Paris: Presses universitaires de France, 1984), 228–246.

34. Letter of artillery commander Hausser the High Commissioner of the Republic, December 27, 1918, ADBR, 121 AL 877.

35. "Troisième rapport sur la mission du M. Henri Hauser auprès des Chambres de Commerce d'Alsace et de Lorraine," January 27, 1919, ANF, F 12 8044.

36. Alfred Sauvy and Anita Hirsch, *Histoire économique de la France entre les deux guerres* (Paris: Economica, 1984), 2:80–84; "Les Mines de Fer de l'Alsace et de Lorraine en 1921," *Bulletin no. 3707, Le Comité des Forges*, 8, AAE C 24/4; Harvey, *Constructing Class*, 139–146.

37. "Troisième rapport sur la mission du M. Henri Hauser."

38. Joseph Rossé, Marcel Stürmel, Albert Bleicher, Fernand Deiber, and Jean Keppi, *Das Elsass von 1870–1932* (Colmar: Verlag Alsatia 1938), 4:55.

39. Georges Delahache, *Les débuts de l'administration française en Alsace et en Lorraine* (Paris: Hachette, 1921), 17.

40. Delahache, *Les débuts de l'administration française*, 17–19.

41. Delahache, *Les débuts de l'administration française*, 18–20.

42. Delahache, *Les débuts de l'administration française*, 18–20.

43. Delahache, *Les débuts de l'administration française*, 18–20.

44. Milliès-Lacroix, *Annex*, ANF F 12 8044.

45. Rodney Edvinsson, ed., Historical Statistics Database, Portal for Historical Statistics, retrieved on January 10, 2016, http://www.historicalstatistics.org/Currencyconverter.html.

46. Harvey Edward Fisk, *French Public Finance in the Great War and Today: With Chapters on Banking and Currency* (New York: Bankers Trust Company, 1922), 186.

47. Wolfgang J. Mommsen, "Max Weber and the Treaty of Versailles," in *The Treaty of Versailles: A Reassessment after 75 Years*, ed. Manfred F. Boemeke, Gerald D. Feldman, and Elisabeth Gläser, Publications of the German Historical Institute (Cambridge: Cambridge University Press, 1998), 535–537.

48. Versailles Treaty, Art. 72; Cornelis Lodewijk and Torley Duwell, eds., *Bulletin de l'institut intermédiaire international*, vol. 9–10 (Hague: H. D. Tjeenk Willink & fils, 1923), 120; Heilperin, *Aspects of the Pathology of Money*, 125–127.

49. André Tardieu, *The Truth about the Treaty* (Indianapolis, IN: Bobbs-Merrill, 1921), 247–248.

50. See the commentary of conservative Louis Marin, the radical socialist Alfred Margaine, and others during the June 22, 1919, session of the budgetary committee of the Chamber of Deputies. Milliès-Lacroix, *Annex*, ANF F 12 8044.

51. David Stevenson, *French War Aims against Germany, 1914–1919* (Oxford: Clarendon Press, 1982), 10–18; Cabanes, *La victoire endeuillée*; Boswell, "From Liberation to Purge Trials," 129–162; Fischer, *Alsace to the Alsatians?*, 128–151.

52. Memorandum from the Director of Commerce of the Directing Council, Emil Hațieganu to the Director of Agriculture, March 22, 1919, ANR Bucharest, Fond Emil Hațieganu, 18/1919.

53. McMeekin, *History's Greatest Heist*, 32.

54. Costin C. Krițescu, *Sistemul bănesc al leului și precursorii lui* (Bucharest: Editura Academiei Republicii Populare Romîne, 1964), 2:288–291; McMeekin, *History's Greatest Heist*, 32; Lucian Boia, *"Germanofilii," Elită intelectuală românească în anii primului război mondial* (Bucharest: Humanitas, 2010), 1–35; Lisa Mayerhofer, "Making Friends and Foes: Occupiers and Occupied in First World War Romania, 1916–1918," in *Untold War, New Perspectives in First World War Studies*, ed. Heather Jones, Jennifer O'Brian, and Christoph Schmidt-Supprian (Leiden: Brill, 2008), 119–150.

55. Krițescu, *Sistemul bănesc*, 2:288–291.

56. Elemér Jakabffy and György Páll, *A bánsági magyarság húsz éve Romániában (1918–1938)* (Budapest: Studium, 1939), 102.

57. Jakabffy and Páll, *A bánsági magyarság húsz éve Romániában*.

58. Peter M. Garber and Michael G. Spencer, *The Dissolution of the Austro-Hungarian Empire: Lessons for Currency Reform*, Essays in International Finance, no. 191 (Princeton, N.J: International Finance Section, Dept. of Economics, Princeton University, 1994), 9–17; Zbigniew Landau, "The Economic Integration of Poland," in *The Reconstruction of Poland, 1914–23*, ed. Paul Latawski (London: Palgrave Macmillan, 1992), 150–151.

59. Garber and Spencer, *The Dissolution of the Austro-Hungarian Empire*, 9–10.

60. Maniu, *Unificarea monetară*, 7.

61. Memorandum to Emil Hațieganu from the Director of Agriculture, March 22, 1919; Lucian Leuștean, *România, Ungaria și Tratatul de la Trianon, 1918–1920* (Iași, Romania: Polirom, 2002), 16–19, 35–37.

62. "Starea de spirit in Transilvania," June 6, 1919, Direcția Generală a Poliției, 3/1919–1920, Consiliul Dirigent, ANR Bucharest.

63. "Cetățeni! Cereți egalizarea coroanei cu leul!," RNA Târgu-Mureș, Direcția Generala a Poliției 4/1920.

64. *Treaty of Peace between the Allied and Associated Powers and Austria* (London: His Majesty's Stationary Office, 1919), 58.

65. Latawski, *Reconstruction of Poland*, 150–151.

66. Latawski, *Reconstruction of Poland*, 101.

67. Treaty of Trianon, Article 189.

68. Decree of the Directing Council on transportation in Transylvania, April 1919, ANR Bucharest, Consiliul Dirigent, 4/1919.

69. Livezeanu, *Cultural Politics*, 129–188; Egry, "Unholy Alliances?"

70. Sándor Pál-Antal, *A marosvásárhelyi utcák, közök, és terek történeti névtára* (Târgu-Mureș, Romania: Editura Mentor, 2007), 10–26.

71. "Starea de spirit in Transilvania," RNA Bucharest, Consoliul Dirigent, Direcția Generală a Poliției 3/1919–1920, p. 29; Vama Santa Mare Papers, RNA Arad, Fond Vama Curtici, 1921/3.

72. Krițescu, *Sistemul Bănesc*, 2:288–291.

73. Krițescu, *Sistemul Bănesc*, 2:288.

74. Krițescu, *Sistemul Bănesc*, 2:288.

75. Alexandru Marghiloman, *Note Politice, 1897–1924* (Bucharest: Institutul de Arte Grafice "Eminescu," 1927), 5:80–81.

76. *Monitorul Oficial* 38 (August 12, 1920): 772; Krițescu, *Sistemul Bănesc*, 2:289.

77. Krițescu, *Sistemul Bănesc*, 2:291.

78. Jakabffy and Páll, *A bánsági magyarság húsz éve Romániában*, 101.

79. *Gazeta Oficială publicată de Consiliul Dirigent al Transilvaniei, Banatului, Maramureșului și părților ungurene*, April 4, nr.22 (1919), quoted in RNA Timiș, Prefectura Jud Timis-Torontal 80/1920.

80. Letter from the director of PHCB Brașov to the director of PHCB Sibiu, March 24, 1919, ANR Bucharest, Consiliul Dirigent, Resortul de Interne, 2/1919.

81. Director of PHCB Brașov to the director of PHCB Sibiu, March 24, 1919.

82. Memorandum, n.d., MNL-OL, Z 223, 24 cs, 71/1.

83. Maniu, *Unificarea monetară*, 16.

84. Office for the Payment of Pensions to the Department of Interior of the Directing Council, Sibiu, September 30, 1919, ANR, Consiliul Dirigent, 1919/3.

85. *Veselia, Revista Umoristica* 26, no. 29 (August 24, 1920): 1.

86. Krițescu, *Sistemul bănesc*, 2:288–291.

87. Garber and Spencer, *Dissolution of the Austro-Hungarian Empire*, 23–24.

88. Krițescu, *Sistemul bănesc*, 2:288.

89. A. Zeuceanu, *La liquidation de la Banque d'Autriche-Hongrie* (Vienne, France : Impr. des Mechitharistes, 1924), 454–456; Garber and Spencer, *Dissolution of the Austro-Hungarian Empire*, 23–24.

90. György Parecz, "A hadikölcsönkötvények beváltása, A magyar postatakarékpénztári betétek kifizetése," in *Gazdasági sérelmeink és kívánságaink* (Dicsőszentmárton, Romania, Erzsébet Ny., 1926), 208.

91. Ágnes Pogány, "A magyarországi közkölcsönök története az első világháború kitörésétől a pénzügyi stabilizációig," *Történelmi Szemle* 44, nos. 1–2 (2002): 65–97; Parecz, "A hadikölcsönkötvények," 208.

92. "Sztrájk a Renner-gyárban," *Ellenzék*, August 19, 1921, 3.

93. Maniu, *Unificarea monetară*, 9; Gheron Netta, *Politica economică ungurească și statele sudestului Europei* (Bucharest: Cartea românească, 1921), 1–8.

94. Bárdi, *Otthon és haza*, 1–105.

95. "Jegyzőkönyv," July 31, 1920, in "Procesele Verbale, 1918–1926," Fond Camera de Comerț și de Industrie, ANR Cluj.

96. Gábor Egry, "The Strangers Within: National Identity, Everyday Encounters and Regionalism in Transylvania, 1918–1944," in *National Identity and Modernity, 1870–1945: Latin America, Southern Europe, East Central Europe*, ed. Viktória Semsey (Budapest: KRE Könyvműhely, L'Harmattan, 2019), 259.

97. Jakabffy and Páll, *A bánsági magyarság húsz éve Romániában*, 101.

98. Maniu, *Unificarea monetară*, 7.

99. Quoted in Jakabffy and Páll, *A bánsági magyarság húsz éve Romániában*, 102.

100. Clark, *Holy Legionary Youth*, 63–65; Máté Rigó, "A felejthető pogrom," *Budapesti Könyvszemle*, Summer 2012, 126–141.

101. E. J. Hobsbawm, *The Age of Extremes: A History of the World, 1914–1991* (New York: Vintage Books, 1996).

102. Zahra, "'Minority Problem.'"

103. Mouré, *Gold Standard Illusion*, 27–49; Barry J. Eichengreen, *Golden Fetters: The Gold Standard and the Great Depression, 1919–1939* (New York: Oxford University Press, 1995), 65–124.

104. Eichengreen, *Golden Fetters*, 29–63.

105. Marguerat, "Les investissements français," 129–131.

106. György Péteri, "Central Bank Diplomacy: Montagu Norman and Central Europe's Monetary Reconstruction after World War I," *Contemporary European History* 1, no. 3 (1992): 233–235; Marguerat, "Les investissements français," 129–131.

107. Marguerat, "Les investissements français," 129–131.

108. Gross, *Export Empire*, 62–64.

109. Mouré, Kenneth, "French money doctors, central banks, and politics in the 1920s" in *Money Doctors: The Experience of International Financial Advising 1850–2000*, edited by Marc Flandreau (London: Routeledge, 2003), 149; Soutou, "Imperialism du pauvre"; Wandycz, *France and Her Eastern Allies*, 3–23.

110. Mouré, "French money doctors," 141–150; Mouré, *Managing the Franc Poincaré*, 1–26.

111. Mouré, "French money doctors," 149; Mouré, *Managing the Franc Poincaré*, 1–26.

112. Henri Mathias Berthelot to "Georges," January 7, 1919, in *General Henri Berthelot and Romania, Mémoires et correspondance*, ed. Glenn Torrey (Boulder, CO: EEM, 1987), 203.

113. Soutou, "Impérialisme du pauvre."

114. Wandycz, *France and Her Eastern Allies*, 3–23; Mouré, "French money doctors," 150.

115. Maier, *Recasting Bourgeois Europe*, 73–76; Kuisel, *Capitalism and the State in Modern France*, 62–71; Richard F. Kuisel, *Ernest Mercier: French Technocrat* (Berkeley: University of California Press, 1967); Slobodian, *Globalists*, 1–90.

116. Máté Rigó, "Transcending the East-West Divide: Towards a European History of Post-1918 Transitions," *Passato e Presente, Rivista di storia contemporanea* 106/2019; Máté Rigó, "Imperial Currencies after the Fall of Empires: The Conversion of the German Paper Mark and the Austro-Hungarian Crown at the End of the First World War," *Central European History* 53, no. 3 (September 2020): 533–563.

117. Judson, *Habsburg Empire*, 442–452.

8. Return Home? Alsatian Industrialists in France and Germany after 1918

1. Fischer, *Alsace to the Alsatians?*, 129–134.

2. Mouré, *Managing the Franc Poincaré*, 1–13; Sauvy and Hirsch, *Histoire économique de la France entre les deux guerres* (Paris: Economica, 1984), 81.

3. Hau, *L'Industrialisation de l'Alsace*, 266–284.

4. Jules-Albert Jaeger, "Les relations avec l'Allemagne et la Sarre," in *L'Alsace depuis son retour à la France. La vie économique: industrie, agriculture, commerce, transports* (Strasbourg: Comité alsacien d'études et d'informations, 1933), 260–263.

5. Versailles Treaty, Article 68, Article 268.

6. "La situation économique en Alsace," [1919], ANF, F 12 8044, 11.

7. Anders E. B. Blomqvist, *Economic Nationalizing in the Ethnic Borderlands of Hungary and Romania: Inclusion, Exclusion and Annihilation in Szatmár/Satu-Mare, 1867–1944* (Stockholm: Stockholm University, 2014), 243–276.

8. Carrol, *Return of Alsace to France*, 118–124.

9. Carrol, *Return of Alsace to France*, 124.

10. "Negociations Franco-Allemand," Minutes of sessions 1 to 39, Baden-Baden, November 5, 1919-July 1, 1920, in Papiers Brugère; AAE 156 QO/2; The delegate of France to the Commission on Reparations to the foreign minister of France, August 12, 1921, AAE, 45RC20 Relations Commerciales (1919–1940) C 22–24.

11. Memorandum, September 18, 1919, ADBR 121 AL 1180.

12. Marcel Koch, "Les courants commerciaux," in *L'Alsace depuis son retour*, 237.

13. Richard S. Fogarty, "The French Empire," in *Empires at War: 1911–1923*, ed. Robert Gerwarth and Erez. Manela (Oxford: Oxford University Press, 2014), 109–129; Bariéty, "Les conséquences."

14. "La situation économique en Alsace," 11.

15. Eugen Jacobi, *Wirtschaftliche Tages- und Zukunfts-Fragen: Vortrag gehalten in der Strassburger Gesellschaft für deutsche Kultur, am 14 März 1918* (Strassburg: Dumont Schauberg, 1918); Ernst Zander, *Der Wirtschaftliche Wiederaufbau von Elass-Lothringen nach dem Kriege* (Strassburg: Karl Trübner 1917), 1–16.

16. Jacques Peirotes, "The Essential Conditions for the Development of the City of Strasbourg," November 17, 1918, ANF, F 12, 8044.

17. Peirotes, "Essential Conditions."

18. Silverman, *Reluctant Union*, 188; Zander, *Der Wirtschaftliche Wiederaufbau*, 21.

19. Gaston Haelling, "Le Port de Strasbourg," in *L'Alsace depuis son retour*, 376.

20. The law was enforced immediately in Alsace-Lorraine as well, even before the peace treaty was handed over to Germany.

21. Maier, *Recasting Bourgeois Europe*, 153–158; Jean Beaudemoulin, *Loi de huit heures, (23 Avril 1919)* (Paris: Dalloz, 1924); Hau, *La Maison De Dietrich*, 151–172.

22. Hau, *La Maison De Dietrich*, 147–154.

23. "Rapport par l'administration Centrale," December 3, 1926, ADD C 43.

24. Gross, *Export Empire*, 139–178.

25. "Conseil de Surveillance" memorandum, December 8, 1922, ADD C 43.

26. Hau, *La Maison De Dietrich*, 163.

27. Hau, *L'Industrialisation de l'Alsace*, 272–274.

28. "Rapport de la Direction Commerciale," December 8, 1922, ADD C 43.

29. Resident general in Rabat, "Note sur le commerce des cottonnades," January 1919, ADBR 121 AL 1283.

30. Jean Marie Mayeur, *La vie politique sous la Troisième République, 1870–1940* (Paris: Éditions du Seuil, 1984), 193–232.

31. Mayeur, *La vie politique sous la Troisième République*.

32. Brocheux and Hémery, *Indochina*, 13–27, 116–180.

33. "Note 3387," Chamber of Commerce and Industry [1921], ADBR 121 AL 1283.

34. "Note 3387."

35. Henri Hauser, "Greater France," *Foreign Affairs* 2, no. 2 (1923): 211–212.

36. Hauser, "Greater France," 224; Friedrich Naumann, *Central Europe* (London: P. S. King & Son, 1916), 1.

37. Charles Regismanset, *L'Exposition national colonial Marseille, 1922* (Paris: Les Imprimeries Françaises Réunies, 1921), 1–9; ADBR 121 AL 1283.

38. Streets-Salter, *World War One in Southeast Asia*, 17–87.

39. Charles Regismanset, *L'Exposition national colonial Marseille, 1922* (Paris: Les Imprimeries Françaises Réunies, 1921), 7.

40. General Commissioner to the Prime Minister of France [1922], ADBR 121 AL 1283.

41. "Note pour Monsieur le Directeur Général," September 26, 1921, ADBR 121 AL 1283.

42. Joseph Chailley-Bert, "Les colonies françaises, conférence donnée en Alsace et en Lorraine en October 1920," 1; ADBR 121 AL 1283.

43. "Note 3387."

44. General Commissioner to Prime Minister of France, ADBR 121 AL 1283; President of the Colmar Chamber of Commerce to the Director of Service and Commerce at the General Commissariat, November 4, 1921, ADBR 121 AL 1283.

45. President of the Colmar Chamber of Commerce to the Director of Service and Commerce at the General Commissariat, November 4, 1921.

46. President of the Colmar Chamber of Commerce to the Director of Service and Commerce at the General Commissariat, November 4, 1921.

47. General Commissioner to Prime Minister of France, ADBR 121 AL 1283.

48. General Commissioner to Prime Minister of France, ADBR 121 AL 1283.

49. Hau, *L'Industrialisation*, 272–274.

50. Hau, *L'Industrialisation*, 272–274.

51. Hau, *L'Industrialisation*, 272–274.

52. Resident general in Rabat, "Note sur le commerce des cottonnades," January 1919, ADBR 121 AL 1283.

53. The resident general commissioner of the French republic in Rabat to the minister of foreign affairs, January 20, 1919, ADBR 121 AL 1283.

54. The resident general commissioner of the French republic in Rabat to the minister of foreign affairs, January 20, 1919.

55. The resident general commissioner of the French republic in Rabat to the minister of foreign affairs, January 20, 1919.

56. Hau, *L'Industrialisation*, 266–267.

57. Hau, *L'Industrialisation*, 266–267.

58. *Übersicht aus Anlass der Fertigstellung Ihres Neuen Verwaltungsgebäudes* (Strasbourg: Adler und Oppenheimer Lederfabrik A. G., 1914).

59. *Mitteilungen des Ausschusses vertriebener Elsass-Lotharinger, Organ des Hilfsbundes für die Elsass-Lotharinger im Reich*, August 14, 1919, 199.

60. Karch, *Nation and Loyalty*, 135–185.

61. "The Factory at Chorzow, Germany v. Poland," *Permanent Court of International Justice*, File E. c. XIII., Docket XIV: I. Judgment No. 13, September 13, 1928, http://www.worldcourts.com/pcij/eng/decisions/1928.09.13_chorzow1.htm; Karch, *Nation and Loyalty*, 135–185.

62. Annemarie Sammartino, *The Impossible Border: Germany and the East, 1914–1922* (Ithaca, NY: Cornell University Press, 2010), 97–99.

63. Gross, *Export Empire*, 220–252.

64. Constantin Buchet, *România și Republica de la Weimar 1919–1933: Economie, diplomație și geopolitică* (Bucharest: All Ed., 2001), 93–110.

65. Buchet, *România și Republica de la Weimar*, 93–110.

66. Gross, *Export Empire*, 68–71.

67. Keynes, *Economic Consequences of Peace*, 71; Norman A. Graebner and Edward M. Bennett, *The Versailles Treaty and Its Legacy: The Failure of the Wilsonian Vision* (New York: Cambridge University Press, 2011).

68. Versailles Treaty, Article 297, (i).

69. Gläser, "Making of the Economic Peace," 392–393; Trachtenberg, *Reparation in World Politics*, viii–ix, 1–45.

70. *Bericht über das 19. Geschäftsjahr*, 4, https://zbw.eu/beta/p20/company/41419/about.de.html.

71. *Bericht über das 19. Geschäftsjahr*, 4; ZBW database.

72. *Bericht über das 24. Geschäftsjahr*, 1–8; ZBW database.

73. *Bericht über das 13. Geschäftsjahr*, 1–6; ZBW database.

74. *Bericht über das 25. Geschäftsjahr*, 1–6; ZBW database.

75. Hans-Joachim Braun, *The German Economy in the Twentieth Century* (London: Routledge, 1990), 33–63.

76. *Geschäftsbericht für das 20., 21. und 22. Geschäftsjahr*, BArch R/3118/31 Zulassungstelle a.d. Berliner Börse, Adler und Oppenheimer Lederfabrik.

77. *Geschäftsbericht für das 24. Geschäftsjahr*, 1–8 in ZBW database.

78. Niall Ferguson, "Constraints and Room for Manoeuvre in the German Inflation of the Early 1920s," *Economic History Review* 49, no. 4 (1996): 635–666.

79. Quoted in Ferguson, "Constraints and Room for Manoeuvre," 637.

80. Quoted in Gerald D. Feldman, *The Great Disorder: Politics, Economics, and Society in the German Inflation, 1914–1924* (New York: Oxford University Press, 1993), 858.

81. Zweig, *World of Yesterday*, 315.

82. *Bericht über das 26. Geschäftsjahr*, 1–4.

83. *Bericht über das 26. Geschäftsjahr*, 1–4.

84. Berkes, "League of Nations and the Optants Dispute."

85. *Geschäftsbericht für das 20., 21. und 22. Geschäftsjahr.*

86. Werner Wittich, "L'Alsace économique de 1913 à 1933," in *L'Alsace depuis son retour*, 21–22.

87. François Uberfill, "Le sort des populations après 1918. Commissions de triage, expulsions, épuration des administrations et des institutions scolaires et universitaires," *Revue d'Alsace*, no. 144 (November 15, 2018): 107–110.

88. Wittich, "L'Alsace économique," 37; Balázs Trencsényi, *The Politics of "National Character": A Study in Interwar East European Thought* (New York: Routledge, 2012), 1–19.

89. Alan Kramer, *Dynamic of Destruction: Culture and Mass Killing in the First World War* (Oxford: Oxford University Press, 2007), 97–107.

9. A Marriage of Convenience? Austro-Hungarian Industrialists in Greater Romania

1. Alice Teichova, Herbert Matis, and Jaroslav Pátek, "Introduction," in *Economic Change and the National Question in Twentieth-Century Europe*, ed. Alice Teichova (Cambridge:Cambridge University Press, 2000), 1–7.

2. Keynes, *Economic Consequences of the Peace*, 273.

3. Keynes, *Economic Consequences of the Peace*, 273.

4. Keynes, *Economic Consequences of the Peace*, 266.

5. Albert Apponyi, "On the Transylvanian Question," in *The Hungarian Peace Negotiations*, ed. E. Cholnoky (Budapest, 1921), 1:136–137.

6. Sándor Keszi and Hillel Kohn, *Exploatarea capitalistă la "Dermata"* (Bucharest: Editura de Stat pentru Literatură Ştiinţifică, 1954).

7. Cornel Ban, "Beyond Anticommunism: The Fragility of Class Analysis in Romania," *East European Politics and Societies and Cultures* 29, no. 3 (August 2015): 643.

8. Similar to the collective memory of 1914; Christopher M. Clark, *The Sleepwalkers: How Europe Went to War in 1914* (New York: Harper, 2013), xxv.

9. Lucian Boia, *România: Ţară de frontieră a Europei* (Bucharest: Humanitas, 2002); Bogdan Murgescu, *România şi Europa: Acumularea decalajelor economice: 1500–2010* (Iaşi, Romania: Polirom, 2010), 212–213.

10. Romsics, *Erdély elvesztése, 1918–1947.*

11. Bogdan Murgescu, "Lucian Boia, De ce este România altfel," in Vintilă Mihăilescu, ed., *De ce este România astfel?: avatarurile excepţionalismului românesc* (Iaşi: Polirom, 2017), 12.

12. Murgescu, "Lucian Boia," 12.

13. Iván T. Berend, *Decades of Crisis: Central and Eastern Europe before World War II* (Berkeley: University of California Press, 1998), 243–244.

14. Murgescu, *România şi Europa*, 234.

15. Lucian Boia, *Cum s-a românizat România* (Bucharest: Humanitas, 2015), 83–87; Vladimir Solonari, *Purifying the Nation: Population Exchange and Ethnic Cleansing in Nazi-Allied Romania* (Washington, DC: Woodrow Wilson Center Press, 2010).

16. Attila Seres and Gábor Egry, eds., *Magyar levéltári források az 1930. évi Romániai népszámlálás nemzetiségi adatsorainak értékeléséhez* (Kolozsvár: NKI, 2011).

17. Boia, *Cum s-a românizat*, 56.

18. Rogers Brubaker, *Ethnicity without Groups* (Cambridge, MA: Harvard University Press, 2004), 8.

19. Brubaker, *Ethnicity without Groups*, 8.

20. Báthory, *Societățile carbonifere*, 10.

21. Anders E. B. Blomqvist, *Economic Nationalizing in the Ethnic Borderlands of Hungary and Romania: Inclusion, Exclusion and Annihilation in Szatmár/Satu-Mare, 1867–1944* (Stockholm: Stockholm University, 2014), 258.

22. Victor I. Slăvescu, *Organizația de credit a României* (Bucharest: Cartea Românească, 1922); Elemér Gyárfás, *Románia hitelszervezetei s az erdélyi magyar pénzintézetek* (Lugos, Romania: Husvéth és Hoffer Könyvnyomdája, 1924), 21–22.

23. Slăvescu quoted in Gyárfás, *Románia hitelszervezetei*, 21–22.

24. DJAN Timiș, Banca Timișoarei "1920/1"; Ioan Boambă, *Banque Marmorosch Blank and Co., Société Anonyme, 1848–1923* (Bucharest: Cultura Natională, 1924), 76–92.

25. "Tabloul Magazinelor," DJAN Cluj, Clujana, 175/1941, p. 27.

26. Zahra, *Kidnapped Souls*, 106–168; Timothy Snyder, *The Reconstruction of Nations Poland, Ukraine, Lithuania, Belarus, 1569–1999* (New Haven, CT: Yale University Press, 2003), 133–153.

27. Ivo Banač, *The National Question in Yugoslavia: Origins, History, Politics*, (Ithaca, NY: Cornell University Press, 1993), 208–222.

28. Hunyadi Attila Gábor, *Cooperative Networks in Transylvania Belonging to Hungary and Romania* (Saarbrücken: Lap Lambert, 2016); Gaucsík, *A jog erejével*, 11–74; Banač, *The National Question in Yugoslavia*, 208–222.

29. Nassim Nicholas Taleb, *Antifragile: Things That Gain from Disorder* (New York: Random House, 2012), 41–80.

30. Gábor Egry, *Etnicitás, identitás, politika, Magyar kisebbségek nacionalizmus és regionalizmus között Romániában és Csehszlovákiában, 1918–1944* (Budapest: Napvilág, 2015).

31. Victor Axenciuc, *La formation et le développement du marché intérieur moderne en Roumanie: Etude et séries statistiques à long terme: (1860–1947)* (Bucharest: Academie Roumaine, 2008), 62–65.

32. Murgescu, *România și Europa*, 214–221.

33. "Erdélyi földgázkincs," *Honi Ipar*, September 1, 1940, 7.

34. "Külföldi részvénytársaságok, " in *Magyar Pénzügyi Compass, 1923–24*, ed. Gyula Kormos (Budapest: Apollo, 1925), 703.

35. Nándor Bárdi, Csilla Fedinec, and László Szarka, *Minority Hungarian Communities in the Twentieth Century* (Boulder, CO: Social Science Monographs, 2011).

36. László Biró, "A Vajdaság a két világháború között: Adalékok a Jugoszláv gazdasági integráció hatásaihoz," in *Vojvođanski prostor u kontekstu Evropske istorije*, ed. Gavrilović Vladan and Boškov Svetozar (Novi Sad, Serbia: Filozofski fakultet u Novom Sadu, 2014), 65–76; Banač, *National Question in Yugoslavia*, 224–225.

37. Gaucsík, *A jog erejével*, 14–18.

38. I. Teodorescu, "Industria în România Mare, Studiu rezumativ al anchetei industriale din 1920," *Buletinul Statistic*, xl, no. 4 (1922): 3–19; I. Teodorescu, "Societăţile pe acţiuni din nouile teritorii, Studiu statistic," *Buletinul Statistic* 1 (1926): 3–55; Ernő Bereczky, ed., *Románia új behozatali vámtarifája, Fém és textilipari cikkek* (Cluj: Lepage, 1926); Axenciuc, *La formation*, 76; Báthory, *Societăţile carbonifere*, 6.

39. "Industria tăbăceriei," *Buletinul Statistic* 1 (1924): 12–13.

40. Báthory, *Societăţile carbonifere*, 9.

41. Zsolt K. Lengyel, *A kompromisszum keresése: Tanulmányok a 20. századi transzszilvanizmus korai történetéhez* (Csíkszereda, Romania: Pro-Print, 2007).

42. Clark, *Holy Legionary Youth*, 7.

43. Elemér Gyárfás, "Az Erdélyi Bankszindikátus megalakulása, helyzete és törekvései," November 4, 1923, MNL-OL K 437–4. csomó 1924-1-342. f. 4.; MNL-OL, K 610. 25. csomó.

44. Gyárfás, "Az Erdélyi Bankszindikátus megalakulása."

45. Gyárfás, "Az Erdélyi Bankszindikátus megalakulása."

46. Gyárfás, *Románia hitelszervezetei*, 21–22.

47. Ștefan Zeletin quoted in Cristian Preda, "From the 'Land of the Donkeys' to the 'Economic Island between the Danube, Dniester, and the Tisza,'" in *Moral, Legal, and Political Values in Romanian Culture*, ed. Mihaela Czobor-Lupp and J. Stefan Lupp (Washington, DC: CRVP, 2002), 241; Daniel Chirot, "A Romanian Prelude to Contemporary Debates about Development," *Review (Fernand Braudel Center)* 2, no. 1 (1978): 115–123.

48. Slobodian, *Globalists*, 27–58.

49. Ștefan Zeletin, *Neoliberalismul: Studii asupra istoriei și politicii burgheziei române* (Bucharest: Editura Nemira, 1997), 350.

50. Oszkár Jászi, *The United States of Europe, Európai Egyesült Államok* (Budapest: Hungarian Europe Society, Magyarországi Európa Társaság: Carneades Bt., 2006).

51. Judson, *Habsburg Empire*, 442–452.

52. Soutou, "Impérialisme du pauvre"; Wandycz, *France and Her Eastern Allies*, 3–23.

53. Mihaïl Manoilesco, *L'Equilibre économique européen: The European economic equilibrium* (Bucharest: Impr. Nat., 1931), 7.

54. Trencsényi, *Politics of "National Character,"* 43–45.

55. Trencsényi, *Politics of "National Character,"* 44.

56. "A kolozsvári Dorna-gyár [. . .]," *Erdélyi Futár*, April 9, 1927, 12.

57. Gyula Horváth, ed., *Dél-Erdély és Bánság* (Pécs, Hungary: Dialóg–Campus Kiadó, 2009), 82–83.

58. Gyárfás, "Az erdélyi románok hitelszervezetei," 78.

59. Gyárfás, "Az erdélyi románok hitelszervezetei," 78.

60. "Magyar-Román kereskedelmi kamara," MOL K 269, Pénzügyminisztérium 416. csomó 467. tétel; Ignác Romsics, *Helyünk és sorsunk a Duna-medencében* (Budapest: Osiris, 1996), 164–167; *Magyar Statisztikai Szemle* (Budapest: Központi Statisztikai Hivatal, 1928), 228.

61. Blomqvist, *Economic Nationalizing*, 243–273.

62. Zoltán Gál, *The Banking Functions of the Hungarian Urban Network in the Early 20th Century* (Pécs, Hungary: Centre for Regional Studies, 2006), 42–54.

63. Blomqvist, *Economic Nationalizing*, 272–276.

64. Horia Maniu, *Unificarea monetară* (Bucharest: Cartea Românească, 1924), 9.

65. Bárdi, *Otthon és haza*, 56.

66. "Külföldi részvénytársaságok," in *Magyar Pénzügyi Compass, 1923–24*, ed. Gyula Kormos (Budapest: Apollo, 1925), 743.

67. "Külföldi részvénytársaságok," 743.

68. "Külföldi részvénytársaságok," 744.

69. "Külföldi részvénytársaságok," 744.

70. Emil Petrichevich Horváth, *Jelentés az Országos Menekültügyi Hivatal négy évi működéséről* (Budapest: Pesti Könyvnyomda Rt., 1924), 1–37.

71. "Refugees" database, Trianon 1920–2020 research project, last accessed October 16, 2020, https://trianon100.hu/menekultek.

72. "Külföldi részvénytársaságok," 722–743.

73. "Külföldi részvénytársaságok," 722–743.

74. Gross, *Export Empire*, 62–64.

75. M. F. to Gyula Boros, November 1, 1924, in "Date monografice," 6/1924, Clujana, DJAN Cluj, p. 60.

76. "Adolf Renner," July 26, 1919, ANR Bucharest, Fond Consiliul Dirigent, Admin. Gen. 9/1920.

77. Memorandum to minister of industry and commerce [Alexander Averescu] [1921], Clujana, 4/1922.

78. Dezső Laky, *Csonka-Magyarország megszállásának közgazdasági kárai* (Budapest: Eggenberger, 1923), 1–32.

79. Philip Cottrell, "Central Bank Co-operation and Romanian Stabilization," in *Business and Politics in Europe, 1900–1970: Essays in Honour of Alice Teichova*, ed. Terry Gourvish (Cambridge: Cambridge University Press, 2003), 107.

80. Attila Gidó, *Úton: Erdélyi zsidó társadalom- és nemzetépítési kísérletek (1918–1940)*, (Csíkszereda, Romania, Pro-Print Könyvkiadó, 2009) 27–49, 470, 475.

81. Daniel Lőwy, *A Kálváriától a tragédiáig: Kolozsvár zsidó lskosságának története* (Kolozsvár: Koinónia, 2005), 431.

82. "Mit kell tennünk erdélyieknek, 1922-ben?" *Napkelet* 24 (1921): 1473; literally, *napkelet* is archaic for "sunrise" and "east."

83. *Riport Újság*, July 10, 1919, 4–5.

84. Péter Ruffy, "Kun Béla erdélyi rokonai elmondják," *Brassói Lapok*, October 22, 1939, 12.

85. Ruffy, "Kun Béla erdélyi rokonai elmondják," 12.

86. Hanebrink, *A Specter Haunting Europe*, 118.

87. Ferenc Kovács, "Hol kukorékol az aranykakas 3," *Romániai Magyar Szó*, November 18–19, 1995, 4.

88. "Szindikátusi szerződés," 6/1924, DJAN Cluj, Fond Clujana.

89. Bárdi, *Otthon és haza*, 106.

90. "Végrendelet," April 19, 1932, DJAN Cluj, Fond Clujana, Secretariat 8/1932.

91. Samu Borovszky, ed., *Magyarország vármegyéi és városai, Torontál vármegye* (Budapest: O.M.T, 1912), 244.

92. "Jegyzőkönyv, Korber féle kalapgyár alakuló ülése," June 5, 1924, Clujana 6/1924.

93. David Sorkin, *Jewish Emancipation: A History across Five Centuries* (Princeton, NJ: Princeton University Press, 2019), 284–285.

94. "Dovadă," October 3, 1924, Clujana 6/1924.

95. Renner tannery to lawyer Alexandru Bodea, February 26, 1923, Fond Clujana, Acte privitor la urcarea capitolului, 4/1922.

96. Memorandum to minister of industry and commerce [Alexander Averescu] [1921], Clujana, 4/1922.

97. Note "Vasile Pop," Fond Clujana, 4/1922, p. 14.

98. Note no. 164 of Titu Popescu to Renner tannery, July 27, 1921, Fond Clujana, 4/1922, 41; "Order," *Gazeta Oficială*, January 17, 1921, 1.

99. Note no. 164 of Titu Popescu to Renner tannery, July 27, 1921, 41; Cluj Commerce Inspection Authority to minister of industry and commerce, [1921], Fond Clujana, 4/1922, 35–37.

100. Note no. 164 of Titu Popescu to Renner tannery, July 27, 1921.

101. Note no. 164 of Titu Popescu to Renner tannery, July 27, 1921.

102. Note no. 164 of Titu Popescu to Renner tannery, July 27, 1921.

103. Note no. 167 of T. Popescu to Renner tannery, July 29, 1921, Fond Clujana, 4/1922, 43.

104. Note no. 167 of T. Popescu to Renner tannery, July 29, 1921, 43.

105. Mihail Manoilescu, *Memorii* (Bucharest: Ed. Enciclopedică, 1993), 1:1–34.

106. Egry, "Unholy Alliances?"

107. C. Bebeș, Director of Foreign Exchange section at Ministry of Industry and Commerce, to Cluj Commerce Inspector, August 8, 1921, Fond Clujana, 4/1922, pp. 15–16.

108. "Visite de M. Lacombe," January 14, 1920, AAE 110CPCOM/98 P/17450.

109. "Statistică," 1921, Fond Clujana, DJAN Cluj.

110. "Statistică," 1921.

111. "Lakásügy," *Erdélyi Munkás*, October 2, 1920, 3.

112. Gábor Egry, "A Crossroad of Parallels: Regionalism and Nation-Building in Transylvania in the First Half of the Twentieth Century," in *Hungary and Romania beyond National Narratives, Comparisons and Entanglements*, ed. Anders Blomqvist, Constantin Iordachi, and Balázs Trencsényi (New York: Peter Lang, 2013), 239–276.

113. Case, *Between States*, 97–149.

114. Balázs Trencsényi, *A nép lelke: Nemzetkarakterológiai viták Kelet-Európában* (Budapest: Argumentum, 2011).

115. Károly Molter, *Metania R.t.* (Budapest: Athaeneum, 1929), 236.

116. Quoted in György Bálint, "Metania R.t.," *Nyugat* 14, no. 1 (1931): 58.

117. Molter, *Metania R.t.*, 241.

118. Emil Kolozsvári Grandpierre, *A rosta* (Budapest: Magvető, 1985).

119. Grandpierre, *A rosta*, 12.

120. Ernő Ligeti, *Föl a bakra* (Cluj-Kolozsvár: Lapkiadó és Nyomdai Műintézet, 1925), 36.

121. Ligeti, *Föl a bakra*.

122. Quoted in Ivan Sanders, "'Transylvanism' and Jewish Consciousness," in *Studia Judaica*, ed. Ladislau Gyémánt (Cluj-Napoca: Ed. Sincron, 1996), 5:65.

123. "A nagyváradi művésznő és a kolozsvári urak," *Ellenőr*, July 18, 1927, 30.

124. "Megperdült a dob Hecht Richárd villája felett," *Brassói Lapok*, December 9, 1929, 7.

125. "Rennerné Halász Baba," *Keleti Újság*, January 17, 1937, 9.

126. "Törzslap, Dr. Farkas Mózes," Fond Clujana, Serviciul Secretariat, 37 / 1943, p. 51.

127. "Törzslap, Dr. Farkas Mózes," p. 51.

128. "Törzslap, Dr. Farkas Mózes," p. 51.

129. "Törzslap, Dr. Farkas Mózes," p. 51.

130. "Végrendelet," April 19, 1932, DJAN Cluj, Fond Clujana, Secretariat 8 / 1932.

131. Pál Ranschburg, "Orvosi bizonyítvány," February 4, 1933, Clujana 37 / 1943.

132. Ranschburg, "Orvosi bizonyítvány."

133. "Véghatározat," Kolozsvár sz. k. v. Főkapitányi Hivatal, August 15, 1918, Fond Clujana, 1 / 1920, p. 20.

134. "A radikális párt kongresszusa," *Világ*, October 15, 1918, 7–9.

135. "Sztrájk a Renner-gyárban," *Ellenzék*, August 19, 1921, 3.

136. Clark, *Holy Legionary Youth*, 4.

137. Livezeanu, *Cultural Politics*, 246.

138. Clark, *Holy Legionary Youth*, 7.

139. Clark, *Holy Legionary Youth*, 63–121.

140. "Román diákzavargások" dosszié, MNL-OL, K 610, 58. csomó, 1–3.

141. ANR, Bucharest, Ministry of Justice (Wallachia and Moldova) 71 / 1927.

142. Teréz Mózes, *Váradi zsidók* (Oradea, Romania: Literátor, 1995), 142–143.

143. *Monitorul Oficial*, 1927. december 18., 22; "Román diákzavargások," 5.

144. Rigó, "A felejthető pogrom."

145. *Monitorul Oficial*, 1927. december 18., 22.

146. *Monitorul Oficial*, 1927. december 18., 22.

147. Dezső Schön, "A váradi zsidók útja," in *A tegnap városa: A nagyváradi zsidóság emlékkönyve*, ed. Dezső Schön, Mose Heller, Rubinstein Sándor, Ödön Grossman, József Gréda and Ottó Rappaport (Tel-Aviv: Nagyváradról Elszármazottak Egyesülete Izráelben, 1981), 121–123.

148. William L. Culbertson to the Secretary of State, December 20, 1927, in *Papers Relating to the Foreign Relations of the United States* (*FRUS*), 1927 (Washington, DC: Government Printing Office, 1942), 3:641–642; "Thirty More Are Hurt in Romanian Riot," *New York Times*, December 11, 1927, 13; "American Reported Hurt in Romanian Riot, Indignation in Hungary," *Washington Post*, December 10, 1927, 3; "A váradi mártírok," *Egyenlőség*, December 10, 1927, 3; Jenő Fráter, "Az erdélyi zsidók hazafiassága," *Egyenlőség*, December 10, 1927, 3; MNL-OL, K 610, 56. csomó / d.1 / VI.

149. "Manifestații," Fond Prefecture Jud. Bihor, 83 / 1927–1928, RNA Bihor.

150. The minister in Rumania (Culbertson) to the Secretary of State, Bucharest, February 18, 1928, 371.1113, Keller, W. N. / 7, *FRUS*, 1927, 3:650.

151. "Manifestății."

152. Gábor Egry, "Navigating the Straits: Changing Borders, Changing Rules and Practices of Ethnicity and Loyalty in Romania after 1918," *Hungarian Historical Review: New Series of Acta Historica Academiae Scientiarum Hungaricae* 2, no. 3 (2013): 449–476.

153. "A radikális párt kongresszusa," *Világ*, October 15, 1918, 9.

154. "Végrendelet," April 19, 1932, DJAN Cluj, Fond Clujana, Secretariat 8/1932, pp. 1–7.

155. "Végrendelet," April 19, 1932, 1–7.

156. "Végrendelet," April 19, 1932, 1–7.

157. "Pótvégrendelet," April 19, 1932, DJAN Cluj, Fond Clujana, Secretariat 8/1932.

158. "Anhauch lovag [. . .]," *Transilvaniai Futár* 11 (1937): 30.

159. Balázs Ablonczy, *A visszatért Erdély, 1940–1944* (Budapest: Jaffa, 2011).

160. "Hagyatéktárgyalási jegyzőkönyv," papers of notary public Dr. Gyula Deák, Kolozsvár, 921/1941, Clujana, DJAN Cluj; "Pótvégrendelet," April 19, 1932.

161. Éva Kovács, "Overcoming History through Trauma. The Hungarian Historikerstreit," *European Review* 24, no. 4 (October 2016): 523–34.

Epilogue

1. Randall Morck, *The Global History of Corporate Governance: An Introduction* (Cambridge, MA: National Bureau of Economic Research, 2005), 1–7.

2. Zahra, *Great Departure*; Hubert, *Deutschland im Wandel*, 9–19, 68–81.

3. David S. Landes, "Bleichröders and Rothschilds: The Problem of Continuity in the Family Firm," *Family Business Review* 6, no. 1 (March 1, 1993): 85–101; Landes, *Dynasties*, 261–273.

4. Tara Zahra, "Imagined Noncommunities: National Indifference as a Category of Analysis," *Slavic Review* 69, no. 1 (2010): 93–119; Maarten Van Ginderachter and Jon E. Fox, "Introduction, National Indifference and the History of Nationalism in Modern Europe," in *National Indifference and the History of Nationalism in Modern Europe*, ed. Maarten Van Ginderachter and Jon E. Fox (New York: Routledge, 2019), 1–14.

5. Nancy L. Green, *The Limits of Transnationalism* (Chicago: University of Chicago Press, 2019), 2–3.

6. David Harvey, *Spaces of Capital: Towards a Critical Geography* (Edinburgh: Edinburgh University Press, 2019), 303–338.

7. "Foreign Direct Investment, Net Outflows (% of GDP) - France," World Bank, accessed April 26, 2021, https://data.worldbank.org/indicator/BM.KLT.DINV.WD.GD.ZS?locations=FR&view=map; Some exceptions include Sandu, *La Grande Roumanie*.

8. Kovács, "Overcoming History through Trauma."

9. Kovács, "Overcoming History through Trauma."

10. Joseph Stieglitz, "Of the 1%, by the 1%, for the 1%," *Vanity Fair*, May 2011, https://www.vanityfair.com/news/2011/05/top-one-percent-201105?currentPage=all; Thomas Piketty, *Capital in the Twenty-First Century* (Cambridge, MA: Belknap Press of Harvard University Press, 2014); "The 1% Solution," *The Economist*, April 15, 2011, https://www.economist.com/democracy-in-america/2011/04/15/the-1-solution.

11. Gábor Scheiring, *The Retreat of Liberal Democracy: Authoritarian Capitalism and the Accumulative State in Hungary* (Cham: Palgrave Macmillan, 2020), 217.

12. Leszek Balcerowicz, *Post-Communist Transition: Some Lessons* (London: Institute of Economic Affairs, 2002), 26.

13. Hau, *La Maison De Dietrich*, 213–217.

14. Harold James, *The Nazi Dictatorship and the Deutsche Bank* (Cambridge: Cambridge University Press, 2004), 76–82.

15. Karl Adler to the mayor of Strasbourg, March 29, 1939, in SB AVCUS, 77 MW 251, Fondation Adler.

16. Zoltán Vági, László Csősz, and Gábor Kádár, *The Holocaust in Hungary: Evolution of a Genocide* (Budapest: AltaMira Press, 2013), 3–16.

17. Timothy Snyder, *Bloodlands: Europe between Hitler and Stalin* (New York: Basic Books, 2010), 1–20.

18. Snyder, *Bloodlands*, vii–xix.

19. Jean Daltroff, "Les Adler et Oppenheimer," *Revue d'Alsace*, no. 136 (October 1, 2010): 178.

20. Daisy Chorin-Strasser and Ferenc Chorin, *Az Andrássy úttól a Park Avenue-ig: Fejezetek Chorin Ferenc életéből (1879–1964)* (Budapest: Osiris, 1999), 143–168.

21. "Document No. 24, Transcript of Romanian Workers' Party Session Regarding the Fate of Sovroms [Excerpts]," in *Soviet Occupation of Romania, Hungary, and Austria 1944/45–1948/49*, ed. Csaba Békés, László Borhi, Peter Ruggenthaler, and Ottmar Trașcă (Budapest: Central European University Press, 2015), 138–141.

22. *A budapesti egységes hálózat betűrendes távbeszélő névsora, 1948 március* (Budapest: M. Postavezérigazgatóság, 1948), 165.

23. György Konrád and Iván Szelényi, *The Intellectuals on the Road to Class Power* (New York: Harcourt Brace Jovanovich, 1979).

24. Zsuzsanna Renner, oral history interview by the author, Cluj-Napoca, December 19, 2017.

25. Renner, interview; Nagy, "Egy kolozsvári nagyüzem múltjából."

26. Judt, *Postwar*, 203.

27. Judt, *Postwar*, 453–636; Stefano Bottoni, *Long Awaited West: Eastern Europe since 1944* (Bloomington: Indiana University Press, 2017), 131–166.

28. Daniel Chirot, ed., *The Origins of Backwardness in Eastern Europe: Economics and Politics from the Middle Ages until the Early Twentieth Century* (Berkeley: University of California Press, 1989).

29. Gyáni Gábor, *Történészdiskurzusok* (Budapest: L'Harmattan, 2002).

30. Richard Joseph Golsan, *Vichy's Afterlife: History and Counterhistory in Postwar France* (Lincoln: University of Nebraska Press, 2000), 124–142; Gábor Gyáni, *Nemzeti vagy transznacionális történelem* (Budapest: Kalligram, 2018).

31. "#2057 [wealthiest in the world] Lorinc Meszaros," *Forbes*, accessed August 31, 2019, https://www.forbes.com/profile/lorinc-meszaros/#5540bd1f4868.

32. "Prévu sans voiture, l'écoquartier des Tanneries est aussi sans ligne de bus," *Rue89 Strasbourg* (blog), January 10, 2019, https://www.rue89strasbourg.com/sans-voiture-lecoquartier-des-tanneries-est-aussi-sans-ligne-de-bus-147074.

33. "La Maison Rouge: 700 ans et une histoire controversée," *France 3 Grand Est*, accessed September 2, 2019, https://france3-regions.francetvinfo.fr/grand-est/alsace/maison-rouge-700-ans-histoire-controversee-1284613.html.

34. Jean-Noël Grandhomme and Francis Grandhomme, *Les Alsaciens-Lorrains dans la Grande Guerre* (Strasbourg: Nuée bleue, 2013); Jean-Noël Grandhomme, *La Première Guerre Mondiale en France*, Mémoires de l'histoire (Rennes: Ouest France, 2002). Exceptions include Uberfill, *La société strasbourgeoise*.

35. A welcome exception to the silencing of expulsions is the Council of Europe's website: "Une Ambassade chargée d'histoire," Représentation Permanente de la France

auprès du Conseil de l'Europe, accessed August 31, 2019, https://conseil-europe.delegfrance.org/Histoire-de-la-Representation-permanente.

36. JP Géné, "Le Sésame de Florange," *Le Monde*, December 21, 2012, https://www.lemonde.fr/m-styles/article/2012/12/21/le-sesame-de-florange_1808408_4497319.html; David Bradby, *Modern French Drama, 1940–1980* (Cambridge: Cambridge University Press, 1984), 238–240; Jean-Paul Wenzel, *Far from Hagondange*, trans. Bernard Bloch (New York: Ubu Repertory Theater, 1984).

37. Géné, "Le Sésame de Florange."

38. "Présidentielle 2017," *Le Monde*, https://www.lemonde.fr/alsace-champagne-ardenne-lorraine/moselle,57/hagondange,57283/elections/presidentielle-2017/.

39. "Call 112," Societatea Complexul Energetic Hunedoara, accessed May 28, 2016, http://www.cenhd.ro; Ilinca Păun Constantinescu, "Shrinking Cities in Romania: Former Mining Cities in Valea Jiului," *Built Environment* 38, no. 2 (2012): 214–228.

40. "Notice of Intent in Relation to Testing the Interest of Potential Investors on the Privatization of Complexul Energetic Hunedoara Company S.A. [*sic*]," Societatea Complexul Energetic Hunedoara.

41. Daniel Ionascu, "Vin americanii: Compania Quintana Minerals vrea să participe la privatizarea Complexului Energetic Hunedoara, care extrage huilă în Valea Jiului," *Adevărul*, December 15, 2014, http://adevarul.ro/economie/afaceri/vin-americanii-compania-quintana-minerals-vrea-participe-privatizarea-complexului-energetic-hunedoara-extrage-huila-valea-jiului-1_548ec7e2448e03c0fdc486ea/index.html.

42. The information referred to the alleged interest of the Vancouver-based Quintana Minerals Corporation in acquiring the Jiu valley's coal mines and power plants; D. Ionascu, "Cum a bâjbâit statul timp de 15 ani încercând să salveze Valea Jiului," *Adevărul*, April 26, 2015, http://adevarul.ro/economie/stiri-economice/analizA-bajbait-statul-timp-15-ani-incercand-salveze-valea-jiului-1_553cd6b3cfbe376e35914506/index.html.

43. Delia Bîrla, "Fabrica de încălțăminte Clujana la un pas de a fi închisă," *Presa Locală* (blog), March 23, 2018, https://www.presalocala.com/2018/03/23/fabrica-de-incaltaminte-clujana-la-un-pas-de-a-fi-inchisa/.

44. Andreea Laza, "Is Cluj-Napoca the IT Capital of Romania?," *Human Direct*, September 27, 2018, https://www.humandirect.eu/blog/2018/9/is-cluj-napoca-the-it-capital-of-romania.

Bibliography

Archives

Austria

Österreichisches Staatsarchiv (ÖeStA), Vienna

France

Archives des Affaires étrangères (AAE)
Archives de la Bibliothèque de Documentation International Contemporaine Nanterre (BDIC)
Archives départementales du Bas Rhin, Strasbourg (ADBR)
Archives National, Paris (ANF)
Archives de la ville et de la eurométropole de Strasbourg, Strasbourg (AVES)
Archives of the Association De Dietrich, Reichshoffen (ADD)
Service des archives économiques et financières, Savigny-le-Temple (SAEF)
Service Historique de la Défense, Vincennes (SHD)

Germany

Archives of the Wissenschaftliches Instititut der Elsass-Lothringer im Reich, Frankfurt am Main (AWIEL)
Politisches Archiv des Auswärtigen Amts, Berlin (PAAA)
Das Bundesarchiv, Berlin (BArch)

Hungary

Budapest Főváros Levéltára (BFL)
Magyar Nemzeti Levéltár, Budapest (MNL-OL)

Romania

Arhive Naţionale Istorice Centrale, Bucharest (ANIC)
Direcția Județeană a Arhivelor Naționale, Cluj (DJAN Cluj)
Direcția Județeană a Arhivelor Naționale, Arad, (DJAN Arad)
Direcția Județeană a Arhivelor Naționale, Timiș (DJAN Timiș)

Switzerland

League of Nations Archives (LoNa), Geneva, Switzerland

Newspapers and Periodicals

8 Órai Újság
A Bánya
Acta Historica Academiae Scientiarum Hungaricae
Adevărul
American Historical Review
American Jewish Year Book
American Journal of International Law
Annales de demographie historique
Annales de Géographie
Austrian History Yearbook
Az Est
Bányászati és Kohászati Lapok
Borsszem Jankó
Bőripari Szemle
Brassói Lapok
Budapesti Szemle
Built Environment
Buletinul Statistic
Bulletin de l'Institut intermédiaire international
Bulletin de la Société industrielle de l'Est
Bulletin de Renseignements
Bulletin, Société des Sciences, Agriculture et Arts de la Basse-Alsace
Business History
California Law Review
Central European History
Comparative Politics
Contemporary European History
Deutsche Außenpolitik
East European Politics and Societies and Cultures
Economic History Review
Egyenlőség
Egyetem, a Kolozsvári Magyar Királyi Ferencz József-Tudományegyetem Társadalmi és Tudományos Közlönye
Ellenőr
Ellenzék
Encyclopédie de l'Alsace
Erdélyi Közgazdaság
Erdélyi Munkás
Ezredvég
Az Est
Ethnopolitics
European Review
European Review of History - Revue Européenne d'histoire
Family Business Review
Forbes

Foreign Affairs
France-Europe Orient
Francia: Forschungen zur westeuropäischen Geschichte
Frankfurter Zeitung
French Historical Studies
Független Magyarország
Gazeta Oficială publicată de Consiliul Dirigent al Transilvaniei, Banatului, Maramureșului și părților ungurene
Geschichte und Gesellschaft
Guerres mondiales et conflits contemporains
História
Historical Journal
Honi Ipar
Hungarian Historical Review
Huszadik Század
Illkirch-Grafenstadener Anzeiger
International History Review
Iron Age
Jogtudományi Közlöny
Journal d'Alsace-Lorraine
Journal des débats
Journal du dimanche
Journal of Contemporary History
Journal of Economic History
Journal of Modern European History
Journal of Modern History
Journal of the History of Ideas
Journal of the Iron and Steel Institute
Journal Officiel de la République Francaise
Keleti Újság
Képviselőházi Napló
Kolozsvári Munkás
Kolozsvári Városi Közlöny
Korunk
Közgazdasági és Közigazgatási Szemle
Közgazdasági Szemle
Köztelek
L'Écho des mines et de la métallurgie
L'Économiste français: journal hebdomadaire
L'Est Républicain
L'Univers israélite
La Caricature, publication de la Librairie illustrée
Le Capitaliste: Journal de la banque parisienne
Le Constitutionnel, journal politique littéraire, universel
Le Monde
Levéltári Közlemények

Levéltári Szemle
Magyar Bánya-Kalauz
Magyar Figyelő
Magyar Gyáripar
Magyar Ipar
Magyar Iparművészet
Magyar Közlemények
Magyar Nyelvőr
Magyar Pénzügyi Compass
Magyar statisztikai évkönyv
Magyar statisztikai közlemények
Magyar statisztikai szemle
Magyar Tőzsde
Medizin, Gesellschaft und Geschichte
Monitorul Oficial
Nagyvárad
Napkelet
National Identities
Népszava
The New York Times
Nouvelliste
Nyugat
Paris-capital: journal financier
Past & Present
Pester Lloyd
Pesti Hírlap
Pesti Napló
Quarterly Journal of Economics
Reichs-Gesetzblatt
Relations Internationales
Review Fernand Braudel Center
Revue d'Alsace
Revue des Sciences Politiques
Revue française de sciences politiques
Revue historique
Romániai Magyar Szó
Schweizerische Bauzeitung
Slavic Review
Slavonica
Századok
Színházi Élet
The Economic History Review
The Economist
Történelmi Szemle
Transilvaniai Futár
Turán

Új Idők
Vasárnapi Újság
Veselia, Revista Umoristica
Világ
Voleur Illustré, Revue pour Tous
Weltwirtschaftliches Archiv

Selected Printed Primary Sources

Adler, Cyrus, and Henrietta Szold. *American Jewish Year Book*. Philadelphia: Jewish Publication Society of America, 1920.

Allen, Mitchell, and Michael Hughes. *German Parliamentary Debates, 1848–1933*. New York: P. Lang, 2003.

A budapesti egységes hálózat betűrendes távbeszélő névsora, 1948 március. Budapest: Magyar Postavezérigazgatóság, 1948.

A Kolozsvári Kereskedelmi és Iparkamara jelentése kerülete közgazdasági viszonyairól az, 1886-, 1887-, 1888-, 1889. Években. Cluj, Romania: Kolozsvári Kereskedelmi és Iparkamara, 1890.

Apponyi, Albert. "On the Transylvanian Question," in *The Hungarian Peace Negotiations*, vol. 1, ed. Jenő Cholnoky. Budapest: M. kir. tudományegyetemi nyomda, 1921.

Arendt, Hannah. *The Origins of Totalitarianism*. New York: Harcourt Brace Jovanovich, 1973.

Armstrong, John Scobell. *War and Treaty Legislation: Affecting British Property in Germany and Austria, and Enemy Property in the United Kingdom*. London: Hutchinson, 1921.

Beaudemoulin, Jean. *Loi de huit heures, (23 Avril 1919)*. Paris: Dalloz, 1924.

Beksics, Gusztáv. *A magyar politika uj alapjai kapcsolatban a magyar faj terjeszkedő képességével és a földbirtokviszonyokkal*. Budapest: Athenaeum, 1899.

——. *A román kérdés és a fajok harcza Európában és Magyarországon*. Budapest: Athenaeum, 1895.

——. *La question roumaine et la lutte des races en Orient*. Paris: Chailley, 1895.

Bereczky, Ernő, ed. *Románia új behozatali vámtarifája, Fém és textilipari cikkek*. Cluj: Lepage, 1926.

Bethlen, István. *Bethlen István gróf beszédei és írásai*. Budapest: Géniusz R.t., 1933.

Bericht des Vorstandes über das 13. Geschäftsjahr vom 1. Juli 1911 bis 30 Juni 1912. Strasbourg: Adler& Oppenheimer, 1912.

Bizony, László. *A keleti határról*. Budapest: Szerző, 1912, 48.

Bleicher, Albert, and Joseph Rossé. *Die einträglichste Plünderung, die je begangen wurde: die Verschleuderung der elsaß-lothr. Industrien u. Bodenschätze; nach offiz. Berichten* Kolmar [Colmar]: Alsatia, 1940.

Boambă, Ioan. *Banque Marmorosch Blank & Co. Société Anonyme, 1848–1923*. Bucharest: Cultură Natională, 1924.

Borovszky, Samu, ed. *Magyarország vármegyéi és városai, Torontál vármegye*. Budapest: O.M.T, 1912.

Bradshaw, George. *Bradshaw's Illustrated Hand-Book to Switzerland and the Tyrol.* London: W. J. Adams & Sons, 1857.

Chirot, Daniel, ed. *The Origins of Backwardness in Eastern Europe: Economics and Politics from the Middle Ages until the Early Twentieth Century*. Berkeley: University of California Press, 1989.

Chorin-Strasser, Daisy, and Ferenc Chorin. *Az Andrássy úttól a Park Avenue-ig: Fejezetek Chorin Ferenc életéből (1879–1964)*. Budapest: Osiris, 1999.

Deák, Francis. *Hungary at the Paris Peace Conference: The Diplomatic History of the Treaty of Trianon*. New York: Columbia University Press, 1942.

Dazet, Georges. *La liquidation des séquestres*. Paris: Éditions et librairie, 1916.

Delahache, Georges. *Les débuts de l'administration française en Alsace et en Lorraine*. Paris: Hachette, 1921.

Delahache, George. *Petite histoire de l'Alsace-Lorraine*. Paris: Libraire Bernard Grasset, 1918, 72.

Delaisi, Francis, René Cassin, and Stéphane Lauzanne. *Les Soviets et la dette russe en France*. Paris: Publications de la Conciliation Internationale, 1930.

Eccard, Frédéric. L'Alsace sous la domination allemande. Paris: A. Colin, 1919.

Eccard, Frédéric, and Louis Renault. *Biens et intérêts français en Allemagne et en Alsace-Lorraine pendant la guerre ouvrage accompagné de la traduction des textes allemands relatifs aux mesures législatives et administratives prises à l'égard des biens français, anglais et alliés et d'une liste des principales enterprises françaises séquestrées et liquidées en Alsace-Lorraine et en Allemagne*. Paris: Libr. Payot et cie, 1917.

Edvi, Illés, ed. *A magyar béketárgyalások: Jelentés a magyar békeküldöttség működéséről Neuilly s/S.-ben 1920 január̈ius - marcius havában*. Budapest: M. kir. tudományegyetemi nyomda, 1920. 3/a:117–118.

Fellner, Frigyes. *A magyar szent korona országai nemzeti vagyonának és nemzeti jövedelmének megoszlása a mai Magyarország és az utódállamok között*. Budapest: Franklin, 1923.Fisk, Harvey Edward. *French Public Finance in the Great War and Today: With Chapters on Banking and Currency*. New York: Bankers Trust Company, 1922.

Grad, Charles. *Wiener Weltausstellung, Bericht über die Industrie des Elsasses*. Colmar, Germany: Buchdruckerei und Lithographie von Camille Decker, 1873.

Geml, József. *Emlékiratok polgármesteri müködésem idejéből*. Timișoara: Helicon, 1924.

Grandpierre, Kolozsvári Emil. *A rosta*. Budapest: Magvető, 1985.

Gyárfás, Elemér. *Románia hitelszervezetei s az erdélyi magyar pénzintézetek*. Lugos, Romania: Husvéth és Hoffer Könyvnyomdája, 1924.

Hauser, Henri. *Les méthodes allemandes d'expansion économique*, 3rd ed. Paris: A. Colin, 1916.

Hellmann, Otto. *Die staatsrechtliche Stellung des Reichslandes Elsass-Lothringen nach seiner geschichtlichen Entwicklung und dem geltenden Recht*. Freising, Germany: Buchdr. von A. Warmuth, 1907.

Hohenlohe-Schillingsfürst, Chlodwig K. V. and Alexander Hohenlohe-Schillingsfürst, *Memoirs of Prince Chlodwig of Hohenlohe-Schillingsfuerst*. Vol. 2, New York: Macmillan, 1906.

Hoefer, Jean Chrétien Ferdinand. *Nouvelle biographie générale depuis les temps les plus reculés jusqu'à nos jours, avec les renseignements bibliographiques et l'indication des sources à consulter*. Paris: Firmin Didot frères, fils et cie, 1855.

Iványi, Emma, ed. *Magyar minisztertanácsi jegyzőkönyvek az első világháború korából, 1914–1918*. Budapest: Akadémiai Kiadó, 1960.

Jakabffy, Elemér, and Páll György. *A bánsági magyarság húsz éve Romániában (1918–1938)*. Studium, Budapest: Studium, 1939.

Jacobi, Eugen. *Fragen der Übergangswirtschaft: Vortrag Gehalten in der Strassburger Gesellschaft für Deutsche Kultur, Januar 1917*. Strassburg: Dumont Schauberg, 1917.

——. *Wirtschaftliche Tages- und Zukunfts-Fragen: Vortrag gehalten in der Strassburger Gesellschaft für deutsche Kultur, am 14 März 1918*. Strassburg: Dumont Schauberg, 1918.

Jászi, Oszkár. *The United States of Europe, Európai Egyesült Államok*. Budapest: Hungarian Europe Society, Magyarországi Európa Társaság: Carneades Bt., 2006.

Jelentés a Magyar Keleti Kulturközpont (Turáni Társaság) két évi müködéséről. Budapest: M.K.K.K. (T.T.), 1918, 20–22.

Katona, Béla. *Magyarország közgazdasága, Pénzügyi és közgazdasági évkönyv 1913. évről*. Budapest: Légrády, 1914.

——. *Magyarország közgazdasága. Pénzügyi és közgazdasági évkönyv az 1917. évről*. Budapest: Benkő Gyula cs. és kir. udvari könyvkereskedése, 1918.

Kempelen, Béla. *Magyar nemes családok*. Budapest: Grill K., 1931.

Keszi, Sándor, and Hillel Kohn. *Exploatarea capitalistă la "Dermata."* Bucharest: Editura de Stat pentru literatură științifică, 1954.

Keynes, John Maynard. *The Economic Consequences of the Peace*. Cham: Palgrave Macmillan, 2019.

Kormos Alfréd, ed. *Pénzügyi compass, 1908–1909*, 18, no. 2, Budapest: Apollo, 1909.

Kormos, Gyula, ed. *Magyar pénzügyi compass*. Budapest: Apollo, 1924, 681–766.

Laky, Dezső. *Csonka-Magyarország megszállásának közgazdasági kárai*. Budapest: Eggenberger, 1923.

Laufenburger, Henry. *Cours d'économie alsacienne*. Paris: Sirey, 1930.

Lévy, Robert. *Histoire économique de l'industrie cotonnière en Alsace: Étude de sociologie descriptive*. Paris: F. Alcan, 1912.

Ligeti, Ernő. *Föl a bakra*. Cluj-Kolozsvár: Lapkiadó és Nyomdai Műintézet. 1925.

Link, Adolf. *Die Deutsche Lederindustrie, Eine Standortsstudie*. Tübingen: H. Laupp, 1913, 15–16.

de Lisle, Thomas Amédée Rouget. *La vérité sur la paternité de la Marseillaise*. Paris, 1865.

Magyar statisztikai évkönyv, 1915. Budapest: M.K.K.S.H., 1918.

A Magyar Szent Korona országainak 1910. évi népszámlálása, 2. rész, A népesség foglalkozása és a nagyipari vállalatok községenkint, Magyar statisztikai közlemények, vol. 48. Budapest: Magyar Királyi Központi Statisztikai Hivatal, 1913.

Maniu, Horia. *Unificarea monetară*. Bucharest: Cartea Românească, 1924.

Manoilesco, Mihaïl. *L'Equilibre économique européen: The European economic equilibrium*. Bucharest: Impr. Nat., 1931.

Manoilescu, Mihail. *Memorii*. Bucharest: Ed. Enciclopedică, 1993.

Menne, Bernhard. *Blood and Steel: The Rise of the House of Krupp*. New York: L. Furman, 1938.

Molter, Károly. *Metania R.t.* Budapest: Athaeneum, 1929.

Nagy, Sándor Galánthai, ed. *Mihók-féle Magyar Compass 1899–1900*. Budapest: Légrády, 1900.

Naumann, Friedrich. *Central Europe*. London: King, 1916.

Netta, Gheron. *Politica economică ungurească și statele sudestului Europei*. Bucharest: Cartea românească, 1921.

Pallas Nagy Lexikona. Budapest: Pallas Ny. Rt., 1895.

Petrichevich Horváth, Emil. *Jelentés az Országos Menekültügyi Hivatal négy évi működéséről*. Budapest: Pesti Könyvnyomda Rt., 1924.

Pinot, Robert. *Le Comité des Forges de France au service de la nation (Août 1914 - Novembre 1918)*. Paris: A. Colin, 1919, 253–254.

Plate, August. *Handbuch für das Preussische Abgeordnetenhaus: Ausgabe für die 20. Legislaturperiode*. Berlin: Moeser, 1904.

Pilisi, Lajos. *A megrohant és felszabadított Erdély*. Budapest: Auktor, 2005, 41–155.

Pinoche, André. *Le Séquestre et la liquidation des biens de sujets ennemis en France et en Allemagne, thèse pour le doctorat sciences politiques et économiques*. Bar-le-Duc: impr. de Constant-Laguerre, 1920.

Pohl, Manfred. *Handbook on the History of European Banks*. Frankfurt: Edward Elgar Publishing, 1994.

Poincaré, Raymond. *Au service de la France, neuf années de souvenirs*. Vol. 11. Paris: Plon, 1974.

Polanyi, Karl. *The Great Transformation*. New York: Beacon Press, 1959.

Procès-Verbaux de la Conférence d'Alsace-Lorraine, 1e–24e séances, 18 février 1915–22 mai 1916. Paris: Imprimerie Nationale, 1917.

Programme de la Fête Ste Cécile de la Chorale de l'usine de Grafenstaden, 14 janvier, 1882.

Régismanset, Charles. *L'Exposition national colonial Marseille, 1922*. Paris: Les Imprimeries Françaises Réunies, 1921.

Rossé, Joseph, Marcel Stürmel, and Albert Bleicher, Fernand Deiber, and Jean Keppi, *Das Elsass von 1870–1932*. Colmar: Verlag Alsatia, 1936.

Schenk, Erwin. *Der Fall Zabern*. Stuttgart: W. Kohlhammer, 1927.

Schön, Dezső. Mose Heller, Rubinstein Sándor, Ödön Grossman, József Gréda, and Ottó Rappaport. *A tegnap városa: a nagyváradi zsidóság emlékkönyve*. Tel-Aviv: Nagyváradról Elszármazottak Egyesülete Izraelben, 1981.

Sebess, Dénes. *Az új agrárdemokráciák*. Budapest: Légrády, 1925.

Statuten der Aktiengesellschaft Adler-Oppenheimer, Lederfabrik Strassburg i. E. Strasbourg: Strassburger Druckerei, 1914.

Simonson, Paul Frederick. *Private Property and Rights in Enemy Countries: and Private Rights against Enemy Nationals and Governments under the Peace Treaties with Germany, Austria, Hungary, Bulgaria, and Turkey*. London: E. Wilson, 1921.

Slăvescu, Victor I. *Organizația de credit a României*. Bucharest: Cartea Românească, 1922.

Somogyi, Éva. *Abszolutizmus és kiegyezés, 1849–1867*. Budapest: Gondolat, 1981.

Suciu, Petru. *Probleme Ardelene, reforma agrară în Ardeal, problema orașelor Ardelene, Clasele sociale în Ardeal*. Cluj: Editura Revistei Societatea de mâine, 1924.

Szentkirályi, Ákos. *Néhány mozzanat Kolozsvár szab. kir. város közgazdasági életének 1909. évi történetéből*. Kolozsvár: Ajtai, 1910, 1–18.

Schenk, Erwin. *Der Fall Zabern*. Stuttgart, Germany: W. Kohlhammer 1927.

Tardieu, André. *The Truth about the Treaty*. Indianapolis, IN: Bobbs-Merrill, 1921.

The Traveller's Handbook for Belgium and the Ardennes. London: Thomas Cook & Son, 1911, 90.

Torrey, Glenn E., ed. *General Henri Berthelot and Romania, mémoires et correspondence 1916–1919*. Boulder, Colorado: East European Monographs, 1987.

Treitschke, Heinrich v. *What We Demand from France*. London: Macmillan, 1870.

Vadnay, Tibor. *A magyar jövő: Közgazdaság- és szociálpolitikai tanulmány*. Budapest: Athenaeum, 1918.

Verhandlungen: *Stenographische. Berichte über die Verhandlungen*. Berlin: Preussische Verlagsanstalt, 1912.

Verzeichnis der in der Bücherei der Firma Adler und Oppenheimer Lederfabrik A. G. Lingolsheim enthaltenen Bücher. Strassburg: DuMont Schauberg, 1917.

Wittich, Werner. *Deutsche und französische Kultur im Elsass*. Strassburg [Strasbourg]: Schlesier & Schweikhardt, 1900.

Zander, Ernst. *Der Wirtschaftliche Wiederaufbau von Elass-Lothringen nach dem Kriege*. Strassburg: Karl Trübner, 1917.

Zeletin, Ștefan. *Neoliberalismul: Studii asupra istoriei și politicii burgheziei române*. Bucharest: Editura Nemira, 1997.

Zweig, Stefan. *The World of Yesterday*. Translated by Anthea Bell. Lincoln: University of Nebraska Press, 2013.

Zundel, Auguste. *1914–1918, Journal de la Grande Guerre vécue à Mulhouse*. Colmar, 2004.

Selected Secondary Literature

Ablonczy, Balázs. *Ismeretlen Trianon: Az összeomlás és a békeszerződés történetei, 1918–1921*. Budapest: Jaffa Kiadó, 2020.

——. *Keletre, magyar! A magyar turanizmus története*. Budapest: Jaffa, 2016.

——. *Pál Teleki (1874–1941): The Life of a Controversial Hungarian Politician*. Boulder, CO: Social Science Monographs, 2006.

——. *A visszatért Erdély, 1940–1944*. Budapest: Jaffa, 2011.

Ábrahám, Barna. "The Idea of Independent Romanian National Economy in Transylvania at the Turn of the 20th Century." In *Nation-Building and Contested Identities: Romanian and Hungarian Case Studies*, edited by Balázs Trencsényi and Dragos Petrescu, 209–226. Budapest: Regio Books, 2001.

Axenciuc, Victor. *La formation et le développement du marché intérieur moderne en Roumanie: Etude et séries statistiques à long terme: (1860–1947)*. Bucharest: Academie Roumaine, 2008.

Bakić-Hayden, Milica. "Nesting Orientalisms: The Case of Former Yugoslavia." *Slavic Review* 54, no. 4 (1995): 917–931.

Balaton, Petra. "Szterényi József erdélyi pályafutása." *Levéltári Közlemények* 82, no. 2 (2011): 146–170.

Balcerowicz, Leszek. *Post-Communist Transition: Some Lessons*. London: Institute of Economic Affairs, 2004.

Ban, Cornel. "Beyond Anticommunism: The Fragility of Class Analysis in Romania." *East European Politics and Societies and Cultures* 29, no. 3 (August 2015): 640–650.

Banač, Ivo. *The National Question in Yugoslavia: Origins, History, Politics*. Ithaca, NY: Cornell University Press, 1993.

Bánffy, Miklós. *The Transylvanian Trilogy: They Were Counted*. Toronto: Knopf Doubleday Publishing Group, 2013.

Bárdi, Nándor. "Az erdélyi magyar (és regionális) érdekek megjelenítése az 1910-es években. Az Erdélyi Szövetség programváltozatai," *Magyar Kisebbség* 2–3, (2003): 93–105.

——. *Otthon és haza, Tanulmányok a romániai magyar kisebbség történetéről*. Csíkszereda, Romania: Pro-Print, 2013.

Bárdi, Nándor, Csilla Fedinec, and László Szarka. *Minority Hungarian Communities in the Twentieth Century*. Boulder, Colorado: Social Science Monographs, 2011.

Bariéty, Jacques. "Les conséquences pour l'économie française du retour de l'Alsace-Lorraine à la France en 1919." *Francia: Forschungen zur Westeuropäischen Geschichte* 3 (1975): 535–536.

Bartha, Ákos. *Populizmus, népiség, modernizáció: Fejezetek a kelet-közép-európai politikai gondolkodás 20. századi történetéből*. Budapest: MTA Bölcsészettudományi Kutatóközpont, 2017.

Báthory, Ludovic. *Societățile carbonifere și sistemul economic și politic al României: 1919–1929*. Cluj-Napoca: Presa Universitară Clujeană, 1999.

Beller, Steven. *The Habsburg Monarchy, 1815–1918*. Cambridge: Cambridge University Press, 2018.

Békés, Csaba, László Borhi, Peter Ruggenthaler, and Ottmar Trașcă, eds. *Soviet Occupation of Romania, Hungary, and Austria 1944/45–1948/49*, ed. Budapest: Central European University Press, 2015.

Berecz, Ágoston. *The Politics of Early Language Teaching: Hungarian in the Primary Schools of the Late Dual Monarchy*. Budapest: CEU Press, 2013.

Berend, Iván T. "A közép- és kelet-európai gazdasági integráció kérdéséhez (Történelmi előzmények)." *Közgazdasági Szemle* (1968): 311.

——. *Decades of Crisis: Central and Eastern Europe before World War II*. Berkeley: University of California Press, 1998.

Berger, Stefan. "Building the Nation among Visions of German Empire." In *Nationalizing Empires*, edited by Stefan Berger and Alexei Miller, 247–308 Budapest: Central European University Press, 2015.

Berghahn, Volker. "German Big Business and the Quest for a European Economic Empire in the Twentieth Century." In *German Big Business and Europe in the Twentieth Century*, edited by Berghahn, Volker, Reinhard Neebe, and Jeffrey J. Anderson. Providence, RI: Thomas J. Watson Jr. Institute for International Studies, Brown University, 1993.

——. *Imperial Germany, 1871–1918: Economy, Society, Culture, and Politics*. New York: Berghahn Books, 2005.

——., ed. *Quest for Economic Empire: European Strategies of German Big Business in the Twentieth Century*. Providence, RI: Berghahn Books, 1996.

Berglun, Abraham. "The Iron-Ore Problem of Lorraine," *Quarterly Journal of Economics* 33, no. 3. 1919, 531–554.

Berkes, Antal. "The League of Nations and the Optants Dispute in the Hungarian Borderlands: Romania, Yugoslavia and Czechoslovakia." In *Remaking Central Europe: The League of Nations and Former Hasburg Lands*, edited by Peter Becker and Natasha Wheatley, 283–314. Oxford: Oxford University Press, 2020.

Bihari, Péter. *Lövészárkok a hátországban: Középosztály, zsidókérdés, antiszemitizmus az első világháború Magyarországán*. Budapest: Napvilág, 2008.

Biró, László. "A Vajdaság a két világháború között: Adalékok a Jugoszláv gazdasági integráció hatásaihoz," in *Vojvođanski prostor u kontekstu Evropske istorije*, edited by Vladan, Gavrilović and Boškov Svetozar, 65–76.. Novi Sad, Serbia: Filozofski fakultet u Novom Sadu, 2014.

Blomqvist, Anders E. B. *Economic Nationalizing in the Ethnic Borderlands of Hungary and Romania: Inclusion, Exclusion, and Annihilation in Szatmár/Satu-Mare, 1867–1944*. Stockholm: Stockholm University, 2014.

Bódy, Zsombor. "Gyár és földbirtok a nagy háborúban és az összeomlásban." 1261–1292, *Századok* 6 (2018).

Böhler, Jochen. *Civil War in Central Europe, 1918–1921: The Reconstruction of Poland*. Oxford: Oxford University Press, 2018.

——. "Enduring Violence: The Postwar Struggles in East-Central Europe, 1917–21." *Journal of Contemporary History* 50, no. 1 (2015): 58–77.

Boia, Lucian. *Cum s-a românizat România*. Bucharest: Humanitas, 2015.

——. *"Germanofilii," Elită intelectuală românească în anii primului război mondial*. Bucharest: Humanitas, 2010.

——. *România: Țară de frontieră a Europei*. Bucharest: Humanitas, 2002.

Bösch, Frank. *Öffentliche Geheimnisse: Skandale, Politik und Medien in Deutschland und Grossbritannien, 1880–1914*. Oldenbourg, Germany: Oldenbourg Verlag, 2009.

Boswell, Laird. "From Liberation to Purge Trials in the 'Mythic Provinces': Recasting French Identities in Alsace and Lorraine, 1918–1920." *French Historical Studies* 23, no. 1 (2000): 129–162.

Bottoni, Stefano. *Long Awaited West: Eastern Europe since 1944*. Bloomington: Indiana University Press, 2017.

Bradby, David. *Modern French Drama, 1940–1980*. Cambridge: Cambridge University Press, 1984.

Braun, Hans-Joachim. *The German Economy in the Twentieth Century*. London: Routledge, 1990.

Broadberry, S. N., and Kevin H. O'Rourke, eds. *The Cambridge Economic History of Modern Europe*. Cambridge: Cambridge University Press, 2010.

Brocheux, Pierre, and Daniel Hémery. *Indochina: An Ambiguous Colonization, 1858–1954*. Los Angeles: University of California Press, 2011.

Brubaker, Rogers. *Ethnicity without Groups*. Cambridge, MA: Harvard University Press, 2004.

Buchet, Constantin. *România și republica de la Weimar, 1919–1933: Economie, diplomație și geopolitică*. Bucharest: All Ed., 2001.

Cabanes, Bruno. *La victoire endeuillée: La sortie de guerre des soldats français, 1918–1920*. Paris: Seuil, 2004.

Caglioti, Daniela L. "Property Rights in Time of War: Sequestration and Liquidation of Enemy Aliens' Assets in Western Europe during the First World War." *Journal of Modern European History* 12, no. 4 (November 2014): 523–545.

——. *War and Citizenship, Enemy Aliens and National Belonging from the French Revolution to the First World War*. Cambridge: Cambridge University Press, 2020.

Cameron, Rondo E. *France and the Economic Development of Europe, 1800–1914*. Princeton, NJ: Princeton University Press, 1961.

——. *France and the Economic Development of Europe, 1800–1914*. Chicago: Rand McNally, 1965.

Cameron, Rondo, and V. I. Bovykin. *International Banking, 1870–1914*. Oxford: Oxford University Press, 1992.

Carley, Michael Jabara. "From Revolution to Dissolution: The Quai d'Orsay, the Banque Russo-Asiatique, and the Chinese Eastern Railway, 1917–1926." *International History Review* 12, no. 4 (1990): 721–761.

Caron, Vicki. *Between France and Germany: The Jews of Alsace-Lorraine, 1871–1918*. Stanford, CA: Stanford University Press, 1988.

Carrol, Alison. *The Return of Alsace to France, 1918–1939*. Oxford: Oxford University Press, 2018.

Case, Holly. *The Age of Questions: Or, a First Attempt at an Aggregate History of the Eastern, Social, Woman, American, Jewish, Polish, Bullion, Tuberculosis, and Many Other Questions over the Nineteenth Century, and Beyond*. Princeton, NJ: Princeton University Press, 2018.

——. *Between States: The Transylvanian Question and the European Idea during World War II*. Stanford, CA: Stanford University Press, 2009.

——. "Reconstruction in East-Central Europe: Clearing the Rubble of Cold War Politics." *Past & Present* 210, Supplement 6 (January 2011): 71–102.

Cassis, Youssef. *Big Business: The European Experience in the Twentieth Century*. New York: Oxford University Press, 1997.

Chickering, Roger. *Imperial Germany and the Great War, 1914–1918*. 3rd ed. Cambridge: Cambridge University Press, 2014.

——. *We Men Who Feel Most German: A Cultural Study of the Pan-German League, 1886–1914*. New York: Routledge, 2019.

Chirot, Daniel. *The Origins of Backwardness in Eastern Europe: Economics and Politics from the Middle Ages until the Early Twentieth Century*. Berkeley: University of California Press, 1989.

——. "A Romanian Prelude to Contemporary Debates about Development." *Review (Fernand Braudel Centre)* 2, no. 1 (1978): 115–123

Chrastil, Rachel. *The Siege of Strasbourg*. Cambridge, MA: Harvard University Press, 2014.

Chuter, David. *Humanity's Soldier: France and International Security, 1919–2001*. Providence, RI: Berghahn Books, 1996.

Cieger, András. *Politikai korrupció a Monarchia Magyarországán, 1867–1918*. Budapest: Napvilág, 2011.

Clark, Christopher M. *The Sleepwalkers: How Europe Went to War in 1914*. New York: Harper, 2013

Clark, Roland. *Holy Legionary Youth: Fascist Activism in Interwar Romania*. Ithaca, NY: Cornell University Press, 2015.

Colli, Andrea. *The History of Family Business, 1850–2000*. New York: Cambridge University Press, 2002.

Conrad, Sebastian. *Globalisierung und Nation im deutschen Kaiserreich*. Munich: Beck, 2006.

Constantinescu, Ilinca Păun. "Shrinking Cities in Romania: Former Mining Cities in Valea Jiului." *Built Environment* 38, no. 2 (2012): 214–228.

Cottrell, Philip. "Central Bank Co-operation and Romanian Stabilization." In *Business and Politics in Europe, 1900–1970: Essays in Honour of Alice Teichova*, ed. Terry Gourvish, 106–144. Cambridge: Cambridge University Press, 2003.

Daltroff, Jean. "Les Adler et Oppenheimer." *Revue d'Alsace*, no. 136 (October 1, 2010): 175–197.

Davis, Belinda. *Home Fires Burning: Food, Politics and Everyday Life in World War I Berlin*. Chapel Hill: University of North Carolina Press, 2000.

Deák, Francis. *Hungary at the Paris Peace Conference: The Diplomatic History of the Treaty of Trianon*. New York: Columbia University Press, 1942.

Deák, István. *Beyond Nationalism: A Social and Political History of the Habsburg Officer Corps, 1848–1918*. New York: Oxford University Press, 1990.

——. *The Lawful Revolution: Louis Kossuth and the Hungarians, 1848–1849*. New York: Columbia University Press, 1979.

Deak, John, and Jonathan E. Gumz. "How to Break a State: The Habsburg Monarchy's Internal War, 1914–1918." *American Historical Review* 122 (2017): 1105–1136.

Dedinger, Béatrice. "The Franco-German Trade Puzzle: An Analysis of the Economic Consequences of the Franco-Prussian War." *The Economic History Review* 65, no. 3 (2012): 1029–1054.

De Grazia, Victoria. *Irresistible Empire: America's Advance through Twentieth-Century Europe*. Cambridge, MA: Belknap Press of Harvard University Press, 2005.

Derix, Simone. *Die Thyssens: Familie und Vermögen, Familie - Unternehmen - Öffentlichkeit: Thyssen im 20. Jahrhundert*. Paderborn, Germany: Ferdinand Schöningh, 2016.

Downs, Laura Lee. *Manufacturing Inequality: Gender Division in the French and British Metalworking Industries, 1914–1939*. Ithaca, NY: Cornell University Press, 1995.

Drecin, Mihai D. *Banca "Albina" din Sibiu, Instituţie nationaldă a Românilor Transilvăni: 1871–1918*. Cluj-Napoca: Ed. Dacia, 1982.

Egry, Gábor. "A Crossroad of Parallels: Regionalism and Nation-Building in Transylvania in the First Half of the Twentieth Century." In *Hungary and Romania: Beyond National Narratives, Comparisons and Entanglements*, edited by Anders Blomqvist, Constantin Iordachi, and Balázs Trencsényi, 239–276. New York: Peter Lang, 2013.

——. "'Der Kampf um Bodenbesitz' Az erdélyi szászok földbirtokviszonyai és a szász nemzetpolitika 1890-1918-ig," *Korunk*. September 2005, 94–107.

——. *Etnicitás, identitás, politika, Magyar kisebbségek nacionalizmus és regionalizmus között Romániában és Csehszlovákiában, 1918–1944*. Budapest: Napvilág, 2015.

——. "National Economy vs. Economic Efficiency? Economic Nationalism, Nationalizing State(s) and Transitory Effects in Interwar Transylvania." Paper presented at the Society for Romanian Studies International Conference, Bucharest, June 2015.

——. "Navigating the Straits: Changing Borders, Changing Rules and Practices of Ethnicity and Loyalty in Romania after 1918." *Hungarian Historical Review: New Series of Acta Historica Academiae Scientiarum Hungaricae* 2, no. 3 (2013): 449–476.

——. "Negotiating Post-Imperial Transitions: Local Societies and Nationalizing States in East Central Europe." In *Embers of Empire, Continuity and Rupture in the Habsburg Successor States after 1918*. Austrian and Habsburg Studies. Edited by Paul Miller and Claire Morelon. New York: Berghahn Books, 2019.

——. *Nemzeti védgát vagy szolid haszonszerzés? Az erdélyi szászok pénzintézeti rendszere és szerepe a nemzeti mozgalomban (1835–1914)*. Csíkszereda, Romania: Pro-Print, 2009.

——. "Regionalizmus, erdélyiség, szupremácia: Az Erdélyi Szövetség és Erdély jövője, 1913–1918." *Századok* 1 (2013): 3–31.

——. "The Strangers Within: National Identity, Everyday Encounters and Regionalism in Transylvania, 1918–1944." In *National Identity and Modernity, 1870–1945: Latin America, Southern Europe, East Central Europe*, edited by Viktória Semsey, 249–271. Budapest: KRE Könyvműhely, L'Harmattan, 2019.

——. "Unholy Alliances? Language Exams, Loyalty, and Identification in Interwar Romania." *Slavic Review* 76, no. 4 (2017): 959–982.

Eichengreen, Barry J. *Golden Fetters: The Gold Standard and the Great Depression, 1919–1939*. New York: Oxford University Press, 1995.

Fear, Jeffrey R. *Organizing Control*. Cambridge, MA: Harvard University Press, 2005.

Feldman, Gerald D. *Army, Industry, and Labor in Germany, 1914–18*. Princeton, NJ: Princeton University Press, 1966.

——. *The Great Disorder: Politics, Economics, and Society in the German Inflation, 1914–1924*. New York: Oxford University Press, 1993.

Ferguson, Niall. "Constraints and Room for Manoeuvre in the German Inflation of the Early 1920s." *Economic History Review* 49, no. 4 (1996): 635–666.

——. *The House of Rothschild: The World's Banker, 1849–1999*. New York: Penguin, 1999.

——. *The Pity of War*. New York: Basic Books, 1999.

——. *The World's Banker: The History of the House of Rothschild*. London: Weidenfeld & Nicolson, 1998.

Findlay, Ronald. *Power and Plenty: Trade, War, and the World Economy in the Second Millennium*. Princeton, NJ: Princeton University Press, 2007.

Fischer, Christopher J. *Alsace to the Alsatians? Visions and Divisions of Alsatian Regionalism, 1870–1939*. New York: Berghahn Books, 2010.

Fitzpatrick, Matthew P. *Liberal Imperialism in Germany: Expansionism and Nationalism, 1848–1884*. Oxford, UK: Berghahn Books, 2008.

Flandreau, Marc, ed. *Money Doctors: The Experience of International Financial Advising 1850–2000*, edited by. London: Routledge, 2003.

Fodor, János. *Bernády György: Politikai életrajz*. Marosvásárhely [Târgu Mureș]: Romania: Lector Kiadó, 2017.

Fogarty, Richard S. "The French Empire." In *Empires at War: 1911–1923*, edited by Robert Gerwarth and Erez. Manela, 109–129. Oxford: Oxford University Press, 2014.

Frank, Alison F. *Oil Empire: Vision of Prosperity in Austrian Galicia*. Cambridge, MA: Harvard University Press, 2005.

——. "The Petroleum War of 1910: Standard Oil, Austria and the Limits of the Multinational Corporation." *American Historical Review* 114 (2009): 16–41.

Paul Freedman, "A dossier of peasant and seigneurial violence" in *The Routledge History Handbook of Medieval Revolt*, ed. Justine Firnhaber-Baker, Dirk Schoenaers. London: Routledge, 2017.

Gál, Zoltán. *The Banking Functions of the Hungarian Urban Network in the Early 20th Century*. Pécs, Hungary: Centre for Regional Studies, 2006.

Galántai, József. *Magyarország az első világháborúban, 1914–1918*. Budapest: Akadémiai Kiadó, 1974.

Garber, Peter M., and Michael G. Spencer, "The Dissolution of the Austro-Hungarian Empire" in *IMF Working Papers* 1992, 066 (1992), A001, 302–310.

Gaucsík, István. *A jog erejével: a szlovákiai magyarság gazdasági önszerveződése, 1918–1938: dokumentumok*. Pozsony, Hungary: Kalligram, 2008.

Geppert, Alexander C. T. *Fleeting Cities: Imperial Expositions in Fin-de-Siècle Europe*. Houndmills, Basingstoke, Hampshire, UK: Palgrave Macmillan, 2010.

Gerwarth, Robert, and Erez Manela, eds. *Empires at War: 1911–1923*. Oxford: Oxford University Press, 2014, 1–16.

Gerwarth, Robert. *The Vanquished: Why the First World War Failed to End, 1917–1923*. London: Allen Lane, 2016.

Gläser, Elisabeth. "The Making of the Economic Peace." In *The Treaty of Versailles: A Reassessment after 75 Years*, edited by Manfred F. Boemeke, Gerald D. Feldman, and Elisabeth Gläser, 371–400. Cambridge: Cambridge University Press, 1998.

Gidó, Attila. *Úton: Erdélyi zsidó társadalom- és nemzetépítési kísérletek (1918–1940)*. Csíkszereda, Romania, Pro-Print Könyvkiadó, 2009.

Godfrey, John F. *Capitalism at War: Industrial Policy and Bureaucracy in France, 1914–1918*. Leamington Spa, UK: Berg Publishers, 1987.

Golsan, Richard Joseph. *Vichy's Afterlife: History and Counterhistory in Postwar France*. Lincoln: University of Nebraska Press, 2000.

Goodfellow, Samuel. "Fascism and Regionalism in Interwar Alsace." *National Identities* 12, no. 2 (2010): 133–145.

Grady, Tim. *The German-Jewish Soldiers of the First World War in History and Memory*. Liverpool, UK: Liverpool University Press, 2011.

Graebner, Norman A., and Edward M. Bennett. *The Versailles Treaty and Its Legacy: The Failure of the Wilsonian Vision*. New York: Cambridge University Press, 2011.

Gräf, Rudolf. *Domeniul bănățean al StEG 1855–1920: Din istoria industrială a Banatului montan*. Reșița, Romania: Editura Banatica, 1997.

Grandhomme, Jean-Noël, Michel Roucaud, and Thierry Sarmant, eds. *La Roumanie dans la Grande Guerre et l'effondrement de l'armée Russe: Edition critique des rapports du général Berthelot, chef de la mission militaire française en Roumanie, 1916–1918*. Paris: Harmattan, 2000.

Green, Nancy L. *The Limits of Transnationalism*. Chicago: University of Chicago Press, 2019.

Grill, Tobias. "'Pioneers of Germanness in the East'? Jewish-German, German, and Slavic Perceptions of East European Jewry during the First World War." In *Jews and Germans in Eastern Europe: Shared and Comparative Histories*, edited by Tobias Grill, 125–159. Berlin: Walter de Gruyter, 2018.

Grohmann, Carolyn. "From Lotharingen to Lorraine: Expulsion and Voluntary Repatriation," in *After the Versailles Treaty, Enforcement, Compliance, Contested Identities*. Edited by Conan Fischer and Alan Sharp. 153–166. London and New York: Routledge, 2008.

Gross, Stephen G. *Export Empire: German Soft Power in Southeastern Europe, 1890–1945*. Cambridge: Cambridge University Press, 2015.

Gyáni, Gábor. *Nemzeti vagy transznacionális történelem*. Budapest: Kalligram, 2018.

——. *Történészdiskurzusok*. Budapest: L'Harmattan, 2002.

Hagen, William W. *Anti-Jewish Violence in Poland, 1914–1920*. Cambridge: Cambridge University Press, 2018.

Hajdu, Tibor, and Ferenc Pollmann. *A régi Magyarország utolsó háborúja, 1914–1918*. Budapest: Osiris, 2014.

Halmos, Károly. *Családi kapitalizmus*. Budapest: ÚMK, 2018.

Hamlin, David D. *Germany's Empire in the East: Germans and Romania in an Era of Globalization and Total War*. Cambridge: Cambridge University Press, 2017.

Hanák, Péter and Éva Somogyi *1867 - európai térben és időben*. Budapest: MTA TTI, 2001.

Hanebrink, Paul. *A Specter Haunting Europe: The Myth of Judeo-Bolshevism*. Cambridge, MA: Harvard University Press, 2018.

——. "Transnational Culture War: Christianity, Nation, and the Judeo-Bolshevik Myth in Hungary, 1890–1920." *Journal of Modern History* 80, no. 1 (2008): 55–80.

Harold William Vazeille Temperley, *A History of the Peace Conference of Paris* (London: H. Frowde, and Hodder & Stoughton, 1920), 2:459–461.

Harvey, David Allen. *Constructing Class and Nationality in Alsace, 1830–1945*. DeKalb: Northern Illinois University Press, 2001.

——. *The Limits to Capital*. New York: Verso Books, 2018.

——. "Lost Children or Enemy Aliens? Classifying the Population of Alsace after the First World War." *Journal of Contemporary History* 34, no. 4 (October 1, 1999): 537–554.

Hatos, Pál. *Az elátkozott köztársaság: Az 1918-as összeomlás és az őszirózsás forradalom története*. Budapest: Jaffa Kiadó, 2018.

Hau, Michel. *La Maison De Dietrich, de 1864 à nos jours*. Strasbourg: Oberlin, 1998.som

——. *L'Industrialisation de l'Alsace: 1803–1939*. Strasbourg: Association des publications près les universités de Strasbourg, 1987.

Healy, Maureen. "Introductory Remarks: Space, Chronology and the Habsburg Home Fronts." *European Review of History: Revue Européenne d'histoire* 24, no. 2 (March 4, 2017): 176–184.

——. *Vienna and the Fall of the Habsburg Empire: Total War and Everyday Life in World War I*. Cambridge: Cambridge University Press, 2004.

Heilperin, Michael Angelo. *Aspects of the Pathology of Money: Monetary Essays from Four Decades*. London: Graduate Institute of International Studies, 1968.

Hewitson, Mark. *Germany and the Causes of the First World War*. London: Bloomsbury, 2004.

——. *Germany and the Modern World, 1880–1914*. Cambridge: Cambridge University Press, 2018.

Hiery, Hermann. *Reichstagswahlen im Reichsland: Ein Beitrag zur Landesgeschichte von Elsass-Lothringen und zur Wahlgeschichte des Deutschen Reiches, 1871–1918*. Düsseldorf: Droste, 1986.

Hobsbawm, E. J. *The Age of Extremes: A History of the World, 1914–1991*. New York: Vintage Books, 1996.

Holec, Roman. *Dinamitos történelem: A pozsonyi Dynamit Nobel Vegyipari Konszern a közép-európai történelem keresztútján: 1873–1945*. Bratislava, Slovakia: Kalligram, 2009.

——. *Dejiny plné dynamitu: Bratislavský podnik Dynamit Nobel na križovatkách novodobých dejín*. Bratislava: Kalligram, 2011.

——. "Economic Aspects of Slovak National Development." In *Economic Change and the National Question in Twentieth-Century Europe*, edited by Alice Teichova, 277–294. Cambridge: Cambridge University Press, 2000.

Horváth, Gyula, ed. *Dél-Erdély és Bánság*. Pécs, Hungary: Dialóg–Campus Kiadó, 2009.

Hubert, Michel. *Deutschland im Wandel: Geschichte der deutschen Bevölkerung seit 1815*. Stuttgart: Franz Steiner Verlag, 1998.

Hunyadi, Attila Gábor, *Cooperative Networks in Transylvania Belonging to Hungary and Romania*. Saarbrücken: Lap Lambert, 2016.

Hull, Isabel V. *A Scrap of Paper: Breaking and Making International Law during the Great War*. Ithaca: Cornell University Press, 2014.

——. *Absolute Destruction: Military Culture and the Practices of War in Imperial Germany*. Ithaca, NY: Cornell University Press, 2005.

Igersheim, François. *L'Alsace des notables (1870–1914): La bourgeoisie et le peuple alsacien*. Strasbourg: Bf, 1981.

Ilyés, Sándor. "Történeti szubkultúrák, csoportkultúrák Kolozsváron a 20. században." *Korunk* 10 (2006): 61–69.

Ionescu, Ştefan Cristian. *Jewish Resistance to "Romanianization", 1940–44*. Basingstoke: Palgrave Macmillan, 2015.

Iordachi, Constantin. *Liberalism, Constitutional Nationalism, and Minorities: The Making of Romanian Citizenship, c. 1750–1918*. Leiden: Brill, 2019.

Irinyi, Károly. *A Naumann-féle "Mitteleuropa"-tervezet és a magyar politikai közvélemény*. Budapest: Akadémiai Kiadó, 1963.

——. *Mitteleuropa-tervek és az osztrák-magyar politikai közgondolkodás*. Budapest: Akadémiai Kiadó, 1973.

Jackisch, Barry A. *The Pan-German League and Radical Nationalist Politics in Interwar Germany, 1918–39*. Farnham, UK: Ashgate, 2012.

Jackson, Peter. *Beyond the Balance of Power: France and the Politics of National Security in the Era of the First World War*. Cambridge: Cambridge University Press, 2013.

James, Harold. *Monetary and Fiscal Unification in Nineteenth-Century Germany: What Can Kohl Learn from Bismarck?* Essays in International Finance, no. 202. Princeton, NJ: International Finance Section, Department of Economics, Princeton University, 1997.

——. *The Nazi Dictatorship and the Deutsche Bank*. Cambridge: Cambridge University Press, 2004.

Janos, Andrew C. *The Politics of Backwardness in Hungary, 1825–1945*. Princeton, NJ: Princeton University Press, 1982.

Jean-Baptiste Duroselle, *Clemenceau*. Paris: Fayard, 1988.

Jeanvoine, Luc. "Conflit intra-allemand sous-jacent au conflit franco-allemand: L'exemple de la S.A.C.M. (1914–1918)?" *Guerres mondiales et conflits contemporains* 265, no. 1 (2017): 33–46.

Jones, Heather, James O'Brien, and C. Schmdt-Supprian. *Untold War: New Perspectives in First World War Studies*. Leiden: Brill, 2008.

Jones, Heather, and Laurence van Ypersele. "Introduction to Part III." In *The Cambridge History of the First World War*, vol. 3, edited by Jay Murray Winter, 181–185. Cambridge: Cambridge University Press, 2014.

Judson, Pieter M. "Afterword" in Miller, Paul B., and Claire Morelon, eds. *Embers of Empire: Continuity and Rupture in the Habsburg Successor States after 1918*. 318–326. New York: Berghahn Books, 2019.

——. *Guardians of the Nation: Activists on the Language Frontiers of Imperial Austria*. Cambridge, MA: Harvard University Press, 2006.

——. *The Habsburg Empire: A New History*. Cambridge, MA: Harvard University Press, 2016.

——. "'Where Our Commonality Is Necessary . . .': Rethinking the End of the Habsburg Monarchy." *Austrian History Yearbook* 48 (April 2017): 1–21.

Judt, Tony. *Postwar: A History of Europe since 1945*. New York: Penguin Press, 2005.

Juhász, Gyula. *Hungarian Foreign Policy, 1919–1945*. Budapest: Akadémiai Kiadó, 1979.

Kaelble, Hartmut. *Industrielle Interessenpolitik in der Wilhelminischen Gesellschaft: Centralverband Deutscher Industrieller 1895 bis 1914*. Berlin: Walter de Gruyter GmbH, 2016.

Kang, David C. "Transaction Costs and Crony Capitalism in East Asia." *Comparative Politics* 35, no. 4 (2003): 439–458.

Kántor, Lajos, and György Kovács Kis. *Kulcsok Kolozsvárhoz: A föl nem adható város*. Kolozsvár: Korunk Baráti Társaság, 2000.

Karch, Brendan Jeffrey. *Nation and Loyalty in a German-Polish Borderland: Upper Silesia, 1848–1960*. Cambridge: Cambridge University Press, 2018.

Katzburg, Nathaniel. *Fejezetek az újkori zsidó történelemből Magyarországon*. Budapest: Osiris-MTA Judaisztikai Kutatócsoport, 1999.

Kauffman, Jesse. *Elusive Alliance: The German Occupation of Poland in World War I*. Cambridge, MA: Harvard University Press, 2015.

Khoury, Philip Shukry. *Syria and the French Mandate: The Politics of Arab Nationalism, 1920–1945*. Princeton, NJ: Princeton University Press, 1989.

Kindleberger, Charles. *A Financial History of Western Europe*. London: Allen & Unwin, 1984.

King, Jeremy. "The Municipal and the National in the Bohemian Lands, 1848–1914." *Austrian History Yearbook* 42 (April 2011): 89–109.

Kirițescu, Costin C. *Sistemul bănesc al leului și precursorii lui*. Bucharest: Editura Academiei Republicii Populare Romîne, 1964, 255–271.

Klabjan, Borut. "The Outbreak of War in Hasburg Trieste." In *Sarajevo 1914: Sparking the First World War*, edited by Mark Cornwall, 233–252. Bloomsbury, UK: Bloomsbury Academic, 2020.

Kocka, Jürgen. "Comparison and Beyond." *History and Theory* 42, no. 1 (2003): 39–44.

——. *Facing Total War: German Society, 1914–1918*. Cambridge, MA: Harvard University Press, 1985.

Kocka, Jürgen, and Heinz-Gerhard Haupt. "Comparison and Beyond: Traditions, Scope, and Perspectives of Comparative History." In *Comparative and Transnational History: Central European Approaches and New Perspectives*, ed. Heinz-Gerhard Haupt and Jürgen Kocka, 1–32. New York: Berghahn Books, 2012.

Komlos, John. *The Habsburg Monarchy as a Customs Union: Economic Development in Austria-Hungary in the Nineteenth Century*. Princeton, NJ: Princeton University Press, 1983.

Konrád, György, and Iván Szelényi. *The Intellectuals on the Road to Class Power*. New York: Harcourt Brace Jovanovich, 1979.

Konrád, Miklós. *Zsidóságon innen és túl: Zsidók vallásváltása Magyarországon a reformkortól az első világháborúig*. Budapest: MTA BTK TTI, 2014.

Koselleck, Reinhart. "Crisis." Translated by Michaela W. Richter. *Journal of the History of Ideas* 67, no. 2 (2006): 357–400.

Kovács, Éva. "Az agrárius beszédmód rekonstrukciója az 1920-as földbirtokreform parlamenti vitája alapján," in *A tudomány és az oktatás vonzásában: Tanulmánykötet Tóth Tibor professzor emlékére*, ed. Zoltán Kaposi, Tamás Lendvai, and Oroszi Sándor. 311–333. Pécs: PTE-FEEK KTK, 2012,

——. "Overcoming History through Trauma: The Hungarian Historikerstreit." *European Review* 24, no. 4 (October 2016): 523–534.

Kövér, György. *A pesti City öröksége: banktörténeti tanulmányok*. Budapest: BFL, 2012.

——. *Iparosodás agrárországban*. Budapest: Gondolat, 1982.

Kramer, Alan. *Dynamic of Destruction: Culture and Mass Killing in the First World War*. Oxford: Oxford University Press, 2007.

Krause, Detlef. *Die Commerz- und Disconto-Bank, 1870–1920/23: Bankgeschichte als Systemgeschichte*. Stuttgart: F. Steiner, 2004.

Kučera, Rudolf. *Rationed Life: Science, Everyday Life, and Working-Class Politics in the Bohemian Lands, 1914–1918*. New York: Berghahn Books, 2016.

Kuisel, Richard F. *Capitalism and the State in Modern France: Renovation and Economic Management in the Twentieth Century*. Cambridge: Cambridge University Press, 1983.

——. *Ernest Mercier: French Technocrat*. Berkeley: University of California Press, 1967.

Kuzmany, Börries. "Habsburg Austria: Experiments in Non-territorial Autonomy." *Ethnopolitics* 15, no. 1 (January 1, 2016): 43–65.

Landau, Philippe-Efraïm. "La communauté juive de France et la Grande Guerre." *Annales de demographie historique* 103, no. 1 (2002): 91–106.

Landes, David S. "Bleichröders and Rothschilds: The Problem of Continuity in the Family Firm." *Family Business Review* 6, no. 1 (March 1, 1993): 85–101.

——. *Dynasties: Fortunes and Misfortunes of the World's Great Family Businesses*. New York: Viking, 2006.

Lengyel, Zsolt K. *A kompromisszum keresése: Tanulmányok a 20. századi transzszilvanizmus korai történetéhez*. Csíkszereda, Romania: Pro-Print, 2007.

Levy, Jonathan. "Accounting for Profit and the History of Capital." *Critical Historical Studies* 1, no. 2 (September 2014): 171–214.

Liber, George O. *Total Wars and the Making of Modern Ukraine, 1914–1954*. Toronto: University of Toronto Press, 2016.

Livezeanu, Irina. *Cultural Politics in Greater Romania: Regionalism, Nation-Building and Ethnic Struggle, 1918–1930*. Ithaca, NY: Cornell University Press, 1995.

Lőwy, Daniel. *A Kálváriától a tragédiáig: Kolozsvár zsidó lskosságának története*. Kolozsvár: Koinónia, 2007.

Mahoney, James, and Dietrich Rueschemeyer. "Comparative Historical Analysis, Achievements and Agendas." In *Comparative Historical Analysis in the Social Sciences*, edited by James Mahoney and Dietrich Rueschemeyer, 3–40. Cambridge: Cambridge University Press, 2003.

Maier, Charles S. "Consigning the Twentieth Century to History: Alternative Narratives for the Modern Era." *American Historical Review* 105, no. 3 (2000): 807–831.

——. *Once within Borders: Territories of Power, Wealth and Belonging since 1500*. Cambridge, MA: Belknap Press of Harvard University Press, 2016.

——. *Recasting Bourgeois Europe: Stabilization in France, Germany and Italy in the Decade after World War I*. Princeton, NJ: Princeton University Press, 1975.

Marguerat, Philippe. "Les investissements français dans le Bassin danubien durant l'entre-deux-guerres: Pour une nouvelle interprétation." *Revue Historique* 306, no. 1 (629) (2004): 121–164.

Marin, Irina. *Peasant Violence and Antisemitism in Early Twentieth-Century Eastern Europe*. New York: Palgrave Macmillan, 2018.

Marks, Sally. *The Illusion of Peace: International Relations in Europe, 1918–1933*. New York: Palgrave Macmillan, 2003.

Martin, Benjamin F. *France and the Après Guerre, 1918–1924: Illusions and Disillusionment*. Baton Rouge: Louisiana State University Press, 1999.

Mathias, Peter, and Sidney Pollard. *The Industrial Economies: The Development of Economic and Social Policies*. Cambridge: Cambridge University Press, 1989.

Mayerhofer, Lisa. "Making Friends and Foes: Occupiers and Occupied in First World War Romania, 1916–1918." In *Untold War, New Perspectives in First World War Studies*, edited by Heather Jones, Jennifer O'Brian, and Christoph Schmidt-Supprian, 119–150. Leiden: Brill, 2008.

Mayeur, Jean Marie. *La vie politique sous la Troisième République, 1870–1940*. Paris: Éditions du Seuil, 1984.

McMeekin, Sean. *The Berlin-Baghdad Express: The Ottoman Empire and Germany's Bid for World Power*. Cambridge, MA: Belknap Press of Harvard University Press, 2010.

——. *History's Greatest Heist: The Looting of Russia by the Bolsheviks*. New Haven, CT: Yale University Press, 2009.

Mendelsohn, Ezra. *The Jews of East Central Europe between the World Wars*. Bloomington: Indiana University Press, 1983.

Menne, Bernhard. *Blood and Steel: The Rise of the House of Krupp*. New York: L. Furman, 1938.

Menyhért, Bálint. "History as an Agent of Growth: Natural Experiments from Central Europe," PhD diss. Central European University, 2017.

Meyer, Henry Cord. *Mitteleuropa in German Thought and Action, 1815–1945*. The Hague: Nijhoff, 1955.
Miller, Michael Laurence. "A Monumental Debate in Budapest: The Hentzi Statue and the Limits of Austro-Hungarian Reconciliation, 1852–1918." *Austrian History Yearbook* 40 (2009): 215–237.
Mitrany, David. *The Land and the Peasant in Rumania: The War and Agrarian Reform (1917–21)*. New Haven, CT: Yale University Press, 1930.
Mommsen, Wolfgang J. "Max Weber and the Peace Treaty of Versailles." In *The Treaty of Versailles: A Reassessment after 75 Years*, edited by Manfred F. Boemeke, Gerald D. Feldman, and Elisabeth Gläser, 535–546. Publications of the German Historical Institute. Cambridge: Cambridge University Press, 1998.
Monaghan, Shannon. *Protecting Democracy from Dissent: Population Engineering in Western Europe, 1918–1926*. Milton Park, Abingdon, Oxon: Routledge, 2018.
Morck, Randall. *The Global History of Corporate Governance: An Introduction*. Cambridge, MA: National Bureau of Economic Research, 2005.
Mouré, Kenneth. *The Gold Standard Illusion: France, the Bank of France, and the International Gold Standard, 1914–1939*. Oxford: Oxford University Press, 2002.
———. *Managing the Franc Poincaré: Economic Understanding and Political Constraint in French Monetary Policy, 1928–1936*. Cambridge: Cambridge University Press, 1991.
Müller, Dietmar. "The Concept of Property in Romania's Economic-Legal History." In *Key Concepts of Romanian History: Alternative Approaches to Socio-political Languages*, edited by Victor Neumann and Armin Heinen, 183–222. Budapest: Central European University Press, 2013.
Murgescu, Bogdan. *România și Europa: Acumularea decalajelor economice: 1500–2010*. Iași, Romania: Polirom, 2010.
Nagy, Botond. "Székelyföld gazdasági fejlődése a 19. század második felében: Határszéli gazdasági környezet és üzleti modellek Háromszéken." PhD diss., Eötvös Loránd University, 2016.
Nagy, István. "Egy kolozsvári nagyüzem múltjából." *Korunk* 16, no. 2–3 (1957): 244–255.
Nagy, Róbert. *Capitalul-forță a transformării: Rolul capitalului german în industrializarea Transilvaniei (1880–1918)*. Cluj-Napoca: Presa Universitară Clujeană, 2011.
Nemes, Robert. *Another Hungary: The Nineteenth-Century Provinces in Eight Lives*. Stanford, CA: Stanford University Press, 2016.
———. "Refugees and Antisemitism in Hungary during the First World War." In *Sites of European Antisemitism in the Age of Mass Politics, 1880–1918*, edited by Robert Nemes and Daniel Unowsky, 236–254. Waltham, MA: Brandeis University Press, 2014.
Nipperdey, Thomas. *Deutsche Geschichte, 1866–1918: Machtstaat vor der Demokratie*. Munich: C.H. Beck, 1990.
Nohlen, Denis. *Strasbourg Architecture: 1871–1918*. Strasbourg, France: Le Verger, 1991.
Nohlen, Klaus. *Construire une capitale: Strasbourg impérial de 1870 à 1918: les bâtiments officiels de la Place impériale*. Strasbourg: Publications de la Société Savante d'Alsace, 1997.
Noiriel, Gérard. *Longwy: Immigrés et prolétaires, 1880–1980*. Paris: Presses universitaires de France, 1984.

Osborne, Eric W. *Britain's Economic Blockade of Germany, 1914–1919*. London: Frank Cass, 2004.

Ouahes, Idir. *Syria and Lebanon under the French Mandate: Cultural Imperialism and the Workings of Empire*. London: I.B. Tauris, 2018.

Pál-Antal, Sándor. *A marosvásárhelyi utcák, közök, és terek történeti névtára*. Târgu-Mureș, Romania: Editura Mentor, 2007.

Pastor, Peter. *Hungary between Wilson and Lenin: The Hungarian Revolution of 1918–1919 and the Big Three*. Boulder, CO: East European Quarterly, 1976.

Péteri, György. "Central Bank Diplomacy: Montagu Norman and Central Europe's Monetary Reconstruction after World War I." *Contemporary European History* 1, no. 3 (1992): 233–258.

——. "Nylon Curtain—Transnational and Transsystemic Tendencies in the Cultural Life of State-Socialist Russia and East-Central Europe." *Slavonica* 10, no. 2 (November 1, 2004): 113–123.

Piketty, Thomas. *Capital in the Twenty-First Century*. Cambridge, MA: Belknap Press of Harvard University Press, 2014.

Pinol, Jean-Luc. "Elites et cercles à Lyon avant et après la première guerre mondiale." In *Eliten in Deutschland und Frankreich im 19. und 20. Jahrhundert: Strukturen und Beziehungen*, 31–60. vol. 1, edited by Rainer Hudemann and Georges-Henri Soutou. Munich: R. Oldenbourg, 1994.

Pohl, Manfred. *Handbook on the History of European Banks*. Frankfurt: Edward Elgar Publishing, 1994.

Poidevin, Raymond. *Les Relations économiques et financières entre la France et l'Allemagne de 1898 à 1914*. Paris: A. Colin, 1969.

Pölöskei, Ferenc. "István Tisza's Policy toward the Romanian Nationalities on the Eve of World War I." *Acta Historica Academiae Scientiarum Hungaricae* 18, nos. 3/4 (1972): 267–291.

Popovici, Vlad. "Elita românească din Transilvania și Ungaria perioadei dualiste în perspectivă istoriografică, între 'național' și 'social.'" In *Elitele puterii: puterea elitelor în spațiul românesc, (secolele XV-XX)*, edited by Cristian Ploscaru. Iași, Romania: Editura Universității "Alexandru Ioan Cuza," 2018.

Preda, Cristian. "From the 'Land of the Donkeys' to the 'Economic Island between the Danube, Dniester, and the Tisza.'" In *Moral, Legal, and Political Values in Romanian Culture*, edited by Mihaela Czobor-Lupp and J. Stefan Lupp, 237–245. Washington, DC: CRVP, 2002.

Preibusch, Sophie Charlotte. *Verfassungsentwicklungen im Reichsland Elsass-Lothringen 1871–1918: Integration durch Verfassungsrecht?* Berlin: Humboldt-Universität, 2004.

Prepuk, Anikó. "Religious Equality and Jewish Emancipation: The Acceptance of the Jewish Domination in Hungary in the 1890s." In *Tolerance and Intolerance in Historical Perspective*, edited by Csaba Lévai and Vasile Vese, 13–23. Pisa: PLUS, 2003.

Preshlenova, Ronmyana. "Austro-Hungarian Trade and the Economic Development of Southeastern Europe before 1914." In *Economic Transformations in East and Central Europe: Legacies from the Past and Policies for the Future*, edited by David F. Good, 231–260. London: Routledge, 1994.

Prosic, Michel. *L'usine créatrice: L'usine de Hagondange, naissance de la vie ouvrière, 1910–1938*. Hagondange, France: Ville de Hagondange, 1996.

Puskás, Julianna. *Kivándorló magyarok az Egyesült Államokban, 1880–1940*. Budapest: Akadémiai Kiadó, 1982.

Rasch, Manfred. "August Thyssen die Katholische Grossindustrielle der Wilhelminischen Epoche." In *August Thyssen und Hugo Stinnes: Ein Briefwechsel 1898–1922*, edited by M. Rasch and Gerald D. Feldman. Munich: C. H. Beck, 2003.

Reill, Dominique Kirchner. *The Fiume Crisis: Life in the Wake of the Habsburg Empire*. Cambridge, MA: Belknap Press of Harvard University Press, 2020.

Révész, Tamás. *Nem akartak katonát látni?A magyar állam és hadserege 1918-1919-ben*. Budapest: Bölcsészettudományi Kutatóközpont, Történettudományi Intézet, 2019.

Rezzori, Gregor von. *The Snows of Yesteryear: Portraits for an Autobiography*. New York: New York Review of Books, 2009.

Rigó, Máté. "A felejthető pogrom." *Budapesti Könyvszemle*, Summer 2012, 126–141.

——. "The Long First World War and the Survival of Business Elites in East-Central Europe: Transylvania's Industrial Boom and the Enrichment of Economic Elites." *European Review of History* 24, no. 2 (March 4, 2017): 250–272.

——. "Imperial Currencies after the Fall of Empires: The Conversion of the German Paper Mark and the Austro-Hungarian Crown at the End of the First World War." *Central European History* 53, no. 3 (September 2020): 533–563.

——. "Transcending the East-West Divide: Towards a European History of Post-1918 Transitions." *Passato e Presente, Rivista di storia contemporanea* 106/2019.

Risacher, Bertrand, and Nicolas Stoskopf. "L'industrie alsacienne dans la Grande Guerre: Un désastre économique?" *Revue d'Alsace* 139 (2013): 77–104.

Ritschl, Albrecht. "The Pity of Peace: Germany's Economy at War, 1914–1918 and Beyond." In *The Economics of World War I*, edited by Stephen N. Broadberry and Mark Harrison, 49–52. Cambridge: Cambridge University Press, 2005.

Robertson, Roland. *Globalization: Social Theory and Global Culture*. London: Sage, 1992.

Romano, Sergio. "Italy in Post-World War 1 Diplomacy." In *Italy and East Central Europe: Dimensions of the Regional Relationship*, edited by Vojtech Mastny. New York: Routledge, 2019.

Romsics, Ignác. *Erdély elvesztése, 1918–1947*. Budapest: Helikon Kiadó, 2018.

——. *Helyünk és sorsunk a Duna-medencében*. Budapest: Osiris, 1996.

——. *Magyarország története a XX. században*. Budapest: Osiris, 2005.

Roth, François. *La Lorraine annexée: étude sur la présidence de Lorraine dans l'Empire allemand, 1870–1918*. Nancy, France: Université de Nancy II, 1976.

Rozenblit, Marsha L. *Reconstructing a National Identity: The Jews of Habsburg Austria during World War I*. Oxford: Oxford University Press, 2001.

Sabahi, Borzu. *Compensation and Restitution in Investor-State Arbitration: Principles and Practice*. Oxford: Oxford University Press, 2018.

Sammartino, Annemarie. *The Impossible Border: Germany and the East, 1914–1922*. Ithaca, NY: Cornell University Press, 2010.

Sandu, Traian. *La Grande Roumanie alliée de la France: Une péripétie diplomatique des Années Folles? (1919–1933)*. Paris: Harmattan, 1999.

Sauvy, Alfred, and Anita Hirsch. *Histoire économique de la France entre les deux guerres*. Vol. 2. Paris: Economica, 1984.

Schama, Simon. *Citizens: A Chronicle of the French Revolution*. New York: Knopf, 1989.

Scheer, Tamara. "Etappenliebe: Belgrad, Cetinje und Lublin unter österreichisch-ungarischer Besatzungsmacht im Ersten Weltkrieg." *Medizin, Gesellschaft und Geschichte* 34 (2015): 35–63.

Scheiring, Gábor. *The Retreat of Liberal Democracy: Authoritarian Capitalism and the Accumulative State in Hungary*. Cham: Palgrave Macmillan, 2020.

Schmauch, Joseph. "Novembre 1918. L'administration française s'établit en Alsace-Lorraine." *Revue d'Alsace*, no. 139 (October 1, 2013): 259–276.

Schuller, Balázs. "Impériumváltás a Zsil-Völgyében, 1918." *Bányászati és Kohászati Lapok* 3 (2005): 35–38.

Schulze, Max-Stephan. "Austria-Hungary's Economy in World War I." In *The Economics of World War I*, edited by Stephen N. Broadberry and Mark Harrison, 77–111. Cambridge: Cambridge University Press, 2005.

Scott, Eddie. "Economic Policy and Economic Development in Austria-Hungary, 1867–1913." In *The Cambridge Economic History of Europe from the Decline of the Roman Empire*, edited by Peter Mathias and Sidney Pollard, 814–886. Cambridge: Cambridge University Press, 1989.

Seres, Attila, and Gábor Egry, eds. *Magyar levéltári források az 1930. évi Romániai népszámlálás nemzetiségi adatsorainak értékeléséhez*. Kolozsvár: NKI, 2011.

Shamir, Haim. *Economic Crisis and French Foreign Policy: 1930–1936*. Leiden: Brill Archive, 1989.

Sharp, Alan. *The Versailles Settlement: Peacemaking after the First World War, 1919–1923*. Basingstoke: Palgrave Macmillan, 2008.

Siegel, Jennifer. *For Peace and Money: French and British Finance in the Service of Tsars and Commissars*. Oxford: Oxford University Press, 2014.

Silverman, Dan P. "The Economic Consequences of Annexation: Alsace-Lorraine and Imperial Germany, 1871–1918." *Central European History* 4, no. 1 (March 1971): 34–53.

——. *Reconstructing Europe after the Great War*. Cambridge, MA: Harvard University Press, 1982.

——. *Reluctant Union: Alsace-Lorraine and Imperial Germany, 1871–1918*. University Park: Pennsylvania State University Press, 1972.

Slobodian, Quinn. *Globalists: The End of Empire and the Birth of Neoliberalism*. Cambridge, MA: Harvard University Press, 2018.

Sluga, Glenda. *Internationalism in the Age of Nationalism (Pennsylvania Studies in Human Rights)*. Philadelphia: University of Pennsylvania Press, 2013.

Smith, Michael Stephen. *The Emergence of Modern Business Enterprise in France, 1800–1930*. Cambridge, MA: Harvard University Press, 2006.

Snyder, Timothy. *Bloodlands: Europe between Hitler and Stalin*. New York: Basic Books, 2010.

——. *The Reconstruction of Nations Poland, Ukraine, Lithuania, Belarus, 1569–1999*. New Haven, CT: Yale University Press, 2003.

Solimano, Andres. *Economic Elites, Crises and Democracy: Alternatives beyond Neoliberal Capitalism*. Oxford: Oxford University Press, 2014.

Solonari, Vladimir. *Purifying the Nation: Population Exchange and Ethnic Cleansing in Nazi-Allied Romania*. Washington, DC: Woodrow Wilson Center Press, 2010.

Sorkin, David. *Jewish Emancipation: A History across Five Centuries*. Princeton, NJ: Princeton University Press, 2019

Soutou, Georges-Henri. "La France et les Marches de l'Est 1914–1919." *Revue Historique* 260: 528, no. 2 (1978).

——. *La grande illusion: Quand la France perdait la paix, 1914–1920*. Paris: Texto, 2015.

——. "L' Impérialisme du pauvre." *Relations Internationales*, no. 7 (1976): 219–239.

——. *L'Or et le sang: Les buts de guerre écnomiques de la première guerre mondiale*. Paris: Fayard, 1989.

Spector, Sherman David. *Rumania at the Paris Peace Conference: A Study of the Diplomacy of Ioan I.C. Brătianu*. New York: Bookman Associates, 1962.

Stark, Gary D. *Banned in Berlin: Literary Censorship in Imperial Germany, 1871–1918*. New York: Berghahn Books, 2009.

Stevenson, David. *French War Aims against Germany, 1914–1919*. Oxford, UK: Clarendon Press, 1982.

Stone, Norman. *The Eastern Front, 1914–1917*. New York: Scribner, 1975.

Stoskopf, Nicolas. "André Koechlin & Cie." *SACM, Wärtsilä, Histoire de La Fonderie (D'Giesserei) à Mulhouse (1826–2007)*, 2007. https://hal.archives-ouvertes.fr/hal-00544984.

Strachan, Hew. *Financing the First World War*. Oxford: Oxford University Press, 2004.

Streets-Salter, Heather. *World War One in Southeast Asia: Colonialism and Anticolonialism in an Era of Global Conflict*. Cambridge: Cambridge University Press, 2017.

Suri, Jeremi. *Power and Protest: Global Revolution and the Rise of Detente*. Cambridge, MA: Harvard University Press, 2009.

Szász, Zoltán, ed. *Erdély története*. Vol. 3. Budapest: Akadémiai Kiadó, 1986.

Szász, Zoltán. "Az erdélyi román polgárság szerepéről 1918 őszén." *Századok* 2 (1972): 304–335.

Taleb, Nassim Nicholas. *Antifragile: Things That Gain from Disorder*. New York: Random House, 2012.

Taylor, A. J. P. *The First World War: An Illustrated History*. New York: Putnam, 1980.

Teichova, Alice. *Economic Change and the National Question in Twentieth-Century Europe*. Cambridge: Cambridge University Press, 2000.

Ther, Philipp. "Comparisons, Cultural Transfers, and the Study of Networks: Toward a Transnational History of Europe." In *Comparative and Transnational History: Central European Approaches and New Perspectives*, edited by Heinz-Gerhard Haupt and Jürgen Kocka, 204–225. New York: Berghahn Books, 2012.

——. "Pre-negotiated Violence: Ethnic Cleansing in the 'Long First World War.'" In *Legacies of Violence: Eastern Europe's First World War*, edited by J. Böhler, W. Borodziej, and J. von Puttkamer, 259–284. Munich: Oldenbourg, 2014.

Thomas, Martin. "French Empire Elites and the Politics of Economic Obligation in the Interwar Years." *Historical Journal* 52, no. 4 (2009): 989–1016.

Tomka, Béla. "Interlocking Directorates between Banks and Industrial Companies in Hungary at the Beginning of the Twentieth Century." *Business History* 43, no. 1 (January 2001): 25–42.

Tooze, Adam. *The Deluge: The Great War, America, and the Remaking of the Global Order, 1916–1931*. New York: Viking, 2014.

Tooze, Adam, and Ted Fertik. "The World Economy and the Great War." *Geschichte und Gesellschaft* 40, no. 2 (2014): 214–238.

Torrey, Glenn E. *The Romanian Battlefront in World War I*. Lawrence: University Press of Kansas, 2011.

Trachtenberg, Marc. *Reparation in World Politics: France and European Economic Diplomacy, 1916–1923*. New York: Columbia University Press, 1980.

Trencsényi, Balázs. *The Politics of "National Character": A Study in Interwar East European Thought*. Oxen: Routledge, 2012.

——. *A nép lelke: Nemzetkarakterológiai viták Kelet-Európában*. Budapest: Argumentum Kiadó, 2011.

Turner, John M. *Trade Development in Latin America*. Washington, DC: US Government Printing Office, 1912.

Uberfill, François. *La société strasbourgeoise entre France et Allemagne (1871–1924): la société strasbourgeoise à travers les mariages entre Allemands et Alsaciens à l'époque du Reichsland: le sort des couples mixtes après 1918*. Strasbourg: Société Savante d'Alsace, 2001.

——. "Le sort des populations après 1918. Commissions de triage, expulsions, épuration des administrations et des institutions scolaires et universitaires." *Revue d'Alsace*, no. 144 (November 15, 2018): 107–128.

Vági, Zoltán, László Csősz, and Gábor Kádár. *The Holocaust in Hungary: Evolution of a Genocide*. Budapest: AltaMira Press, 2013.

Vagts, Detlev F. "Coercion and Foreign Investment Rearrangements." *American Journal of International Law* 72, no. 1 (January 1978): 133–148.

Van Ginderachter, Maarten, and Jon E. Fox. "Introduction, National Indifference and the History of Nationalism in Modern Europe." In *National Indifference and the History of Nationalism in Modern Europe*, edited by Maarten Van Ginderachter and Jon E. Fox, 1–14. New York: Routledge, 2019.

Varga, Bálint. *The Monumental Nation: Magyar Nationalism and Symbolic Politics in Fin-de-Siècle Hungary*. New York: Berghahn Books, 2016.

Vincent, C. Paul. *The Politics of Hunger: The Allied Blockade of Germany, 1915–1919*. Athens: Ohio University Press, 1985.

Vogler, Bernard, and Michel Hau. *Histoire économique de l'Alsace: croissance, crises, innovations: vingt siècles de développement régional*. Strasbourg: Editions la nuée bleue, 1997.

Wahl, Alfred. *L'option et l'émigration des Alsaciens-Lorrains, 1871–1872*. Paris: Ophrys, 1977.

Wahl, Alfred, and Jean-Claude Richez. *La vie quotidienne en Alsace entre France et Allemagne: 1850–1950*. Paris: Hachette, 1993.

Walker, Mack. *German Home Towns: Community, State, and General Estate, 1648–1871*. Ithaca, NY: Cornell University Press, 1971.

Wallerstein, Immanuel Maurice. *Unthinking Social Science: The Limits of Nineteenth-Century Paradigms*. Philadelphia: Temple University Press, 2001.

Wandycz, Piotr Stefan. *France and Her Eastern Allies, 1919–1925*. Minneapolis: University of Minnesota Press, 1962.

Watson, Alexander. *Ring of Steel: Germany and Austria-Hungary at War, 1914–1918*. London: Allen Lane, 2014.

Weber, Max. *Economy and Society: An Outline of Interpretive Sociology*. Berkeley: University of California Press, 1978.

Wehler, Hans Ulrich. *The German Empire, 1871–1918*. Leamington Spa, Warwickshire, UK: Berg Publishers, 1985.

——. *Krisenherde des Kaiserreichs: 1871–1918. Studien z. dt. Sozial- u. Verfassungsgeschichte*. Göttingen: Vandenhoeck u. Ruprecht, 1970.

Wempe, Sean Andrew. *Revenants of the German Empire: Colonial Germans, Imperialism, and the League of Nations*. New York: Oxford University Press, 2019.

Wenzel, Jean-Paul. *Far from Hagondange*. Translated by Bernard Bloch. New York: Ubu Repertory Theater, 1986.

Wessel, Horst A. *Thyssen & Co., Mülheim a.d. Ruhr: Die Geschichte einer Familie und ihrer Unternehmung*. Stuttgart: Franz Steiner Verlag, 1991.

Wolf, Nikolaus. "Was Germany Ever United? Evidence from Intra- and International Trade, 1885–1933." *Journal of Economic History* 69, no. 3 (2009): 846–881.

Wolff, Larry. *Woodrow Wilson and the Reimagining of Eastern Europe*. Stanford, CA: Stanford University Press, 2020.

Woronoff, Denis. *François de Wendel*. Paris: Presses de Sciences Po, 2001.

Zahra, Tara. *The Great Departure: Mass Migration from Eastern Europe and the Making of the Free World*. New York: W. W. Norton, 2016.

——. "Imagined Noncommunities: National Indifference as a Category of Analysis." *Slavic Review* 69, no. 1 (Spring 2010): 93–119.

——. *Kidnapped Souls: National Indifference and the Battle for Children in the Bohemian Lands, 1900–1948*. Ithaca, NY: Cornell University Press, 2008.

——. "The 'Minority Problem' and National Classification in the French and Czechoslovak Borderlands." *Contemporary European History* 17, no. 2 (2008): 137–165.

Zilch, Reinhold, and Jürgen Koppatz. *Okkupation und Währung im Ersten Weltkrieg: Die deutsche Besatzungspolitik in Belgien und Russisch-Polen 1914–1918*. Goldbach: Keip, 1994.

Index

Page numbers followed by letters *f*, *m*, and *t* refer to figures, maps, and tables, respectively.

www.ingramcontent.com/pod-product-compliance
Lightning Source LLC
Chambersburg PA
CBHW030135160526
45176CB00018B/679/J
9781501764653